Managing
Medical
Authority

Managing Medical Authority

How Doctors Compete for Status
and Create Knowledge

Daniel A. Menchik

Princeton University Press

Princeton and Oxford

Published by Princeton University Press
41 William Street, Princeton, New Jersey 08540
6 Oxford Street, Woodstock, Oxfordshire OX20 1TR

press.princeton.edu

All Rights Reserved

Library of Congress Cataloging-in-Publication Data

Names: Menchik, Daniel A., author.
Title: Managing medical authority : how doctors compete for status and create knowledge / Daniel A. Menchik.
Description: Princeton : Princeton University Press, [2021] | Includes bibliographical references and index.
Identifiers: LCCN 2021036891 (print) | LCCN 2021036892 (ebook) | ISBN 9780691223544 (paperback) | ISBN 9780691223568 (hardback) | ISBN 9780691223551 (ebook)
Subjects: LCSH: Medicine—Practice—Management. | Physicians. | BISAC: SOCIAL SCIENCE / Sociology / General | BUSINESS & ECONOMICS / Organizational Behavior
Classification: LCC R728 .M477 2021 (print) | LCC R728 (ebook) | DDC 610.68—dc23
LC record available at https://lccn.loc.gov/2021036891
LC ebook record available at https://lccn.loc.gov/2021036892

British Library Cataloging-in-Publication Data is available

Editorial: Meagan Levinson & Jacqueline Delaney
Production Editorial: Ali Parrington
Text and Jacket/Cover Design: Pamela L. Schnitter
Production: Erin Suydam
Publicity: Kate Hensley & Kathryn Stevens
Copyeditor: Anne Cherry

Jacket/Cover Credit: Cover photo by David Schalliol

This book has been composed in Verdigris MVB Pro Text and Arial

10 9 8 7 6 5 4 3 2 1

For my parents, Paul and

Bettie, and brother, Jeremy

Contents

It's a truism, and pervasive trope, that medicine has authority. Under medicine's authority we are pried open, prescribed potentially dangerous drugs, and subjected to risky treatments. We often pay high prices for medical care, shouldering massive debt to pay off medical expenses. And we accept physicians' pronouncements, in concert with those of other medical stakeholders that range from nurses to pharmaceutical companies. On occasion, patients may personally and collectively rally to influence the decisions of these stakeholders. And we have the right to decline physicians' services or propose that they offer us different ones. Yet, empowered as we might be in light of new access to information, when on the gurney we'll defer. As scholars have shown, this deference is important for medicine's control. And so, the strongest symptom of medicine's authority is that its stakeholders have created and can manage what counts as sickness and health, and can continue to define these conditions.

This book takes part in an ongoing conversation about the great control medicine claims over our bodies, minds, and lives, and how doctors and other stakeholders manage it. Sociologically speaking, how medicine manages its control is a question of its authority. Based on the historical record of the waxing and waning of acceptance toward not only specific diagnoses and treatments, but also over-time shifts in the dominance of the homeopathic and osteopathic movements, medicine is not eternally assured its authority, but rather must continuously renew and reinvigorate it. Scholars of medicine's legacy have offered historical evidence of medicine's victories—for instance, doctors' movement of care out of the home and into hospitals over which they were able to maintain control. Even with this retrospective affirmation of medicine's dynamism, the scholarship still lacks a departure, beyond single historical accounts or synthetic treatments, to build a portrait of ongoing and organized activity among medicine's stakeholders. And so I asked, How is the authority of medicine controlled, managed, and socially organized? This question has become somewhat more important now that social scientists studying medicine have become more aware of, and have paid more focused attention to, the huge project of social organization that is medicine itself. How does this project constantly respond to social changes, whether developments in technology, workplace initiatives, or payment processes?

My interest in the question of how medicine manages its authority was only amplified as I did my field research. It became apparent that some prevalent sociological understandings about authority had serious limits in light of the data I was gathering. I compared these data to my experiences as a teacher, in which I noted that teachers were encouraged to work with outside certification boards (though largely uninterested in doing so). And I noted research that showed that teachers had a hard time controlling what knowledge was taught in the classroom unless they had a working relationship with stakeholders outside the classroom: administrators and sometimes parents. What I saw in my data on doctors was a way of organizing authority that was similarly complicated, but more centered on extra-organizational relationships with peers who intermittently met in geographically and temporally distant venues. And I wondered, since I was seeing this "outside" orientation of doctors, how it might be important to the management of authority, and whether it had something to do with their concerns around responding to technological and other changes. I was also observing a lot of work done by individual doctors themselves to establish what and whose knowledge should be deemed authoritative.

I had assumed that I could understand authority by studying the hospital alone. I had assumed that doctors had little recourse regarding hospital decisions, and that the interests of industry would dominate doctors' practices. And I had assumed that doctors were constantly in tension with those in other professional groups, such as nurses, and with those in subfields of medicine different from their own. None of these assumptions proved to be the case, and my observations raised more questions needing explanation, particularly about the degree of clinical uncertainty I observed. In fact, I observed doctors expressing some uncertainty about what to do when making decisions with patients. But I saw something quite different in their arguments about how medical work should be understood and carried out. I observed that some doctors were quite confident and bold as they shaped the understandings of both trainees and local and visiting peers. Similarly surprising, to me, was that in their shaping, I also observed differences in approaches—and even descriptions of anatomy—among those I had assumed were trained similarly.

Still, I had no idea how these differences in approach, ones reflecting the core of medicine's authority, were adjudicated. I understood only later that there was much more to know about what happened outside the walls of the hospital, in places where new knowledge was being presented and unlikely collaborations were taking place, but where there were also clear divisions among communities of physicians with different approaches and data, and with different ideas about whether they should seek to innovate or follow their field's leaders. To better understand these physicians, I went multiple times to venues organized by corporate actors and the professional association of the doctors my study centered upon, cardiac electrophysiologists (EPs), and tried to understand differences across venues in patterns of work. But many questions remained.

Specifically, it wasn't clear how the doctors I observed reached agreement on what would be defined as a medical problem, and what solutions were appropriate—a process I would later come to refer to as "organizing indeterminacy." I saw that leaders in medicine vigorously discussed, and sometime disagreed on, how doctors throughout the field should understand what problems patients were experiencing (e.g., shortness of breath, fainting) and what solutions (e.g., medication, device implants, surgery, "watchful waiting"), should be undertaken by their physicians. These doctors' problems and solutions were being discussed, supported with evidence, and contested. And I saw that these discussions occurred in particular in venues set up for just that task, not unlike grand rounds, and mortality and morbidity meetings—rituals that sociologists have demonstrated as organizing attention in central venues in which doctors manage errors.

A set of questions surfaced that motivated a new way of understanding doctors' management of authority: How do experts control whose knowledge is intended to inform practice? How do particular doctors manage how this knowledge is used? How is knowledge worked out between them, and with other stakeholders, in an ongoing way? What are the relationships between doctors' practices with patients and their activities elsewhere? And how well does our current understanding of the work of experts fit with doctors' actual practices? This book offers my answers to these questions. In revealing what happens behind the scenes, the interactions that patients never see but are central to medicine's ability to maintain its authority, this project is the culmination of my efforts to study places in which the work of managing authority gets done, where knowledge is presented and evaluated—including many places new to the literature.

During these efforts, my observations led me to think differently about how we conceptualize work, driving me to pay more attention to the many experts involved. This meant paying attention to not only doctors but also device reps, and not only those standard-setters working in top-ranked hospitals but also everyday clinicians in private practice. I looked at those who participate in processes that happen again and again, and thus make those processes effective in managing authority and the other needs of work. So, in addition to providing an analysis of the way medical authority is managed, I mean this book to detail one sociological approach by which social life can be studied, especially the kind of life that is organized among individuals who work in individual places and perform individual tasks, but are also aware of the importance of maintaining a more collective social presence in what we refer to as "medicine."

Finally, what I saw made me think differently about the craft of fieldwork itself. This book is the product of the happy accident that I was able not only to be embedded in the hospital itself, but also to follow doctors to other places where they carried out professional work (what I call "venues"), so that I could pay attention to how these places are tethered together by continually reinforced cross-venue connections to enable these experts to socially create and shift medical problems and solutions. I could only understand these connections by going to these venues outside the hospital, a kind of venturing uncommon among social scientists concerned with understanding medical work. And as I spent time with medicine's many stakeholders in the multiple venues in which they worked, it was evident that while sociology's approaches to ethnography in workplace venues like the hospital were invaluable, I still needed to think a bit differently not only about authority but also about ethnography.

The pursuit, then, in my research and the pages that follow, was of three goals. One goal was to develop an account of the relationships between, and changes in, key organizational, professional, and corporate stakeholders involved in managing medicine's authority. A second goal was to develop a theoretical vocabulary that affords scholars of professions and organizations, when looking at subjects beyond the entity we call medicine, the capacity to make sense of the range of processes and experts contributing to occupational projects. A final goal was to develop and pilot an approach to ethnography that makes this kind of investigation possible.

Acknowledgments

This project started with the collection of data in graduate school; it was at first my dissertation work, and, as I continued to work in the field and to think more about what I had found, gave rise to the realizations that became this book. I owe thanks to many people for their support and criticism, and intend to acknowledge as many as the space will allow.

I must thank people for contributions that have run deep, and it is only in continuing the process of my work that I have viewed the full value of their enthusiasm and demands for clarification. I want to start by acknowledging Madeline Arnot and John Beck, who, in my master's program at the University of Cambridge, gave me intensive training in qualitative methods and more generally introduced me to the joys of theory and empirical research in sociology.

Years removed from my time at the University of Chicago, I still see my advisors in my work, sometimes in unexpected ways. One of my advisors, Andy Abbott, modeled what a scholarly life could be, and always helped me see what was interesting in my work. A good puzzle was all he needed to get going on a rich conversation. Sometimes our meetings involved mostly tightening my prose. (Work remains.) Another advisor, Ed Laumann, opened up a universe of sociological ideas. He also pushed me to compare EPs with members of other occupations, leading me to also study general cardiologists (chapter 2) and internists (chapter 4). The third member of my committee, David Meltzer, was a valued source of feedback and friendship, whether it was discussing a paper at 2 a.m., or helping through the morass of anxious IRB administrators. And, as someone who is both a social scientist and a physician, he gave me important insight into the perspective of doctors—it was, in a sense, like getting two surgeries for the price of one.

I am also grateful for University of Chicago graduate school colleagues who stimulated laughter and intellectual challenge. These "multiplex" ties were unfathomably fun and distracting, in defusing the mortification process inherent to graduate school. Greg Liegel, Rafael Santana, Paki Reid-Brossard, Zack Kertcher, and Bobby Das all kept things going when the going slowed. So too did Jessica Feldman, Melissa Kew, Zohar Lechtman, Linda Lee, Etienne Ollion, Gawin Tsai, Monica Lee, Misha Teplitskiy, Ben Cornwell, Dani Wallace, Chad Borkenhagen, Len Albright, Michal Pagis, and Stefan Bargheer. Jen Karlin, Adam Baim, and Betsy Brada were valued guides to the anthropology of medicine. As friends with whom I share my interests and work, Lei Jin, Sida Liu, Xiaoli Tian, and Josh Pacewicz have been important in providing feedback long after we left Hyde Park.

Also at Chicago, Don Levine thoroughly introduced me to the need for rigor in building and engaging sociological theory, and from early days onward he was a solid source of critical feedback. I honed my style for the vignettes in a small seminar with Walter Kirn. Stimulating workshop commentary from John Levi Martin came at exactly the right time. Saskia Sassen provided early funding and a shared curiosity in the potential of Internet communication as a research subject. Kristen Schilt was a big help with market matters. Informally, I received helpful thoughts from Linda Waite, Mario Small, Dingxin Zhao, Lis Clemens, Terry Clark, Ron Burt, Kate Cagney, Ryon Lancaster, Cheol-Sung Lee, Hans Joas, Karin Knorr Cetina, James Evans, Jean Comoroff, and Michael Silverstein.

Oxford University offered a lively community for finishing the dissertation. Tak Wing Chan was a valued colleague and sounding board for early ideas. I'd also like to thank Michael Biggs, Grant Blank, Tomas Farchi, Kate Hamblin, Jaco Hoffman, Sarah Harper, Bernie Hogan, Noortje Marres, and Monika Krause for various forms of colleagueship. Liz Martin and the rest of the Nuffield College librarians were most hospitable during my days laboring through at least a third of the dissertation on the tower's fifth floor. Helen Hughes Brock, my unexpected neighbor, offered fine tea and stimulating conversations about her father and 1950s sociology at Chicago.

A number of colleagues have read the book manuscript, or portions, and have done me the service of asking pointed questions and offering penetrating observations. An interdisciplinary group comprising Wendy Espeland, Marisa Brandt, John Waller, and Sanyu Mojola interrogated the entire text, chapter by chapter, in the MSU History Department's august seminar room. At a spirited "pre–author meets friends" lunch at Reading Terminal, a group of colleagues took a few hours from ASA to offer very helpful, if contradictory, comments on the first chapter and on chapters closely related to their own interests: Vanina Leschziner, Clayton Childress, Claudio Benzecry, Mariana Craciun, Terry McDonnell, Craig Rawlings, Hannah Wohl, Steve Hoffman, and Emily Erikson. Beyond these book workshops, Larry Busch read and returned each chapter with dozens of comments, and was helpful in suggesting connections to scholarship in science studies. Tom Gieryn offered pages of feedback on the manuscript, and I'm grateful for his reiteration of the importance of control in authority. Thanks to Ezra Zuckerman for his comments on ideas I shared on knowledge and decision-making. I valued my conversations about the book's progress in occasional ASA lunches and walks with Stefan Timmermans, who also offered helpful feedback on an early book prospectus. Gary Alan Fine was generous with his comments over many ASA and Chicago dinners, and at his lively ethnography workshop. And Ann Mische provided incisive commentary at the Junior Theorists' Symposium, where I presented some ideas about the social organization of coalescence.

The final stages of research and writing were at Michigan State University, a wonderful place to work, earn tenure, and to advance an academic career. For book-improving conversations and comments, thanks to my supportive colleagues in sociology, especially Steve Gold, Cathy Liu, Tom Dietz, Aaron McCright, Vladimir Shlapentokh, Ken Frank, Soma Chaudhuri, Zak Neal, Xuefei Ren, and stef shuster. I am also appreciative of the reading group discussions and general collegiality of those across campus in Lyman Briggs College: Naoko Wake, Sean Valles, Jerry Urquhart, Georgina Montgomery, Rich Bellon, Jim Smith, Bob Bell, Megan Halpern, Kevin Elliott, Rob Pennock, Mark Largent, and Elizabeth Simmons. Various vignettes and chapters were read and improved by the many members of my undergraduate senior seminars, those in my graduate course on authority and medicine, and by my exceptional undergraduate RAs: David Lawlor, Adithya Bala, Maya Giaquinta, Justin Hudson, Brielle Komosinski, Raquel Zwick, Alyssa Corpus, Connor McCormick, Tess Andrews, Mithil Gudi, and Catrina Stephan. For further comments on various parts of the text, thanks to Ashley Lyons, Rachel Kamins, Emily Calderbank, and Callista Rakhmatov. Sociology PhD student Megan Penzkofer drew on her experiences as a medical student and as a PhD candidate in sociology, and improved the final product. At the University of Arizona, our sharing of the beauty of the Sonoran Desert helped, but more important were the conversations with my new colleagues, which contributed in important ways to my finishing touches on the work. Beyond those venues already named, I have benefited from discussions of this work at University of Hong Kong, Chinese University of Hong Kong, Northwestern, Notre Dame, University of Michigan, and UCLA.

Ethnographers live our projects with those we scrutinize, and I am grateful to the doctors who were charitable enough to invite me into the venues where they managed their occupational project, and to allow me to observe—even to provide me with a white coat. Even if I cannot thank by name all of those who have contributed to this study, I hope to do so through getting their stories right. I am appreciative of their willingness to include me in the many venues they frequent, at a time in which much discussion of doctors is highly ideological and politicized. I hope that I have had little effect on their venues and occupational project stemming from the notes and pictures that were taken—because I deeply appreciate the access I have been given, and hope that future ethnographers might be afforded a similar level of access in medical and other venues. These doctors expanded my concept of what constitutes being professional; it's with great appreciation that I leave my white coat hanging in the closet to remind me of their contributions.

I also appreciate those physicians who were not part of my study but corrected, clarified, and contributed to my understanding of medicine more generally: Mindy Schwartz, Eric Whitaker, Vinny Arora, Mark Siegler, John Yoon, Caleb Alexander, Elmer Abbo, Harvey Golomb, Nicole Artz, Ari Levy, and Chad Whelan. David Rhine, a cardiac electrophysiologist, served as an expert source for many text- and phone-mediated consultations on terminology-related matters. Thanks should also be given to Superior Hospital administrators for the quantitative data they provided on their patient base. Betsy Bogdansky was a very helpful guide to the Heart Rhythm Society archives in Washington, DC. (I thank Kyle and Jonathan for giving me couches on trips to those archives, and my cousins Cindy and Ellen for giving me beds for annual meetings both sociological and medical.) I appreciate the staff of the American College of Cardiology, American Heart Association, and the Heart Rhythm Society, and the chairs of several guidelines committees, for opening up and facilitating the opportunity to observe multiple in-person meetings and also their biweekly virtual meetings.

I am also grateful to those working in industry for letting me into events whose dynamics have received much more speculation than close study. During a time when doctor-industry relationships are under critical scrutiny, it might have seemed risky for these companies to open their doors to a sociologist. And so, thanks too are owed to the program and educational directors who allowed me into their fellows' meetings and hands-on events, and for letting me call to later clarify and confirm my observations.

I'd like to also thank photography collaborators David Schalliol and Carlos Javier Ortiz for the good humor and comradeship as we explored all the exotic spaces described in these pages. Their images perfectly captured what I tried to convey, while also shaping how I understood the venues we traversed.

I owe a special debt, that unfortunately can never be repaid, to Charles Bosk, who sadly passed away this year. With Chuck, with whom I met every year, whether in Chicago, Oxford, or wherever the ASA was being held that year, I found the finest form of collegiality. It is impossible to overstate how great a loss he represents for the scholarship on the social organization of medicine. Bosk's first book, *Forgive and Remember*, inspired the typography of this book. And his spirit is inseparable from it.

I benefited from crucial funds from National Institutes of Aging and AHRQ Health Services Research training programs, and a dissertation grant from the Foundation for Informed Medical Decision Making. I also benefited from University funding through the Chicago Center of Excellence in Health Promotion, and the Charles R. Henderson dissertation fund. I'd also like to thank all the funding bodies and the postdoc committees that did not fund my project, because their applications and interviews forced me to expand my purview to answer bigger questions. And I've valued immensely my intermittent sparring with Kathy Cochran on dimensions of this work, from writing, to argument, to the semiotics of images. I thank Meagan Levinson for her enthusiasm for this book's possibilities, and for shepherding it through the publication process, as well as three Princeton University Press reviewers for close reads of a big book. One of these reviewers, who turned out to be Peter Bearman, gave extensive and very helpful comments, for which I am grateful.

My parents, Bettie and Paul Menchik, sparked an interest in ideas from early days. My younger brother, Jeremy Menchik, a fellow social scientist, has been a solid source of humor and advice in navigating the scholarly world. Elizabeth Landauer was also a major source of prodding and laughter. I am also grateful that Oliver and Max, even as they have not withheld their puzzlement over the many episodes of work "the book" seemed to require, have reinforced (and enforced) the importance of play. Finally, my wife, Maria, was willing to interrupt her own research trips and, in light of her own work as a scholar, has taken on a considerable burden in sharing, sometimes disproportionately, household tasks. (I hope I've done my fair share of the cooking.) And, as a fellow alum and adherent to the Chicago belief that conflict brings inspiration—and maybe even truth—she has frequently expressed skepticism about my early arguments, alongside skepticism that this book would ever emerge. But this honest skepticism is the best kind of support, and I wouldn't enjoy this give-and-take more with anyone else.

Managing
Medical
Authority

one

Introduction

Organizing Indeterminacy across Tethered Venues

A long tradition of scholarship beginning with Everett Hughes reminds us that professions have authority. In his examples, the experts who govern us define what is a crime and how it should be punished; for example, the clergy, who have expertise in salvation, define what is a sin and how one responds to it. In medicine, various stakeholders including doctors define physical or mental conditions as healthy or unhealthy, and how they should or should not be managed. To put it another way, as experts do their work, they see and establish what for them, as professionals, is a problem they are meant to solve. When experts are managing problems, then, these problems are not "natural," but instead are created by those experts, who also create the solutions.[1]

If experts are able to manage their authority well, they will have support from clients as they do their work, and from other stakeholders with whom they work, and will continue to occupy their position of social influence. This project is an attempt to understand how it is that medical experts in particular manage their authority so that they do not have problems with patients and others who have a stake in medicine. More particularly, it is an attempt to understand how together, physicians and other expert stakeholders, maintain medicine's authority.

The management of authority has consequences if not done well. Historical scholarship on medicine, as well as everyday observations, suggests why medicine's authority might not always be a given, and also the potential consequences of the profession's inability to manage authority. Medical practices have not always worked, and sometimes still don't. Medicine, sometimes not far from bloodletting, involves much trial and error. Technologies break, and kill people. As a consequence, some patients may reject the value of medical solutions—for instance, vaccines. Doctors may find that, as they treat patients, the diagnoses and treatments they would usually support are not right for the case. Hospitals may seek to control the kind of work doctors do. This problem with reputation sparked the emergence of the allopathic medicine movement.[2]

This project differs from earlier work on what authority is and how it is originally obtained, as framed by Hughes and the many he influenced: I ask how authority is continuously managed. For instance, what is the role of individual professionals in managing medicine's authority? How are competing claims for authority adjudicated by individual practitioners when they need to make a practical decision? And what are the practices that doctors regularly engage in to maintain the authority of the collective?[3]

This book is the product of my work to understand the connections between the individual interests of these stakeholders and the collective consequences for their patients and themselves. That goal, and questions including those posed above, require attention to the processes physicians use in an ongoing way to maintain authority. As we will see later, when doctors manage their authority, they are managing different aspects of their work and relationships with others in their occupation, as well as with patients, including creating new practices, and evaluating and adopting technologies. This approach offers a new perspective on the management of authority, and tests some basic assumptions about physicians' tasks that have been isolated from the broader scope of work they do with their credentialed peers and other stakeholders to manage medicine's authority in what I will refer to as an "occupational project" shared by all the stakeholders.

This book is an ethnography, and as such it focuses on individuals, and all they might do to establish, reinforce, and implement practices. But it also focuses on a compelling account of the relationships between individual actions and their collective consequences, and it accounts for persistent and consequential processes and connections among those who perform different work and periodically meet in various venues, including venues often obscured in ethnographic work. As I'll explain in greater detail below, I use the term *venue* to capture places that are formatted for focused tasks that involve joint activities, are attended during specific periods for particular events, and serve to organize work on some dimension of the collective project that those attending are at least minimally motivated to strengthen. Rather than examine a single venue or compare venues, as is often done, I study consequential linkages between them, examining the relationships among a set of venues that are interconnected, or "tethered."

The venues I observed were a hospital's wards, the operating theater (which they and I refer to as the "lab"), and boardrooms; industry-sponsored fellows' training programs and hands-on meetings for physicians to learn new technology; and annual meetings of the professional association.

The multiple venues I observed allowed me to understand how doctors define what counts as a medical condition and perform medical interventions to treat those conditions. What I saw was a very complicated relationship—and which has not been revealed in previous studies—between authority, cross-venue collaboration, and making new knowledge. The next step for this study, then, is to take a quick look at a particular venue that lets us see joint activities in medicine in all their complexity. Then I will read this vignette through the conceptual vocabulary this book proposes.

The Live Case Presentations at the Annual Professional Association Meeting

The vignette below describes individuals who perform many of the tasks involved in managing authority, gathered at a conference organized by the Heart Rhythm Society. Many of these practices seem foreign to what I understand as medical work. Specifically, several of the problems they have to face in this venue broaden the scope of their work beyond working with their hands or developing new knowledge.

When I get to the venue, which is the annual meeting of the professional association for certain specialized cardiologists—cardiac electrophysiologists—and take my place with the attendees, I recognize that some of their tasks are familiar, if at a completely different scale. I'm sitting in a 10,000-seat auditorium, featuring an immense Jumbotron screen. It's the largest conference room in the country's largest convention center. We're about to watch a live case presentation, in which some well-known physicians are working together to demonstrate new knowledge and allow others to critically examine it. Specifically, selected presenters are directing surgeries from their home operating theaters—or "labs"—in which they operate, in real time, on real patients, while these surgeries are broadcast into the auditorium.

The live case presentation is a centerpiece and the most popular event of the international annual conference. The master of ceremonies and a row of internationally distinguished cardiologists sit on the stage, but everyone's eyes are fixed on the forty-foot screens behind them. To keep up with the state of expert knowledge, EPs in the audience have arrived from the institutions where they usually do their work, and those who can't attend have paid hundreds of dollars for on-demand access at home. They are here to learn about new territory being charted, but also to marvel at these sometimes-transnational performances. Given the pulsing music, and the rise and fall of audience members' cell phone

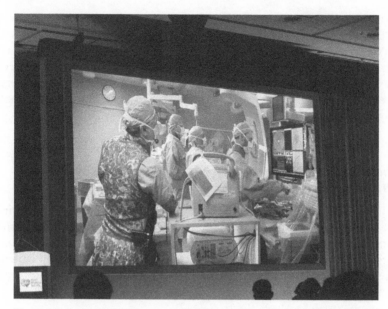

Figure 1.1. An operating theater, or "lab," in which an electrophysiology procedure is being performed. Although it is not the live conference described in the vignette, it has a similar audience size and composition. The doctors being watched are dependent on screens to ensure they address the patient's problem, and, for purposes of validating their observations in their home labs, the doctors watching the screen from the conference rely on watching the mediated doctors. Photograph by Carlos Javier Ortiz.

cameras, to me, at least, it feels less like a conference than a rock concert.

The first presenter is Dr. Kellogg. Her procedure involves a new way of pacing the heart to prepare for a pacemaker. She is the only speaker in the presentation, but behind her are two nurses, a technician (or "tech"), and an advanced student ("fellow"). Another fellow stands at the bedside, with hands on a lead he's snaked up the femoral artery into the patient's heart. Dr. Kellogg next introduces "our friends from Medscape and Medicore," the medical device company representatives who are always at the bedside during procedures, there to clarify the affordances of new technologies, offer a hand, and gather intel on how doctors like the technologies and whether those doctors can use them safely.

One of the purposes of Dr. Kellogg's presentation is to point out a new solution to a recognized problem. Dr. Kellogg grounds her work in recent scholarship, and she mentions another case her team will soon publish, based on an innovation they developed in their lab. She describes the lab's "neat double-alligator technique" for collecting and visualizing EKG signals from the lead, which is a kind of antenna that carries electrical signals. She also demonstrates her new way of pacing the heart, called "His bundle" pacing, performed from a different location than usual. This approach allows doctors to more precisely program a pacemaker to fix the rhythm of an abnormal heartbeat, by electrically activating both of the heart's ventricles, rather than one alone. On one screen, we see slides of EKGs, images of anatomy, and results of clinical research. On the foot of many of the slides that contain elegant images of the anatomy she is treating, Dr. Kellogg has acknowledged another respected standard-setter for providing the images. On another screen is an ongoing live image of the lab itself, the true testing ground for any medical procedure. It offers a view of the hands of the fellow performing the procedure as well as the team enabling their use. Displayed on yet another screen is a real-time digital capture of a fluoroscopy of the patient, an X-ray image of the movements of the heart. Dr. Kellogg provides a verbal interpretation of both the EKGs and the fluoroscopy for the audience and panel, and points out the atrial lead, which, she notes, was placed "at the suggestion of an astute representative from Medscape."

Some questions with direct and straightforward answers are asked by doctors who already use these techniques, and by the moderator. As the fellow screws a lead into the patient's heart, an audience member asks whether the patient will be safe if they must get an MRI scan at some point in the future. He is concerned about whether Dr. Kellogg's new direction is compatible with his everyday routine. "The 38/30 lead is not MR conditional. How much of a problem is that?" Dr. Kellogg responds: "OK, that's a good question, and we got confirmation from our Medscape rep here that the lead is MR conditional at this point." After she gives a thumbs-up to the camera, she redirects attention back to the lab's innovative technique of displaying the jagged EKG on the same screen as the map of the heart they've made, yet another image they make to track their progress on the procedure. "Having used our neat double-alligator technique, you can see the position of the lead on our 3-D map there." It's an innovation that affords the physician the ability to see more, and that Dr. Kellogg believes will offer colleagues a valuable way of interpreting information on their patients' hearts.

The expert panelists begin to ask questions about the direction proposed, ones that reflect their own positive and negative experiences. A key issue involved in the task of pacemaker implementation is that the screwed-in lead can become dislodged from the heart's wall, requiring a new operation. Dr. Strauss asks, "How often do you encounter the issue of the lead falling off?" Dr. Kellogg repeats the question, and admits, "I would say that probably for most of us, in the initial experience the answer is, 'More than we would have liked.'" Dr. Kellogg is willing to acknowledge that she, like doctors with less experience, encounters challenges when undertaking a new procedure. She indicates that she's still working out a strategy. Dr. Strauss is paying attention not only to the screen but also to the audience, and he endorses using *his* approach with the lead. Their other panelists endorse their own approaches, in turn.

After answering all these questions, Dr. Kellogg once again takes center stage. As a riposte to the others' attempts to validate their own track records, Dr. Kellogg makes a display of success: she finishes the narrative of the case by showing, and defining, its completion; turning back to the fellow, she asks him to show one last X-ray image and set of EKGs. She finishes by describing her good result: "We checked our threshold and it looks like it's .3 at 1.0 milliseconds." That level signals success, and she reinforces it for the audience. The audience members' cell phone cameras bob for a final set of screenshots.

Amid the applause, the master of ceremonies issues his praise: "Well done, congratulations."

□ ■ □

The cameras now move to another lab at Cityview Hospital. In this case, the presenter is Dr. Passer, but doing the procedure is not a fellow, but rather Dr. Stimm, who is Cityview Hospital's EP program director and a well-known expert in ablation. Ablation is the practice of using a catheter to create scar tissue in the heart so that it doesn't trigger or sustain an abnormal rhythm. Dr. Stimm is focused on the case, but also on the international viewing audience. The procedure Dr. Stimm will perform is more complex than the first one we observed, and is considered innovative for its use of two existing technologies not ordinarily used together. These technologies are usually used for different procedures than today's, but Dr. Stimm wants to show that when used together they can solve new problems that cannot otherwise be addressed with existing technologies.

Unlike Dr. Kellogg, who was directing a fellow to perform a procedure that has become fairly routine for her lab and has been made accessible to non-experts, Dr. Stimm's procedure requires more specialized knowledge than most EPs hold. The other physicians on the screen are also esteemed for their particular niche in the laboratory; when Dr. Lindbaum, one of the panelists, brings up a question on anticoagulation, we can see Dr. Passer, on the screen, turn and ask his colleague Dr. Long, who has specialized knowledge in the area.

Dr. Stimm has selected the case because the conference audience comes to be wowed, and this one truly fits the bill. As he later put it, in an interview with me, people want a live case to be "a little bit like NASCAR, where you watch it to see a crash." But ultimately, he said, doctors performing live cases strive to select a patient with whom they can succeed; they want to show that their group does high-quality work. Before this patient was chosen, three others were considered and rejected: one with cardiac anatomy that was too large, a second whose wife objected, and a third who didn't reliably show up to appointments. Somehow this patient was comfortable—or made to be comfortable—with the potential risks.

The camera first zooms in on Dr. Passer, who describes the catheters they'll use, and then onto Dr. Stimm's hands, which loom large on the screen. They hold and flip the handle of the ablation catheter, to demonstrate how he will soon apply light pressure on its small knob.

Behind the star power of Dr. Stimm is a support network that reaches beyond the members of his lab. Dr. Lindbaum recognizes when Dr. Stimm is struggling to place his catheter where he can pick up important signals. This struggle occurs despite Dr. Stimm's earlier efforts to prepare for a smooth performance, which he initiated the moment he was invited to carry out the presentation in front of thousands. As he recounted to me later, in an interview, "Before we went live, we put a wire in a nice place and took it out, so we knew we could get there. When we went live, I couldn't get it back there." Fortunately, Dr. Lindbaum had visited his lab the week before to observe the innovation, and as he sat on the dais at the conference he was able to help Dr. Stimm save face during the live procedure. Dr. Stimm said, "Steve Lindbaum texted [my lab colleagues] to put the endo wire in further. I did that, and it went right in; that's what allowed us to get the wires together." Such on-the-fly support from a colleague in a far-flung venue will be remembered; as Dr. Stimm later put it, "I owe him now."

Arrhythmia eliminated, Q&A begins. The conversation turns to post-procedure experiences. Live cases like these are venues where experiences that look like complications can actually be recast as common occurrences, and even expected. There is a back-and-forth, with doctors sharing their own experiences with patients whose procedures didn't follow the same trajectory as Dr. Stimm's. Dr. Lindbaum asks about a possible complication that has to do with how long to keep a drain in the patient's chest after a procedure: "How often do you see the pericardial effusion the next morning?" Dr. Passer answers: "We keep the drain in until we see no drainage. However, sometimes they come back with [fluid]. Is that a unique experience, or are we the only ones to see that?" Other panelists jockey to share their similar experiences. Dr. Strauss responds, "Sometimes it happens, if they have heart failure." Another panelist affirms in a way that helps those in the audience, who may eventually perform these or similar procedures in their home labs, interpret and justify their own experiences: "Sometimes that happens, and they need support for a few days. So keeping a drain for a few days is a good idea." At this point, the direction forward does not seem clear, but something else is clear to me: even once new solutions are proposed for problems that physicians tackle, those solutions may not always work.

The master of ceremonies ends on an aesthetic note. "Beautiful outcome there. Congratulations. Very courageous case."

The applause of the audience thunders through the room. Regardless of where the audience members are watching from, the conference center or their homes, all now know what innovations—and what challenges they create—are coming from one of the top programs.

□ ■ □

The next morning, the third and last case is performed in a recently redesigned lab across town, at Superior Hospital, where the matter of dexterity becomes more complicated. This hybrid lab is new, low-lit, and holds robotic technology that enables collaborations between those on the vanguard of both cardiology and cardiac surgery. Dr. Torstal, the director of the electrophysiology program, introduces Dr. Balter, a cardiac surgeon who "just celebrated his 300th robotic procedure in three and a half years." Behind the crossed-armed Dr. Torstal, in the remote laboratory, we can see the robot's metal fingers tweezing into a beating heart.

Dr. Torstal intersperses his descriptions of their next plan with the word *disruptive*, a term that means "pioneering" among the au courant business school set. He notes that the current procedure is based on a "first-in-man" procedure—that is, one previously tested only on animals—that he published as a case report in electrophysiology's top journal. Dr. Torstal describes the part of heart he's operating on: "This might be an area that has truly never been accessed in human beings. Any comments from the expert panel?" From the conference stage, Dr. Strauss asks Dr. Balter how he does the procedure safely, while pointing out his own strategy. Dr. Torstal comments approvingly, "Wow, that's slick."

Suddenly, a seemingly uncontroversial subject—the existence of a piece of anatomy—becomes a matter of contestation. When one of his fellows shows him the map of the heart they've made, Dr. Torstal acknowledges and calls into question the position of those who, as he puts it, believe in something called "macroscopic channels." "There does appear in the area there—*if you believe in the macroscopic channels*, the area we didn't map—you can see there is a potential broad isthmus between the scars." He then mentions leaders in the field who were skeptical of the value of examining these so-called channels, and "had a nice paper in *JACC [Journal of the American College of Cardiology]* several years ago saying that isolated diastolic potentials offered a better case for ablation than what you got from just looking at those channels macroscopically." After asking the expert panel for their impressions, he gets validation—and the last word: "It's a good point—I think you need to combine both, you need to look for the channels, but you really want to see those isolated diastolic potentials, which you have here."[4] Thus, anatomy, especially anatomy one's rivals will reference to justify their practices, seems to become a matter of belief.

Similarly, other questions about medicine appear to afford a chance for an individual physician to set a professional agenda— and to also signal their distance from industry. Such opportunities are usually seized by central leaders in electrophysiology, whom I call "standard-setters." These leaders can be distinguished from doctors who are a bit more peripheral—I'll call them "clinicians"— and who comprise much of the live case's audience. When Dr. Torstal answers the next question, from a clinician who asks what technologies he advises using for a procedure, he asserts that no doctor should be tied to one medical device company. Even if his embrace of "disruption" suggests in part an appreciation of what technology companies may offer, he has distanced himself from physicians who appear unjustifiably exclusive with the technologies they use. A different clinician asks him about the advantages of the mapping system he is using. "We use all three systems. The advantage of this system is—" He takes a moment to reassert the importance he places on choosing whichever technology suits the particulars of the case at hand. "I personally, to editorialize, think that we should choose the shape of a mapping catheter tailored to the arrhythmia of interest."

More cell phone cameras rise and fall, and a clinician I've approached says she plans to share her photos with colleagues and administrators "back home," despite the fact that a recording of the event is included with her conference registration.

The moderator signals he is aware of the suspense and general entertainment value that this live case has created: "Dr. Torstal, we've given you five extra minutes in this session. It's an encore; they're holding up lighters in the audience."

Even with the enthusiastic extension, Dr. Torstal remains restrained. He primes the audience to be prepared for the possibility of a "steam pop," in which a bubble forms during the process of burning, or ablating, the heart, which can marginally increase the possibility of perforating the heart. Later, he reiterates this concern. "Again I want to remind the audience that if you see a steam pop, don't be too alarmed—everything's quite superficial. [There may be a steam pop] because there's no cooling."

The moderator congratulates and thanks Dr. Torstal and the experts. No steam pop has occurred, and the fellows have begun stitching the sutures. In closing the moderator reaffirms the role of chance: "We wish you good luck."

Getting to Authority: Organizing the Indeterminacy of Expert Knowledge

In many ways, the vignette is a setting similar to the classic representation of medicine's authority in so many paintings, such as Rembrandt's *The Anatomy Lesson of Dr. Nicolaes Tulp*, or Eakins's *The Gross Clinic*. I turn to these paintings now because they are iconic representations of some of the raw material of authority. These paintings depict an operating theater in which top physicians, demonstrating points of anatomy, are surrounded by people in tiered seating. These doctors are using their resources in time and energy to define and reinforce definitions of sickness and health, respecify anatomy and diseases, and share expertise—that is, teaching. Some have earned the right to teach and demonstrate, while others are there to observe and defer.

The scenario depicted is familiar to many sociologists studying medicine, too, who have seen, for instance, how the ritual of grand rounds allows surgeons in a hospital to observe their colleagues' virtuosity with high-risk patients, and to collectively review the generalizable principles that are emerging for the surgical management of disease. The paintings show us authoritative experts who get to perform the riskiest medical tasks, and others who are watching them, as they reinforce and sometimes shift the profession's understanding of the body, illness, and treatment.[5]

These pictures not only hang in world-class museums but are also reproduced on the covers of some of the most influential social science works on medicine. But there is much that the pictures obscure. They don't show that in the face of a high degree of risk, medicine is characterized by a wide variance of plausible options for dealing with that risk. They don't show the give-and-take among medical experts who question each other and suggest competing approaches. They don't show that medicine is, to a great degree, indeterminate with regard to the boundaries of expert knowledge and accepted practice. As shown in the vignette and in the data presented in this book, organizing this indeterminacy is important because there is a project around it, one that extends to other venues.

Some features of the vignette help to illustrate this idea of indeterminacy. First, in contrast to the static account offered by the paintings, we see in the vignette repeated instances where the presenting doctor constructs others' view of their work. For instance, when Dr. Torstal recasts the steam pop as relatively benign—or at least justified in light of the benefits of his procedure—he is offering for his colleagues a way to understand a particular dimension of EPs' work. And he calls into question the existence of "macroscopic channels." But what sort of processes are involved in a situation in which someone is both shaping understandings, but also giving space to those who push at his preferred understandings?

We can see indeterminacy a second time when the doctors in the vignette demonstrate their expertise alongside other stakeholders and tasks, which the paintings also obscure. We see in the vignette, for instance, the interesting fact that Dr. Kellogg looks to medical technology reps on the stage for knowledge that she and the observing clinicians both lack. Overall, what's the significance of the fact that they are performing multiple tasks and working with unexpected stakeholders like companies?

And we see indeterminacy a third time, in the presenters' references to those far beyond their labs, and to their knowledge, distinct connections also not suggested by the paintings. What's the significance of the fact that the presenters are linked by digital feeds to the audience at the conference venue and to those watching from remote locations? In the paintings we have a range of people in the audience, and some are talking to each other.

How do we make sense of the fact that Dr. Stimm's colleague in the conference venue was sending text messages to the lab, offering him advice that ultimately enabled him to execute the procedure successfully?

Finally, in the vignette we see indeterminacy in shared understandings of how medicine itself should be understood, and in efforts to help shape that understanding. For instance, on the foot of many of her slides, Dr. Kellogg has acknowledged another respected standard-setter for providing the images she uses. And in Dr. Torstal's presentation, we saw him seeking to shape understandings about technologies, when he suggested how decisions about catheters should be made. How should we make sense of the fact that these experts appear less uncertain about what they are seeing than they are actively shaping what other experts involved in medical work should be saying and doing?

This book is intended to explore this indeterminacy of knowledge, practice, and the occupational project itself. It stretches across many venues, to show how in the face of this indeterminacy, powerful experts go about managing their authority by managing the conceptualization and implementation of their occupation's core ideas of problems and solutions. For sociologists, there are many potential payoffs of looking at the ongoing organizing of authority in medicine. Such a focus can allow us to understand the individual's role in managing authority. We can then account for why there are differences in practices across places. We can understand how authority can persist regardless of stratification inside of medicine, and how physicians at different social locations differently contribute to the authority of the group. We can identify why some treatments that are considered effective at one point might later be considered problematic. We can go beyond demonstrating that medical work is unsystematic ("it's complicated" or "nuanced" or "messy"), and show, especially in terms of its relationship to science, some principles through which it is organized. And this focus can provide a way of thinking about how knowledge is considered by a group given privileges to create and vet it, and how we should understand what knowledge is accepted. Finally, a potential practice benefit beyond sociology might follow a focus on the fact that they do manage authority, and how: it provides a basis for trust. What we might see is that giving doctors the right to manage their authority serves public interests more than otherwise thought.[6]

Yet, because the processes I use to observe and study interaction are new, we need a vocabulary for understanding what is happening. To take our scope of inquiry beyond the immediate conversation, I ask: How else might what we have seen in the vignette be related to authority? To answer this question, in what follows I will continue to read the vignette using theoretical constructs I propose will be valuable for understanding authority, namely, organizing indeterminacy, problems and solutions, the occupational project, and tethered venues.

The Process of Organizing Indeterminacy of Expert Knowledge

From the perspective of a sociologist, what we saw in the vignette might look like managing uncertainty, that is, the application of expertise to particular circumstances. When we talk about individuals with uncertainty, we are referring to situations where members of a group must make a decision and are not sure either how the group understands the knowledge base related to that decision, or whether that knowledge applies to the specific decision at hand. The managing of that uncertainty is a process of trying to apply expertise in working through a particular case. And we can see some of that in the vignette, for instance in Dr. Stimm's concern about whether his procedure would be successful. Similarly, we saw Dr. Kellogg ask colleagues about how long to put a drain in a patient's chest after a procedure, which reflects her uncertainty about whether challenges involved with this practice can be traced to the patient or to the procedure.[7]

I differentiate this process of organizing indeterminacy—which involves processes of active definition, control, and construction—from well-studied processes of managing uncertainty. Organizing indeterminacy in medicine is a process of defining and changing the way anatomy, disease processes, and medical practices writ large should be understood by colleagues and the public, while managing uncertainty is a process of working through a particular case about which one is uncertain regarding those details of anatomy, disease processes, and medical practices. Organizing indeterminacy involves controlling people to shape medicine itself. Individual physicians are actively working together in an occupational project not only to understand medicine as it has been handed down to them, but also to *construct* medicine itself in light of constant social changes. They are working as individuals, but they are also collectively contributing to the practice of medicine itself, because they are allowing people to see their work and comment on it. In contrast, managing uncertainty happens once the work of labeling is done. It is a term often used to describe the individual's state of understanding, rather than the individual's work in shaping others' understandings.

The data, taken as a whole, show a picture different than that of managing uncertainty. The vignette shows an open, but noticeably organized, physical and conceptual space, in which a whole range of ideas about medicine is entertained. It's a situation offering a range of potential directions that physicians could have taken, and a range of diverse positions on knowledge that people might potentially agree on; a moment prior to the carrying out of the tasks. In that situation, multiple different doctors were attempting to use language, people, and material resources to shape thinking and behaviors about medicine. And the germ of that idea is behind the work done by this book.

My reference to openness captures the idea that for these experts in medicine, it is a given that people can disagree—different opinions can exist in the same space. In the vignette, we can see openness in the fact that in certain circumstances there may not be a single, widely shared, way of understanding a social and physical fact, but rather, different perspectives on the way the EPs' work might be understood. In the state of indeterminacy we saw in the vignette, individuals have a relationship with that work that is conditional. The vignette highlights contestation, even over the existence of a specific location on the human heart and the use of existing technologies. The conditional relationship to work can also be observed when technologies change, resulting in new signals to be seen, understood, and addressed, and new opportunities for treatments.

The most interesting quality about the data offered in the vignette is that despite the indeterminacy about what the profession's knowledge was, is, and could be, this was also a systematically managed event. And, as I saw later, there were features common across different venues—in particular, the systematic management and the building of the knowledge base. I saw a condition in which individuals who are reliant on a knowledge base are *also* actively working to shape that knowledge base, and how others interpret information that is part of that base. They are renewing, refreshing, and reinvigorating a knowledge base.

I describe these processes together as organizing indeterminacy, which involves claim-making (including labeling), advocacy, examination, refinement, and accommodation of the views of others. These stakeholders were differently advocating for surgical versus pharmaceutical versus behavioral interventions, and they were differently claiming the superiority of one particular school of thought (what Crane referred to as an "invisible college"), often tied to their training program. And all were seeking to convince peers and students of a particular mode of interpreting an EKG or even recognizing an anatomical structure or physiological process; for example, Dr. Torstal's indicating to the audience that they might understand the patient's problem as involving either "macroscopic channels" or "isolated diastolic potentials," depending on what they believed. They were refining and reinforcing different approaches and best practices for the clinicians in the audience. The doctors were choosing to label standards for the tens of thousands of viewers paying to watch in person, via the live feed, or through the videos they purchased "on-demand" online, or on a portable hard drive, to learn about breakthroughs and gain continuing medical education credits. In the vignette, the labelers were defining the boundaries of the open, indeterminate physical and conceptual space of medical work. This indeterminate space doesn't exist independently of those who label it; and so, although it might be described as the proverbial "gap" in knowledge, it is not.

Having gotten a partial view of the cast of characters we'll encounter in this book, we can now take a closer look at how their collective efforts contribute to the management of authority. The choices made by the vignette's doctors are similar to the organizing processes captured in observations of grand rounds in a hospital, but their pioneering choices have a global scope, involving rare and often tricky conditions, for which no map exists. And we see, consistent with what scholars have demonstrated regarding the hesitancy of senior physicians to sanction colleagues, that nothing's punitive—no one's getting blamed for unpredictable events. Rather, the peers of these senior physicians recognize and make concessions for inevitable complications that might happen in this space of openness, maybe even letting them organize indeterminacy by relabeling events that initially seem negative (such as Dr. Torstal's steam pop). No one is guilty for raising an objection or question, because new ground is being broken; those who speak up are trained to organize indeterminacy. Overall, the vignette offers a snapshot of what the leaders of cardiac electrophysiology are doing, as practitioners of medicine, to organize themselves and a knowledge base.[8]

Creating Problems and Solutions

When physicians shape indeterminacy at both individual and collective scales, they produce medical authority. And medicine, like other areas of expert work, trains its members to do this shaping, and to understand that it is a part of their work. They have enough to do in the fast-paced and high-stakes environment of their day-to-day work on the wards and in the operating theater. How do they manage the constant pressure of change, for instance, the indeterminacy generated by introduction of new technology, or the pressure of a new disease on matters of the heart? Together, they organize it by labeling problems and solutions.

This process of labeling cannot be organized by individuals alone. Professional authority doesn't exist unless a range of stakeholders buy into it, sharing an at least provisional idea of what the professional group's work is. Those people are different, and the tasks are too—there are different tasks done in different venues, and those venues necessitate that different people work to carry out these tasks, and that the acceptance of subordinates is at times necessary. In the live case presentation, we're seeing alternative interpretations about how peers should approach how they gather and interpret information in everyday work. In subsequent chapters in this book, we're going to see other tasks; for instance, in medical device company meetings, the synthesis of a range of research and clinical data into support for using a particular technology; and in annual meetings, the endorsement of a particular school of thought. How are people, tasks, and venues connected in terms of how indeterminacy is organized?

One way to think about what happened at the conference observed in the vignette is that indeterminacy was defined by individuals, and organized in a way that had the potential to shape the understandings of those inside and outside the professional group. Scholars of professional work, and of social problems generally, have used different terms for this basic social process, from "diagnosis and treatment" to "labeling" to "social problems." Sociologists have recognized that this process is central, for instance, to the control of people who are considered different, whether in the work of the criminal justice system or in the work of the professions. And labeling has also been understood to make it possible to socially process individuals in these systems of criminal justice and health care. More important, it has been recognized that this process plays a role in the further development of those systems.[9]

The terminology I use, "problem and solution," is continuous with this language, yet broader, as I seek to reinforce that a homogeneous set of experts—that is, a set of similarly trained and credentialed professionals—are not just taking an existing task by relying on a set knowledge base. Rather, a wide set of stakeholders from across professional groups are continuously generating those problems and solutions themselves. Even if it describes a general social process, the language "problem and solution" closely tracks the terminology used by scholars of medicalization, those concerned with laying out the contours of medical authority. On the one hand, medical professionals, often alongside stakeholders such as industry, and patient advocacy groups, label problems: should a heartbeat with a certain EKG reading be called an arrhythmia or a consequence of too much caffeine under stress? Should a set of behaviors, such as distractibility or forgetfulness, receive the diagnostic attribution of attention deficit disorder, or of being twelve years old? They create these classifications for a collective group, both inside and outside medicine. On the other hand, professionals also label solutions: whether it should be medications or school recess that is needed to address attention deficit disorder; whether surgical intervention or meditation should be used to treat arrhythmias.[10]

This focus on ongoing shifts in problems and solutions reflects a key way this book departs from previous literature on medical authority. In their studies of medical authority, Freidson and Starr were focused on explaining how physicians make, in Paul Starr's terms, their "definitions of reality . . . prevail as valid and true." This project is informed by a different question that is equally if not more important: *How* does a wide set of stakeholders continuously organize the processes of defining how medical work should be understood? This question arises because, unlike Freidson and Starr, who were trying to understand the social organization of medical authority by looking at a very small set of stakeholders, primarily comprising and centering physicians, this account is centered on a wider group of professionals. And unlike theirs, my question is process-oriented. While they used synthetic or historical approaches respectively, this ethnographic account focuses on the people and places continuously organizing medical work. And therefore, it is centered more on a wider range of ongoing processes at work, offering a way to conceptualize and understand the management of authority in the present and into the imagined future.[11]

This book will begin to examine this adjudication process central to medical authority. Other questions arise, for example, how does the social organization of authority work so that someone can identify a problem and solution, comfortably pronounce on it, and, at the same time, also acknowledge that people are going to possibly disagree with it? Dr. Torstal's comment suggests that part of the labeling process is knowing that it's possible to disagree with a label once it is made by an influential doctor. It suggests that there are some processes yet to be identified that allow work to continue even when strong differences exist. Later in the book I pursue how doctors like him go about socially organizing their work to try to fill the indeterminate space of defining problems and solutions, while also leaving it open, and I will consider the space's consequences.

The Social Organization of the Management of Authority: The Occupational Project

It's time to acknowledge that in one way, the vignette could be somewhat misleading. Specifically, it might suggest that the process of creating problems and solutions is an individual project of particular doctors. But, if we think about the vignette a little more closely, we can see that it is showing us a social project, in which we see ties to industry, and physicians with different opinions deciding to come together in this venue of the conference, to share their positions, contest each other's positions, and propose new positions. This section focuses on paying attention to a social project of a particular type: the occupational project. This concept of occupational project captures a range of tasks that constitute work; as we'll see in subsequent chapters, for doctors these tasks include, for instance, maintaining relationships with invisible colleges, accessing resources for clinical trials, and naming anatomy—tasks performed with an eye toward the future of the group. These tasks contribute to processes of establishing problems and solutions with a range of stakeholders—including ones often thought of as "external"—as these stakeholders manage authority.

I introduce this concept of occupational project because it is a way in which we can examine more broadly the range of processes that may contribute to managing authority. In an important way the vignette has focused us on the steps taken by a few prominent people on the stage, but looking at the occupational project brings our attention not just to shop-floor tasks of work, not just to the positions of prominent people, and not just to the efforts of credentialed professionals aiming at a unitary goal, but also to the actions of interdependent stakeholders that are centered on taking the profession into the future.

The vignette also shows us characters new to ethnographic studies of medicine and the professions, and, in contrast to other works, positions them as constitutive of, and not external to, medical work. What we see in the vignette is a diverse group, taking on multiple new tasks, and engaging in unexpected collaborations. They also interact in ways that show us a bigger kind of project, in which different kinds of knowledge are integrated and integral. First, and most striking, was the presence of those typically thought of as not from the world of professions, but of business. The relationship doesn't seem one-sided; those company reps appear to be neither exerting strong influence on doctors nor affording those doctors much influence over them. And Dr. Torstal, in advocating for maintaining relationships with multiple companies, suggested the value of having an arm's-length relationship with any given company. But the device company rep, whose expertise came from having a foot firmly planted in the company, appeared to be a key partner in innovating. Second, given the cost of the live cases described, there was likely some cooperation from hospital administrators. (Indeed, in a later conversation Dr. Stimm relayed that the procedure cost his university tens of thousands of dollars to organize, as it involved getting advanced camera equipment into operating rooms not prepared for the performance, and reducing considerably the number of procedures the hospital could conduct that day.) The vignette shows collaborations occurring among stakeholders in and from a range of venues—some normally considered to be "outside" the profession.[12]

The vignette also shows that in addition to undertaking the task of ablating arrhythmias, the diverse group of stakeholders is engaged in many other behaviors that can be understood as tasks, ones involving a different knowledge base. As we saw, Dr. Kellogg was spreading a colleague's observation, sharing slides that she had received from a fellow well-known EP standard-setter. Also, rather than performing the procedure herself, which might be more efficient and effective, she was taking the extra time necessary to educate fellows. We saw that Dr. Stimm had to select a patient carefully as he performed the task of ablation, in order to ensure his contribution to the success of the procedure in an operating room that can be said to be global. And physicians we often think of as working toward different goals, in different jurisdictions, were working toward similar goals and seeking to manage tasks together: Dr. Torstal and the cardiac surgeon were helping each other complete their tasks and build their reputations. A diverse group of stakeholders was performing a range of tasks that may appear completely irrelevant to the central one they were trained for, that their professional jurisdiction has claimed, and that they must perform on the front lines, but these other tasks also have the potential to be consequential for the problems and solutions the profession can create.[13]

The case study-based scholarship on expert work and knowledge production suggests that this diversity of stakeholders is significant in socially organizing the management of authority. That literature, which focuses on expertise and laypeople, has also shown us that different venues are important. Indeed, this literature was part of my motivation for visiting some key venues in which these stakeholders might assemble. The literature's relevance to physicians' work, which involves collaboration with a range of stakeholders, is clear; doctors periodically visit several venues with varying recurring social dynamics, where they perform tasks that are both global and local, including training subordinates, selecting clients, managing patients, testing new technology, cultivating new colleagues, adjudicating each other's claims to knowledge, and forming electrophysiology-wide practice standards.[14]

Like much of that work, this study's focus on knowledge locates it not only in people but also in things (e.g., technologies). In addition, it analyzes the work of physicians and other stakeholders across many venues in which efforts are oriented toward ensuring that they shape the knowledge discussed and used there. While capturing the range of stakeholders involved in the shaping of medical work, the case study work raises some new questions about how we should think about how individuals hold together as a collective, and remain connected, as they continuously respond to changes and shape future work in ongoing ways. How, then, should we think about how they authoritatively work out the details of their project? This project seeks to capture the ways that different stakeholders develop and maintain authority-strengthening connections across venues. But if we don't use the terminology used by scholars of the professions, how should we conceptualize the set of stakeholders involved?

Here we return to the concept of the occupational project, which I see as the solution to the problem. I am using the word *occupational* because I want to account for the working relationships between the professionals and the wide range of people they deal with, including those in areas not traditionally thought of as being organized by expert knowledge. The tasks of managing authority do not involve a set knowledge base that is held by one group, but rather one that is constructed by a range of stakeholders, whose alliances may be stronger or weaker according to time and place.[15] This attention to time is one reason I am using the word *project*, because I want to capture that the work is ongoing and future oriented, and sometimes involves alliances that shift. Especially when discussing professionals, projects involve agency in the sense of choices and intentional action; they include, for instance, choosing to use and endorse a technology, or to help an employer raise its standing in competitions for prestige. Some social work must be accomplished in order to manage tasks, and also to set the rules for how things get done and can change. A future orientation underpins this defining; those in an occupational project want future insiders and outsiders to use their terminology and technology, and to look first to its practitioners' expertise. As technology changes, experts must change the way tasks are organized. The term *project* implies, too, that as policies change— such as a hospital's policies for financially supporting a set of doctors, or allowing companies into the building—experts' relationships with their occupation's stakeholders might have to shift. The future orientation of the occupational project is directed at the profession's capacity to retain its say on what constitutes a problem and solution for a community.[16]

It's possible for a multidisciplinary group with a diverse set of tasks to be operating in a state of indeterminacy and not get much done. The defining characteristic of an occupational project is that this group of stakeholders has resolved to organize indeterminacy on subjects for which their skills are relevant. As we saw in the vignette, future approaches were proposed. Clinicians had come from all over the globe to see these new procedures described, in Dr. Torstal's terms, as "disruptive." The future was onstage. The standard-setters were taking the risk of presenting live cases and using new methods, to talk about technologies that will eventually allow them to address problems for which there are currently no solutions. This attitude toward the future is further evidenced in the fact that we are observing the intentionally organized dissemination of knowledge; the event is being recorded and will be shared on the Internet, as well as archived for those who are not there seeing it and will feel the imperative to do so.[17]

At its core, maintaining authority in medical work is about sustaining deference from those outside the occupational project, to the problems and solutions that have been defined under the banner of "medicine." The profession must get, and maintain, distinction from key stakeholders, which range from patients to companies to the state. Authority resides in the group of people doing the work, which particularly includes, but is not limited to, doctors. Expert work involves a division of labor, albeit one that involves interdependence and collaboration. And so it involves multiple goals and activities, including raising funds, attracting collaborators, and evaluating opportunities.

Scholars' more recent observations about the nature of expert work have implications for the way I use the term *authority*. In this book, authority refers to what a group has when it can keep control over what people in and around an occupational project should be doing. I am talking about authority in a particular sense, one that has to do with management. Authority reflects those stakeholders' knowledge, their skills, their technology, and their rhetoric with those they serve in key venues.[18]

This use of authority is not meant to suggest that authority is rooted in rights or claims; rather, it is oriented toward an understanding of authority as processual. Authority confirms, momentarily, how some group should think about things—and rethink them, into the future. Therefore, it determines what they can or should do. In other words, my understanding of authority addresses questions like What's the nature of the decisions the group members are making? and How do their decisions contribute to their ability to move into the future?

This conceptualization of authority follows from recent scholarship and changes in the nature of the relationship between physicians and "outside" stakeholders, that suggest that authority has become more complicated. In studying medical work, Freidson and Starr approach authority in a way that excludes stakeholders such as industry, because they use a traditional way of defining "professional." The language of "occupational project" reflects a much broader set of stakeholders. When one types *catheter ablation* into the Google search engine, results two through four point to the websites of the National Heart, Lung, and Blood Institute, the Mayo Clinic, and the American Heart Association. Revealingly, the first link points to a site created and maintained not by any professional association but by Medtronic.[19]

I study different venues, stakeholders, and the relationships between them because I am interested in capturing how these individual stakeholders relate to the collective groups to which they belong, as well as how the content of authority may be reinforced through the occupational project. Authority may be threatened by ongoing social changes, including those involving technologies created only in part by those trained in medicine. The demands on physicians as caregivers, and other experts, are constantly changing; technological capabilities increase, disease trends develop, and patients' lifestyles and experiences change. In response to these shifts, standard-setters need to create new knowledge, and clinicians need to be guided by new knowledge. In other words, medicine's stakeholders are involved in an ongoing process of proposing and reinforcing new problems and solutions. As I will describe below, we do not yet understand how these stakeholders develop the control necessary to maintain authority, and whether we can identify a systematic process underpinning the organization of that control.

We see from the vignette that indeterminacy with regard to knowledge of medicine is connected to the making of that knowledge. The vignette shows an open space that is flexible conceptually, in that it allows those in it to do the work of presenting new knowledge, but also physically, in that it is a place where they can see and be seen. Our next step is to notice that this open venue is gesturing to and connected to other venues.

Venues and Tethers

Having settled the matter of a definition of the occupational project, at least provisionally, the next step is to look at what its stakeholders *do*—all the different kinds of work conducted by all the stakeholders. So, it makes sense to look at as much of what we would call the "practice" of medicine as we can see. If we are to tie the occupational project to management of authority, we need to observe many places, and understand how those places are interconnected in that occupational project. Each of these places is a venue where participants meet to engage in focused tasks that in some particular ways shape and sustain the different social projects that can contribute to the occupational project. I will also scrutinize what I call tethers, that is, persistent cross-venue linkages that facilitate the efforts of those participating in a social project to set and contest its problems and solutions. Theorizing work in this way foregrounds the importance of culture in the concept of authority.[20]

The vignette is our first snapshot of the work done by doctors, but it implies, either directly or indirectly, the existence of other venues that the doctors are tying together. Dr. Kellogg, in using slides that contain the images shared by a fellow leader in the occupational project, demonstrates that she is interpreting her work in a way that resonates with that of respected peers working in other labs. Dr. Torstal uses his preemptive neutralization of a potential steam pop to reaffirm that he's done many of these cases in his home lab, without incurring the negative outcomes that his peers and audience might ordinarily expect. And we even see the clinicians in the audience use their cell phone cameras for pictures of procedures deemed successful by standard-setters, in order to share news of innovations with local colleagues and support arguments about purchasing technology that will help them generate similar results. Another way we can think about what we saw, then, is that the vignette is implicating, either directly or indirectly, the existence of other venues that their inhabitants are tying together.

My notion of tied-together venues is informed by, but addresses limitations in, the concept of "worlds," which, as initially applied by Howard S. Becker to "art worlds," is used to describe how people with different skills get other people to help them get things done. This idea is innovative in its focus around tasks and projects in places like the construction of an art opening, or the staging of an opera, where it is necessary to understand how members of an occupational project maintain authority. It is centered also around the language of "project"; as Becker notes, it involves "real people trying to get things done, largely by getting other people to do things that will assist them in their project." Becker's concept is particularly valuable for understanding the construction of one-off events in particular spaces, such as the performance of a play or the creation of an artwork. It offers the concept of convention, which points to the usual roles taken by people—for instance as it relates to scripts that organize the enacting of gender roles in relationships—in those specific spaces where coordination is necessary.[21]

Yet this focus on events does not provide a conceptual vocabulary that would allow us to understand connections across spaces for accomplishing a single complex task, and see how these places are connected in the service of the future-oriented dimensions of expert work. As Becker pointed out in his discussion of performance artists, a director may have to collaborate with actors and funders, and their actions in those venues tend to be focused on present goals, just as it could be said that the doctors presenting the live cases are focused on the successful completion of a certain surgery, in that moment. But the conceptual needs are different for studying the ongoing management of authority; understanding the project of professionals involves understanding work in the context of a much longer time horizon, as well as a range of individuals who have their own visions of the future of that enterprise (there may be, for instance, new practitioners who need training). And, beyond this theoretical justification, what I came to see during the course of my years of research was that the doctors were doing much more than thinking of the present moment, and that it is important to follow them as much as possible into the many venues where they mentor trainees, negotiate for resources, expand their referral base, influence the practices of clinicians, and shape guidelines.

And so, in observing these scenes in which participants seek to shape understandings and strengthen claims by tying together important meeting places, we can see there's more to be done if we are to understand the relationship that must exist between individual and collective in accounting for the management of authority. Although I am using the language of occupational project (rather than the more narrow language of profession), my goal is not to discount the fact that there exists something about professions that involve peoples' coalescence: that is, how a group holds together and strengthens itself while continuously carrying out its work. When sociologists use the word *coalescence* it tends to refer to onetime victories such as the use of credentials and licenses, and onetime experiences of training (or "socialization") in a formal institution. It is also assumed, at times, that coalescence just happens. The nature of coalescence, the processes involved, and its association with our focus on the professions, remain largely unexamined. Specifically, we may still want to build in the capacity to understand how our subjects' understandings reflect and influence those in other spaces. Since parsing out the qualities of the professionals themselves is inadequate to show their more complex social relationships and interdependence around local tasks, this book is organized around the places—venues—in which they do their work. These are places, I will argue throughout the book, where their occupational project is furthered to continuously strengthen their case for the social permissions they have been granted.[22]

Venues provide affordances for a potentially wide range of specific task-centered social interactions, and, taken together across the rich variation in work-related tasks, they provide affordances but also limitations on permissible interactions. As I use the term, the venue is a social space where people meet to carry out work, affirm knowledge claims, monitor each other's progress, and keep each other apprised of changes in techniques and tools. A classroom is a venue. The operating room is a venue. The conference described in the vignette, like a hospital, may contain multiple venues. As we will see in subsequent chapters, in venues participants format the tasks, the roles, and the opportunities to interact. They do this formatting to accomplish organizational and professional goals, and demonstrate particular skills, by defining tasks of work that are appropriate to the venue. Venues also place limits on what can be discussed, what is observed, who attends, and what role a person is allowed or expected to play. For example, doctors understand that representatives of a medical technology company are welcome in an operating room to teach how their technology is used, but not in the boardroom where administrators are discussing how to reduce the appearance of conflicts of interest. And so, they are places where one is likely to observe interdependencies between those trained, and often working, in professions we would consider different and potentially oppositional. As noted above, what we casually refer to as "medicine" embraces a huge range of activities carried out in venues that are medical in nature, but also ones that are less centered around medical tasks.[23]

These venues are connected by tethers, persistent cross-venue linkages that are reliably useful in facilitating the efforts of those participating in a social project to set and contest its problems and solutions. Tethers allow participants to do things that strengthen projects of their own and the group, working within the open space of indeterminacy. Tethers capture the idea that there are personal and professional relationships across the venues that people use to tie together the otherwise discrete tasks that might be called the work of the profession. Sometimes a tether is used in the service of generating and changing a shared knowledge base, and sometimes it is used in the service of collective action. There are many examples, including language, material, and human ones. To take a linguistic example, if a physician speaks of "macroscopic channels," the matter of belief described by Dr. Torstal, they are tying themselves to those in other venues who accept this language as a matter of course. And with his use of the business register, Dr. Torstal projects himself as someone who, elsewhere, can identify promising innovations, and also support people with the same foresight. Dr. Kellogg notes that her decision to place a lead in one of the heart's chambers was based on the suggestion of an "astute" company representative, signaling that the ties she has with companies are constructive of exceptional practices. She also uses the medical technology person by having them ask audience members a question to tether to those in the audience who might use technology. And she uses those sitting in the audience, on the edges of their seats, to go back to their home labs and spread the gospel.

It is worth noting that the concept of tethers and venues reflects a certain perspective on studying culture, a feature of which is attention to where culture is located. The subject of culture is of course a vast and well-trodden one, debated for centuries by diverse scholars across disciplines. While the concept is important to the notion of tethers and authoritativeness discussed below, it would be distracting and peripheral to this project to discuss in detail that literature's particular relationship to the concept of authority. The closest analogue to how the concept of culture is engaged here is in Michael Silverstein's attention, not to what is "culture," but to the way culture presents itself to humanity, which confronts the question of *Where* is culture. And, as this book demonstrates in its attention to venues, it might be possible to understand people's conceptions of medicine's problems and solutions as authoritative—in the sense of having shaped relevant stakeholders' understanding of the work—in light, at least partially, of the venues from which those enumerations emanate. It is in these venues, and the tethers between them, that the culture of medicine emerges, and where connecting that culture to authority begins. And in its attention to tethers, then, this book finds culture to be used in forms that range from the linguistic to the material, circulated across venues of interaction, and imminent and constitutive of task-centered work.[24]

By paying attention to tethers and venues, it is possible to see the active role of professionals in managing the structure and the content of their work across locations in the occupational project, offering tools for understanding the active work involved in organizing indeterminacy. We can see their value in the process of organizing indeterminacy by recognizing that members of an occupational project offer problems and solutions that are not self-evident but rather essentially contested. Without studying multiple venues, for instance, it might be difficult to make sense of failures in attempts at social control—for instance, as we will see in chapter 4, when a hospital's attempts at asserting control cause doctors to seek jobs elsewhere. And specifically examining tethers can show us how doctors are able to carry out and shift pioneering practices about which they might, at times, feel personally uncertain, as well as how they might organize indeterminacy for peers and followers. More generally, moving across venues allows us to keep our eyes on both experts' individual responses and the multiple collective consequences, different units of scale reflected in the distinguishing here of uncertainty and indeterminacy.[25]

Finally, attention to the connections among venues and stakeholders can help us answer questions for which the interest of scholars has been evergreen: what is the relationship between those pursuing their own self-interest and the stability of group they constitute? Durkheim and Marx, in their studies of work, of course took up the interest of classical liberals in this question. It's also familiar to scholars of work who have taken up these questions of social control in terms of professional self-regulation. Early work by Freidson on this subject examined a group of clinicians in a private practice setting with little evidence of professional control, finding a "live and let live" philosophy among practicing clinicians. Later work by Bosk re-inforces the presence of these attitudes among attending physicians, while demonstrating the presence of hierarchical control processes in attendings' teaching relationships with subordinates. In part perhaps because social scientists have studied single practice settings, there's rarely been any indication of extra-organizational control. Perhaps if we look differently, we might observe more.[26]

The Ethnographic Approach

The concepts sketched above were developed through an approach to ethnographic observation centered around attention to distant influences on the ethnographic here-and-now. This approach differs from one involving being embedded in one or two venues.

For many years I have been embedded in multiple venues where doctors carry out a broad range of tasks, including work involved in organizing their occupational project. I found, as the vignette illustrated, that venues are implicitly interconnected in complex ways. We can see that in the venue of the live case presentation, or the "virtual" lab. I was describing there not only what the standard-setters and their fellows were doing with their hands, which can be properly called practicing electrophysiology, but also how the clinicians in the audience raised questions, and how the medical representative helped the work. Those relationships, between teacher and student, core and periphery physicians, doctor and device rep, must be cultivated and reinforced somewhere. The real and implied presence of those different places where they do different work suggests the payoff from not simply examining action on the "shop floor" of the clinic, or comparing dynamics in several venues. That the vignette revealed a working link, or tether, between the home lab and conference meeting suggests potential new ways of looking at venues and ways their participants are oriented to other venues. It's a potentially productive perspective, not least because of how medicine is organized in the globalized high-tech present.

The literature that both directly and glancingly addresses authority has not yet captured the dynamism in medical authority. The most common approach to understanding professions is the creation of synthetic, stylized accounts of the work of their medicine alone or of multiple professions. Some scholars, like Freidson, who uses an ideal typical approach, pull together multiple accounts of medicine, capturing the experiences of a massive group in schematic terms. Abbott took a similar tack, creating a conceptual vocabulary by synthesizing areas of work from librarianship to law. Even as it removes professionals from the place and time in which they work, the synthetic approach was compelling for its time, and remains useful today because it offers an encompassing account that spans the venues where work is carried out. And the synthetic approach is also compelling if we are to look at "pure" cases of those trained with a homogenous body of expertise, rather than the range of knowledge reflected in an occupational project.[27]

However, while valuable for proposing commonalities and differences across those considered to be in different professions, the synthetic approaches of earlier scholars can't offer insight into the ongoing interactions and interdependencies among people who share an occupational project but bring different perspectives. Because they seek syntheses, these scholars' interest is not in studying individuals in a group of people whose expertise has shifted and will continue to change, who respond to and enact transformations in the standing of their profession, and who frequent venues not always defined as "professional" in nature. It doesn't situate the decisions of individuals in terms of the everyday pressures they experience, and it assumes that the motivations of individuals mirror those of the profession. Because they are looking for standard qualities across groups, they can't capture that there are very different rates of attrition from the occupation, stratification processes, and degrees of consistency in terms of dominant tasks performed across groups. These approaches tell us less about processes through which individuals shape each other's understandings of the culture of the occupational project in particular places. It is only by seeing how subjects regularly work in and across usual venues that we can make sense of how they might manage the occupational project in light of everyday pressures. This multivenue ethnography that's attuned to processes helps show the perspective of those who are making decisions to do the social organizing that is important for managing authority.

It is true that some sociologists have looked ethnographically at processes underpinning medicine's social organization, but they have done so by adopting a primary focus on a single hospital, or by making comparisons across them. These study designs do not capture the sense of a broader occupational project. For instance, some ethnographic work on physician training does examine multiple venues in one hospital, from the classroom, to training teams, to mortality and morbidity meetings and grand rounds. But it does not account for the interdependence between those in the hospital and those working in other venues. Other work, primarily focused on physician training, compares the experiences of incipient professionals across hospitals with different missions and thus patient bases (e.g., academic and community hospitals). Comparative studies can show variations in what might be called "top-down" effects, in which subjects in two different venues are compared in terms of their response to a policy. Or they might take a "bottom-up" approach, examining differences in the training experiences of two groups of people who work in different hospitals but are treated as similar in terms of background. Yet this comparative work gives the impression that professionals are socialized "once and for all," and in a way that doesn't reflect the diversity of career types in the vignette, as well as the fact that physicians might change after their training. It also tends to obscure the ways that medical professionals work actively to link these venues.[28]

Others have looked at the doctor-patient relationship. I pick up on that approach, but I triangulate that relationship with other relationships that are going on at the same time, examining the doctor-patient relationship as it is inflected by the doctor-doctor and doctor-trainee relationships in the context of the hospital. This choice follows from my focus on authority. The decision to study venues comprising other stakeholders reflects the inability of individual doctor-patient interactions alone to shape authority, and the role of expertise. The literature shows, and the physicians themselves assert, that the work of definitions of problems and solutions, and their shifts, cannot be validated by individual patients. Specialized physicians would claim that even non-specialized physicians would be unable to understand sufficiently the range of factors involved in these definitions and shifts. Judgments about knowledge in an occupational project reflect the judgments of a specialist group, one that can construct a belief system that defines certain things as problematic, and potentially solvable. My interest is in what the doctors are doing in their process of social organization, which means I'm more interested in what they are doing with each other and other stakeholders.[29]

Medicine is an apt subject for developing this venue- and tether-centered approach to ethnography, because the tasks of work in medicine are many, and they are located in and across many venues including those involving quite distant influences, and because its stakeholders develop and maintain many interconnections, via tethers, across the venues. Physicians perform many tasks, and they cannot do all these tasks in an operating room; like the device reps in the vignette, they serve as teachers but also have some tasks of scientists and, especially with patients, salespeople. To understand the management of their authority I found it necessary to understand ways those tasks differ among members of the occupational project and across venues, as they are conducted not just by doctors but also by industry reps, administrators, and those working with the state (malpractice attorneys). Studying medicine in this way allows us to see some of the individual-collective relations that are hard to observe in one venue, such as processes of coalescence and social control.

This book therefore takes a methodological step, in an effort to show how the organizing of authority is supported at different venues. Specifically, I seek to look at how individuals are moving across venues that are tethered together, as though on a plane, and using these tethers to organize indeterminacy in a way that strengthens the occupational project. This helps us understand how tethering contributes to the coalescence of a group that we call a profession. In doing so, I consider whether it is possible to extend a tradition of Chicago-school ethnography, which focuses on the importance of time and place, to account for relationships with venues outside the workplace, and—in light of efforts to conduct global ethnography—outside the city; relationships that others have argued Chicago ethnography is unable to capture. Thinking in terms of horizontal tethered venues, rather than either the more common and hierarchical imagery of the "micro" and "macro" "levels" or the promissory socialization model, privileges the dynamism of social life.[30]

On the Occupational Project and Venues of Cardiac Electrophysiology

The key questions of this book are answered in a theoretically informed and systematic ethnographic study of tasks performed by cardiac electrophysiologists (EPs). EPs are not interventional cardiologists (who open clogged arteries and sometimes implant stents), nor are they cardiac surgeons (who perform open-heart procedures). In contrast, EPs use ablation catheters to burn or cool parts of the heart to repair abnormal rhythms. They might also regulate the heart by implanting defibrillators and pacemakers. The EP tasks I observe also include managing patients, socializing trainees, performing surgical procedures, learning new knowledge and techniques, and discussing the process of creating guidelines for the occupational project more generally. At times I juxtapose these specialized cardiologists with those in less-specialized areas. This book strategically analyzes doctors in "Superior Hospital," a top-ranked tertiary-care teaching institution. EPs also welcomed me to join them across a number of different venues outside of the hospital that they said they regularly attended, and I also attended these venues independently. I was with these doctors as often as possible, working as a participant-observer.[31]

In planning my observation of tethered venues I soon became conscious of the importance of close attention to venue selection, using inductive and deductive strategies. Working inductively, I reviewed the study participants' schedules and noted the usual events and their venues. I chose to follow doctors in these venues, because the venues themselves are regular features of the profession's work that are directly linked to the referral network important to competition. This approach has some limitations; when ethnographers are working in one venue, they will miss direct observations in another that may be significant for understanding the initial one. In this case, I had reason to believe that information on the management of authority would be spread across venues that are hard to observe, such as conference calls in which international colleagues discuss research findings that should be included in professional guidelines. And it is also true that professionals' schedules may include events that have little influence on decisions or outcomes that are important to subjects. In partial response to these challenges, working deductively, I worked to find optimal venues to include clinicians I would not see in Superior Hospital. In this case, I knew that the doctors who are best reputed among their colleagues in academic medicine are usually active in research and interested in publishing unique patient cases. Therefore, it made sense to rule out city- or state-based medical society meetings because I was able to interview and observe clinicians in industry meetings, and medical society meetings didn't include the kinds of subject matter that standard-setters care about. (For instance, I knew, based on my understanding of observing physicians' interactions with patients, from interviews and observations, that interactions with patients before procedures were of minimal importance for the relationships among colleagues in the lab and elsewhere.)[32]

My account of the work of cardiac electrophysiology is broad with regard to venues, but like other ethnographies, it is necessarily narrow. For instance, I study doctors primarily in one subspecialty of medicine. Moreover, electrophysiology is skewed in some meaningful ways. For example, it is fairly white, which is not uncommon in American medicine. Less common, however, is its sex composition; even as some other medical subfields have approached or reached sex parity, EP remains 90 percent male. Because of this skew, I have pointed out when my argument is potentially affected by qualities of the group (as in chapter 2).

It is also the case that even if cardiac electrophysiology work has some particularities, no single field of medicine includes all areas of work in medicine as a whole. Conversely, as mentioned, a synthetic approach would have been limited in accounting for the agency of those individuals who continuously reconstitute medicine. I felt that EP exposed a number of dimensions of the occupational project of doctors, with its ability to capture economic matters, as well as the tasks of both the knowledge-based internal medicine tasks, and the active hands-on tasks of procedures of the type we saw in the vignette. And, among the many problems addressed by doctors, heart-related medical conditions represent the number one cause of death in the United States. The array of traits described here makes EP an important domain as a proof of concept, letting us see all the potentially germane players across subfields.

Also of importance, studying cardiac electrophysiology offers a way of studying venue-specific tasks potentially involved in the management of authority. One such task is that of participating in university-based training programs. After medical school, EPs, like other physicians, do three years of residency in the venue of the hospital. They rotate through subspecialties in the hospital and they work in teams led by an attending physician, which include senior residents who supervise interns (junior residents) and medical students. The team goes on rounds, which is the process of caring for patients on the hospital wards. In the last year of their residency, most doctors apply for a fellowship within a specialization, and usually go to another hospital for that fellowship. In cardiology, a field in which physicians find, treat, and prevent diseases of the heart, doctors will complete a general cardiology fellowship program that lasts three more years. If a doctor wants to become a specialist such as an EP (known among cardiologists as "electricians" because they manage electrical disorders), or an interventional cardiologist (referred to by EPs as "plumbers," because they clear clogged arteries), they then embark on an additional one- to two-year fellowship program. During the fellowship, they begin to go to conferences, and maintain relationships with those who have influenced them in their career, as they build new relationships.

After completing university-based programs, cardiologists usually follow one of two tracks. Although all of these tracks, often called "career types," share some basic tasks, they nonetheless involve relatively different patients, teaching roles, and conference experiences. While I'm not studying the careers of individuals themselves (e.g., Charles Drew, Florence Nightingale, Jonas Salk), I am interested in how careers are organized. First, the doctors whom I have called the standard-setters take a path that combines patient care, research, and the teaching of students, residents, and fellows, usually at a university hospital. They often will participate in, or even lead, clinical trials or other kinds of research with new technologies or techniques. In their academic venues, they will often meet in the morning to discuss new research in the field. They present their ideas and research at industry-sponsored conferences and annual meetings. Other cardiologists, the "clinicians," tend to perform routine procedures and make more money. They work in private practice settings and community hospitals. They rely on conferences to develop their networks and acquire the latest knowledge. While each type of physician relies on referrals from general internal medicine physicians to acquire patients, the clinicians might further refer complex patients, or "cases," to the standard-setters.[33]

To demonstrate the similarities and differences between EP and other occupational projects, I compared EPs with other doctors, and situated them in an occupational project that shares qualities with those of doctors with different tasks. I'm studying what they do as they conduct their work of all kinds, in and across its many venues. And so, even if this study is not explicitly comparative, to juxtapose electrophysiologists with those in other occupational projects in light of the theory of authority management sketched here, I do compare them with general internal medicine doctors and at times those in other subspecialties, such as general and other interventional cardiologists, who have tasks and regular venues that differ slightly.

I focus on the occupational project of a set of interdependent doctors and other stakeholders, very loosely organized around matters of the heart.

There are other ways of doing this, which can be seen in the several flavors characterizing scholarship on authority in medicine. It would be possible to study authority by foregrounding specific social problems (autism, abortion, attention deficit disorder) and their solutions, which has the affordance of demonstrating the social organization of the rise and fall of cultural attention, or neglect, directed to a specific issue. This approach, one often followed in the study of medicalization, tends to conceal which candidate understandings were not pursued. Or, in a more Foucault-inspired way, it would be possible to look at the discourses alone. However, such an approach conceals information about the humans authoring and spreading those discourses.[34]

Of course, different research questions fit different approaches to answering questions of social organization. Since my interest is in capturing the way people who organize indeterminacies may adjust or ignore each other's approaches, may hold together or fall apart, I centered this study on these people and the multiple places where they periodically meet and seek to reinvigorate their authority. My justification for studying the occupational project is that it allows me to answer most directly the question of how authority is organized. This broader project in which multiple people are involved and studied is what it takes to produce the management of authority of a group. It also captures the multiple scales at which individuals, situated at different social locations in the community, work to further their own goals and those of a collective, in the present and into the future.

The Argument

I argue that authority is managed, among individuals, by those who work interdependently within venues, and engage in collegial competition for status and other resources across venues. These individuals are firmly situated in an overall occupational project, where doctors and others label problems and solutions by using tethers across venues to control patients and colleagues. They establish what counts as up-to-date knowledge or best practice at any particular time, under the control of a largely physician-led, multiheaded leadership structure that has developed a process for organizing indeterminacy. Physicians, standard-setters especially, compete to have recognized and validated their invested-in problems and solutions for organizing indeterminacy, ones that often reflect approaches of those in their invisible college and thus serve their career goals. Other stakeholders who are traditionally considered "outside" the profession, including representatives for the state, companies, and the hospital, themselves support these physicians' competition and are also incorporated into the leadership of the occupational project; so much so that they shape work and have an important role in the process of organizing indeterminacy. Lastly, the competition for status and other resources, rather than impeding the management of the occupational project, seems to make it work effectively, for it enables EPs as a group to tolerate and benefit from the efforts of some individuals to organize indeterminacy in their way.

In this system in which authority is managed, then, the pursuit of status has a more collective consequence—it is a process that serves to organize who speaks for the occupation, in light of the work's essential indeterminacy. The existence of the competition has the consequence of adding up to create constant reinforcement of doctors' ways of understanding and doing things, and of offering up new problems and solutions. As a result, the use of tethers across venues furthers and strengthens the occupational project, and better prepares all involved for looking forward into the future.[35]

The Chapters

I have organized this book into six empirical chapters, each relating to one of the significant venues I studied. I also divide the book into two parts. Chapters 2–4 describe work in venues inside Superior Hospital: the wards, where attendings socialize residents in their teams and groom patients; the EP labs, where doctors divide labor and perform cases; and the bed management meetings, where doctors work to secure hospital resources. Chapters 5–7 describe venues outside the hospital, where standard-setters interact closely with clinicians: industry-sponsored meetings where leaders of the occupational project describe best practices; industry-hosted hands-on technology training programs; and international conferences where technologies are marketed and standards are adjudicated and reinforced. Chapter 8 describes how my observations support my argument that authority is managed in a collegial competition across venues in which doctors and others in their occupational project label problems and solutions by using tethers to control patients and colleagues. Chapter 8 also proposes some implications of this research. I end with a methodological appendix.

Chapter 2 takes us to the venue of Superior Hospital's residency program, where respected attending physicians are training resident physicians and introducing them to processes involved in authoritatively establishing an approach to practice. The chapter highlights differences between two attending physicians who work in occupational projects with alternative ways of labeling medical problems and their solutions.

Chapter 3 takes place in Superior Hospital's EP morning meetings and operating rooms, where doctors divide labor and perform cases, revealing several principles for how doctors interact with others and organize indeterminacy. These processes include sharing presentation slides, dividing labor in a lab according to level of expert skills in niche areas of focus, passing down one's approach to fellows, and cultivating "good hands."

Chapter 4 moves to another venue in Superior Hospital, the administrative offices where the bed geography meeting takes place. It shows how doctors manage changes in administrators' goals for their workplace in order to gain some control over both hospital resources and the ability to perform their tasks in a fashion consistent with their occupational project.

In chapter 5 we explore the first venue outside the hospital: industry-sponsored meetings where leaders describe best practices in terms of the process of executing specific medical procedures, but also in terms of supporting peers and taking precautions in selecting cases. In this venue, advanced fellows and early-career clinicians are learning standard-setters' definitions of key problems and solutions.

Chapter 6 shows us the venue of industry-hosted hands-on technology training programs. This venue provides a closer look at everyday clinicians, especially those in their mid- and late-career stages. It offers a look at some of their tethers to standard-setters, and how these everyday doctors become aware of, and can learn the tactile skills for, carrying out new procedures.

Chapter 7 takes us to the annual meeting, which includes presentation venues like the one in the vignette. This chapter focuses primarily on four of these subvenues: the exhibition floor booths of medical device makers, the debates among standard-setters, the social events where doctors socialize and share gossip, and the meetings where doctors assemble to discuss the creation of standards.

Chapter 8 ties these chapters together and reiterates the argument, drawing conclusions based on the evidence of how medicine's authority is actively managed in an ongoing way, among all the many stakeholders involved. It discusses what it looks like to understand the management of authority in and across multiple venues.

In the methodological appendix I detail my involvement with the people and venues I observed, and then describe the methodological problems I faced and the insights I came to about ethnography, including the casting of the ethnographer as a problem, using tethers to help with access, deidentification, and subject self-consciousness.

The data presented here, then, suggest the promise of deriving from the case of medicine a theory of managing authority that reflects the complexities of modern expert practice, including the different places where experts meet, work, and talk about different topics with different people. Not only does this approach represent a shift in perspective from the recent literature but it returns us to an earlier way of studying medicine that affords the development of general theory. Social scientists have offered a wide range of justifications for studying medicine's many characters, from the pharma reps to the doctors to hospital administrators. Some scholarship in medical sociology considers medicine important for its own sake. In contrast, other scholarship studies medical work with an eye toward contributing to a subfield of sociology, such as organizations or professions. While this second approach is closer to my own, I take a direction that is different still, specifically following early scholarship on medical work with an interest in offering generalizations about other subjects studied by sociologists, such as socialization, failure, diffusion, power, culture, or the self. Returning to a kind of analysis from sociology's less-specialized days means that my observations about medical people and venues can teach us much for understanding core questions of social life more generally.[36]

two

Superior Hospital's Inpatient Wards

Grooming Patients and Socializing Trainees

Some doctors may be able to organize indeterminacy before an international viewing audience, as we saw in chapter 1. But most do this work day by day when they put on the white coat and do their work with patients in clinics and operating rooms. Doctors are able to do this work with patients in part because of their past training, and in part because of doctors' current privileges: patients are dependent on doctors for access to validated knowledge, resources, and skills. But patients' dependence on them is not enough. If doctors are to maintain their authority, they also need patients' belief, so that they can carry out in everyday practice procedures like those established in a venue such as the auditorium in which the live case was held. Patients don't expect doctors to fix everything that disturbs their health, but rather to "do all they can." Doing all they can requires some control over their task of caring for the patient. How do doctors shape patients' belief in their ability and in the procedure they recommend? How do doctors communicate to patients what specifically patients must do for doctors to accomplish their tasks? And how do physicians enlist patients' support in fulfilling the expectations they have crafted about what success looks like?[1]

This chapter examines the venue of the inpatient wards in the home hospital. In this venue, doctors reinforce their approaches to organizing indeterminacy; once they've established problems and solutions reflected by at least some members of the greater occupational project, they groom patients to accept this approach to organizing indeterminacy, and socialize trainees to implement their plans. Grooming is a physician's efforts to shape patient behavior to improve the chance of a process and outcome consistent with how their field has organized indeterminacy. Efforts to groom patients seek more than mere compliance (with their personal expectations), or adher-

Figure 2.1. Outside the lab, these are the white coats doctors are likely to put on to perform any of their tasks with patients. This chapter concerns inpatient wards, but the coats are worn everywhere, even in hands-on meetings sponsored by technology stakeholders. These were photographed at one such meeting. Photograph by David Schalliol.

ence (to a proscribed set of behaviors). Grooming shapes patients to behave in specific ways so that doctors can to do what their occupational project requires if they are to succeed at using their problems and solutions to define the course of care. To groom, then, doctors focus on ameliorating negative priors, smoothing resistance, creating belief, and prescribing behaviors that people must follow to get better. They also seek to socialize trainees to carry out this work on their behalf. Because those residents might only be on their service for a few weeks to a month, this socialization is not intended to be a long-term shaping.

In this chapter, we follow two doctors, both "attendings," during their time on the wards, as they groom patients and socialize trainees, doing so in ways that support how their occupational project has organized indeterminacy. Both doctors are cardiologists, and therefore both are seeing patients whose problem has been defined by their referring internist as broadly heart-related. But they see their patients differently. One of them, Dr. Kellogg, is what I call an "intensivist," a subspecialist whose solutions usually involve proposing and conducting hands-on interventions such as ablation or placing a pacemaker. The other, Dr. Walker, I call a "deliberator," someone who is less specialized and whose solutions usually involve proposing that patients take medicine and modify their everyday lifestyles. Dr. Kellogg and Dr. Walker differently lead a single team in different ways, using different practices, and both of them gain buy-in with the cardiology patients admitted to the hospital. Both of them can groom patients well, and so they can predict and explain their patients' outcomes, helping them to reinforce the problems and solutions they have sought to establish.[2]

This chapter compares these doctors' approach to grooming as a way of formatting patients based on place in the referral chain, trajectory of care, and management of time as a tool for action. Their approaches reflect several qualities of time: stages, duration of contact, and its discursive qualities. When off the wards, these attendings see patients at different stages in patients' trajectories of care. Deliberators, the general cardiologists, see patients earlier in the referral chain, and are unlikely to perform specialized procedures. In the most general terms, their first instinct is that the solution is medication and a lifestyle shift. In contrast, intensivists are seen further down the referral chain. Because doctors earlier in the referral chain have attempted all of the less-invasive approaches, such as medication, intensivists are more likely to perform procedures. Their first instinct involves a non-invasive surgical intervention (ablation) or a device (pacemaker or defibrillator). The comparison shows that different work needs to be done to execute, and to train students to do, the organizing of indeterminacy demonstrated at the annual meeting presented in chapter 1.

Off the wards, doctors who don't perform interventions strategically use time as a tool for action, often even deciding that a patient's problems will not necessitate medical care. Dr. Walker attempts to groom patients to take their medicines and be linked to a support system; he doesn't fix patients with his hands. These deliberators may prescribe a drug that usually works on other patients and, depending on patient response, substitute for those drugs others in the same class. This longer-term process of arriving at an accepted patient plan also involves much more effort in consultations than is required in Dr. Kellogg's compliance-inducing declarations. For Dr. Kellogg, less time and effort are spent in treatment on the ward; for intensivists, the treatment efforts are centered on operating room (or "lab") interventions.

When on the wards, these attendings see the same patients, who are all admitted to the cardiology service and not sorted according to needs that might usually be treated by one cardiology subspecialty. This chapter, which focuses on the EP interaction style by way of comparison, will show that the cardiologists end up grooming individual patients differently based on their usual tasks off the wards, which differ according to feedback loop speed of those tasks. Ninety percent of the doctors' time is spent off the wards, in their outpatient clinics and venues where they train fellows. The patients on the wards that teams are treating, or "rounding on," are ill, but not acutely. They are likely to exhibit a range of cardiological issues, and have been admitted to the hospital's ER or transferred from another hospital. Because they have entered the hospital this way—and thus any doctor on call that month can be responsible for treating them—it's possible to say that patients' medical concerns are "held constant" across the month. However, each type grooms similar patients differently, and socializes trainees differently, even though the patients they see on the ward do not meaningfully differ.

In investigating how Dr. Kellogg's intensivist practices and Dr. Walker's deliberative practices inform the content of their authority, some larger questions arise. First, assuming that a patient's expectations are important because the doctor needs them to accept their approach to a task, an approach they've worked out across venues, what happens when the patient is resistant, and the doctor can't quickly shape their expectations? Second, how do areas of medicine with different tasks get their definitions of indeterminacy accepted? How is the language different in formatting a patient for the doctor's tasks? If there are differences in strategies for gaining compliance, how do we understand general principles of managing authority behind these alternative strategies?

Grooming Patients and Socializing Trainees

Doctors relate to patients in different ways to produce the same result: patient grooming. Grooming happens sometimes through fear-inducing pressure, or strongly worded advice (Dr. Kellogg's approach below). Other times, it involves giving patients the impression of input through ongoing negotiation (demonstrated below by Dr. Walker). Having explainable results allows doctors to reaffirm the benefits of their occupational project's approach to organizing indeterminacy.

In most cases, these attendings rely on, and thus must socialize, other team members and paraprofessionals to assist in grooming a patient. In particular, the grooming ability of residents is highly valued because they are the doctors who first receive patients in the academic hospital's emergency room. Important ties between managing everyday work and managing professional authority are revealed when we examine how attendings socialize trainees to accomplish these everyday tasks, and how these tasks are ultimately accomplished. These ties of duty and discipline are learned by new doctors as they themselves learn to use fear and empathy to educate the patient on the benefits of adhering to plans they've established in conversation with their attending.

How do doctors influence the perception of success and failure in the eyes of the patient? The first problem is how to get a patient to set realistic expectations for their medical decision. By expectations, I mean the patients' idea of an acceptable outcome in their particular case. Sometimes patients feel similar or worse when they leave than when they enter the hospital. In these instances, doctors would like a patient to feel that they received "the best possible care," and to acknowledge that their post-hospitalization discomfort is normal or standard. To influence these sentiments, doctors must have information on the field's predictions and deliver this information to the patient effectively. The second problem is one of shaping patients' behavior, both inside and outside the hospital. To better ensure their effectiveness, they need patients to relinquish control in the hospital and possibly adopt a new lifestyle once they leave. Doctors need patient compliance in order to apply knowledge that they have personally developed and learned from the training and writings of international leaders.

In the hospital, these goals for patients are pursued most strongly by the physicians who have completed their formal training. As we will see, the attendings will simulate their interactional practices with patients when they interact with residents. This can be nerve-racking for students, because they know that they are being evaluated for their ability to use knowledge. They are learning that the position of physician is also one of culpability.

Below are two different conversations that I observed while shadowing a team of training residents for one month. These two conversations, about setting up patients to receive Lasix, a drug that helps rid the body of excess sodium and water, represent two different styles of patient grooming and trainee socialization, practiced by an intensivist (Dr. Kellogg) and a deliberator (Dr. Walker). These doctors lead a team comprising a senior resident (Dr. Nethers), two interns (Drs. Hoffman and Norhoff), and a medical student. This team works on the cardiology ward for the whole month, first with Dr. Kellogg and then with Dr. Walker. I present vignettes describing how they approach the same task—in this case deciding on the use of Lasix for their patients.[3]

Dr. Kellogg

On rounds on the first day of the month with my team, Dr. Kellogg, an EP, finishes up her conversation with our first patient.

"We're going to switch you over to a Lasix drip. OK? OK?" The patient pauses. "Say OK."

The patient demurs. "OK."

With strides as strong as her assertions, Dr. Kellogg leads the team out the door. "See you later."

Here, and in other interactions with patients, Dr. Kellogg uses the same rhetorical approach as her electrophysiology colleagues to encourage patients to participate in treatment plans. She uses imperatives to help her patients (and watching residents) reach what she often appears to consider a foregone conclusion. She needs them to feel confident in her expertise, in case she decides that an intervention is appropriate.

As an intensivist who spends most of her time conducting hands-on interventions, when working on the wards Dr. Kellogg needs patients to submit trustingly to the treatment she feels will be in their best interest while in the hospital. To get their immediate compliance, she is unambiguous in telling patients what she thinks will help them most. Unfortunately, patients do not always listen. So she expects her trainees also to develop the firmness she has mastered.

For example, in one interaction, Dr. Kellogg presents records of a patient who had just been treated and discharged healthy. She models this firmness with trainees to teach them how to act with patients who need a procedure during their stay, even though only some of the patients they see in their cardiology rotation will ultimately need the surgical interventions she conducts. She questions her intern using the same pressure-eliciting register she used with the patient:

"What do you see in this EKG?"

Multiple queries of "Anything else? Anything else?" follow while the intern hems and haws, making unconfident stabs at rapidly decoding the jagged heartbeat tracings.

The barrage of queries finishes with "Thanks to you, the patient died."

Dr. Kellogg needs compliance from the patient and, in order to get it, uses the same interrogation approach with trainees. Success with her procedures and teaching requires trust and responsiveness.

Dr. Walker

In the second half of the month, the team is headed by a different cardiologist, Dr. Walker. His expectations for patients are different from Dr. Kellogg's, because off the wards he sees patients who have more chronic cardiological issues. As a general cardiologist who usually needs patients to cooperate beyond the hospital stay, solving their problems often requires longer-term lifestyle shifts. On his first day as the head of the team we visit a patient with heart failure. Dr. Walker asks the patient, "Well, tell me what your thoughts are."

The patient, during the early days of his stay in the hospital, was reluctant to question the doctors, merely stating that they should do more to confront his problems. Now, after a month, however, he erupted with agitation: "My thoughts are, well, I'm tired of being a guinea pig. I told [Dr. Nethers {the resident}] that what they usually do with the fluid I have is use Lasix and Zeroxolyn. It might be slow, but it did the job. You all keep giving me different junk, and it's not doing a thing."

Dr. Walker replies, "Why don't we do this, then. Would you like us to switch you back [to Lasix]? The reason that they arrived at a new regimen is, when we tried the previous one, we didn't feel we were getting as much of a response. I think that sometimes, things change. And we might now be at a point where things might work. Why don't we switch you back over to the Lasix today? Is it OK if we use the IV form? I think you still need that. Let's do that. I think it's worth a try. So we can switch you."

By providing the patient with information on his rationale for preferring certain drugs and making sure that the patient feels heard, Dr. Walker conveys to the patient the importance he places on compromise.

He continues, "My only concern about the Zeroxolyn is that it made your electrolytes low. But we have other IV medications, like Diaril. This has a similar use. We just made a switch to the IV format yesterday, and got some progress, about half a liter. And before we hadn't made much progress. So why don't we move to Lasix today? I saw the heart failure people yesterday, and they said they'd like to try heart pressure tests. I know for you it has been a real odyssey. You have been here a long time, and you feel like you hadn't made a lot of progress. I know, it's frustrating. I want you to keep your mind open about checking pressures again. The heart failure specialists think this is important. Tomorrow we can think about whether there is a role for the pressures. That sound OK? As good as a plan could be after you've spent a month in the hospital?"

The patient mumbles a response, sounding like, "I guess so."

Dr. Walker: "Well, it's a frustrating problem. We think progress has been made overall, but has plateaued over the last few days. It takes time. Sometimes the heart weakens, so past therapy doesn't work. You know your body well, so I think switching to Lasix makes sense. Anything we can do to make you more comfortable in the meantime?" Leaning over him, he picks up the head of his stethoscope. "Can I take a listen?"

The consultation is complete. By compromising with the patient on the drug, Dr. Walker has modeled for the medical students how negotiation, not medical knowledge alone, is crucial to success in gaining compliance. He has also attempted to give the impression to the patient that even if he remains uncomfortable, his condition will be consistent with what medicine can achieve.

> Huddled with his team outside of the patient's room, Dr. Walker exposes his own socialization approach, suggesting to them how to negotiate in a way that will encourage the patient's ongoing compliance.
>
> Dr. Walker: "Well, I tell you, if the patient's so focused on the Lasix and Zeroxolyn, I would be happy to sorta make a deal with him. Sometimes it's the medication, and sometimes it's the physiology—it's such a moving target with these people."
>
> Intern: "The only reason we stopped Zeroxolyn in the first place was to help the natremia, after all."
>
> Dr. Walker: "So we could say, 'OK, you can get Zeroxolyn if you do a right heart cath, that would be a gain for us.' I think using this drug would be relatively neutral from a medical standpoint. . . . We'll need high doses: 600 over 20."

Dr. Walker is quick to adjust his medical plan when he perceives that longer-term benefits will come from accommodating to the patient's requests.

On another day I see Dr. Walker telling a story about his own days in training, which involve tasks with patients who are much more acutely ill than those he now treats.

> "I was in the Cardiac Care Unit with 2nd year resident, and this guy comes up to the unit, short of breath, gurgling, heart failure, gurgling. I'm thinking, What to do? Bruce comes in. Folds his arms. He says, 'This guy needs to be intubated.' I think, Wow, he's so decisive. So the anesthesia doc comes up, goes by the bed, and turns to Bruce. Bruce is in the corner. Half my height, has his arms folded looking very confident. And anesthesia guy turns and says, 'You got any Etomidate?' Bruce says, 'Nurse, get him some Etomidate.' So the nurse goes running out to the front. Bruce says, 'Yeah I'll get you some Etomidate,' just nodding his head as he watches. So the nurse comes back, Bruce says 'Here's your Etomidate,' anesthesia guy says 'Thank you,' and gives it to him, does the intubation. And Bruce is still nodding. So we get back to the desk, and I turn to Bruce and I say 'Listen, what is Etomidate?' He says, 'I have no idea.' That's the day I learned what it took to be a resident."

Even if he learned the "strong and wrong" philosophy—a philosophy characteristic of the work of intensivists such as Dr. Kellogg, and which will be discussed further in the following pages—on his way to becoming a cardiologist, Dr. Walker uses it only on rare occasions. To ensure patient compliance in order to provide necessary care, doctors need deference, but that can take many forms.

Doctors' Different Work with Subfield Tasks Shapes How They Socialize Trainees and Groom Patients

Patients and trainees bristle over Dr. Kellogg's terse intensivist delivery and embrace Dr. Walker's accessible deliberator approach. These two styles of interchange with patients are often perceived to represent character attributes that are sometimes thought to be beneficial for professional success. Although different kinds of work attract different personalities, the story isn't so simple; even trainees without an inclination to perform certain kinds of work start acting similar to others who perform tasks with feedback loops of the same length.

In the vignettes above, attending physicians sought to groom patients and socialize trainees, doing so in a way that reflects how they organize indeterminacy. Through these modes of management, attendings reinforced the kinds of problems and solutions they use *off* the wards; in the case of the EP, the grooming supports her interest in conducting an intervention, in which she will perform a procedure, and in the case of the general cardiologist, the grooming supported medical management, which will be primarily carried out by the patient. In these two contexts, the vignettes below look more closely at how the work in their subfields will shape the ways in which these doctors get patients to defer. These doctors are performing the same general task with patients and residents, but grooming takes different forms depending upon whether a deliberator or an intensivist is at the team's helm.

How the Intensivist Assertively Gains Patient Confidence While Socializing Trainees to Be Decisive

Dr. Kellogg, as with other cardiac electrophysiologists, must frequently respond spontaneously to unexpected events and new information provided during the hands-on execution of a case in her laboratory. As we saw in the vignette at the opening of this book, the work of Dr. Kellogg and her colleagues in the electrophysiology laboratory is to implant pacemakers or defibrillators, extract electronic leads and other device components if they deliver excessive shocks or fail to work when appropriate, and ablate the heart in an effort to correct electrical signals forming abnormal cardiac rhythms. She needs to be granted freedom to pursue pathways that emerge long after the patient becomes unconscious. For that she needs deference and full information on a patient's condition. In these laboratory settings outside the residency team, Dr. Kellogg's usual decision-making processes resemble those she models for the trainees in rapid-fire interactions that allow her to assess residency team members. Electrophysiologists' work demands a high level of coordination and a low margin of error once the patient is on the operating table. Their tasks are incredibly time sensitive.

The work of intensivists in the lab requires them to act intuitively and deliberately, so they need to groom patients and paraprofessionals to act in a way that supports their responses to these fast feedback loops. The behavior of an intensivist is event-centered, and they must quickly interpret patient changes in front of a team consisting of a doctor completing a fellowship, a nurse, and several assisting technicians.

Dr. Kellogg requires predictability in these interactions because she depends on the immediate availability of good information. For example, she must evaluate recommendations from the industry representative at the bedside who assists with the procedure by clarifying the features of the technology. Intensivists must ensure both that the device is suitable for the patient's anatomy and also that it does not include unnecessary features. Intensivists have a deep understanding of a limited range of tasks, and, given the risk in these tasks, want as much predictability as possible.

When outside the laboratory and with the residency teams, Dr. Kellogg and her colleagues interact with trainees in a style that maps on to the kind of fast feedback loops they have when performing ablation and implanting pacemakers. Their goals are to gain assent from patients and prepare trainees to respond rapidly. With their everyday tasks in the operating room, the feedback loop is short. Even if the feedback loop with her trainees' patients is longer when they are on the ward than on the gurney, she nonetheless adopts the intensivist mode for teaching purposes.

One grooming strategy used by Dr. Kellogg is to presume patient compliance to her solutions as a default condition, rather than offer up options: "We're going to do x, and we are more likely to be more successful if we do that." As part of her personalized approach to informed consent, she may then briefly hedge, saying, "If you're adamant about not doing this, we're going to respect your wishes," but would go on to indicate to the patient that their test result suggested that her initial recommendation would be immediately beneficial for achieving a particular outcome.

Her second strategy is to use stark metaphors to recommend health behaviors to patients. A favorite: "By eating all of this canned food, it's like you're screwing off the top of a salt shaker and pouring it down your throat."[4] With these tactics, she and other intensivists attempt to send a clear message about the risks of not changing a behavior, while smoothing any potential resistance from the patient to treatment. For patients whose heart problems cannot be managed with a device or ablation, intensivists may not recommend a procedure but rather changes in lifestyle.

The doctors will then choose to frame in blunt terms the consequences of ignoring their advice. Dr. Kellogg bluntly conveys this message: "If you decide not to take medicines, that's your choice. If you don't take this medicine, you could have a large heart attack."

While the central tasks of an intensivist are to gain patient confidence and to perform procedures correctly, the most essential underlying task is to communicate effectively. Trainees are expected to know how to communicate information effectively to their attendings, peers, and patients. They must learn to hold their composure even in tough circumstances, answer questions about a device or procedure without stuttering, and communicate to patients that they know the process and consequences of an operation. The doctor has successfully executed the task of getting patient compliance if the patient knows what to expect, and will comply even if the process is painful. In their operating room procedures, especially, intensivists must be ready to change strategies after interpreting new information.

On the wards, Dr. Kellogg seeks to expose students to potential complications so they can personally anticipate outcomes and rapidly adjust course. She suggests that trainees need to respond quickly and perform a resolute and highly polished case presentation if they are to gain the buy-in of both the patient and fellow colleagues, and make themselves confident that their experience is sufficient for action. As she taught during rounds one day:

> In your verbal interactions with people, it's important to know what you're talking about, but it's also very important to convey to the other person that you know what you're talking about. That you're confident about what you're saying, and not hemming, hawing, saying, "I don't know, I don't know." Just make a guess and put your stake in the ground. . . . And there's this expression, "Be strong and be wrong." It's funny because it's a little bit backwards, but the hyperbole is meant to emphasize the importance of being confident in what you say. And also feeling like you've done enough research and that you have gone through the rationalization in your mind so thoroughly that you are convinced that what you're saying is correct. And so, because you've gone through that exercise, you don't have to know everything, have all the experience, but you have to at least have gone through the process so thoroughly that you can put your stake in the ground.

A doctor's strong response affects both herself and the patient. On the other hand, by being strong, even if wrong, Dr. Kellogg is better able to control whether patients accept the content of her assertion, that is, whether they defer to her decisions and define success in her terms.[5]

The importance for Dr. Kellogg of firm communication in grooming a patient for attending-conducted medical treatment was conveyed in her teaching style. To simulate the pressures of their usual procedures when not on the wards, intensivists engage in Socratic questioning—in medical parlance, "pimping"—trainees in their before-rounds case presentations, forcing them to learn to decode information very quickly, as if they were mid-procedure. By exposing trainees to new information in a fashion analogous to how electrophysiologists interact with the patient, Dr. Kellogg is preparing trainees to communicate effectively, while also preparing them to change strategies if necessary. Her respective pedagogical strategy involves interrupting their case presentations. Dr. Kellogg's strategy, exercised on the wards and in meeting room prior to rounds, creates pressure on residents to concisely arrive at a diagnosis.

> Dr. Kellogg: "So, I think a useful format is to start with the problem, and then, your assessment of that problem. In your presentation yesterday, all of those elements were mixed together. So, she's a new dilated cardiomyopathy. Based on her history and the test we got yesterday, including a negative stress test and a negative TSH [thyroid-stimulating hormone score], she is most likely a pericardiomyopathy. From a symptoms standpoint, what do you think her volume status is?"
> Intern: "I don't think—"
> Dr. Kellogg (interrupting): "So your options are euvolemic, hypovolemic."
> Intern: "Well—"
> Dr. Kellogg (interrupting): "So, do you think she's hypovolemic, euvolemic?"
> Intern: "Euvolemic."
> Dr. Kellogg: "Well, based on what you're telling me, she didn't diurese, and was not euvolemic yesterday, so she's unlikely to be euvolemic today. So, assessing people's volume status is a skill for you to work on."

Through these sequences, intensivists reenact the challenge of gathering data, evaluating its relevance, considering its consequences for different potential outcomes, and taking action. Even though their pimping is occurring on the wards and not in the operating room, attendings want trainees to understand the kind of pressure they might experience under more dire circumstances.[6]

From her further statements, it is clear that Dr. Kellogg appreciates polished speech for practical as much as pragmatic purposes: "There is a general format in which people expect to receive information, and while there are variations on that theme, there is a basic structure that, if adhered to, economizes and also clearly communicates what you think is going on with the patient." She seeks a presentation with a beauty like that of a mathematical proof that employs the fewest steps necessary. Her succinctness is mirrored in her overall responsibility as well as the nature of her procedural expertise—verbally, procedurally, and clinically, her world is one of succinctness.

When her leadership of the team ends, Dr. Kellogg will often tell trainees to become more comfortable presenting in the "strong and wrong" style. Reflecting these comments, intern Dr. Hoffman felt she became more assertive over the course of the month:

> I mean, the things that she said at the halfway mark were to take more ownership over the patients—instead of asking Dr. Kellogg what she wanted to see, just give her an idea, say what I want to do. I think part of the reason I wasn't doing it was I didn't want to be like—and she used the right words—"you don't want to be arrogant about it." And I said, "I didn't want to say 'I'm doing this,' knowing you've got 10 or 12 more years of experience, with you then saying 'no, we're not.' So I'd usually say 'we could increase this' or 'we could increase that.' And I think these would be things that either one of us would be OK with . . ." She said "you're not going to offend me if you say 'we're doing this.' If you're wrong you're wrong—it's fine. But just say it that way." So I think I changed and became a little more assertive.

Dr. Kellogg encourages trainees to define claims they felt were assertive as "appropriate" rather than "arrogant" so that they, in turn, can transform how a patient understands his or her condition. As studies of acute caregiving have corroborated, patients will welcome, if not expect, such strong assertions.[7]

While it is difficult to use ethnography to draw conclusions about causal relationships, it is worth noting that in response to Dr. Kellogg's socialization approach, interns spoke decisively and also spent a considerable amount of time reviewing the scientific literature, and using it to defend their decisions with patients. First, when confronted with the pimping of intensivists, they formulated strong-and-wrong responses along with a specific case presentation format. One resident described her motivation for preparing for presentations with Dr. Kellogg: "The times that you feel like an idiot on rounds, I can tell you, you go and you read because you just don't want to be an idiot again." A medical student indicated he was highly conscious of Dr. Kellogg's expectations for how he should consider the relevance and consequences of patient data, given how often he had been sanctioned on his oral presentations. "She told me, 'Don't think out loud, don't say what you're thinking. It is more professional to not say anything.' She says it's more professional if I process things first before I say them. And if it's not relevant, don't say it. She said, 'Make yourself look good and not bad.'" The medical student anticipated that his concern for saving face would be achieved by working with teammates. Consequently—and as was the case with his other teams—he and a resident habitually crammed for case presentations late into the evening, often staying overnight at the hospital (against Superior's medical school policy) during the half month in which they worked with Dr. Kellogg.

Second, when working with intensivists, the trainees would often draw on the familiar strategies of information collection they cultivated in medical school. They prepared presentations together and, in the face of intensivists' pimping, deployed scientific findings in case presentations. An answer beginning with "Dr. X does it this way . . ." is unacceptable to all intensivists, who require the independence of thought involved in responding to an intervention's contingencies. Once they decided what they wanted to do, and felt that the patients would accept their decisions, trainees would look first to databases with summaries of expert opinion, such as UpToDate, which then might lead them to scientific studies published in the Medline database. Their ultimate goal was to locate articles based on the longitudinal, multicenter, prospective, "landmark" clinical trials that constitute cardiology's knowledge base. They also frequently sought out the guidelines synthesizing the current consensus on a topic. Sharing the motives of doctors who take pictures of others' slides at the "late-breaking trials" presentation in the annual meeting and share those pictures with administrators in their home hospital, these residents could use the research findings as tethers to support their goals in the team—here, of saving face. Here their task demanded support, and the residents used findings they collected in their off hours to create that support.

Intensivists need compliance from patients in a procedure but also from team members in a lab. And because of their need for predictability, the intensivists provide positive feedback to trainees if they get reliable information, and negative feedback if they don't get it. Trainees' responses to the intensivists' socialization strategies most closely resemble what the trainees learned in medical school—that is, amassing and deploying knowledge in reliable and predictable ways for those testing them. After consulting with each other, they draw on skills developed in their preclinical medical training, where they were expected to memorize information such as anatomy. This makes them realize they need to deliver decisive statements in a form that will reassure both patients and interdependent professionals of their competence. From the intensivist's perspective, in so doing the trainees will become more confident, and confidence is important in the tasks carried out by the intensivist off the wards, in procedures.

How the Deliberator Grooms Patients Toward Lifestyle Changes while Teaching Negotiation

In contrast to what intensivists demand from their trainees, deliberators do not allow the same level of reliance on familiar short-term strategies. The work of the deliberator differs from that of the intensivist in multiple ways: it's not to provide a quick answer but to find the best answer over time; it's not to be in control of the patient but to gain the buy-in of the patient; not to visualize the right solution for the patient but to adjust in converging on a pragmatic solution. The deliberator experiences a different level of uncertainty in decision making, as patients might have a whole range of cardiological issues, if indeed their problems turn out to be related to the heart at all. General cardiologists like Dr. Walker groom patients in a way that foregrounds a range of individualized quality-of-life and disability-related concerns that may develop over time.

Deliberators frame problems broadly, and rely on patient feedback for making decisions about care. The primary tasks of Dr. Walker, along with other deliberators, involve few procedures; instead, he largely ends up providing his patients with medication to treat their cardiac concerns. He is concerned not only about the immediate outcomes of invasive valvular surgery but also longer-term ones. And so, while he fits the folk notion of the "good doctor," his behavior is just as strategic as Dr. Kellogg's.

On the wards, general cardiologists may emphasize that trainees must anticipate more possible outcomes into the longer term. For instance, if they are working with an elderly patient who might get a valve replacement, they have to consider the side effects on their long-term mental capacities. Because deliberators are working with patients on a longer timetable, they expect trainees to examine patient symptoms more deeply and holistically than simply drawing on results of cardiac tests. Dr. Walker is not looking for short-term solutions and quick fixes; instead, he realizes his journey with his patient is long-lasting and may contain a variety of future outcomes. Thus, he wants trainees to help teach patients to take some responsibility for their own health.

Dr. Walker gives the patients the impression that he has been successful if he has been able to help them manage their own health. In managing patients on the wards he prefers to recommend lifestyle changes and the use of medications over procedures—indeed, he may often need to convince patients that procedures will not help them feel better, or may lead to unexpected new concerns. So when Dr. Walker sees a patient, he will spend time defining what is "normal" and what is pathological. To delimit these areas of concern he may need to contextualize the problems a patient is experiencing—pointing out, for instance, whether and how experts sitting on the field's guidelines committees would treat the patient's sources of discomfort. Dr. Walker sits down at the bedside of a worried patient.

"Have you ever felt your pulse, and feel it going fast? Do you feel any abnormality there? I know, it's hard to know." After the patient nods affirmatively, and indicates "it used to go just away, but yesterday it didn't," he reassures her. "Well, I'm glad you're here. I think what we can do is, we can really ease your mind about these a lot. So far we don't find anything that makes us particularly worried about your heart. We did some blood tests, and there's no evidence of a heart attack or anything like that. Palpitations can occur for a lot of different reasons. Sometimes, palpitations can occur when heart beats faster, in a normal way . . . but your body experiences that and reacts to that, even though the heart's doing what we expect it to do, sometimes the reaction to that can be . . . you experience some of these complications."

The patient listens intently to Dr. Walker's reassurance about his colleagues' usual take on her palpitations. He continues, helping her anticipate and interpret the fact that symptoms won't necessarily go away and may indeed return. "So that's sort of a nice situation; if we can do the test to confirm there is no problem with the heart, we can send you home with a lot of confidence. [We] can't maybe say these will never happen again, but [that] when you have them, you can say 'I've been checked out, this is not the big heart attack that's obviously a concern.'" The patient reaffirms "it frightened me," and Dr. Walker takes care to recognize her concerns. "I know it did, I know it did. And that's why I'm glad you're here. So we're going to take it very seriously, and do a couple of tests today, to look into your heart. One of them will be an ultrasound of your heart, okay? And the second is what we call a stress test . . . we have you walk on a treadmill and take some pictures before and after, so we can see if you have any evidence of blocked arteries in the heart. I anticipate that we won't find anything that will give us a real clear reason for the palpitation. . . . What I've found in a lot of folks that have palpitation like this, if we can do a full heart workup, and we can tell you that there is not an abnormality of your heart, then many times that helps a lot, because even when you feel some of those symptoms, you can have the confidence that there is not something terrible going on." With a reassuring tone, Dr. Walker tells the patient we will be back soon to check on her.

Dr. Walker, like Dr. Kellogg, frequently uses metaphor. Metaphors speak to the patient's understanding of the world. They are therefore useful for the doctor seeking to define patients' expectations for what they can reasonably demand from medicine. Rather than inducing deference through fear, however, Dr. Walker seeks to identify with and try to get the patient to engage in inconvenient and perhaps uncomfortable behavior, in part by using metaphor. In proposing a patient wear a Holter monitor—a wearable device worn to record heart rhythms and capture irregular heartbeats—he compares his challenges with those that are more mundane: "The problem with palpitations, it's a little bit like when you take your car to the shop and the mechanic doesn't hear the noise when he's driving it around. . . . Sometimes you have them at home, but then you come to the hospital, and even though we have you on a heart monitor and so forth, you don't have any [in the hospital] so we're not able to pick them up. This is a way we that can have you wear something for about a month, and if you have [palpitations] you can push a button . . ."

Dr. Walker may find the metaphor of the auto mechanic useful for establishing shared understanding, because he deals with humans (who vary more than do cars), and he needs them to cooperate and feel reassured if he is to help them manage their conditions and thus generate the impression of success. This may reassure them they are controlling and improving their lifestyle and symptoms in a way that moves them toward taking full advantage of medicine's capabilities. Later in the day, we see him ask a patient:

> "The other thing that I think is really helpful in these kinds of situations is . . . do you do any kind of exercise program?" When the patient replies that she doesn't, and is afraid that it might spark more palpitations, Dr. Walker is quick to disabuse her of her misconceptions: "I find that in people who have palpitations like this, if you can get on a regular program where you're doing some walking each day, if you can find like half an hour a day, what I find is that people who are on a regular exercise program experience less palpitation. They get used to having their heart rate up at a certain time during the day, and for the rest of the day it says "I'm not gonna have any of these extra heartbeats. . . . If there's anything at the end of the day that makes us concerned about exercise, we will let you know. But I don't anticipate that's gonna be the case. I think that an exercise program will be good for stress reduction and a lot of different things, and could really make a big difference."

Beyond encouraging lifestyle changes, deliberators will often reinforce to elderly patients their evident previous success if, as he puts it, they have "lived to their eighth or ninth decade without yet having encountered me." He gives patients his definition of success, regardless if that success is shaped by actions unrelated to medical care, as medicine will receive credit for returning patients to that state.

The emphasis deliberators place on effective communication is equally as strong; however, the reasoning is quite different. Deliberators must not only gain patient trust but maintain it over an extended period of time. And so, successful deliberators must induce a degree of self-motivation in the patient. For example, because Dr. Walker's patients must follow longer-term medication regimens, he must coax a higher level of buy-in from them. Therefore, he must negotiate with his patients over management strategies. Here, maintaining the confidence of the patient lies in effectively communicating to them that the doctors really do not know what will work best for them. Only through collaboration, coupled with patient feedback, can the doctor fix his or her problems. Thus the salve for the patient is in communicating feelings and concern, demonstrating that no decision is frivolous.[8]

Dr. Walker's goals for training residents involve teaching them to change patients' behavior to accord with broader medical guidelines. Dr. Walker indicated in interviews that a goal underpinning his interactions with subordinates was to push them to interact with patients in order to gather information and develop provisional, adjustable plans. Treatment trajectories for deliberators ultimately differ considerably between patients because they are likely to tell each their condition was unique. To reduce the amount he had to speculate about outcomes, Dr. Walker might even suggest that some measures be delayed in response to a patient's objections, often with the intention of reaching a compromise based on a longer-term goal. For example, when a resident proposes a new treatment regimen and the patient protests, Dr. Walker may agree with the resident's proposal that the new regimen will accomplish the task more quickly, but will have the greater concern that the patient won't adhere to the new regimen over time.

Deliberators need innovative ways to manage patient conditions. Because of this need for innovation, deliberators require team members to collaborate in ways that might shake loose a new idea. For example, in situations where Dr. Walker doesn't end up taking the resident's suggestion, Dr. Walker feels that the discussion itself is important. Consequently, Dr. Walker expects team members to be open to a range of possible directions for treating and securing the compliance of a patient. Many things can happen to patients between office visits: they can be noncompliant; a new, more acute problem could arise; or they can improve on their own.

Furthermore, the deliberator's tasks involve goals that can be quite ambiguous, ranging from an interest in preventing procedures for those with limited capacity to give informed consent, to a focus on improving quality of life. Thus, team members must observe by the bedside as he works through a treatment plan with his patient by taking in information the patient provides in order to arrive at a plan.[9]

Given Dr. Walker's tasks, he seeks to use knowledge effectively in collaboration with others through an inclusive discursive approach. He allows—if not expects—trainees to experiment with various kinds of knowledge without predetermined plans or extensive justification. As Dr. Walker explains:

I generally take the approach in the training environment that my job is to watch the overall care, make sure it is going in the right direction. So if somebody feels they want to get an additional test here, an additional test there, I let them explore that a little bit. Provided it's not something that's dangerous, I let them go there and find out where they end up with that test, even if I've been there and know it's not going to help us. . . . The times you run into trouble with residents is frequently with the brightest ones who are overreaching or are more confident than their level of training would suggest they should be.

In contrast with demands placed on intensivists, deliberators have more time available when making decisions. Contrasting his job to that of the intensivist cardiologists, Dr. Walker explains, "So, it's sort of different urgency, in a sense, a different level of risk that comes into the equation. If I'm reading an echo, and it looks like the fellow didn't read it correctly, we have a few hours to teach him why that isn't correct."

Furthermore, Dr. Walker expects dialogue in decisions; trainees who display overconfidence remove the attending from the process and, in doing so, prevent him from bringing his knowledge to bear on final decisions. Without that option, he may not be able to reflect the recent changes in cardiology in his practices.

To ensure that interns can interact with patients to instill greater self-reliance, Dr. Walker consistently asks his interns to work together as a group. To begin to envision outcomes, he feels the team should float a range of diagnoses and approaches to management. He also observes how subordinates tolerate the uncertainty of making a decision and tries to teach them how a range of considerations can emerge through informal conversation that might be obscured by unambiguous delivery.

By the bedside, Dr. Walker will also teach team members what to pay attention to when examining a patient with a stethoscope, point out the swishing sound of an abnormal heart, and tell them the meanings of the crescendos they hear. The process of unraveling the more puzzling symptoms discovered on rounds is a great pleasure for Dr. Walker, and he frequently jokes about the possible questions that novices should ask, such as, "Does she have a pet bird? Has she recently traveled to the Southwest?" Finally, he asks, with a quizzical tone and dramatic pause, "Does she work . . . in a foundry?"

After watching Dr. Walker, trainees learn to shape expectations, and to make decisions, collaboratively. Trainees do their utmost to avoid being forced into a conclusion before they can consult with their attendings.

To be able to manage patients according to the needs of their cardiology attendings, the residents must keep the patient in bed. After recently switching to work with Dr. Walker, Dr. Nethers listens to the patient tell his story, after hearing the case report from her intern, Dr. Geld. The team's attempt to groom the patient will suffer not by delaying a decision, but rather by not shaping expectations, neglecting to involve Dr. Walker.

From the patient, an engineer, the questions continue. He has asked to see images of his arteries. Dr. Nethers stalls. "It's a coordination problem—only certain computers will play them."

After the patient repeats his request, she uses another tack. "The problem is that you may not be able to understand them, need someone to walk you through them." Channeling her intensivist attendings, she says, firmly, "You're going to be here for a few days."

With equal force, he says, "No." His family starts laughing.

Dr. Nethers stands up from beside the bed, saying, jokingly, "Oh well, my job is done, I can just leave."

The patient persists. "No, I asked Dr. Geld to do the stress test early, so I can look at it and go home early."

"OK, let's go through this again. I like Dr. Geld a lot, he's very, very good. But he's not in charge. I'm not in charge." To reframe the meaning in patient terms, Dr. Nethers moves from the ambiguous and medical to the concrete and lay. "Dr. Walker is in charge. And you had a big heart attack—well, a moderate heart attack—but you had a significant heart attack, so we don't want to rush the decision."

Recognizing the traction she's developing, and aware of the potential problems that occur when they must rely on others for important decisions about their patients, Dr. Nethers informs the patient of the organizational obstacles to responding to the patient's discharge requests. Patients like this may also have the education that enables a greater capacity to access or generate the expertise to interpret data themselves.[10]

"If you get the stress test early, the earliest you get it read is 3:30. So, my team is on 30 hours straight starting this morning, and we leave at noon, or 1, or 2. We are supposed to leave at 30 hours to do our best; that leaves us at 1 p.m. That means we have to rely on other physicians that don't know your story as well as we do to clear you—to discharge you, which we get very nervous about, with your history of having had a heart attack, and knowing that you have disease in these other vessels, and knowing that, it's probably likely that there will be some problem with the stress test."

Dr. Nethers then opens up a chance for the patient to negotiate by referring to further clinical information from an interventional cardiologist. "I was also told by Dr. Lozar that the other arteries weren't as bad, but there was some block. He said that maybe we can tackle this with some medication, or we may need intervention. You would have a choice—if it's intervention you can go home, recoup, and come back."

After the patient, seemingly satisfied on the occasion of having become even more informed than when he entered the hospital, says he sees value in both options. His wife intervenes, saying, "I guess what he's trying to ask is, what do you think?"

Finally, Dr. Nethers punts. "I'm going to leave that up to Dr. Walker, because it really depends on whatever the stress test shows. I think . . . again, Dr. Walker is an attending, and I'm a little resident. I still have a lot to learn to get to his level, plus I'm not going to be a cardiologist, so I'm not going to learn all that."

Dr. Nethers provides the results of the tests the team had ordered, and the specific locations of the blockages, which influenced the options they posed. Better-educated patients, even if they recognize the value of expertise, require different tactics for grooming. Their socioeconomic status outside of the hospital leads them to feel they deserve a relationship closer to that of a colleague rather than a subordinate. Therefore, strategies of information control are especially important for these patients, and they take a different form. To gain patient consent, Dr. Nethers must account for patients' differing expectations. Some will defer only once they've seen diagnostic tests, while others will be satisfied by seeing the white coat alone.

Seeking to distance himself from his ailment and relate with his doctors as more of a peer than subordinate, as middle- and upper-class patients often do, the patient asks about Dr. Nethers's evidence base: "Have you seen the pictures?"

Dr. Nethers wants to control the information the team has already collected and not interrupt the tests they planned with Dr. Walker. The images also represent a bargaining chip. "So this will be an issue; if you get discharged tomorrow, when I'm not here, I won't be able to show you the images!" She laughs and continues, "No, I think it's great. I think it's wonderful that you're curious and interested. It's good for your health. And you're an engineer so I can even more understand your concern . . . my sister's an engineer, so I understand where you're coming from."

The patient's daughter follows up. "So, he gets the stress test, but you don't know when it will come back."

Dr. Nethers: "Tomorrow. Dr. Walker will personally read it. And if he thinks it's OK to discharge, we'll call the team who is covering for the night, who we'll tell that Dr. Walker will call, and—if you're OK to go—will write up the paperwork for you to go. But otherwise, you probably won't hear anything, which means you're staying. And we'll address it in the morning."

The patient's daughter asks, and Dr. Nethers answers questions about how the doctors interpret the stress tests the patient will take, what kind of heart attack her father had, and when they will finally be able to see the images. She has a long call day ahead and needs to complete her already mounting duties, so she needs to be the primary person in the room who is taking on the clinical perspective. She grasps her stethoscope and steps toward the patient. "I need to examine you, I need to talk to some more patients if you don't mind. You can't have any questions now?" Everyone laughs, and she moves in and listens to his heart. "Well, you probably could, but . . . give me a break for a little bit." Amid everyone's laughter, she waves good-bye as we slide into the hallway.

Dr. Nethers, en route to involving Dr. Walker, seeks to convince the patient that his lay interpretation of his body is inferior to their expert analysis. She must manage his interest and expectations and make him comfortable with how she and the team have defined his medical situation. At the same time, she seeks to deter him from forming alternative decisions by looking at images of his arteries, and works to reinforce his confidence in the team by referring to her consultation with another expert, Dr. Lozar. In this respect she seems to have internalized an aspect of Dr. Walker's deliberative style, though without having mastered his ability to communicate convincingly in order to gain patients' trust.

Dr. Walker emphasizes discussion and negotiation over fear when modeling decision making for trainees. Each member of Dr. Walker's team needs to develop his or her own understandings of patients. To help them begin to cultivate the relevant interactional skills, in case presentations he does not "pimp," but rather probes. As Dr. Hoffman noted, "[Dr. Kellogg] had a particular order for the case presentation and expected all the previous patient information we had; whereas with [Dr. Walker] it was like 'oh great, you have the echo report!' With her [Dr. Kellogg], if you don't have the echo report, that would be inconceivable. With him [Dr. Walker], if you had it, it was like a bonus." They reported feeling that he had few demands that he consistently expected in terms of specific knowledge. Additionally, he was prepared to use whatever patient knowledge the team could find to work with them in assembling a picture of the patient and inductively deciding on next steps. In interviews, Dr. Walker emphasized the value of recognizing uncertainty and exploring multiple potential solutions. Here, he responded to trainees during case presentations:

Dr. Walker: You know, this is one where you get nine different attendings that will have a slightly different opinion on this. None of them are right or wrong. The way I always think about it, if you're perioperative and you go to cath somebody, I'm not sure if putting someone who is demented on the cath table and asking them to cooperate is a safe bet.

Resident: So medical management is right, in this situation?

Dr. Walker: I'm just giving you my opinion. Part of the process is for you guys to make decisions, and do what you want, and if I think any of it's dangerous—like, if you order a stress test with someone with a thrombus—then I'll let you know. But short of that, there's not either a right way or wrong way to do this, so do what you want to do.

Dr. Walker rarely interrupted or corrected his subordinates during their case presentations. The way he sought to teach doctors to confront tasks required that he model reflection as well as direct trainees to propose individualized treatment directions and remain aware of the relationship between their judgment in the moment and their judgment a minute later, after considering other information. The teams never received, nor were they expected to provide, an unambiguous indication of what constituted proper treatment. They frequently hedged in their case presentations, suggesting that the differences between the intensivist's and deliberator's tasks lay in their ability to easily envision the possible outcomes of the treatment plan they propose.[11]

Once again, it's unreasonable to draw conclusions about causal relationships about the relationship between socialization strategy and trainee response. However, with deliberators, it was clear that trainees developed information-management strategies that reflected the time pressures that attendings like Dr. Walker imposed. During call nights, residents were less likely to search for information from databases or from the patients, and more likely to go to bed earlier, because most of the information they need will emerge in interaction with the team during rounds or from patients themselves (who are also asleep). When research findings from databases were introduced into the discussion of patients' treatment plans, it was usually because Dr. Walker brought it in.

In terms of the use of information, trainees observe that deliberators, in contrast to intensivists, discourage deductive decision making using knowledge from the literature on clinical trials. Consider an episode from one of Dr. Walker's first days of service with the team we've already discussed above. These team members expected that he would disagree with the management of a patient. One intern, Dr. Geld, used strategies he had developed in medical school to respond to intensivists' tasks by self-confidently invoking findings from a study as he attempted to justify his decision to Dr. Walker; however, he was met only with resistance. The second intern, Dr. Hoffman, made a similar attempt and was similarly rebuffed. After listening to the barrage of evidence, Dr. Walker patiently gave his own opinion by quoting another set of articles from specialty cardiology journals that were not known by those in early stages of general training. Dr. Walker was unimpressed, and, as the team would soon learn, the use of abstract and analytic knowledge that was decontextualized from the patient's circumstances was unwarranted with Dr. Walker. Describing these early attempts, the resident on the team, Dr. Nevins, described how she thought Dr. Walker saw the trainees' actions, with chagrin: "Even if they were strong, they were wrong!" Deliberators' tasks involve considering a range of patients' behavioral and clinical traits, as well as observations gathered over time. During this period, the trainees would generally develop an ad hoc relationship with the literature. When they work with the deliberator, their motivation for reading changes and is driven by a concern for reducing general uncertainty about cardiology. They believe Dr. Walker values a doctor's capacity and willingness to adjust—rather than perfect delivery—when grooming a patient.

Dr. Walker's tasks have a relatively long time horizon, and so his approach to grooming patients involves a conversational style. The strategies he uses to groom patients parallels those he uses to socialize trainees. Furthermore, those trainees come to learn to include information provided by patients, rather than information they retrieved from databases, to demonstrate their abilities.

Conclusion

Being a physician involves more than the ability to learn medicine's knowledge base. A doctor must be able to anticipate the consequences of treatments while using her experiences and expertise to earn her patients' confidence. Notes must be combined into music.

To reach the outcomes described in their journals and conferences, and to use the respective diagnoses and treatments, doctors must actively groom patients in a way that allows them to practice their specialty with results that line up with those in their occupational project. Although doctors with usual tasks that vary in the length of feedback loop have their own processes of projecting these outcomes, each keeps one eye on how members of their field have organized indeterminacy. Dr. Kellogg, the intensivist, must gain the confidence of the patient. For Dr. Walker, the deliberator, it is important for patients to change their behavior. Attendings, then, groom patients in a way that reflects how they perform tasks, whether that involves the solution of sending patients to get procedures or putting them through a course of drug therapy. Trainees seek to ensure that the attendings shaping the field—for whom more is at stake, reputation-wise—are able to make the final decisions by both preparing patients and ensuring that they remain malleable to the team's needs. Attendings socialize their trainees, and speak to patients, in a way that facilitates completing tasks according to the problems and solutions in clinical tasks in their area of cardiology. While for continuity with previous work I've used the term *socialization* to describe students' responses to attendings, the behavior they exhibited is much more contingent than is suggested by the term; a more appropriate term might be *short-term socialization*. In the case of intensivists, if they can get the patient to comply, then perhaps they can perform the procedure that helps build their own reputation as well as the field's. This interest, and interactional form, is generated and reinforced in venues outside this one.

The broader difference in time horizons is consistent across fields; in contrasting the errors of EPs with those of general cardiologists, the electrophysiologist Dr. Stimm said, "we commit crimes of commission, they commit crimes of omission."

Published research findings are used differently in attendings' efforts to groom patients and train subordinates. When Kellogg sees trainees' gaps in knowledge, she can influence them to read up and deliver strongly. When Walker sees trainees' overconfidence, he can watch them more closely. Further, the attendings' different short-term socialization approaches led trainees to support some uses of knowledge over others. Information management is important—not the information itself, but how it is used and how its use is authorized. The physicians want to define what information is important and relevant. By doing so, doctors are able to define success and failure within the profession.

The attending strengthens the cardiology program by being able to groom patients, because it allows them to train residents, conduct clinical trials, and perform demonstrations like those seen in the live cases. Although the content of the subordinates' practices may be somewhat different across attendings, the real differences in the treatment of the non-acute patient admitted to the wards happens when the patient moves off the wards and into the attending's clinic or into a procedure. Having the skill of grooming provides doctors with patients who are well suited for EP or general cardiology care, for case studies, and potentially for enrollment in clinical trials (instead of simply through referrals).

Before moving on, a note about gender is warranted. Some might think about Dr. Kellogg's approach as reflecting the fact that she is a woman in a male-dominated field, rather than being an approach reflecting the nature of her tasks. So, it is important to revisit a claim made here, one that will be affirmed in subsequent chapters: each attending's approach to grooming and socialization stems from their everyday non-ward tasks. In the case of

Dr. Kellogg those tasks are procedures, including implanting devices and ablating the heart. Since it may be suggested that Dr. Kellogg's approach to grooming stemmed from her minority status in a profession that is 90 percent male, I wondered if her pedagogy reflected "hegemonic masculinity."[12] To investigate this concern, I observed six teams, including three led by electrophysiologists, finding Dr. Kellogg's approach pervasive in EP-led teams. Because Dr. Kellogg was the only woman EP (out of six) at Superior Hospital, I was unable to observe others. What I could say is that her abilities are similar to others', having been trained in a top program. Further, her grooming and socializing approach is consistent with other intensivists; as will be seen in chapters 3 and 4, she socializes residents in a fashion parallel to that of her EP colleagues Drs. Buntin and Bellard. To be sure, there were some outliers within types: the oldest EPs were less demanding of subordinates than were the younger ones. However, within tasks, the approach to grooming was remarkably consistent among men and women, older and younger, more and less experienced.

As we will see in subsequent chapters, physicians will use these trainees and cases as tethers. They train and place residents in other programs, present novel cases in lab meetings and industry-sponsored conferences, and incorporate those compliant patients into clinical trials. These cases of success help them diffuse their particular approach and, more generally, strengthen the occupational project.

three

Cardiac Electrophysiologists in the Lab

Achieving Good Hands and Dividing Labor

We saw in chapter 2 how doctors groom patients on the wards to facilitate practices and results that line up with their occupational project, doing so according to the length of the task's feedback loop. These key initial discussions between patient and physician are helpful to understand doctors' work of controlling trainees and patients in applying the solutions in their approach to organizing indeterminacy, but they constitute only a small component of its underlying process.

The next career stage involves socially organizing their lab to ensure that they perform high-quality everyday work in the operating room itself—procedures that are, in their terms, of the "bread-and-butter" variety—as well as work considered innovative. That work, as we'll see by focusing in on the tasks of the cardiac electrophysiologist, includes the solutions of implanting pacemakers or defibrillators, extracting electronic leads and other device components if they deliver excessive shocks or fail to work when appropriate, and ablating the heart in an effort to correct electrical signals forming abnormal cardiac rhythms. It also involves developing a division of labor among colleagues who are known for their strengths in particular niches of the occupational project.[1] It's a division of labor that involves specialization but also interdependence, such that it is in everyone's interest to combat the threats to its stability originating from those working in other venues, such as hospital administration.

Having discussed both general cardiologists and EPs, then, this chapter is shifting to focus on EPs. At this stage, attendings have progressed through medical school, residency, and fellowship training, and are training their own fellows and now performing the everyday work of EP, which involves regular communication with those in other venues.

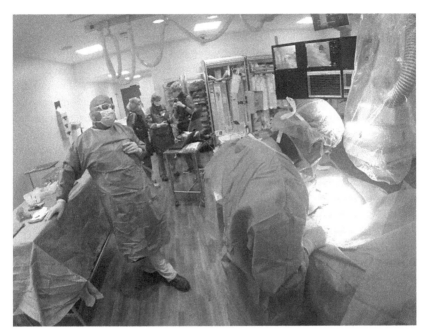

Figure 3.1. A procedure done in a lab. The EP fellow whose hands are on the patient is "closing" post-procedure, and only one set of hands is needed for this task. Photograph by author.

In the meetings of the labs, standard-setting attendings collectively organize work so that they can each define problems and solutions, and pursue their area of specialty for which they are recognized in the greater occupational project. This chapter, also set in Superior Hospital, reintroduces us to many characters from the live case. Ben Stimm is the director of the lab. His specialty in EP, and in the lab, is ablation. Mark Buntin performs some ablations and implants devices but is the only one who extracts leads. Joe Bellard implants devices and conducts ablation, using an approach developed at a well-known program that differs from the one Dr. Stimm trained in. Andrew Long primarily implants devices, as does Sandra Kellogg. As they perform their tasks in their niches, each is exposed to different patient needs and tests new technologies in those areas. They socialize electrophysiology fellows, who have recently finished their cardiology fellowship and have arrived to spend two or three years training in the lab.

Although this chapter zooms in to examine the everyday tasks of the intensivists in the EP lab, a lab with its own culture and norms, it would be wrong to see it as a closed world. The lab is situated in the hospital, and in controlling their tasks, the doctors use multiple tethers that connect this lab to other venues: to industry-sponsored meetings, and to international conferences. As mentioned, practices need to be successful in this venue to be accepted elsewhere, so standard-setters frequently publish and present in other venues their case studies of struggles and success with patients. Simultaneously, activities outside of the lab bear on solutions used inside. For example, case studies shared by colleagues, clinical trials, and scientific guidelines all impact local work. As I will discuss in later chapters, accounts of these practices tether the venue of the lab to venues such as the industry meetings and annual conference; when doctors travel to these venues they are expected to demonstrate their successes with the tough cases that they have been referred, the research they have conducted, and the fellows they have attracted and trained.

Attendings also maintain ties with colleagues external to Superior Hospital, often with those who share a niche, which encourages them to further differentiate from local colleagues according to their relative expertise with the tasks of the profession. The differentiation among attendings in the lab and their respective ties with doctors in other respected labs starts to bring into focus some of the key links between the everyday practices of standard-setters and the "best practices" published in the guidelines. Their interest in distinction in the local venue of the lab is synergistic with being recognized in the broader occupational project.

This chapter addresses the relationship between two key abilities that physicians must have: the ability to adopt new technologies or practices and the ability to organize and work within constraints set by their laboratory, colleagues, and hospital. It also suggests how attendings socialize training EPs to develop these abilities. It takes us to two key venues inside the lab: the operating room and the weekly a.m. meeting.[2] There we're going to see two processes of coordination and interdependence that strongly organize indeterminacy: the process of gaining technical and procedural support from subordinates in a way that allows attendings to use and develop "good hands," and the process of gaining and reinforcing support from other standard-setters for specialization in a niche. If attendings gain the predictability in the lab that enables good hands and builds esteem among colleagues in their group, their practices can be adopted and maintained in ways that enable these standard-setting physicians to be relatively competitive in their efforts at organizing indeterminacy. They can gain support from the hospital (which has its own goals) and continue to shape problems and solutions with patients there and colleagues in the profession. To see how that works, we follow several doctors from the live case back to their lab.[3]

Coordination of Multiple Tasks in the Lab

It is 3 p.m. in October, and I've slogged through a serious winter storm, one that drove dozens to abandon their buried cars mid-commute, to get to the hospital I've studied for four years and have come to call home. I'm on my way to observe an operation. I'm there to observe the doctors, and I put on my white coat, which, even if conspicuously embroidered *Daniel Menchik, MA*, above *Sociology*, still lets me blend into the background as I join the physicians in their daily interactions with patients.

The guard waves me past the suited industry reps registering at his desk. Opposite a group of differently outfitted, white-coated residents in a coffee bar selling off the day's remnants, a family reads hallway advertisements lining the hospital's newer glassed wing: "Superior Hospital for Cancer Therapy," "Superior Hospital for Complex Surgery," and so on. As I walk deeper into the hospital, the images on the walls shift; the ads stop and I walk past dusty portraits of famous physician scholars, the standard-setters in their fields.

I head to the electrophysiology lab, where the basic task is to do a procedure that involves burning a patient's heart or implanting in it a device. I change into scrubs and a white coat. In addition to the attending and fellow, I find, oddly enough, a woman in clicking high heels, wearing assertive makeup and exhibiting a triathlon physique. Like me, Diana was given access to observe. She is a representative who is proposing a solution to the problem of arrhythmias the EPs manage. To gain some control, she practices her pitch on me; at least she will persuade the ethnographer, if not the doctor: "the world's smallest, thinnest, high energy devices. Look how thick it is. It's, like, 50 percent thinner than the others. Best technology in a long time. We're excited."

Outside the lab, Diana and I see doctors talking to one another. Dr. Bellard encounters us on his way to Lab 2 to do his procedure. He hears Diana's pitch, and it's similarly ineffective on him. Scrubbing his hands, he volunteers his interpretation. "They are all the same. They try to make it sound like each product is so much better than the others. It's a fucking pacemaker. You know what I mean? They are all patenting and licensing. The bottom line is, the patient is eighty-five years old, for God's sake. If the patient will be climbing Mount Kilimanjaro, and the oxygen requirements suddenly drop, or increase, it's like this device will provide a third leg. Or a parachute." Dr. Bellard's display is surprising because he often depends on the reps to get and learn new technologies that let him stand out among other doctors. But he laughs and throws aside the crumpled towel. "You know? Like, do I have ass written on my head?" Walking past me he smirks at the rep. "Right, Diana?" "Whatever you say, Dr. Bellard."

Arriving in the EP lab's operating room, I see that Dr. Stimm is implanting the pacemaker while Adam, the fellow, watches. The smell of burning flesh pervades the room. I poll participants for an analogy, but the technicians, nurses, and doctors are stumped; nothing smells like this. The scent hangs as I stretch to see the burning tool cutting through the subcutaneous fat covering the "pocket" where the defibrillator will be implanted. Smoke rises from this slot above the patient's breast, a pink incision with splotches of white fat and charred scabs where the electric knife has deepened the scalpel's cut. The patient is awake but not aware: here, the art of anesthesia is in sedating the patient sufficiently to block pain but not so much as to affect the heart's rhythm. The attending inserts his fingers into the incision to open it. He slides his fingers inside to ensure the device can fit. All along, the fellow is poised, itching to use his hands, even in the most routine EP procedure.

Dr. Stimm's movements are fast and deliberate; all the while he is talking, describing the reasoning behind his decisions in order to help the fellow understand the patient the same way he does. As Dr. Stimm continues to work with his hands, his stare shifts between the patient and the six monitors mounted on an arm above the patient. There, EKG and X-ray images index the position of the catheters slithering through the axillary vein toward the wall of the heart, into which they will eventually be screwed. The heart will soon be accelerated and slowed based on commands given by the attending to the device representative, who stands and operates the device programmer, which sends electrical signals to a wire that paces the heart.

The coordination of the procedure is complex, and as elegant as Dr. Stimm's hands. He is simultaneously coordinating two critical things: the relationships among the lab members and their performances of their roles. The fellow follows the hands of the attending, who himself is staring at the monitor. The nurse is nimbly moving between recording the patient's blood pressure and his own selections for the upcoming fantasy football draft. The technicians are waiting for the fellow's order for a scalpel, as moving too far away to hand it to the attending may earn them excoriating criticism. The device representative is poking at her BlackBerry with diamond-ring-adorned fingers and noisily chewing gum. At the end of the case, during the testing phase, she intermittently calls out the rate that the device is pacing the heart and waits for the attending to order a new rate.

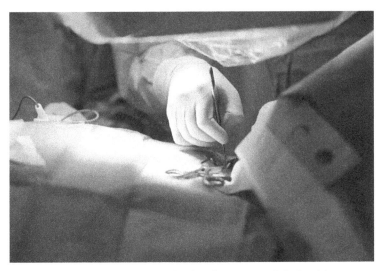

Figure 3.2. The attending is using his hands to accomplish the delicate procedure of cutting through layers of skin, alternating between using a regular and electric scalpel. The electric knife solves the problem of the need to control bleeding, by cauterizing vessels as it cuts. What we don't see is that he exercises the same delicate movements with that knife. Photograph by Carlos Javier Ortiz.

I am shifting from leg to leg in search of any somewhat comfortable posture for standing with twenty-five pounds of lead wrapped around my waist and over my shoulders and around my neck. All six of us in the OR wear this radiation protection, some for upward of eight hours every day, and I envy the occasional observer who appears in the control room wearing only scrubs and a lab coat. My movement is slight for other reasons: even if participant observers are technically immune from sanctions, it never fully feels that way. So, I too have a role in the lab—that of being invisible or at least not in the way.

Moving back into the control room to take some notes, I survey the exchanges from behind a window. A speaker pipes in talk from the OR, letting me listen as I watch. The move is driven less by the desire for subtlety and more by the chairs, offering a temporary reprieve from the radiating ache of my lower back. A fellow is there doing wrist exercises with a spring-coiled handgrip in one hand and navigating cnn.com with the other. I get a "hey" as he returns to the news. I slide past the books of research study protocols, the dusty VHS video recorders, and the button that I have become informally charged with pushing to silence the alarm indicating five more minutes of X-ray radiation has been emitted, past the pile of industry-branded pens discarded on the counter and the branded pads of paper advertising the latest positive trial of their product, and twist the knob on the speaker system that channels a stream of sound from the lab, one I'll filter into my field notes.

Five minutes later, I walk over to the control room for Lab 2, where more burning is taking place. Without interrupting their conversations, the team made thorough observation of the door, of me, and of my notebook. I put it away. The tech there is seated in front of a computer presenting an image (intended to represent the heart being burned) of an egg-shaped orb with brightly multicolored tubes emerging from its side. The fellow is beside him at the terminal. He captures several screenshots he will use in PowerPoint slides for an upcoming conference. Dr. Buntin has placed burns around the circumference of the pulmonary vein, in an approach that his colleague Dr. Stimm has described to fellows both in the lab and elsewhere. A jagged line on the EKG has smoothed, and Dr. Buntin has twisted the catheter to target another line and area of the heart.

The procedure is routine for Dr. Buntin, but it reflects an ongoing concern for the patient, who seeks reassurance now that the surgery is complete. Dr. Buntin asks questions and waits for answers, responding to questions slowly and making sure his answer registers. He is focused; the patient can detect when he is in a hurry. For authoritativeness with the patient, he no longer needs the patient's compliance and reassurance; rather he needs to be responsive and help the patient know what he should expect after being discharged home.

Controlling Team Members for Predictability, and Developing a Local and National Reputation

The vignette is what I observed. However, there are many activities that easily go unnoticed, at least until one pays attention to qualities of social organization that underpin a procedure's smooth execution, and that enable doctors to keep doing tasks their way and being recognized for doing so. These activities involve doctors' securing control in their lab tasks, from control related to carrying out the task itself, bringing in new approaches, or for clinical trials. Further, they seek to maintain and strengthen their standing and connections with those outside of the lab, including ensuring that they can use preferred solutions. In doing so, they must manage the tension between teaching an approach based on their own training and approach to organizing indeterminacy, and one based on teaching trainees to think independently.

Controlling the Lab to Organize Good Hands

Regardless of their manual dexterity, physicians can't practice their skills to maximum positive effect without control of the lab. Specifically, in the lab they need a certain predictability if they are to demonstrate the "good hands" valued by other physicians. A successful procedure is about both using the technology and being aware of the social features of managing the team.[4]

With EPs' tasks, the contributions of these elements to success are similar with both ablations and device implants. With ablations, the EP's view of the patient's anatomy is mediated by both an X-ray image (fluoroscopy) activated by a pedal on the floor, his hands on the catheter, and the map that the doctor and a tech have created to replicate the anatomy of the heart. The EP must be able to locate areas of the heart and burn them with a catheter snaked through an artery near the patient's groin, up into the heart, and across the hole they have made to puncture the interatrial wall that will provide access to the pulmonary vein. These more complex procedures, such as the ablation of atrial fibrillation, or "afib," require confidence about one's own approach in the relatively minor elements of the procedure, such as gaining access to the cephalic vein. They require a smooth and fluid execution that anticipates the impact of each movement on the patient and reflects their ability to shift strategy if complications occur. With devices, they must evaluate the device recommendation from the industry representative at the bedside—whom they use as a tether to the company, which is constantly changing its technologies—who assists with the procedure by clarifying the features of the technology and helping test it in the patient. EPs and their fellows must ensure that the device is both suitable for the patient's anatomy and also that it does not include unnecessary features. They must also constantly monitor the jagged tracings of an electrocardiogram that at any moment might reveal excessively fast or slow beats.

Both here and in the vignette it's possible to see that the physician's body is important, but the dexterity of the electrophysiologist is a small dimension of accomplishing a procedure. Learning these everyday clinical practices involves repeating the same act until it becomes instinctive. Spines warp to reflect the demands of constantly bending over. Calluses quickly harden. Not only must technology be managed but also social relationships with subordinates, technicians, and industry reps in the lab; with other attendings in the group who have their own niches and approaches to organizing indeterminacy; and with the fellows who will soon carry the group's culture elsewhere. Electrophysiologists also demand predictability in interacting with other members of the lab because they depend on the immediate availability of good information. The skill of good hands cannot be developed without the social context of coordinated teamwork.[5] EPs must direct the nurse to deliver sedation if the patient expresses pain. As we saw in chapter 2, the behavior of EPs, who are intensivists, is event centered, and they must quickly interpret patient changes in front of a team. These doctors demand responsiveness from their team—whether in terms of doing as they say, doing it quickly, or simply acknowledging them—and are highly sensitive to whether they get it. Their tasks also involve preparation for surprises; responsiveness is especially important in both avoiding and responding to more acute situations, such as those involving a heart perforation. Attendings require responsiveness in routine challenges, as circumstances can shift due to an unanticipated discovery of an infection or difficulty with gaining access to a vein. Compliance of staff is a matter of standing at attention, and also of following every step and offering all the help they can.

And so, predictability in a number of areas is important for EPs because they need to reduce variability in procedures as much as possible in order to organize indeterminacy in a way that lets them use their solutions in light of the inevitable unknown and unpredictable things that occur in any procedure. The team that surrounds the attending is constantly changing; an attending will work with a different combination of nurse, tech, and fellow for each procedure. Thus, the attending must ensure that everyone is aware of his or her preferences. Given the social dynamics inherent in a venue that requires ongoing coordination, how does the doctor perform procedural tasks well in response to feedback? How does the doctor manage the complicated social relationships? How does the doctor gain sufficient compliance from others in the lab to maintain status with those distant colleagues who may visit the lab to observe, and the local ones who are dependent on consistent quality from his hands?

Intensivists have a deep understanding of a limited range of tasks and, given the risk they recognize in these tasks, want as much predictability as possible. Attendings' management of a medical situation involves making decisions about knowledge and the performance of authority in a rapid-fire setting. They must frequently respond spontaneously to often-unexpected events and new information provided during the hands-on execution of a case in their laboratories. At the same time, the EP must remain sensitive to patient feedback. Electrophysiologists' work demands a high level of coordination and permits a low margin of error once the patient is on the operating table. Their movements are intuitive and deliberate only if they can rely on predictability from their associates around the operating table.

Failures in organizing these relationships may create complications or other clinical signs of substandard performance.[6]

In order to manage good hands, then, doctors work to organize the lab's physical format as well as its social tone or climate. Technicians ensure that favorite catheters are removed from the cabinets, sterilized, and placed on the equipment cart for the attending. This setup protocol is formalized in an "EP reference book" for teaching new techs about the preferences of their attendings. Preferences range from catheter tip sizes to specific brands. Technicians memorize these preferences and preemptively prepare the preferred equipment. The director, Dr. Stimm, is especially picky. He will remove a pencil from the holder soon after a case starts, and he expects it to be sharpened to a fine point. Techs customize computer programs solely for the catheter signals he expects to see. And they know what tone to set in the lab, turning on the music if the attending is Dr. Buntin and leaving it off if it is Dr. Stimm.

When attendings establish control over a lab, they can choose their approach to procedures, reinforce the importance of these techniques to fellows and colleagues, and enable the staff to anticipate their particular needs. Since cardiac electrophysiology is a young field, with procedures such as catheter ablation developed only in the past thirty years, doctors between major centers may use different techniques and practice them in slightly different ways. Some of these differences are uncontroversial, such as whether the doctor should use a cephalic cut-down or a subclavian venipuncture approach to implant a pacemaker or defibrillator. However, in other procedures, approaches are controversial and contested, especially in the area of ablation for atrial fibrillation. The EP's preference for an approach, when one exists, was most likely developed in the lab in which they were trained. Over time, many will meld approaches to personalize their ablations.

In part because they have different approaches to organizing indeterminacy, most practitioners vary slightly in the steps used to prepare the patient before a procedure. Consequently, they need the techs and nurses assisting them to know who is boss. Because Dr. Bellard uses the cephalic cut-down procedure, a more time-intensive approach than Dr. Kellogg's, his procedures inevitably take longer. He uses the approach as a tether to the well-known lab in which he was trained, and, as he often reminds fellows, using it allows him to incorporate new techniques into practice as they are updated. He must therefore calibrate paraprofessionals' expectations accordingly, with a seriousness meant to keep the command structure stable. While coordination is necessary for most tasks, except for the end-of-the-year parties, the attendings reinforce the social distance. In this case, Dr. Bellard is imposing a hierarchy; the technicians can't fraternize with Dr. Bellard.

> Steve, a technician, tries to bond with Dr. Bellard. "So, can you step it up? Kellogg was from slash to stitch in one hour."
>
> Dr. Bellard quizzically replies, "Huh?"
>
> Steve continues, "Yeah, you can beat her. Bet you a buck, bro."
>
> He goes for a fist bump, and Bellard declines.
>
> Dr. Bellard: "Huh? Call me Dr. Bro." He looks at me before walking out of the room. "Gotta keep these guys in line."

For attendings seeking compliance, technicians' speed is more important than their knowing to sharpen pencils and select the proper music. Attendings impose and create stability in the lab hierarchy because it allows them to predict both the duration and dynamics of the case. More locally, the doctors try to be respectful of their colleagues' time in the hospital, as the two labs they primarily use are shared among the five doctors, and they know that a delay will often send them or their colleagues home after 9 p.m.

Turning to other team members, the EPs will in fact accept the guidance of industry representatives, if selectively. They will keep up if they actually listen to the representatives to see what they need to know. If a representative knows about a new technology, then the EP will listen, because representatives have specialized expertise with the devices. Although patients only occasionally seek details about devices, doctors need to be prepared with information to back up their approach to organizing indeterminacy by appearing to be aware of all the new technology. Representatives are aware of technological developments that the doctors don't follow and, since they are often former nurses with experience in clinical care in EP, they know how to test the thresholds governing when devices will activate. But EPs can evaluate the knowledge that is being deployed and judge, given their usually more intimate understanding of the evidence representatives quote, whether the venues in the study quoted actually resemble their own.

Even as they may accept help from device representatives, sometimes co-opting their services to help teach fellows, attendings will also maintain distance. Representatives provide the devices, leads, and screws for implantation, and help test the device after it is implanted. Attendings may also seek to appropriate those reps' services in the interest of socializing fellows.

> Bob, the representative from Medicore, gives Dr. Bellard a long pacemaker lead.
>
> Dr. Bellard immediately responds, "What is that? Did you ask me?"
>
> Bob defends himself. "That's what you usually use."
>
> Dr. Bellard says, "Well, you should have asked me. Don't say 'you usually do this.'"

Bob demurely responds, "I should have."

Dr. Bellard hits his stride. "Bob, Bob, Bob, it's only because you brought in bagels today, man. You're on my good side now."

Bob brightens up. "That's why I bring them in, they offset everything else."

Dr. Bellard stops him. "I wouldn't say they offset this. It's your attempt to. You should ask the fellows. Make them think about what type of lead they want."

Attendings scold fellows when it seems they have become too close with the reps and thus may have put themselves in a position that compromises their ability to appear independent. In part this is because, to the Superior doctors, the technologies sold by the companies vying for their business are largely indistinguishable. (As Dr. Moore put it, in an interview, "a defibrillator is almost like a commodity now. There's wheat, soybeans, and defibrillators.") One company works each case, and each wants to be invited back. They especially want their newer and more specialized technologies in the hands of the high-status EPs, given the potential publicity bought by such product placement; they can advertise to other EPs if a certain EP uses their product successfully. And, as will be described in chapter 6, even though companies don't want to give the impression that they have developed excessively close relationships with their doctors, they would like fellows to hold them in high regard and be as committed to their training. Because of this, the attendings socialize the fellows to use their critical judgment regarding not only the technology but also the blandishments of the representatives.

Attendings center on establishing control with fellows in the lab for other reasons: they need to pass along their signature techniques. An EP's lineage is a badge of pride, indexed in their instruction to fellows and advertised in discussions at conferences outside the lab. To be sure, attendings want to ensure their trainees are prepared for changes in technology and are able to show their own critical judgment. But even if the attending wants the fellow to have many techniques at their disposal, they will want to ensure the fellow is able to carry out practices in the EP's own unique way.[7]

The apprentice-like nature of the fellowship creates a tension between learning an attending's approach and showing the attending you are both an independent thinker and someone who can learn from an expert. The fellowship stage contains some of the expectations for apprentice-like behavior Bosk shows that surgeons expect from residents, but involve more expectations of autonomy, perhaps because fellows are at a more advanced stage of training. These lessons may involve learning methods for a case's preparation as much as its execution.

Dipu and Dr. Bellard are standing by the sink outside of Laboratory 1.

"Did you scrub, Dipu?"

Dipu gestures toward an antiseptic gel on the wall. "I used that other gunk."

"Did you scrub first? You need to scrub for five minutes on your first case."

Dipu answers, cautiously, "The other time I did that, someone said, 'Why are you doing this?'"

Dr. Bellard quickly responds, "No. It's simple. I know nobody else here but me—no one else does my procedures, I don't do anyone's procedures."

He turns to me. "They always like to compare. 'Well, so-and-so doesn't do it that way. I've never had to do it that way.' Well, you have to do it that way now."

Turning back to Dipu, "OK, how old are you? You're like thirty-something years old, father of a child. It goes back to second grade—if that person told you to jump off a bridge, would you do it? I mean you have a brain, and if you have a reason and say, 'Well, the reason that I do this is because data suggests that you don't need to scrub, and according to this study here, there is a three percent reduction in the infection rate if you use this approach,' well, that's *academic*, man, that's intellectual, now we're having a conversation. When you guys say, 'Well so-and-so said to do it this way,' I don't give a shit who 'so-and-so' is. Just like if I say something, and you go to another doc and say 'Bellard does it this way,' they aren't going to give a shit. 'Who's Bellard?'"

Dipu responds, "So the infection rate is three percent lower?"

"I don't know!" Dr. Bellard snaps. "You've got to find out. You need to make yourself a little more credible. Don't say, 'Well so-and-so does it this way.'"

Dipu responds "So if there's a paper that says wash your hands this way . . ."

"Yeah, do it, come up with a paper, with data. We're in academics here, we're scholars. You read every night, I think. I hope." Dr. Bellard pauses for a moment. "I know you don't, you're full of shit."

Although the attending is training his apprentice to learn his practices, he also wants Dipu to assess critically the available options and propose a well-reasoned argument. And he's not going to make it easy on him; socialization is as much a stress test as it is a process of communicating content.

I linger with Dr. Bellard. "Well, if he brought to the table an argument based on the literature, would that work?"

"Yeah," Dr. Bellard replies, and Dipu claims, "he's very reasonable," scurrying into the laboratory.

Dr. Bellard yells after Dipu, "Just don't tell me that you do something because someone else says to do it. You're thirty-three years old and the father of a child and married and at the third level of your training—you gotta be able to question things more than just copying."

I ask Dr. Bellard if it would indeed be adequate to respond by quoting a clinical trial.

"Well, maybe. Because they might quote some data and you say, 'Well, I don't care.' That was only one study. How many patients followed? That's not data, what makes it data? I've been doing it this way for years. This is how we did it where I was trained."

He laughs, snapping on his latex gloves. "Either way they can't win."

The attending expects a fellow to work with enough teachers to be able eventually to use whatever approaches best fit the job. This sampling is familiar in residency, where trainees rotate through subspecialties, but, as Dr. Bellard reveals, some attendings consider this process important in fellowship.

> If trainees challenge an attending on something they are generally squashed, [as] that attending is already set in his ways and has enough evidence and knowledge to either support or refute whatever it is that's being brought up. And that is a sort of teaching, and the trainee then takes on that understanding, there's nothing that's left open-ended for him to make his own judgment on. So the trainee takes on, essentially, a piece of you. . . . Here it's more of an apprenticeship than a fellowship, and we're not going to change that.

It may seem contradictory that Dr. Bellard is asking the fellow both to follow his orders and to think for himself. But, even if we understand Dr. Bellard's pimping as a reflection of the interest standard-setters have in fellows taking orders in training, the act reveals itself to encourage sufficient mastery in a variety of techniques that they can choose from later. And critical judgment is important, because it allows the doctor to treat the patient with the right procedure for the problem, which secondarily leads to a good outcome, which reflects well on the doctor, which then finally reflects well not only on the fellow but ultimately on the attending who trained the doctor.

None of this is to say that the literature is unimportant to attendings, who, in fact, will take care to teach fellows how to use it to update their practices.

> Dr. Bellard brings up on the computer a paper published in April, and points out the lead author, Dr. Marcum, the director of Dr. Bellard's fellowship. "Just so you have some idea where it's coming from." He reads the abstract to Mike and emphasizes the result.
> Mike responds, "So that's what I thought, that the R-wave had to be greater than 50 percent of the total QRS to suggest that it was coming from the LV."
> Dr. Bellard walks through the EKG in front of Mike. "So this is relatively narrow. And now we should look at this result from the paper. See, there are three references."

Like trainees, Dr. Bellard uses the literature as a tether to teach fellows how to update practices, but also to read the data in a way that is similar to others sharing his approach to organizing indeterminacy. On one hand, he wants to make sure that his trainees interrogate new evidence to ensure its relevance to a particular patient. On the other, he draws their attention to the work of Dr. Marcum, his mentor, to pass down a way of reading the EKG, in the hopes that his approach will retain the respect it is currently afforded, and that his approach to problems and solutions is passed on.[8] His interest in fellows developing independent judgment, then, is stronger in relation to their relationship with device reps than with their attending.

Physicians' Control of Their Cases Is Important for Their Reputation and for Their Collaborations with Outsiders

We have seen Bellard's efforts at control, demonstrating the benefits attendings feel that standardization offers for obtaining good outcomes, and the ways attendings seek to teach trainees to think for themselves (and also draw on articles that strengthen the attending's approach to organizing indeterminacy). Attendings need to control their labs and want to teach their trainees to follow their preferred best practices. A further reason for those priorities is that they are conducive to establishing trust with colleagues across the profession with whom they have to collaborate on clinical trials in order to gain broader authority.

Examining how EPs outside of Superior think about clinical trials suggests some indication of why it is important to manage their labs, and how they use those trial protocols as tethers to develop that control. Dr. Halvane is the most senior member of the pioneering lab I visited in France, one that made a paradigm-shifting discovery involving how atrial fibrillation should be ablated. But if he, like other EPs, is to earn membership in the network of those who conduct the trials published in top medical journals, they must maintain a reputation for being able to control their lab. Top doctors who lead clinical trials around the world need both reliable partnerships and the assurances that tasks are performed in similar physical and social spaces.

One way their standing is influenced is by successfully contributing to clinical trials. In individual physicians' venues, the EPs at Superior are monitoring colleagues, to know where they have room to make new knowledge and also where colleagues in the professional group are succeeding, or possibly failing. Just as scholarship on physician socialization has shown that trainees who practice in ways that hurt the profession are severely punished, attendings punish existing and potential collaborators who fall short.[9] The home lab illustrates the significance of status competition in strengthening the occupational project through the case of multicenter clinical trials, which require adjudication of claims to skill, knowledge of best practices in the lab, and adherence to protocol in multicenter collaborations. Dr. Halvane, one of the most respected EPs in the world, describes the challenge of evaluating who should be invited to participate in the multicenter clinical trials he leads:

> It's not that easy to know what's going on in other people's labs. But there are ways to get a pretty good idea of what's going on in the lab. Discussing with those guys. Discussing with other guys who have been visiting them. Actually visiting the lab helps. You see the people working. You see if they are fast, if they are sure, if they are skilled—that's something you can appreciate. You look at the operator, that's what matters.

"Knowing what's going on" is related to the process of trying to create solutions to new problems the professionals have raised, ones they expect to eventually work more than 90 percent of the time. He continues, discussing the consequences of failure:

> You know, it is very easy to kill a study. This is especially true if you have someone not doing what you expect him to do. . . . You have to realize that if you have a complication when you are pioneering something, you will face the court and there will be no expert to say what you did is reasonable, that it's recommended by this scientific society or whatever. [The recommendation] simply does not exist. It's a period of time where you are very vulnerable.

Doctors pay attention to how others are doing things, because in order to develop field knowledge, occasionally one needs to collaborate on trials. Professionals at the apex of the field, such as Dr. Halvane, are especially sensitive toward their colleagues' abilities and keenly aware of the constant risk of status loss and damage to the occupational project. The solutions developed by standard-setters are important, not least because a key basis for medical malpractice is a failure of the treating doctor to adhere to the standards of the profession.[10] Clinical trial protocols, then, serve as tethers that strengthen standard-setters' efforts to gain buy-in for their approach to organizing indeterminacy.

The people making new knowledge are at risk, but it is mitigated to some extent by the fact that people watch one another and have ties to mentees, people who watch one another and support minimizing the possibility of risk. The stakes are high; as Dr. Stimm put it in reference to a new technology developed by a colleague and now being studied in trials: "he has to be very careful because his reputation could be tarnished in the end if it turns out that this is a bust." When deciding on a partner who might be proposing a new solution to profession-defined problems, Dr. Stimm will frequently choose to work with former mentees. After all, the EPs at Superior have sought to strengthen the occupational project by educating these trainees in their approaches to practice. Further, Dr. Stimm and his colleagues will watch each other to detect sufficient skills and adherence to protocol, and they will do their best to avoid partnering with someone who does not enroll enough patients or whose patients have complications. They feel pressure because if these trials fail, others will feel able to level invalidating and thus status-deprecating claims about the investigator's idea. Further, those negative trial results will be reported to and noted by the federal government, with consequences for a professional group that are more durable.

Maintaining Esteem among Colleagues in a Group

As we've seen, it's not automatic that someone can use solutions that they've pioneered and would like peers elsewhere to adopt. The opening chapter's vignette of the live case showed that standard-setters occupy niches and have an international following of doctors who watch them at the conference, take pictures of their slides, and even pay to watch at home. And the first half of this chapter shows control, the composition of good hands, in a way that involves ties outside of the hospital. But they need support, in particular in the form of referred patients. Other EPs refer patients to EPs if they fear they are unable to treat them successfully, or if the patient needs specialized skills they can't provide. For their continued innovation—the creation and use of solutions—the control just discussed is important, but without patients, and of a certain type, physicians won't become eminent. Unlike in areas of basic science, for instance, the medical profession is not organized to allow doctors to gain prominence just through teaching, sharing slides, conducting research, or speaking, but requires them also to maintain credibility through providing patient care. How is the hospital's group of EPs organized to support one another's efforts to set the solutions for their occupational project?

The example of Dr. Bellard reinforces that it is very important to standard-setters to have the space to practice their signature approach. As we have seen, attendings need support from group colleagues to attract referrals and perform these practices. Programs like Superior Hospital, which have doctors who are higher status than those at Dr. Bellard's initial employer, comprise physicians who are especially interested in preserving their approaches in the field through speaking, research, etc. Each colleague wants to be referred patients from non-Superior EPs who have judged their own skills inadequate to treat the patient safely. How, then, does such a group divide up tasks so that each doctor can reinforce that they are the appropriate person to carry out a particular type?

One key to answering this question takes us back for the moment to the lab. When it comes to discussing practices in the group, the other doctors—who may or may not be in the same operating room—must nonetheless recognize each other's skills in controlling and executing procedures. Acquiring an innovation or adopting a new procedure is part of a division of labor in which EPs must demonstrate their competence with the five physicians who share the two Superior Hospital labs. In doing so, doctors continuously seek to strengthen their standing with local peers. Maintaining their standing is going to require that they be able to practice in a way that is in line with how they describe their work to those in the global conferences and training events occurring outside the hospital. By being able to take on rare cases, they are then reciprocally able to increase their status in those external communities, making them competitive relative to others in their subfield who are also seeking to have their mode of organizing indeterminacy influence the occupational project. Such recognizable and specialized expertise will also attract companies who will give them the chance to try new technologies.

The specialized knowledge and experience of each of these attendings give them what can be described as "esteem in a niche." Specialization in the group allows physicians to enhance the quality of their practices, a well-known effect. But this department-level division of labor is also important because physicians have to receive enough referred patients to accumulate the capital of cases to share at meetings and to distribute to colleagues in slides used to disseminate knowledge. Those with esteem in their niche can inform practices that are highly observable by others in the lab. Together, the lab then becomes a microcosm of the occupational project.

Given the different frequency with which individuals conduct each procedure, some doctors will hold stronger feelings about the technology and practice that should be adopted than others. In the hospital, grounds for

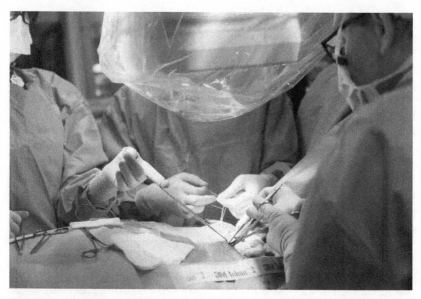

Figure 3.3. Closing up after the basic procedure. This is a job for the fellows, with the assistance of nurses, under the supervision of the attending. Photograph by Carlos Javier Ortiz.

respect in their niche, as well as their knowledge of procedures and new literature being conducted by colleagues in other institutions, must be continually reinforced among Superior EPs in the weekly morning conference. These morning demonstrations are often given by the person with esteem in a niche. Subjects may be interesting cases, new research, or a report on recent developments in an area. In addition to introducing new knowledge, attendings will socialize fellows.[11]

Slides Enable Sharing of Information and Signaling

The first way to see how these doctors organize esteem in a niche, is by examining circulated slides. And the a.m. report is a venue where they use these slides as tethers, where they carve out a niche and maintain their leadership with respect to their profession's problems and solutions by using slides, everyday deference to peers, and the socialization of subordinates. The attendings are embedded in a network of specialists inside their niche but outside their hospital, who share PowerPoint slides describing their latest work and, in doing so, keep their more distant colleagues apprised on their research and unique cases. Dr. Frank Moore, the lab director who has trained hundreds of electrophysiologists in the field (and Dr. Stimm's mentor), describes it this way:

Figure 3.4. At an a.m. meeting at Cityview, a high-status physician presents to internal medicine residents, cardiology fellows, EP fellows, and attendings, who pay close attention to the slides. Photograph by David Schalliol.

Some people ask me for slides. They will say "good physiology talk," "flow was good," and they may say "Can I share your slides?" . . . But if I want to show Ben's slides or a talk he gave on SVT that showed beautiful examples that he had from his lab, as a courtesy I would ask him, and at the bottom I would say "courtesy of Ben Stimm" just to say "You gave me a slide, it was a perfect example, and I couldn't find one that beat it, so here's a good way of describing it."

And sometimes two colleagues will be on the same lectern, using each other's computer, and there will be shared information. So, there will be times where I'll be with Bill Samuels; we have all our talks together at a particular fellow's symposium each year. Recently, I wanted to show a slide of his in Europe. I put not only "courtesy of Bill," but I called him specifically, sent him a copy of the slides, and said "Can I show this slide of this information? Are you ok with it?" This was a pretty PowerPoint with multiple things coming in. And obviously it took a lot of time to make. So I thought I'd give credit, and he said "Oh, I'm just thrilled to have you show it, and the fact is you don't have to say anything." But, given the work that was done to prepare it, you give people credit. Mike Adler is at the Mayo clinic, and he does a lot of work on genetics, and he says, "It does irk me when someone says 'give me a copy of your slides so I can show them,' and you know they're not going to say where they got them from. And I know they are not appreciating how much time it took creating this."

Presenting shared slides, then, allows standard-setters to show they are doing their procedures in a way that is in line with top members of the field, and are demonstrating that they recognize the importance of recognizing colleagues' contributions to the field. Like trainees, then, standard-setters also use research findings as tethers. Presenting top doctors' slides (with attribution) communicates that the attending is a trusted colleague. Approximately 75 percent of the talks I attended inside and outside Superior Hospital included other doctors' PowerPoints. These experts circulate the details of interesting cases using these slides, and they preface their presentations by stating, "I received these slides from . . ." Slides signal users' membership in an elite club, which helps presenters' credibility in claiming they have the special skills that would justify occupying a niche. Presenting these slides also signals you are separated by such a small amount of social distance that you can successfully request these. Dr. Moore continues: "Just having the slide at all is a sign [saying] 'I got this slide from Frank Moore. I'm his best friend.'" He laughs. "No, it's fine, it's great. It's a signal. A lot of that happens; there is a whole process of making sure people know that you're 'in the know.'"[12]

Slides, then, help physicians locally and in the occupational project. They can share case studies. They can give updates about their new technologies and abilities with using them. And, in addition to signaling friendships with physicians in high places, the slide-sharing network allows the doctors to signal expertise, thereby allowing them to attract the kind of patients that will let them ensure their findings are replicable. This replicability is a prerequisite for making slides that colleagues show elsewhere. The legitimacy that the network of shared slides provides helps them establish a protocol for their procedures. It also lets the doctor conduct publishable trials like those discussed by Dr. Halvane, a practice that will bring them notoriety in other venues, which will create demand for those slides. To carry out investigations that the doctors hope will lead to discoveries, they must gain the buy-in of colleagues.[13]

Leading from a Niche

Showing slides is helpful for sustaining ties outside and circulating news, but it tells us little about the work in strengthening a niche that must be done locally, as when attendings respond to peers in front of fellows. As mentioned above, Dr. Buntin is often consulted when patients need their leads extracted, and he seeks to maintain this niche.

We are in the morning meeting speaking about the conditions under which a device and infected leads should be extracted from a patient. It's a delicate procedure that only a single other EP in the city will conduct. Dr. Buntin emphasizes that they should be concerned about the staph [*Staphylococcus aureus*] infection.

Dr. Long responds quickly. "That's interesting. Would you advocate taking out devices in all patients that develop any kind of bacteremia?"

Dr. Buntin chuckles, and stares at Dr. Long. "Andrew, I don't operate in absolutes." He continues, chuckling to himself, "I absolutely do not operate in absolutes."

Dr. Buntin clarifies his opinion on how colleagues should think about extractions and is wary of others' unambiguous claims about a procedure that he lectures about all over the country. He knows well that what constitutes the cutting edge is always moving. He also resists generalizations despite the fact that he has developed some of the most important practice standards, through research with thousands of patients. Aside from belittling colleagues that question them, specialists like Dr. Buntin also defend their expertise by noting the case studies they've published, demonstrating the volume of patients they've received as referrals, and mentioning the frequency with which they are invited to speak.

Even as trainees use the guidelines to make a case, the guidelines can serve as an obstacle to physicians' use of their approaches to organizing indeterminacy with trainees. Guidelines that the federal government uses to reimburse hospitals may conflict with those formulated by the profession, a community that also contains conflicting perspectives. Having sat on guidelines panels at the international meetings, the attendings want to socialize fellows with the understanding that a similar group of physicians will arrive at different conclusions according to time and place, and that the standards can thus be influenced by politics. Dr. Buntin's attitude toward the guidelines reflects his standing in his niche.

A problem has arisen in the a.m. conference as they discuss how to deal with conflicting recommendations from two different sets of guidelines for the same practice: anticoagulation during ablations. Dr. Buntin says the federal guidelines recommend remaining on aspirin.

Pausing a moment, Dipu contests this, "Not the afib guidelines."

Dr. Buntin sighs, and argues that although there exist conflicting perspectives in the standards, his approach—which happens to align with federal reimbursement standards—should be used by the fellows. "I understand that. They're misguided there. My recommendation is that you should not stop the aspirin. University D gives you a false impression to give Warfarin alone. But Medicare pays you if you keep them on aspirin. It's very pragmatic in my estimation. You can argue on either side—it's a level of evidence 'C'—but I think that if your ability to get paid for what you do is going to hinge on your quality . . . the line's been drawn in the sand."

Dipu restates his claim, affirming that the level of evidence for the guidelines is low. "This is from the new guidelines. Just came out last year as a class 3b indication. Low-dose Warfarin with or without aspirin."

Dr. Buntin leans back in his chair clasping his hands behind his head. "You know, it's a risk-benefit ratio you have to individualize. Consider people with liver problems. Gotta take it on a per-case basis, because from a medico-legal standpoint, your peers are going to look at this. You have a foot to stand on in either case. Use your best clinical judgment. That's essentially what the disparity between these two guidelines is telling you—use your best judgment. Why they can't come to consensus with a method seems silly to me because guidelines are written by the same societies. It goes to show you the politics of guidelines—and believe me there is a lot of politics in guidelines. And a lot of conflicts of interest. Remember that."

Attendings are aware of guidelines developed by their professional societies as well as reimbursement standards put into place by the state that reward their adherence to some of these standards. The proposed practices in these standard-setting efforts are not always consistent, but a decision must be made. Thus, Buntin, using the tether of the federal reimbursement standards, is arguing that it is necessary to ensure that decisions are consistent with his approach to organizing indeterminacy.

The EPs' standpoints toward individual procedures, then, accompany an eye toward the way their results are connected to affect the occupational project. A key concern for Superior doctors is to bring in referrals, and to be successful in treating them. Reputations are also affected by patient outcomes, because outcomes create a perception of one's skills and the field's capacities, influencing the doctors' abilities to set expectations for what problems and solutions they can establish. Dr. Long often provides advice to fellows attending industry events, where he points out that poor results will put at stake their personal reputations in a venue, but also create risk for the occupational project more generally. As Dr. Long puts it at one such event, discussing the importance of making sound judgments about accepting referrals: "Successful procedures are expected. . . . Most of the time you go in—most procedures with the exception of AF ablation—you literally have greater than a 90 percent chance that you're going to succeed. And in medicine it really ought to be that way; we should not be taking patients when on a consistent basis they have a 60 percent or 50 percent chance of success."

Dr. Long is also speaking on behalf of medicine, with advice about strengthening the occupational project; as he notes, conducting procedures with a less than 60 percent success rate creates a problem for medicine more generally. Their solution needs to be a greater than 60 percent success rate, along with patients who can afford them this success. Patients, then, are used as tethers with the potential to show that the field is healthy. He's also suggesting what young physicians should be doing as they begin participating in the occupational project: they should succeed, because everybody associated with this person will be affected. If a doctor practices careful judgment in a way that strengthens the profession, he is more likely to deny competitors the capacity to invalidate his practices as damaging to the profession's authority. Inability to compete with other standard-setters, then, hurts both the individual and the group.

The Stakes of Losing Control

I've described the circumstances of ongoing control and predictability in the lab. But one way to see its importance to EPs' efforts to strengthen their home lab and occupational project, is in a case study. Dr. Bellard came to Superior from his first job as an attending at another academic center. Rather than use three catheters for an ablation, as is common for those who train at University A with Dr. Malcolm (Dr. Stimm's teacher) he was trained to use five catheters to perform the procedure (including one inserted into the patient's neck).[14] The benefit of the extra two "antennae," as they often put it, is that from the outset of the procedure they can gain more information on the nature and origin of the arrhythmia. The solutions that Dr. Bellard pioneers reflect this approach; the case studies he presents and publishes involve using five catheters. At this previous employer, the lab that didn't recognize his comparative advantage, what will below be called "esteem in a niche"—or do so sufficiently early on for Dr. Bellard's liking. Thus, he had some trouble when his approach to organizing indeterminacy rubbed up against that of a senior attending in his department. Now that he has moved to a program that is more well known, he intends to make sure that he is able to practice and teach fellows his method. After I asked him why he left his previous job, Dr. Bellard answered with an anecdote:

> The head of the lab had worked at University A, where Ben [Stimm] was, and had never put in a neck line. So I was putting in a neck line, and he had come in and was wondering what was going on, and I said, "I'm just putting in a neck line real quick" and I went to change the camera, and he came and pulled it out of the neck and goes "we don't put in neck lines. If you do it in the leg, you can get a reading in three seconds." And it was in front of the nurses, in front of the fellows, and I had just started—I was only in my third or fourth month, and I was bringing this new technology and procedure, afib ablation, to the program. Which is something that you need to have the buy-in and support of the director for. And when the program director comes in and pulls out one of your lines, and totally slams you in front of everybody, you have no credibility.
>
> So I had to go into his office and say, "Let me tell you something. If you ever come into the room again when I'm doing a case without asking permission, we have some issues, number one. Second of all, don't you ever disrespect me like that in front of the fellows, and in front of the nursing staff. I have to have their complete respect, so that when I ask for things and when things need to be done in the room, they respect what I say and do it without resistance." And he is going "ya, ya," and was kinda disgruntled. And here was the kicker, he said, "All you guys from University B, all you like to do is just fuck around, just map and fuck around." Well, we take all the time to get really focused and look around, and as far as I'm concerned that's how we trained, that's how we do things. Is it more meticulous? Maybe. It's all in the way you look at it. University A guys are different in that sense. I wouldn't say that Ben [Stimm] is less meticulous, it's just that the University A guys kinda roll with whatever information they gather [with three catheters] rather than go and look for it. But we have got all that information in there so we're kinda covered at all times, instead of having to look for it.

Dr. Bellard has the high level of dexterity necessary for good hands, but more than physical prowess is necessary to demonstrate his skills to distant colleagues and local trainees. As shown here, he considers it very important to practice as he was trained. He also indicates the importance of using the tether of a technology and procedure he learned in University B. When he presents cases at the annual meetings, he shows slides with readings from five catheters. It would be possible for Dr. Bellard to learn the more minimalist approach to practice; he was trained in one of the most competitive and prestigious EP fellowships in the world by Dr. Malcolm, who is one of the most esteemed EPs in practice. However, Dr. Bellard wants to give fellows the option to perform ablation as he learned, rather than as Dr. Stimm, his colleague, teaches. And, comparatively speaking, he will improve his standing in the lab group and field by continuing to practice Dr. Malcolm's signature style.

Furthermore, without the director's support at his previous hospital, he felt it impossible to control lab members enough to, for instance, bring in new practices such as afib ablation. He felt that he was also losing the respect of paraprofessionals. Only by having their respect would he get the rapid responses he needed to carry out the procedure in the manner for which he is recognized. Consequently, Dr. Bellard felt there was no alternative but to leave the hospital for new opportunities that would allow him to use his approach to organizing indeterminacy. Dr. Bellard's experience in his previous program demonstrates the importance of a physician's being able to use the solutions for which he is known; doctors gain standing by distinguishing themselves through signature approaches. Upon his arrival at Superior, Dr. Bellard was allowed to have control over his lab in order to demonstrate his good hands in using the five-catheter approach.

Hospital-Directed Collective Action to Raise Peers' Esteem, and Support the Group

One way to see that their attendings organize in terms of niches is by observing whether peers support others' claims about their niche. Do they band together to support the needs of individuals? Below, as a second case, we will see the group band together to support and enhance Dr. Long's control and success with procedures in his niche.

The attendings are specialized in distinct areas and often receive relevant case referrals that allow them to employ practices and technology they've pioneered. But in fact, allocating this local form of status is a way of helping groups cohere around the shared interest in enhancing each other's standing and raising the profile of the group. Although attendings compete with each other to maintain each's standing as experts in their niches, they band together as a group to further shared interests. These interests include enhancing the group's reputation (and thus each doctor's individual reputation), attracting referrals, lobbying for new technology purchases, and voicing concerns on hospital policies.

Because Superior's doctors are known for their skills, and thus must treat patients with unusual anatomy or conditions that referring doctors feel uncomfortable handling, they often require specialized technologies. Dr. Stimm knows that the group's reputation for treating these patients strengthens the program. As technology purchases often involve a range of hospital and industry stakeholders, these interactions frequently occur over email. The exchange below shows how purchasing decisions occur. In the first email, Matt Bennett, the administrator in purchasing, has been contacted by Diana Devers, the industry representative for Medscape.

```
From: Devers, Diana
Sent: Wednesday, September 03, 2008 6:58 PM
To: Matt Bennett
Subject: RE: Medscape CRDM contract addendum

Matt:

I hope you enjoyed the long holiday weekend.
Thank you for getting back to me. There are a
few products that are very unique to the
industry and do not fall into your existing
categories.
    Specifically, our new LV lead for Bi-V devices
that was designed to enhance the ability to be
successfully implanted, deliver therapy and
minimize risk of dislodgement. This is the very
first LV lead [of its kind] to be developed,
approved by the FDA, and commercially released.
The lead is backed by strong clinical evidence
and data. The FDA is requiring special training
to all physicians prior to use because of its
unique benefit and approach.
    I would be happy to have the contracts
department write up an addendum and [sales rep
colleague] and I would like to sit down and
discuss these product differences with you.
When would work best for you?

                            Regards,
                            Diana
                            Medscape, Inc.
```

The director of purchasing will forward these initial emails to Dr. Stimm, which usually sets off a chain of comments exchanged solely between attendings. When able to present a united front, Dr. Stimm will then represent the group back to the hospital. In this case, the team is discussing a technology used in device implants, which are conducted most frequently by Andrew Long and Sandra Kellogg. Though devices are not in his niche, Dr. Stimm—who will have to defend the purchase to the hospital—is skeptical initially.

```
Team,

Please see below.
   I do not consider [this] LV lead different
enough that we should pay more for it. Does
everyone agree with me?
                              —
```

Andrew Long voices his disagreement.

```
I'm not sure [that I agree]. I just used it
today and it was the only lead that was stable
in a large posterolateral branch. Plus, it is
the only lead [of its kind] on the market
currently.
                              Andrew
```

Dr. Stimm, because he estimates that he puts in an LV lead every two months, said in a side conversation that he doesn't implant devices frequently enough to experiment with different ones. So he consistently looks to Andrew Long, who often leads clinical trials on new technologies, for advice on devices. As he puts it, "I would value Mark [Buntin]'s opinion on a new tech involved in lead extraction. But if it came to a new LV lead I would value Andrew Long's opinion. . . . I would go to him first, because he's doing them. It's a simple example, but, it's a new tech: how did we adopt it? Someone in our group that we respect thought there was value in it." Here, Dr. Long's opinion is most valued, as he is doing the highest number of procedures and is therefore relatively best known for their solutions. If that person supports a technology purchase, Dr. Stimm will recognize the merits of the colleague's point, if obliquely, and then present that decision to the hospital.

In this case, Dr. Stimm switches from being skeptical with colleagues to being persistent with administrators. As he writes to the purchasing director, after finding out the price, "We need to have access to this lead. An extra $700 for this particular lead is not unreasonable."

If a doctor with esteem in their niche wants a new technology, then the group will pressure the hospital to make a deal with the company. The group has learned of this technology during pitches from the representative during other procedures, and may thus provisionally approve of the purchase. Yet discussions are more extensive when the new technology has not been bundled with the leads and devices that already have been priced according to a previous agreement. In cases like this, adoption involves financial risk; the hospital must preemptively purchase equipment, taking the chance that the leads will go unused on the storage room shelf if attendings change their minds. However, EPs need to have a range of equipment available in case they need to switch technologies or strategies mid-procedure. So, for the doctor to carry out risky procedures referred from colleagues and illustrated in shared slides, and for the hospital to maintain its status as a site that handles tricky patients, investments in new technologies must be made that can accommodate the problems of these complicated patients. And after the team presents itself as a united front—one that unites them also with the manufacturer—the investments are usually made.

Conclusion

In the way it delimits the shaping of problems and solutions, the EP group serves as a kind of microcosm of key processes in the occupational project. When it works, members are able to support each other's solutions, referral stream, and efforts to maintain their niche by organizing indeterminacy. To maintain their good hands, standard-setting doctors control the operating theater, seeking to create predictability that enables them to run clinical trials, train fellows, and influence distant peers by means of sharing case studies. Doctors sharing a hospital group will divide labor according to those niches, and exchange slide presentations with others who share a niche but work in different hospitals, presentations with images and descriptions of how they've organized indeterminacy with recent cases in their area. In their meetings, those with esteem in a niche describe their niche's latest problems and solutions, and in so doing they socialize fellows. When they must show hospital officials the importance of purchasing the technologies they need for the latest problems and solutions, they will band together to support the way their members have organized indeterminacy.

It is common inside and outside the medical profession to describe "good hands" as a relative judgment of one person's skills. But this recognition crucially depends on one's ability to manage the social context of the task; the doctor must control the lab and its staff in order to increase predictability, reduce variability, and ensure responsiveness so that procedures are likely to be successful. Control is so important that, as seen in the episode with Dr. Bellard, practitioners will switch institutions to work with others who let them use their preferred techniques. Looking back to chapter 2, then, it is clear why Dr. Kellogg's sanctions differed so markedly from those of Dr. Walker. Since an EP's dexterity with a catheter relies on their ability to manage a group, and their associates need to salute the flag, attendings develop their leadership style accordingly.

Beyond seeing these leadership modes in action, in this chapter we also saw how results from clinical trials are discussed by those far away from the international meetings, where guidelines are formulated. Across venues, slides serve as tethers used to strengthen one's approach to organizing in-determinacy. Among other messages they share, these slides communicate that accounts given by standard-setters also work in everyday practice. Given this web of ongoing evaluative relationships, it is unlikely that such standards will be credible without exhibiting some success in the clinical setting. The slides Dr. Moore describes were shared after he shared a lectern with another standard-setter who organizes indeterminacy in a similar way, when presenting in the fellows programs I will discuss in chapter 5.

Finally, this chapter shows specialization as an organizing principle for how doctors interact with others and how they control authority. In the midst of new techniques and new guidelines being proposed, the attendings need to maintain a position where they, occupying their niche, can sample from the range of available approaches for diagnosing and treating cases in their niche. Since they specialize while still being aware of each other's skills and needs, they are able to collectively work to secure the hospital's coop-eration when they feel they need to buy new technologies. This approach is particularly effective when the financial stakes are relatively low and the nec-essary expertise for the task held by doctors.[15] But, as shown in the next chapter, the hospital cannot always be influenced when various groups of doctors in a hospital are competing for finite hospital resources, such as beds, which are sought by other occupational projects.

There are other questions remaining that can't be answered here, but they have explanations that will be explored in greater depth later. It may not be clear now why slides are so important to those outside the local peer group, but will be seen when we jump to fellows conferences. We can't ex-plain why guidelines are given short shrift, but will see when we observe dis-cussions at the annual conferences. And we can't explain how information is shared about trustworthy collaborators until we see what fellows share and hear when they leave the local hospital to travel to those events. Finally, what are the limits of standard-setters, in terms of their capacity to control their tasks?

four

The Case of the Bed Management Program

Bureaucratic Influences and Professional Reputations

Physicians, like other service workers, need clients that will help them demonstrate the strengths of their approaches. As we saw in the introduction's opening vignette, Dr. Stimm had to consider and reject three patients before he identified one who would let him demonstrate his abilities for an international audience. He and colleagues seek to apply all the knowledge they've learned in training and with patients as well as expand that knowledge by working on the tough cases that come through the doors of a top-ranked academic center. In particular, specialized doctors, who have reputations that sustain high referrals, want to apply their knowledge to patients their colleagues have sent from elsewhere. By doing so, the doctor can satisfy these peers while also attracting cases sufficiently interesting to present at meetings like the one described in the book's opening vignette, and the venues described in upcoming chapters.[1] For the hospital, well-insured patients allow it to afford advanced technology and renowned physicians, both of which raise the hospital's prestige. But a large group of patients highly attractive to the hospital may not be the most interesting to the doctors; the concerns of administrators may conflict with concerns of the physicians. At the same time, executives must be careful in their efforts to reduce the size of the hospital's front door. If a hospital restricts its doors, doctors may be left without the patients needed for training fellows, conducting clinical trials, and writing case reports through which they shape the future of the occupational project. What happens when doctors' efforts to use tethers, organize indeterminacy, and strengthen the occupational project are obstructed?

Processes of managing authority, then, involve managing more than a doctor's relationships with their patients, trainees, or peers—they also involve doctors' ties to other professionals and administrators in a workplace. Those administrators can put the doctors' status at risk. Based on the previous chapter, one might conclude that the interests of Superior Hospital and the doctors would align. Indeed, the hospital should be interested in having doctors practice in ways that allow them to establish widely followed problems and solutions, letting them compete most effectively in their own reputational marketplace. After all, the hospital benefits from the publicity garnered by curing a puzzling patient. But the relationship between doctor and hospital is considerably more complex, and the doctors' occupational project may be strengthened, or weakened, by their relationship with the hospital. In some circumstances, specific goals that the hospital has as it pursues prestige—for instance, its public standing as measured by published *U.S. News & World Report* (*USNWR*) rankings—may conflict with physicians' efforts to control tasks, generate individual status, and shape the future of their occupational project. If and when public symptoms of the resulting tension emerge, the reputations of both the physicians and hospital might be damaged. In other circumstances, the favored tasks of each may be symbiotic, with the tasks that help the hospital improve its standing also serving as ones representing the effort doctors make to perform tasks in a way that generates professional status. A natural next step, then, is to begin to consider how venues and people that are not involved in direct patient interaction influence the management of authority.

To do so, I will offer a case study that suggests how the doctor-hospital relationship bears on doctors' management of medical authority, and examine how the doctor-hospital relationship differs between cardiology and internal medicine doctors. Because cardiologists need referrals to perform high-quality work and to distinguish themselves in published case studies and clinical trials, whereas internal medicine doctors must coordinate care to manage patients effectively in the hospital, each group manages tasks through different means. The following case study illustrates how the management of medical authority is generally supported or suppressed by the nature of the doctor-hospital relationship, and its bearing on physicians' pursuit of status. Case studies allow us to probe the broad range of factors that may condition a relationship. This chapter explores the case of a new Superior Hospital program intended to enact a process of managing beds through a central system. This new program for managing beds represents a way of confronting one key problem of any organization that processes people, throughput, that is, moving people in and out effectively. It also involves an issue not yet addressed but crucial to managing medical care: controlling financial costs to the hospital. Accessing patients who need care in Superior's high-ranking areas, and who are well insured, helps the hospital maintain its goals for prestige while managing costs. But, although the hospital competes for prestige with other hospitals, and doctors compete for status with other physicians, only some of its throughput goals are shared by physicians.

In the case study we will see that, ultimately, the implementation of the program favored the daily tasks of some doctors (in internal medicine) but not others (in cardiology), showing again that doctors who work in different occupational projects have different needs for tasks. Their different responses indicate that, when it comes to their ability to manage medical authority, doctors whose tasks are differently structured will vary in how they are affected by—and feel they must respond to—hospital programs. For the doctors whose tasks were not privileged, the cardiologists, the changes impacted their personal goals of performing high-quality procedures and garnering status amongst colleagues outside of the hospital. The negative impact of the bed management program led the EPs to leave Superior Hospital.

Different Responses to the Hospital's Efforts to Manage Beds

As an introduction to the case study, I describe some responses of physicians to a new administrative policy. I begin with the bed policy's backdrop: an effort to improve in the rankings and build a new hospital. The following two vignettes show how general internal medicine and cardiology physicians respond to the key features of the hospital's revised "interdisciplinary rounds." The first depicts a regular bed management meeting, illustrating the benefits internal medicine doctors see in the program. The second depicts an email thread among cardiologists, doctors who opted not to attend the bed management meetings, illustrating some reasons for their opposition to the new program.

The Administrative Context for the New Bed Policy

As I walk through the building, I look down the hallways and outside the windows, and am constantly reminded that the hospital has its eye on its own standing as it serves its trustees. Renderings on construction fences depict a new children's hospital. Soon the hospital will have an addition that houses the private rooms and flat-screen TVs necessary to keep its competitive edge. Leaving the lobby and entering the hospital's oldest building, I pause at an oak-paneled conference room to observe a monthly meeting. The discussion is surprisingly different from what I had previously imagined a hospital discussion to be. The room is set up with a long table, with notepads and pens at each seat. The event, ostensibly, is meant to manage patients and beds. There's no PowerPoint presentation, which is surprising, given what I hear.

In this conference, eyes are rapt on the chief medical officer, who kicks off the conversation about managing beds. "The trustees at the last meeting latched onto the fact that we didn't make our goal of increasing our amount of private-payer patients by three percentage points. We went up two percentage points last year, which you remember added 16 million to the bottom line." The vice president of nursing jumps in. "Remember that the trustees are soon to vote on the new children's hospital going forward, and will also be asked to make a huge contribution to the future success of our building, probably six figures or more." The discussion ends with a report from the president. "We have to put pressure on ourselves to shrink down certain pieces of our portfolio and redeploy them. I spoke to fifty other academic CEOs and showed them the PowerPoint slide indicating our data for return visits is aberrant to the rest of the health system consortium. If we were stockbrokers we would be thrown in jail for churning. We don't think, 'Why am I seeing this patient this year?' or 'Maybe they could see someone else.' So we're correcting a long history and culture in this hospital, and have to rely on each other. And the big leverage point is trust and communication, neither of which are in big supply here."

The doctors see a different problem, and a different solution. The meeting breaks up and I fall into lockstep with a physician whose section's beds have recently been cut. Not everyone accepts the CEO's language. "Convicted for churning? I'm thinking, 'Listen, man, I'm taking care of the patient, I know how often I need to see them.' It sounds like he was talking about widgets more than about humans." I nod, trying to appreciate his impressions of what we'd witnessed of the machinations behind running a top medical center.

Bed Management in the Internal Medicine Quadrant

At the internal medicine quadrant bed management meeting, five or six regular attendees discuss how the bed assignment program is meant to increase throughput speed by getting the patients well enough to move out of the hospital. Bonnie and Susan, case managers, are responsible for connecting patients with outpatient facilities—linking, for instance, patients with kidney failure to dialysis centers. Matt, a social worker, matches patients with longer-term care facilities such as nursing homes and rehabilitation centers. Ranah, an administrator, sits before a computer terminal with pictures of all the hospital's beds, each flagged with information as to whether it is vacant, occupied, or being cleaned between patients. Colleen, a nurse practitioner and supervisor of the nurses on the ward, is there to ensure there is an appropriate number of nurses working. At the head of the table sits Donna, the bed director, another administrator who reports to Superior Hospital executives and is accountable for maximizing the number of beds that are empty and cleaned by noon. Finally, also present is Dr. Abraham, an attending in charge of the bed management program for internal medicine. Dr. Abraham has more medical expertise and a higher level of seniority than the others in the room. Therefore he also has the greatest capacity to mobilize other resources in the hospital for any tests or treatments the interns need in order to discharge patients. Further, while all the members of the occupational project at the table can exert pressure on interns who have come from the wards to report on patients, he can exert more.

In this episode, there is a crisis: all the beds in internal medicine are full, and there are three people waiting to be admitted from the emergency room. Patients must be discharged. An intern in internal medicine says that one of the patients cannot be discharged until an interventional radiologist uses a needle to drain fluid from the patient's abdomen (a procedure known as paracentesis).

Dr. Abraham: "We really really need beds today, so if there is any possibility the paracentesis could be done early enough so that—"

Intern: "Yeah, it was scheduled for 9, only issue is she needs 4 units of FFP [fresh frozen plasma]—"

Dr. Abraham: "Need 4 units of FFP for a para?"

Intern: "She's got liver failure and her INR [international normalized ratio] is like 2.4, so we got to get it down to like 1.5 or so."

Dr. Abraham: "So, to be honest, I take care of these patients all the time, I'm on the hospitalist liver service, the most I'd give her is 2 units of FFP. And who is doing the procedure? You or the procedure team?"

Intern: "The para is being done by IR [Interventional Radiology]."

Dr. Abraham: "Yeah. Call the procedure service, and see if they'd be willing to do it without an INR goal of 1.5. . . . IR are Nazis when it comes to their requirements for INRs."

The intern is trying to get his patient off the floor. And Dr. Abraham, an attending with experience treating patients, is motivated and able to help. Dr. Abraham is a hospitalist, a physician who works exclusively in a hospital, who can mobilize help from the procedure team or his colleagues, or simply conduct the procedure himself. So, the intern asks for clarification. "You think she'd be OK after 2 units?"

Dr. Abraham: "I guarantee you that if you did the para without the FFP, she'd probably be fine. I shouldn't say guarantee. If you did the procedure safely and appropriately, etc., etc., etc., the risks are pretty low for a para. I wouldn't worry if it was 1.6 or 1.8. I've done paras with INRs of 3."

Intern: "The only reason we did 4 is that IR wanted 1.5 . . ."

Dr. Abraham: "I understand. OK. You know what, give her the FFP now. And go back upstairs and first thing you do is call the procedure service and see if they'd be willing to do it with the 2 units of FFP. And if so, cancel IR and just have the procedure service do it. I bet they will do it with 2 units, and I bet they probably won't require an INR check."

Intern: "OK."

Dr. Abraham: "That being said, I hope that in the near future, your team will be more comfortable doing paras on your own so you won't be hostage to the Nazi aspects of IR. What I'm concerned about is if you don't get the para done till 7 or 8, then you might feel nervous and want to keep her overnight. And we really, really need the bed. So, if for some reason IR can't do it by 2 or 3 o'clock, and procedure team can't do it by 2 or 3, I actually want you to page me. I'll get one of my colleagues to do it."

The intern leaves the meeting, after thanking Dr. Abraham.

Training internal medicine doctors frequently have problems accessing consultants, those physicians who hold key skills for their tasks. Additionally, the physicians are comfortable with nonmedical necessities driving the care; interns are content to follow the goals of the group and to rely on the hospitalist's knowledge base. They, too, want patients discharged quickly, as it may allow them to shave a few hours off a thirty-five-hour shift.[2]

Bed Management in the Cardiology Quadrant

Cardiologists found less benefit from the hospital's use of the meetings to intensify bed management than did internal medicine doctors. These doctors need little assistance from other professionals in managing and discharging patients, because they have all the specialized knowledge needed to make these decisions, and also because they don't discharge to outside institutions. Further, and as described in chapter 3, specialized cardiologists like EPs generate status when they accept and treat patients who have been referred for clinical trials; when they train and place fellows as faculty and clinicians; when they perform successful cases; and when they generate, circulate, and publish case reports based on colleagues' referrals of challenging cases. Cardiologists' tasks leave them less concerned about discharge than admission, especially EPs and interventional cardiologists, who are at the end of the referral chain, and do not require that their patients be placed in other institutions after their procedures. They described the program as a conscious effort to cut the number of beds for their patients. Cardiologists initially came to the meetings, which had similar participants as internal medicine's.

Superior Hospital's electrophysiologists rely on empty hospital beds because they perform invasive procedures that frequently require at least a day of recovery. Knowing these beds are available allows them to reassure referring clinicians that their patients will be well-cared for. More beds also allow them to increase the probability of encountering a puzzling patient and of having the required number of patients for clinical trials and an adequate number of fellows to train. Because these cardiologists depend on their respective personal networks, and because they live in a city with intense competition for their procedures, their reputations are important for attracting opportunities. After approximately four years of the bed management program, the allotment of beds for surgery and cancer rose to 50 percent (from 43 percent) and 30 percent (from 24 percent) respectively, while the percentages for internal medicine and cardiology patients dropped to 13 percent (from 23 percent) and 7 percent (from 10 percent).

With these cuts, most attendings were angry and forbade trainees to go to the meeting. How, then, do we study a nonevent? To do so I draw in part on emails provided by Superior cardiologists who identify the salient issues behind their rejection of the meetings.

The cardiologists' anger is evident in their responses toward Superior Hospital's attempts to control the patients admitted onto the wards. Dr. Spangler, a cardiology attending in charge of the bed management program for the cardiology unit, indicated that the following exchange was representative of the kind of messages that his colleagues found problematic, given their unhappiness with the hospital's restricting referrals.

The hospital deploys the Emergency Medical Treatment and Labor Act (EMTALA) to restrict patient transfers, diminishing the cardiologists' control over their work. This federal law is intended to ensure that patients who come to inadequately equipped hospitals will be able to access facilities with resources they need. The law requires adequately equipped hospitals to accept patient transfers as long as the patient in transport does not pass one with similar capacities. Soon after the bed program began, Superior Hospital respecified the way it adheres to EMTALA. This transcript highlights rival concerns between the hospital and the doctors. The hospital is concerned with resources while the doctors are concerned with losing cases that they traditionally use to strengthen their professional relationships and maintain their fellowship program.[3]

From: Spangler, Brian
To: [Cardiology Faculty]
Sent: Thursday, April 22, 2007 10:52 AM
Subject: <no subject>

Two new developments from your friends in Discharge
    1)   There has been a significant clarification of the EMTALA regulations that govern the transfer of emergency patients from outside hospitals.
    We [in discharge] have used these criteria to transfer patients who need a procedure that can only be performed here without regard to their ability to pay. In other words if the patient met EMTALA criteria (see below)—we bring them. The clarification is that these criteria should only apply to patients in an outside hospital emergency room, NOT inpatients.
    So we will no longer accept inpatients from other hospitals that are uninsured even if they need a procedure that is not offered at the sending hospital. The patients will be referred to County Hospital. Individual exceptions for therapies that are uniquely offered at Superior (not available at County or elsewhere) will be considered.
    2)   The hospital will no longer be accepting [neighboring state] Medicaid patients of Any type.
    These announcements will be coming soon—I wanted to give you a heads up to see if any of you felt that these patients were important either for training volume or training case variety. If so, we need to provide objective

```
data to support this and then we can propose
exceptions to the rule.
                                    Brian

---------

For your reference—these are the EMTALA
screening questions—

Does the patient have an emergency medical
condition?

Is the patient unstable despite treatment?

Does the unstable patient with an emergency
medical condition require inpatient services
available here that the transferring facility
does not provide to any patient or cannot
provide to this patient at this time?

Do the benefits of transferring the unstable
patient with an emergency medical condition
outweigh the risks associated with the
transfer?
```

The problem of restricting referrals from primary care and general cardiologists is especially acute in cardiac electrophysiology and interventional cardiology, which are areas at the end of cardiology's referral chain, whose doctors may not be contacted before patients are vetted in by Spangler. Though hospital administrators don't say explicitly to the cardiologists that they can't bring patients in, they are implicitly doing so by stating that patients can be transferred to Superior Hospital only if they are not admitted elsewhere. Because it hurts their ability to do their work, the bed management program has a particularly adverse effect on the cardiologists.

The cardiologists' angry response to the program can be seen in the following emails to Dr. Spangler, from the directors of each program, Dr. Ben Stimm and Dr. Jeff Lorenzo.

```
Brian,

I understand the financial considerations, but
unfortunately, every case is important for
fellow training volume. A few questions:
    1.  I suspect patients who need a
[pacemaker lead] extraction for life
```

```
threatening infection could be considered to
meet EMTALA criteria. But how do we learn what
is offered uniquely here vs. at NSH [North Side
Hospital] related to cardiology?
     2.   It is rare that we are called when the
patient is in the ER, it is usually after the
patient is hospitalized.
     3.   Who is responsible for asking the
EMTALA questions below? If it is the physician
receiving the call [from their colleague], the
hospital must recognize that a policy that
requires the physician to ask these questions
is going to introduce just one more reason for
a referring to not call us with all of their
cases. I believe that we should be allowed to
always say "yes" so that we can maintain a
good relationship with the referring physician
and leave the dirty work of refusing the
transfer to the hospital bed desk. Remember,
the policy is the hospital's, not the
physician's.

                         Thanks,
                         Ben
```

It was clear that, to the director of the EP program, the approach of admitting only the referrals for which Superior was uniquely suited would fray the EPs' relationships with the local community of colleagues from whom they are forced to refuse transfers. These often challenging cases are used as tethers in relieving peers from around the country from tough cases they would prefer be placed in Dr. Stimm's expert hands; approximately 65 percent of Superior's EP patients come from referrals outside the hospital. In addition to helping referrers, these patients serve as tethers that strengthen the occupational project in other ways; when EPs accept transfers, they can ensure that their patients aren't treated by other doctors who also treat arrhythmias, the cardiac surgeons, who are often in competition with EPs and use a very different, and more invasive, approach.

Dr. Jeff Lorenzo, the director of Superior's interventional cardiology program, shares with Dr. Stimm a concern about fellow training volume.

```
I believe we need to see as many ACS [acute
coronary syndrome] patients as possible for
training purposes, and too few come through
our own doors. Many, but not all these patients
```

```
are referred from the ER, but I also do not
want the role of gatekeeper, and do not want to
lose any such cases.
```

A major motivation for accessing these beds was for the patient volume necessary to train fellows. The minimum number of patients for training fellows comes from the recertification boards in the profession, who require that fellows have conducted a minimum number of procedures before they can be certified. Since multiple procedures cannot be performed on the same patient during the same visit, a reduced number of beds necessarily reduces the number of fellows who can be accepted and trained. Such atrophy limits the number of trainees that attendings may place as either faculty in their colleagues' academic departments, or as members of physician groups who might refer their toughest cases to Superior doctors.

These doctors need some control over their patient base. To that end, they advocate a return to the previous "always say yes" policy. The Accreditation Council for Graduate Medical Education (ACGME) requires a high volume of procedures to sustain the fellowship, and Superior Hospital doctors are highly aware of these numbers. Soon after these emails, the EP department was, in fact, placed on probation by the ACGME because of its low volume. Since probationary status is the first stage in the loss of a fellowship program, having this designation may signal to future fellows that they should steer clear.

How a Hospital's Efforts at Control Can Affect Physicians

Hospital administrators face financial, professional, and political problems and multiple competing demands. First, due to variations in insurance coverage, the hospital makes money on only some of its patients, while others cause it to lose money. Therefore, to deal with the financial problem, hospital administrators develop multitiered cost systems for maximizing reimbursement from insurance companies by cross-subsidizing costly patients with ones who are better reimbursed. Second, hospitals face problems attracting and retaining high-status physicians, who require advanced technology and complicated patients that will help them refine and reinforce their approaches to organizing indeterminacy. These standard-setters need a diverse patient base in order to train residents and fellows, to solicit cases that may garner notoriety, and to attract patients as research subjects who provide them with the ability to obtain funds for conducting clinical trials. The hospital shares some of these goals, especially that of attracting puzzling patients whose successful treatments can be publicized, but is also concerned with maintaining and increasing their revenue. The third issue is the hospital's political problem of responding to state policies for accepting patients. It must solve these problems without breaking the law. If they want to prioritize not only the complex patients with the potential to raise their prestige, but also revenue, they need policies like EMTALA that let them legitimately limit how narrow they can make the hospital's doorway.

We need to ask, then: what organization-level relationships need to be managed so that doctors can do work that will allow them to carry out their tasks and organize indeterminacy? And how much control do doctors have over these relationships?

The Problems of Reimbursements, Prestige, and Location

The doctors seek to attract complicated and interesting patients. This goal is shared by the hospital, provided it is uniquely able to care for that patient (and is reimbursed accordingly). The status of cardiologists—though not the internists—depends to a great extent on their abilities to perform and publicize their expert procedures. The hospital's prestige rests on similar grounds—to compete in its ranking system, academic hospitals also need high-status physicians in its areas of investment, to conduct fancy procedures and disseminate news on these accomplishments.

Yet complicated patients, at least those without private insurance, tend to be more attractive to the doctors than to the hospital. The stronger the reputation of a hospital, the greater its revenues tend to be, in part because it can attract a higher proportion of patients with high-quality insurance.[4] Consequently, because Superior Hospital is paid by public and private insurers on behalf of its clients, the hospital's reputation is linked more closely to the insurer. Thus, doctors and hospitals may not benefit from the same pool of patients.

Attracting those well-insured and puzzling patients directly or from referrers comes through raising one's rankings. The *USNWR* system rewards hospitals with subfields that are near the top of the rankings, but punishes those with slightly less stellar performances across a number of subfields. For instance, if a hospital is in the top ten in six areas (out of sixteen), such as cardiology, oncology, pediatrics, gastroenterology, rheumatology, and urology, it is included in *USNWR*'s "honor roll," even if its psychiatry department is below average relative to competitors. In contrast, the hospital will not crack the honor roll if the hospital is in the *top twenty* in twelve areas. Although a bureaucracy and its professionals are always codependent for prestige, the *USNWR* ranking system leads the hospital to benefit disproportionately from the success of doctors in its highest-ranked specialties.[5] The hospital will then make human and physical capital investments in those areas in which it has a comparative advantage; recruiting top physicians and purchasing novel robotics in those specialties trumps improving nursing capabilities in lesser-ranked ones.[6]

The government sets reimbursement levels according to the relative supply of medical services in a geographic area, with the hospital's highest reimbursements coming from tasks they are uniquely able to do: the most specialized services, ones that raise Superior Hospital's national profile. For instance, at the time of the bed management program, Superior Hospital generated money on the double-balloon endoscopy because it was uniquely able to conduct that procedure. Its unique capabilities and high reimbursements then make it more capable of attracting those high-status specialized doctors and patients that generate prestige. Compared to a community hospital, the overhead paid by Superior means that treating patients there costs an average of 60 percent more.[7] In contrast, Superior Hospital loses money for all government-pay obstetrical care and deliveries, which do not require the specialized skills they have invested in. For these conditions, Superior Hospital ultimately subsidizes a large proportion of the care that is provided. Other area hospitals generate positive revenues because their costs are below their reimbursement levels.

Table 4.1 describes patient types and revenue amounts for Superior Hospital in 2006, the approximate date the program began. The vast majority of its surplus is derived from a relatively small number of patients. As the table illustrates, to optimize its finances the hospital is incentivized to attract and develop strategies to admit patients who are complex and privately insured.[8]

As the table indicates, the net revenue from hospital patient visits is then about $80 million. It is spent on "organizational slack," the capacity to absorb changes in its environment without changing its core activities. It allows the hospital to have a bed available if a high-status physician wants to transfer in an uninsured patient of a referring clinician. It frees beds for cases in which one of its physicians thinks that it is valuable for teaching or research purposes. It allows Superior to operate, like most of its competitors, at approximately 75 percent capacity. Thus, unlike a hotel, the most profitable or successful hospital is not necessarily the most full.[9]

Reimbursement would be less of a problem if Superior Hospital were located in a more affluent area with a greater concentration of hospitals. However, its niche in the city's ecology is one of extremely concentrated poverty and sparse medical facilities. Compared to the city as a whole, Superior Hospital's region has in excess of 50 percent more low-income residents. Twenty-nine percent live below the poverty level, and more than 20 percent live between 100 and 199 percent of the poverty level. The region contains a large swath of the city's patient population that receives public insurance benefits or no benefits at all.[10] Because Superior Hospital is located in a low-income area of the city with high levels of cardiovascular disease, and because there is a correlation between low income and cardiovascular disease, it therefore attracts poorly insured or uninsured patients with

Table 4.1. Privately Insured Complex Care Patients Subsidize Others in Superior Hospital in 2006

	Complex Care	General Care
Private Patients	3,840 visits	86,400 visits
	+$165.6 million	+$94.8 million
Government Patients	6,720 visits	120,000 visits
	− $90 million	− $87.6 million
Total Patients	**10,560 visits**	**206,400 visits**
Revenue	=$75.6 million	=$7.2 million

multiple conditions that require long hospital stays. Thirty-six percent of Superior's patient base is on Medicaid, whereas the median level of Medicaid-insured patients among the city's other large hospitals in town is 15 percent. To intensify these pressures of place, in the last twenty-five years, many nearby hospitals had closed their ERs, and seven had shut their doors permanently.

Before the Bed Management Program

Superior Hospital did not always have a deliberate strategy for handling the environmental pressures of reducing costs and increasing prestige. Before the bed management program emerged in the mid-2000s, cardiologists could control bed assignments; Superior Hospital had a well-known "always say yes" policy for admitting patients into its beds, and was filled with patients referred by doctors and hospitals from all over the country. And, with patients needing specialized care also came "dumps" from other organizations: the sick refugee from Cambodia with just enough money for a plane ticket, the criminal offender impossible to place in a nursing home or dialysis center, or the Friday admission to a neighboring hospital unwilling to pay its nurses higher weekend salaries (and thus "unable" to care for patients they were legally required to admit).[11] Open beds could be assigned to any patient who arrived by foot or ambulance.

This laissez-faire approach became a problem for reasons tied to both the financial bottom line and the doctors' needs. The hospital's image began to suffer among the doctors it trained and employed, and with those physicians wanting to refer patients. Protests over the patient mixture came from clinician educators, respected researchers, and students who reported spending a month in their ob/gyn rotation without delivering a baby.[12] Most patients in the world, and therefore most patients in the random assortment that came to Superior under the old regime, do not have private insurance, and therefore the hospital was not maintaining a high-enough reimbursement rate. And so, their unpredictable patient flow lacked the well-reimbursed patients with conditions that the hospital's hoped to treat in light of its human and physical capital investments. Because of a lack of beds, the subspecialties that made Superior "a World-Class Patient-Centered Integrated Academic Medical Center" could not get their patients admitted. The USNWR rankings fell. It became crucial for the hospital to reorganize its environment.

In the same way that EPs spread knowledge via slides and divide responsibilities for patient care according to their niche in the electrophysiology lab, the hospital also needs a dynamic system for allocating beds and a way of sharing information among professionals to facilitate throughput. In a way, these two entities are nested; doctors have their own sphere, but are still in the hospital. Yet, at that time the cardiology department was not at the very top of its field's rankings, and the EP group, for which Superior was well respected, could not rely on separate USNWR rankings for its subspecialty because there weren't any.

The hospital executives decided that developing an international reputation involved ensuring that beds were available for valued patients. What would it take, hospital executives asked, to create the prestige and the space to attract these interesting, privately insured patients, and then to discharge them quickly? An organizational solution involving bed management seemed necessary for overcoming the disjuncture between the personal motivations of doctors and the collective needs of the hospital.

The Mechanics of the Program

In response, Superior Hospital implemented the bed management program to monitor and control admissions, match patients to beds, and expedite discharges. The program had three components that relate directly to the physician-hospital relationship: a system for allocating beds according to hospital priorities, a public relations campaign that helped support those priorities in the community, and the addition of a throughput component to the usual "interdisciplinary rounds" attended daily by members of a team managing patients on the wards.

In altering these meetings to emphasize the throughput component, the program involved bed reallocation, not expansion; the problem was one of patient quality over quantity, so opening more beds would not improve matters.[13] Additionally, and in contrast to the hospital's practices before the bed management program, the attending leading the meetings could not fill another section's beds; beds assigned to one quadrant by the ER's discharge administrator could not be converted to beds governed by another quadrant. Additionally, no more patients could be accepted once a quadrant reached capacity.

First, the administration implemented a system that would allow the hospital to admit patients selectively and thus ensure that it would not take on too many patients whose care would be inordinately expensive relative to revenue they generated. A central characteristic of the resulting program was that the number of beds in the hospital would be unevenly divided into four groups: multispecialty services (surgery), cancer, general internal medicine, and cardiology. Patients would initially be matched to those beds according to a protocol administered by a hospital administrator who worked in the emergency department. Because of the relative position of emergency room doctors in the medical pecking order—these doctors would have little success in attempting to reject the transfer of a specialized surgeon's patient from a cross-town colleague, for example—two physicians from each hospital section were chosen to moderate conflicts.

The new system of bed management solved many problems encountered in patient intake by transferring control of Superior Hospital's environment into the hands of administrators instead of physicians. Like airplanes circling for an available runway, patients without an available bed on an inpatient ward matching their condition would accumulate in the emergency room until a bed opened. But, like air traffic control centers facing a tornado, hospitals can take measures to respond to pressure. They can exercise their legal right to declare themselves full (on "bypass") and thus close their doors to the ambulances that might bring them patients who were acutely ill but poorly insured. This protects the hospital from short-term environmental changes, such as the closure of a nearby emergency room or entire hospital, while leaving a bed available for a patient transferred for high-payout procedures, like a double-balloon endoscopy. Thus, the hospital was able to match patient volume to the skills of staff members it felt would best assist in improving its standing.

Second, Superior Hospital created a public campaign, which involved generating support from the local community, despite the fact that the program limited the number of beds available to individuals with illnesses that were prevalent in the local community. Superior Hospital needed a warrant to create its new bed management program so that it could raise its status and revenue by attracting and managing "complex care" patients with private insurance—essentially redefining its use of the "community" to describe not neighborhood patients but those who would help the organization attain its goals for prestige.[14] Consequently, it secured a substantial federal grant to help it partner with other emergency rooms and state-funded federally qualified health centers in surrounding neighborhoods.[15] In meetings with skeptical community members, it promoted partnerships with these neighborhood centers and created a system for channeling internal medicine patients from its emergency room to these outside facilities. Administrators and physicians sought to build support for these initiatives in off-campus meetings organized in venues such as local art spaces, museums, and churches. Additionally, it partnered with a private hospital in an affluent suburb, one likely to offer a higher proportion of patients with private insurance. To redefine further its patient base, Superior also opened a Center for Customized Healthcare in a new facility two blocks from its primary competitor in an affluent part of town. Most advertisements on public transit were removed, reflecting its shift away from patients who likely would not be privately insured.

Third, administrators sought to manage the everyday patient discharges by requiring interns to attend bed management meetings in their quadrant, and asking for updates on when patients will be discharged. Superior Hospital developed morning meetings by altering an existing practice known as "interdisciplinary rounds," consisting of a group of paraprofessionals who met to discuss the discharge needs of the patients managed by the interns. One of the two interns who represents a team on the ward attends the specialized daily meetings held by each quadrant. Each day, the interns review the section's vacant and occupied beds, discuss patients' progress and expected discharge plans, reexamine the test results, consider hospital policy, and reach a verdict on disputes that arise between colleagues. These meetings are not arbitrary or accidental. They are orchestrated, involving a protocol that processes the patient in a standardized fashion for billing. In addition to discussing plans for placing patients in outside facilities, the participants check to see if the patient has the health coverage necessary for the treatments they need. These events are institutionalized, in a way; the residency program expects interns to attend interdisciplinary rounds so they can be trained in what the Accreditation Council for Graduate Medical Education (ACGME) calls "systems-based practice." Hospital executives modified these meetings to control both (a) the distribution of conditions that are seen in the hospital(ensuring they match the beds allocated) and (b) the number of days a patient stays in the hospital (reducing them). The hospital uses its discharge meeting to share patient information among those with the networks and expertise necessary for action.[16]

The concern for reducing patients' days in hospital is especially important to administrators; a hospital must move patients through their stay within the number of days for which it will be reimbursed by the state or insurance company. Hospitals are given the incentive to discharge patients as quickly as possible; the Diagnosis-Related Group (DRG) system for reimbursement used by most public and private insurers pays the hospital a flat fee on the basis of a condition. The meetings, then, are also necessitated by the offshoring of medical care into nonhospital venues (dialysis center or skilled rehab facilities) and by the lack of uniform policies across insurers. Since the meeting's architects are concerned with financial matters, patients requiring a long stay are dangerous. In a system in which the state pays for patients' hospital stays, patients—such as the one in this chapter's internal medicine vignette—would be risky only organizationally.

In these meetings, the intern wants to get in and out fast, leaning on paraprofessionals to take care of what is often considered to be the "scut work" of logistics. Whereas everyone else stays for the entire one-hour meeting, interns come when they are able and leave after reporting on their patients. Yet it's the interns who receive most of the room's attention—the hospital is set up to give them, if not the final say, then considerable control over practice decisions. Based on the information received from interns, paraprofessionals will begin the involved process of matching needs with qualified staff. The social worker may need to consider whether a preferred nursing home match has recently been sent, in their terms, a "good" patient (on Medicare or private insurance) or a "bad" one (on Medicaid), and allocate the subsequent one accordingly. It may mean coordinating outplacement with a dialysis center, nursing home, or a family who, at 8 p.m., might prefer waiting until the next day to make the seventy-five-minute drive to the hospital.

The meetings proceed by auditing the section's beds, which must be accounted for, cleaned, and quickly turned over. This conversation is facilitated by a dynamically updated computer terminal whose "Census Report" for the ward is printed and distributed in the beginning of each meeting. On the Census Report, the admission date is indicated, serving as a stark reminder of how long the hospital has been paying for the patient's care. The hospitalist notes if the attending physician is a junior faculty member; they are more likely to accept his prodding to speed up patient discharges. Finally, there are flags to indicate if the patient is a hospital employee, needs their hospitalization kept secret, has an infectious disease, or is a security threat. These flags indicate to the discharge team the kinds of pressure that can be applied.

Over the six years the program was in place, the average length of time patients remained in the hospital dropped by a half day per patient. At the same time, the percentage of patients with private health insurance rose by four percentage points. Each percentage point represented 8 million dollars in hospital revenue. Even though the poorly insured patients with chronic conditions continued to come to Superior Hospital, their costs were offset by the higher percentage of beds allocated to patients that could pay, and thus allow the hospital to raise its prestige. The hospital could do the multiorgan transplant and complex cancer treatments for which it was well known. By the administration, the program was considered a great success.

The Different Responses of Internal Medicine and Cardiology to the Bed Management Program

Even if the program's central architects were edified, the enthusiasm for the program was not unanimous. The fallout from the program differed by group: it was embraced by general internists, rejected by cardiologists. The internists were happy to delegate discharge tasks to hospitalists, social workers, and case managers; they enlist the help of paraprofessionals to process medical records and expedite tests so that patients can quickly be placed in a facility or sent home. In contrast, EPs could not receive patients suited to their personal skills. The details of the reception are revealing of each group's needs for carrying out their tasks and in a way that reflects how their doctors organize indeterminacy.

Internal Medicine

A lot of the internal medicine patients are so complicated . . . and these people are really tricky. For instance, it's someone who has chronic renal failure and a rheumatological condition, and they're on Coumadin—those people are multiply managed, and those endpoints are softer, because a lot of times those people go home and they're still pretty chronically ill—so in some ways it's really critical to get the discharge plan. . . . When you're the primary care doc you're the only one who knows how to work the system. So, for instance, I can do most anything—I know how to call the ER and talk to that person, I know how to call the bed desk.

In cardiology, you can get by without having the people there because it's you who will make a decision. . . . I think the cardiologists don't take any bullshit, whereas the internal medicine doctors—some of our patients are like tar babies, they get in this vicious loop. So [those doctors] just go along to get along.

—SUPERIOR HOSPITAL INTERNAL MEDICINE DOCTOR

For internists, high-quality care requires hospital-wide coordination. After admitting patients through the emergency room or outpatient clinics within the hospital—few of Superior Hospital's internal medicine patients are referred from outside hospitals—internists establish a treatment plan and begin working with venues like nursing homes, dialysis centers, and outpatient rehab facilities on discharge plans. Treatment in nonhospital institutions often continues for their patients once they leave the hospital. Help in slimming the bed census and speeding discharges is welcomed as internal medicine doctors confront the challenge of managing "social admits," those patients who have come to the hospital simply for authorization to use public funds to pay for admission to nursing homes and rehabilitation centers. As a consequence, the general internist's fiduciary relationship with a patient is distributed among those with multiple skills and institutional contacts. They can control the tasks by using other specialists as tethers, inside and outside the hospital.

The pressure on the interns begins their first day in the program, June 30. At 10 a.m. the two interns file into the meeting room, which is filled with the social workers, case managers, and nurses affiliated with the program. The interns' eyes dart back and forth between the seats available at the table, where social workers, case managers, and nurses are seated, and those along the wall, where they can sit together. They choose seats along the wall, near the exit.

> Dr. Williams begins by telling the trainees what those in the discharge meeting expect. He says, "OK, have you done this before?" The interns shake their heads.
>
> The intern reads off the name of the first patient on his census. "Michael Blaine—NE 968. He's a fifty-year-old gentleman who got assaulted in the head with a brick. There's also end-stage renal disease. He's got a lot of social issues. I think he's been convicted several times. Got a history of alcoholism."

While everyone wants to move patients efficiently through the hospital and into outside facilities, Dr. Williams wants to ensure that their desire for efficiency doesn't compromise medical concerns. As the discussion continues, the case manager turns to the issue of cost, bringing up the point that Mr. Blaine has no insurance.

Dr. Williams returns the conversation to issues of importance to diagnosis, treatment, and placement. Foreseeing the problems that will come with influencing a dialysis center to commit to Mr. Blaine, Dr. Williams clarifies: "A new dialysis?"

> The intern continues, reporting the plans for treatment. "So we're getting a perma-cath."
>
> Matt: "Does he have any family?"
>
> Intern: "I'm unsure, because when I asked him, 'Where do you live, who can I contact?' He's like, 'My uncle' and I go, 'Is there anyone else?' I go, 'What's his cell phone number, how can I get a hold of him?' He's like, 'I don't know.' So I'm going to try to figure that out. This was yesterday. He's a little belligerent, and his mood changes."

Matt: "Is it because of the head injury, or just him feeling really bad because he hasn't gotten dialyzed?"

Susan, the case manager, picks up an earlier thread: "He's getting dialyzed today?"

Intern: "Yes."

Bonnie, another case manager who has worked at Superior Hospital for more than thirty years, smiles. "Well, better book him in for a while."

Everyone laughs. The intern looks puzzled. Donna, the bed director, says, "Oh, Bonnie."

Dr. Williams, having come to understand this administrative variety of gallows humor, is unable to resist the chance for catharsis over the case's challenges. "Looking for an August first discharge, then?" People laugh harder.

Dr. Williams lowers his voice and levels with the intern: "He's going to be potentially really tough to get a dialysis chair. That's why you're hearing all of this swirling, because he's a new dialysis. Sounds like he has some issues that are going to make people not feel comfortable giving him a chair."

Bonnie, cognizant of the whole range of services the hospital must provide before a dialysis center will accept a patient, asks if the patient is showing symptoms of drug withdrawal. The intern indicates that the patient hasn't shown any signs of withdrawal in the two days he's been in the hospital. The social worker, recognizing the complications of discharging the patient, then turns to Bonnie and asks if she thinks he's homeless. Bonnie points out that it's a strong possibility, considering that the patient is giving his uncle's address but he doesn't know the number. The social worker's concerns persist.

Matt: "And you say he has a record of some kind?"

Intern: "Um, yeah."

Bonnie: "Did you write that in your notes?"

Intern: "I haven't written it yet."

Bonnie: "Well, I . . ."

Intern: "I know, I gotta write that down."

Bonnie: "I mean, if you write that down, he's not going to get in anywhere, I can tell you."

Intern: "Oh, OK, I haven't written it down yet, but I'm not sure—"

Bonnie and the nurses and case manager share nervous laughter. Bonnie turns to the issue of convincing outside institutions like dialysis centers to accept complicated patients. "I don't want to be shady or anything, it's just once you document all of that, even if it's in the remote past, then his chances of getting placed anywhere are just like out the window."

> Intern 2: "So, should we never write something like that?"
> Bonnie: "No, I'm not saying never."

> Dr. Williams steps forward with a lesson on grooming patients to maintain good relationships between patients and the hospital. "No, no, no. Basically what you want to do is, if it's relevant to the medical issue at hand, then of course you need to document it. Um, but you also want to recognize that everything you put in that note people will be looking at, and making lots of interpretations about. So if someone were convicted thirty-five years ago for something, and it has no relevance to what you're doing, do you need to carry that forward and label them that? So you just have to think about what it is you're documenting. So, with this one, obviously, the alcohol is probably very related to the clinical situation. So today, you documented that. You don't want to not document something that is clinically relevant. So, that's all. It's nothing you can do, this is a tough patient, and we see a lot of them, and this one is going to be particularly tough, but that's OK."

After going through their patient lists, the interns thank members of the meeting and return to the wards. As we walk together after the meeting, Bonnie explains the problem presented by this patient.

> "The dialysis centers put it all together and say 'somebody doesn't have insurance, is a drug user, and has been convicted.' They will say they cannot accept the patient. Basically, once you give a chair, it's very difficult to get them out. It's three days a week every week for the rest of their life. So it's a long-term commitment for whatever dialysis center takes him. . . . For a new dialysis, we really can't discharge until we have a stable dialysis home for him. That's where the tension comes in. 'Cause we're stuck, we're totally at their mercy." Bonnie raises her voice and looks at me. "We want to make it *honest* but make a strong case."

Discharge decisions are complicated by institutions outside the hospital. Dr. Williams and Bonnie know from experience that interns benefit from, and will be grateful for, help with patients like Mr. Blaine. The meeting's members have the resources and knowledge necessary to help with what interns consider "nonmedical" challenges. A frequent topic of discussion is conjuring up ways to discharge patients who frequently do not comply with orders and thus require supervision. These patients also offer few new learning opportunities and end up sapping morale. But interns know little about, and care little for, the negotiations in managing and discharging patients with features that, organizationally speaking, render them deviant. For these doctors, maintaining authority involves the ability to move a patient through the hospital, and into other organizations.

Thus, the trainees invite and are accustomed to being assisted by paraprofessionals in grooming patients. First, paraprofessionals will consult each other in establishing a plan to manage disruptive behavior, grooming patients into adherent hospital residents. To groom patients—those considered especially challenging because they can be difficult to treat—the hospital will work with the patient to develop a contract to orient their health behaviors during and after their hospitalization. Here is one such document, deidentified:

General Medicine Team

Bill Marcus Building

Superior Hospital

Superior Hospital ("SH") provides comprehensive care to patients. As a patient of Superior Hospital, we request your cooperation with the following guidelines and encourage you to set forth your expectations for your medical team below:

1. Maintain an atmosphere of mutual respect, behaving in neither a verbally nor physically confrontational manner in any interactions with SH medical staff.
2. Follow the floor rules as outlined by your medical team and nursing staff, such as alerting your nurse if you plan to leave your room for any reason.
3. Press the nurse call button and ask for assistance if and when you choose to leave your bed and/or your hospital room. You must wait until your primary nurse responds to your call before leaving the floor.
4. Alert the nurse in the event you experience any new symptoms, or any worsening of existing symptoms.
5. You may not disconnect yourself from any IV tubing, such as a PCA pump, through which you are receiving your medication.
6. You may not leave the floor for up to one hour after receiving your pain medications, whether through IV or PCA delivery.
7. Upon discharge, take your medications only as prescribed by your medical team (when applicable). Please communicate any

questions or concerns, such as side effects or dose questions, to your provider or nurse.

8. Fill and re-fill your prescriptions in a timely manner. We will give you enough medication to last a fixed amount of time, usually 30 days. Make sure you allow adequate time for refill requests. If you plan to have the Sickle Cell Care Team follow up with you in our clinic, you will need to have an appointment set up with the team within the time frame required <u>before your prescription runs out</u> so that we can refill your prescription before you have a lapse in medication. Once you are a clinic patient of some standing, <u>call the clinic one (1) week before your prescription runs out.</u> We will not tolerate repetitive "emergency" calls for drug refills. We will not honor walk-in requests for medication refills. The clinic phone number is: (XXX) XXX-XXXX.

9. Keep your medication in a safe and secure place. Stolen medications should be reported to the police and to your provider immediately.

10. Refrain from using illegal drugs or abusing alcohol.

11. Try two relaxation techniques for ten (10) minutes each before requesting a PRN [medication taken "as needed"], or, when home, before taking a PRN.

12. Fully participate in treatment and follow your provider's medical advice.

The guidelines, then, begin with what the team expects. After rhetorically setting the context for how everything the patient writes will be understood, the document includes the expectations authored by the patient.[17]

I expect my medical team to:

1. Give Respect if wanting to get respect
2. Do right by me—as in figure out the reason for my pain get it under control and talk and treat me as an adult.

It is important for my medical team to know this about me:

4. I treat other as they treat me
5. I can respect people wishes concerns, etc. as long as they speak to me like an adult.

Stress and negative thinking may bring on a pain crisis. Relaxation techniques that work for me are:

7. Listen to music
8. Watch TV
9. Stay to myself and relax

I acknowledge that I have received, read, and understand this document. I agree to follow these terms of care and understand that failure to follow these terms can result in discontinuance of medication, treatment, and dismissal (discharge) from the Superior Hospital.

Signed and dated 5/31/XXXX by patient.

□ ■ □

Many contribute to the accomplishments of internal medicine doctors' tasks, with patients especially given a certain amount of input. Ultimately, this input reinforces the physician's grooming, because it sets mutually constructed expectations for behavior on the wards. (The form also indicates the physician efforts at grooming may come off as pedantic; the patient's concern about being treated as "an adult" is mentioned twice.) And while the patient retains control over some activities—like the TV and music—the doctors are able to successfully complete their tasks, which involve diverse personnel, ranging from a nurse to a sitter to a security guard. These patients, like the "social admits" who enter the hospital without any chance of improving, largely in order to be admitted to an outside facility, are labeled by paraprofessionals early in their stay. Paraprofessionals negotiate, and enforce, the documents and processes that facilitate the doctor's success.

Paraprofessionals provide further assistance by connecting patients with institutions outside of the hospital. To establish a patient's relationship with a dialysis center, the social workers require knowledge from interns corresponding to characteristics in the "risks/barriers" column below. Figure 4.1 describes how the hospital manages potential risks posed by patients.

Because these "bad" patients lower morale, internal medicine doctors value paraprofessionals' assistance for doing high-quality work and discharging them from the wards. Over time, having had to manage care across different venues, residents share advice that can enhance their capacity to control tasks on the wards. As Armando, a resident, said: "You learn to bring orders straight down to interventional radiology. You should then make small talk with Pat, the secretary there. Don't call, because she'll say that there are twenty people in front of you. When you talk to her, talk to her about her cats."[18]

The work of internal medicine doctors is enhanced by providing the hospital with the vital information needed to facilitate long-lasting relationships with outside institutions. As illustrated above, there is some concern around labeling patients as drug users or homeless or having a criminal record, because then they might not be accepted by the center. The social worker, Mike, realizes, however, he can overcome patients' (noncriminal) qualities because he engages in a long-term exchange relationship with the centers, using as tethers those they've developed relationships with. As he describes in an interview:

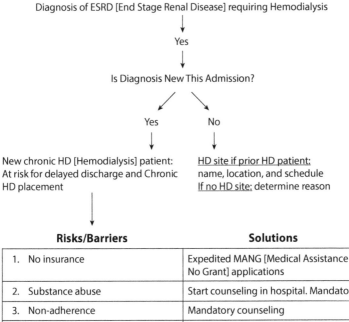

Care Intervention Algorithm for End Stage Renal Disease

Diagnosis of ESRD [End Stage Renal Disease] requiring Hemodialysis

Yes

Is Diagnosis New This Admission?

Yes   No

New chronic HD [Hemodialysis] patient: HD site if prior HD patient:
At risk for delayed discharge and Chronic   name, location, and schedule
HD placement   If no HD site: determine reason

Risks/Barriers	Solutions
1. No insurance	Expedited MANG [Medical Assistance No Grant] applications
2. Substance abuse	Start counseling in hospital. Mandatory
3. Non-adherence	Mandatory counseling
4. Violence	Mandatory counseling
5. No family support	Setup of support prior to d/c [discharge]
6. No transportation	First week of transport setup prior to d/c
7. History incarceration	Refer to SW [Social Worker] for screen and supports
8. No PCP [Primary Care Physician]	Refer to Resource Center for PCP appointment
9. No appointment for surgical access of Fistula or Graft	Must have appointment for graft or fistula prior to d/c
10. Left Prior Site without proper transfer process	Talk with site pt. [patient] left and progress to Renal Network as needed

Figure 4.1. Flowchart for Action with Patients Needing Kidney Dialysis. Shared by Bonnie, Superior Hospital case manager.

Particularly if you have a background of sexual assault, the nursing home could reject you. It is built into the law that they will not be accepted. Also, they know there are good patients and not so good patients. They consider [factors like this] because they commit for life.

There's all this concern about connecting nongeriatric patients with geriatric patients. There is a 53-year-old patient from a nursing home who is now in prison because he bludgeoned his 73-year-old roommate with a clock radio. So it's things like that that make nursing homes pause when they consider taking younger patients who have drug and alcohol histories. Because it sets them up for things like that.

The nursing home will say, "Ok, you gave us a bad one, now you need to give us a good one: a Medicare patient, or whatever." There may be a few times where I'll give nursing homes two not-so-good ones in a row. But they know that down the line something better will come along. So it usually works out like that. They can't take all uninsured patients, because they'd go out of business. Just like us. We can't take all uninsured patients because we'd go out of business. But in the last year or year and a half, they began to say no.

Because the labeling work of internal medicine doctors involves moving their patients into and through organizations, they are motivated to lean on social workers for throughput needs. If a patient is not accepted, they must remain at the hospital, which pays high prices as host. The social workers can, and must, help the nursing homes maintain their reputations with the public; to attract "good" patients, they can't have too many "bad" ones.

In internal medicine, other members of the hospital possess both crucial knowledge and key connections for placing patients. Ties must be managed with outpatient rehabilitation centers, nursing homes, and dialysis centers. The residents use others at the meeting as tethers for organizing indeterminacy in the way their attending decides. The social worker, case manager, and nurse can assist with connections to resources, and the hospitalist can even potentially intervene in a protracted case. In internal medicine, then, the interns participate in the meetings of the bed management programs because they value the help paraprofessionals provide in discharging patients to outside hospitals, a major dimension of quality care.

Cardiology

The bed geography program? Biggest waste of time. I would never tell an attending he couldn't admit someone. I can't believe there are two attending cardiologists that work on that. I would disband it immediately. Triage of beds? Geez. It's a nurse's job.
            —DR. MARK BUNTIN, SUPERIOR HOSPITAL
                ELECTROPHYSIOLOGIST

The internal medicine doctors who collaborate with paraprofessionals must deal with throughput issues and are rewarded for "getting things done," so their jobs were made easier by paraprofessionals who assemble at the meeting. The work of cardiologists, including their process of gaining status, is constructed differently. Far fewer of their patients arrive through the ER. And the most valued patients—those referred by colleagues—faced additional hurdles in being admitted. The relationships cardiologists have with referring doctors is crucial, as referred patients help these doctors raise their standing in their occupational project. However, to control tasks, they need beds. And so, as described above, the Superior EPs sought to subvert the bed management program by not attending its meetings. They also began to apply other pressures on Superior.

Superior's new policy on beds strained what had been a reasonably positive relationship between the cardiologists and hospital. Feelings were hurt, loyalties questioned. The doctors were angry and they had questions. Why were other specialties given more beds? Will this threaten our accreditation? Would we have enough patients to train our fellows? Enough to lead and participate in clinical trials?

Interns went to the discharge meeting when the bed management program was first rolled out, but even then, they communicated their attending's disdain for it. They would deploy evasion techniques such as saying that they "needed to speak with their attending," or deploy scientific findings that supported their team's decisions, evidence that was usually accepted in the meeting. Cardiologists' efforts in the discharge meetings were counterproductive to the hospital's goals. When interns attempted to resist using the protocol intended to sort patients into the four hospital areas, they created constant difficulties for the administration, which eventually had to develop a strong mediator for an independent examination of the cardiology section's plans.

The cardiologists' aversion to the program is made clear in the extract below, where I interview the chair of cardiology, Dr. Sam Armstrong, who arrived several months before the bed management program was implemented. I begin our conversation by asking how the program has affected his section.

> Well, very adversely. Basically, when I came here two years ago, the pledge was to keep a certain number of beds open, but the reality, when you get rid of all the sanitizing speech, is that they don't want people from the neighborhood coming to this medical center, so they shrunk the beds to make it difficult. That's a very coarse tool to manipulate human movements. It's like making the door on your house four feet tall to keep out all the people that are five feet tall. I mean, it's going to make it uncomfortable for all the people that are four foot two as well. And so in the course of trying to find private paying patients, they've basically made it hard to get in here. I mean, even if you remove those concerns about the ethics of dealing with human beings—[and it's like] we're forgetting the

Hippocratic oath or why any of us got into medicine in the first place—
the problem with that is there's a certain critical mass . . .

Dr. Armstrong's voice trails off, amid his general discussion of how the program has influenced what patients the cardiologists have been able to see.
He pauses, gazes out the window, and resumes his response, invoking a different metaphor to indicate how the problem of managing beds has influenced a hospital's most specialized and notable work.

You know, a hospital's a really complex organism, and it needs certain
types of food to keep it going. It needs patients, for example, not only for
the patient's sake, to make them better, but it needs patients to train the
next generation of doctors. The imaging labs need a certain volume
pull for competency, even for staffing, you know, if it's always busy,
you can staff for that. [But, this arrangement is] like trying to run a
restaurant that's only busy at noon—I presume, I've never done it—
but I imagine that's probably complicated because you need people for
a really short time, but they've got to get dinner on the table, for two
hours, they've got to fly. I've seen when it doesn't work well and people
just walk away from the restaurant, they don't come back. And so we are
struggling to bring in patients that are private payers, while we live in a
very poor part of the city, and when you cut the number of beds, what has
happened is the bulk of patients that do have legitimate, serious, life-
threatening heart problems that we're delighted to look after, now all of
those people aren't there, so there are fewer downstream revenues or
even patient follow through in echo, EP, and all those other programs.

One of the reasons that cardiologists have trouble with the hospital's efforts
to restrict referrals, is that they face a competitive market and few of their
services are highly specialized. Dr. Armstrong continues:

This is a complicated city. You've got 50 places that do heart work—yeah,
five zero—and I don't mean places that do a little bit of heart work, but
places where you can get a heart bypass. And so when you're in that kind
of environment, to assume that I will go to the best restaurant downtown
because it's the best, well, I'm not sure. Also, what does the best mean?
Second, how do you find out it's the best? And third, as you well know, if
you type in "best restaurants in [town]" ten websites will pop up and they
don't all list the same restaurants, and if you actually tracked it back,
you'd find that people are actually paying to be listed—so they may not
be the best but they're certainly the most proactive in town. And that's
the same with medical centers. So if you have a heart problem and you
want to see someone, how do you know where to go? And if you live on

the east side you're gonna have to drive past Landsford, Cityview—not to mention a whole bunch of private hospitals—to get to us. So even if we are better—and arguably for many procedures a competent person at many centers could do the work—it's a big jump to assume you would come all the way over here. That you'd come to an area that you don't live in, one that also has a bad reputation, to get your health care.

So any efforts of the cardiologists to bypass EMTALA are going to be very difficult. However, like heart surgeons rerouting circulating blood past a clogged artery, the cardiologists have strategies for bypassing administrators. Dr. Spangler notes that the cardiologists may trick him into admitting patients who have little or no insurance and are not acute. They say, "the patient truly needs to come here" when they actually just want to maintain ties with their clinician colleagues at other institutions. They then claim that better prospects, "good" [privately insured] patients are coming down the road. Dr. Spangler says he will give them one chance, but that he will blackball the physician if caught lying and those private patients don't come through. A second strategy is that Superior Hospital attendings will tell their patient to leave their other hospital AMA (against medical advice) and come straight to the Superior EP laboratory or the intensive care unit.[19] Once they are in "the unit," the medical-legal officials are concerned with an adverse event, so the cardiologists are able to keep the patient.

Although their workarounds are sometimes successful with getting patients initially admitted into the ER, the workarounds will not always help get patients from the ER to the wards, or into recovery beds once procedures are complete. The following emails, shared with me by the director with the intent of revealing his opposition to the discharge program, show a case of EPs' frustration with postprocedure bed placement.

```
Ben,

Getting beds today was a nightmare. To say I,
as well as the EP Staff, am frustrated is an
understatement.
     We had a patient that was an elective
ablation of Mark's. The procedure was completed
and the patient was recovering in our bay at
10:00 am.
     I was paged by Dr. Spangler that the bed
situation was bad and we were unlikely to get
beds until late in the day. I spoke to you at
that point and you had discharged our patients
from the previous day by 8AM. We had a full
```

schedule with our bays occupied. We also had
patients in non-bay areas waiting for
procedures.

We also had an ER patient that was a CV/
TEE, who had threatened to walk out of the ER
due to frustration of waiting for a bed and
lack of communication. I asked the ER RN to
speak to the patient personally. She agreed to
stay after I assured her she would be well
taken care of, more comfortable and her care
expedited in the EP Lab. (this pt. is a
physician herself)

This patient had a bed reservation
scheduled from ER yesterday. She had already
spent one night in the ER. The hope was that
she could be discharged after the CV, but
Dr. Buntin needed to admit her. The bed
request was never rescinded pending the
decision by Dr. Buntin. I first tried calling
the charge nurse who informed me [. . .] they
had no beds, no chance of beds, and that they
couldn't take our patient due to being on
bypass.

. . .

I also find it troubling that they were just
going to leave us hanging without a bed for our
patient, by telling me if the ER couldn't help
us, we just didn't have a bed. Our staff is
scheduled for 10 hour shifts, starting at 10
AM. They are wonderful, and have stayed
multiple times until, 8, 9, 10 PM waiting for
beds. I can't ask them to stay 16–24 hours to
monitor a patient overnight.

Martha
[Lead EP nurse]

The fact that Martha's patient was left in the ER for multiple days—likely
half-naked—demonstrates the severity of the admissions problem for EPs.
In this swatch of a three-page email, we see that even patients who likely
have high-quality insurance (i.e., physicians) suffer. Poor experiences such
as this, undoubtedly reported back to referring physicians, will do little to
improve the reputation of the doctors and hospital.

The head of the lab concurs with Martha's objections. His email is a public display intended to show the consequences of the program on patients'

perceptions of the hospital and of EP. Since he also wants to communicate most broadly that he is ready to unilaterally send patients to other hospitals in which he and his colleagues consult, he sends this email to the entire cardiology faculty, the chairs of the cardiology section and of internal medicine more generally, the executive in charge of the cardiology budget, and the physician-executive who has established the discharge system.

```
RE: closure of EP lab for elective cases
Date: Wed, 29 Oct 2008 20:06:16 -0600

Dear Martha,

I am very sorry we are increasingly having
this experience with our EP patients. This is
unfair to our staff—but mostly to our patients.
    I cannot accept a system where our patients
who are scheduled for elective EP procedures do
not have an inpatient bed assignment or a bed
available in a recovery unit before the case
starts. I cannot in good faith send patients
who come in from out of town for an elective
procedure, that has been scheduled for weeks,
to the emergency department, especially when
there is a chance that even that undesirable
option might not be available when the ED is on
bypass.
    Starting Monday we are closing the EP lab
to all elective outpatient cases. We will
reopen the EP lab when a Superior Hospital
policy is established that guarantees that our
outpatients will have a bed assigned to them,
or at least a recovery unit bed available to
receive them, before the case starts.
    Please contact all of our patients and
cancel all elective outpatient EP procedures
until further notice. I will review each
patient's chart with you to be sure that cases
that are urgent are not postponed. Some of
these cases will be rescheduled at Suburban
Hospital. I will contact our referring
physicians tomorrow.

                    Thanks,
                    Ben
```

This email is a clear symptom of the strain cardiologists felt from the program, exposing how Superior's prestige-pursuing policy was experienced by the cardiologists. In this and the previous passages, Ben Stimm says, point blank, that the cardiologists' interests come first.

Because workarounds are not always successful, and in light of this status-depleting episode, for several years the EPs had begun cultivating partnerships and admitting privileges at hospitals like Suburban, which alleviated some, but not all, of their problems. These partnerships, in which Superior physicians went to these hospitals and carried out procedures, were developed in response to requests from these hospitals, and offered access to the EPs and their fellows a new pool of potentially interesting patients. It also offered the opportunity to build their reputations by assisting cardiologists who felt unqualified or uninterested in taking on the risk of these challenging cases. The EPs continued to conduct off-site procedures as they continued to lose control of the beds, whose numbers continued to drop.

Still, these workarounds and evasion tactics were not always successful. In an interview, Dr. Stimm describes a status-diminishing occasion, discussing how the bed management program's change from a "just say yes" policy for admitting patients began straining relationships with colleagues in the city.

> We've already gotten burned. Phil Cavins is at Methodist [Hospital]. He called me and said, "Can you see this guy about a defibrillator?" Well, he probably should send that patient to County Hospital, but there's reasons he doesn't: because he's afraid they're not going to get good care, or might have to wait 6 months. So he calls me and I just say yes. Then I get a phone call from Dr. Astrid, who's in charge of managing how many Medicaid patients we see in clinic, and he asks, "Do you really need to see this guy?" and I'm like, "No I don't really need to."

Dr. Stimm is one of the best EPs in the city, but implanting a defibrillator is generally considered a routine procedure, making it hard to justify a transfer. Even if this patient turns out to have unusual anatomy, a case cannot be made for Dr. Stimm's unique advantage. Dr. Astrid's orders came because Medicaid reimbursements are relatively low, and the hospital would lose money without raising its prestige.

> And so he tells me I need to call Dr. Phil Cavins back and say I don't need to see his patient. So then the patient gets the message that we said OK and then we said no. And I'm the messenger for the hospital—that's the worst part.
>
> And then they have the national meeting in town for the Association of Black Cardiologists, which [Superior cardiologist] Kevin Wilson is a

founding member of. In front of all these cardiologists from all over the country, Phil Cavins stands up and says "I can't get my poor patients care even at Superior Hospital anymore. They said they'd see a patient and they found out he has Medicaid and they won't see him." And Kevin Wilson was just very upset.

I agree with the mission, but we shouldn't be penalized because the public health system is inadequate. So we try to help patients out by taking care of them. The hospital can't stay afloat only taking care of Medicaid patients—but it's the way they go about it.

To maintain his standing in the city—and that of his department—Dr. Stimm would like to take the patient. Doing so is in the interest of maintaining a positive relationship with Dr. Cavins; in the future he might receive more puzzling patients from this clinician, or want to recruit him for a clinical trial he leads. Not only did the rejection cast Superior Hospital cardiologists in a bad light to the rejected patient, but the highly public fallout did little to improve the reputation of the hospital's cardiology program.[20]

Based on his colleague's experience at the national meeting, Dr. Stimm felt that his reputation had been marred by working in a department that rejected the transfer request of a local. And he didn't have the resources he needed; as Dr. Stimm puts it, the hospital's approach "kills people in fields that are very dependent on volume. We need to do 10 cases to get one interesting one." When Dr. Stimm says the approach "kills people," he's talking about doctors whose reputations suffer when they can't get cases they can use as tethers. When he says "interesting," he is cognizant of the importance of having a case that could be used to share their approach to organizing indeterminacy, supporting their approach when giving a conference talk, or publishing a case report. These often-challenging cases relieve clinician referrers from around the country of tough cases. As he put it, the inability to accept transfers would hurt the reputation of the EPs, because "[your hospital is] not going to be a referral center, and being a referral center is part of your status."

Although, as mentioned, the bed allocation program was ultimately phased out, damage had been done. Ben Stimm, the head of the lab, decided to leave. So too did Sandra Kellogg, and Andrew Long.[21] In an interview conducted one year into his new job, Dr. Stimm offered, without provocation, that "[he had] not had a big problem getting patients transferred here. It also has not been an issue if I'm in clinic and I want to admit a patient through the ER." He brought this up in response to a question on his feelings about his new job, a response that reinforces the primacy of ties to colleagues for one's practices. Consequently, he and his colleagues were able to accept all patients, diminishing the chance they would again be again be denounced before one of their professional associations.[22]

Doctors found that their ability to provide control over accepting complex cases and assisting colleagues was compromised. They left Superior for a lower-prestige hospital, where they would be able to do what was necessary to continue practicing in a high-quality way that would let them continue furthering their careers. The doctors left because the situation seemed unambiguously better elsewhere, although the decision involved clear benefits and costs. The benefits were clear; doctors rely on beds because of longstanding commitments to referring colleagues, clinical trial partners and sponsors, as well as professional organization–established standards for the minimum number of hours of training for fellowships. These were the resources they would have received if Superior had not instituted the bed management program; getting more patients into Superior wouldn't have raised their pay, as they were salaried. Yet costs existed: the competing hospital was lower in prestige than Superior, and thus would at least initially not be a usual stop on the scholarly lecture circuit. The EPs would lose at least half of their patients because of HMOs' practice rules and "restrictive covenant" clauses that made it impossible to communicate with patients upon changing jobs. And there were other considerable inconveniences for moving to the competing hospital, such as commute length and increased hospital oversight.

The cardiologists' exit made sense; they don't want to damage the occupational project by breaking tethers used to organize indeterminacy their way, such as those represented in patient referrals, as in the episode described here. These physicians, as noted in chapter 3, seek enough patients so they have sufficient choice to select those who will yield them their ideal solution: a 90 percent success rate. At the same time, by not helping a colleague—and not simply declining to take all patients in need of medical care, but rather appearing to discriminate—they dented the occupational project.

In sum, Superior Hospital pursued prestige through the bed triage meetings in the interest of attracting private-payer and "interesting" patients for those fields that were already highly ranked. The hospital's pursuit of prestige in a ranking system—one with a particular set of rules that constrained the EPs' ability to accrue status with stakeholders outside their hospital—created a backdrop of strains such as the beds. The administrative action of reducing beds was controversial; it is one thing to engineer a supply chain, but enacting one in a hospital is another matter entirely. And, perhaps because the physicians stopped attending the meeting, over the years in which I observed the interdisciplinary cardiology discharge meetings, the cardiology section showed no progress in its efforts to reduce discharge times.

So, the bed program limited Superior's doctors' efforts to establish problems and solutions in ways discussed previously, where they define arrythmias and practice in a way that lets them shape standards. But a different kind of problem is also evident here: that of disparities in health care access. Their decision to leave Superior for a lower-prestige hospital is unsurprising in light of the fact that Superior doctors have accepted as their own those problems supported by the Association of Black Cardiologists: "To promote the prevention and treatment of cardiovascular disease, including stroke, in Blacks and other minorities and to achieve health equity for all through the elimination of disparities." Ultimately, they also faced a social justice problem, in light of medicine's public face, which involves addressing the problem of underinsurance through seeking to take all patients without regard to ability to pay.

In contrast to internal medicine, then, the fiduciary relationship in cardiology involves paying close attention to the relationship with referrers in addition to patients. The experience of the cardiologists with the bed management program shows us that a field's dependence on referrers can be a liability when its home organization emphasizes its own prestige and reimbursements, rather than those in occupational projects that help little in its attempts to reach its goals.

Conclusion

In its ability to lay bare key features of social order, a new policy is like a natural disaster.[23] This case offers a look into what holds different tasks of medical work together, showing what is valued at the time and in the context of medicine's reimbursement and ranking systems. It also shows that using tethers is important for strengthening doctors' efforts, but that their use looks different across areas of medicine. In efforts to deliver high-quality care, physicians with different tasks are differently affected by hospital programs. Specifically, the policy lets us see what is necessary to control tasks across areas of medicine: in internal medicine the tethers are to social workers and administrators in outside venues, and so the doctors are minimally affected by the bed management program; in cardiology the tethers are largely to venues outside the hospital, and thus are strongly influenced by the program. The comparison reinforces that control, using tethers, is central to the managing of authority. Further, doctors' pursuit of status can align or clash with the hospital's goals depending on a profession's dominant tasks. In exploring these areas, it is clear that the hospital's pursuit of revenue and prestige adds to their doctors' status—and thus helps them manage their tasks—or does not.

Even if revenue was increasing, the prestige of Superior Hospital was dropping, according to the *USNWR* rankings. (Several years after Drs. Stimm, Long, and Kellogg moved to Cityview Hospital, its cardiology ranking rose, and the hospital entered the honor roll for the first time in decades.) Although these cardiologists were gradually replaced, Drs. Buntin and Bellard left two years after the others. Many other doctors outside cardiology left for Cityview Hospital and other city hospitals in protest of the program itself.[24]

The administrative efforts of a hospital can powerfully influence care, but they are not always hegemonic. And those who are concerned with the highest-quality care and generating high status, the physicians, are not always going to dominate those concerned with economic success and the prestige of the organization. Rather, they are interdependent. Interests align when an organization is in a position to reward doctors in their own status rankings and the *USNWR* rankings. Beyond the potential implication of the case that it is harmful for doctors to lose their status, it reinforces the fact that managing authority is not an aftereffect or a precursor; it is integral to the work of doctors. Furthermore, the case shows the importance of organizational venue: for doctors, managing medical authority involves navigating their institutions' pursuit of prestige.

Superior Hospital was willing to undermine the status of its cardiology section in the hope of raising the hospital's prestige more generally. In the case presented in this chapter, when Superior Hospital sought prestige through fields other than cardiology, it damaged the standing of its own cardiologists. Specifically, as discussed above, they were accused of racial discrimination in front of many important members of their profession. Consequently, three out of the five EPs moved to a hospital that was willing and able to allocate its resources toward assisting doctors in generating the status they felt was unattainable at Superior Hospital. The remaining two left Superior within two years. While, as noted in chapter 3, the hospital was willing to purchase new technologies that could help the EPs manage the complex patient, their less-complex and publicly insured patients were considered too expensive. In contrast, at Cityview they could practice in ways consistent with their approach to organizing indeterminacy. Thus, this case demonstrates how equilibrium in physicians' ability to manage medicine's authority can be reestablished when other facilities accommodate doctors who are unable in one venue to realize their goals in organizing indeterminacy.

Finally, this chapter also demonstrates how tethers are used to strengthen the occupational project across venues. We saw patients used as tethers to non-Superior stakeholders, with their use varying between internal medicine and cardiology physicians. General internists rely on attracting and creating "good" patients to use as tethers in strengthening their relationships with organizations they must also discharge "bad" patients into. In seeing the experience of the internal medicine doctors—who are much like the deliberative cardiologists, though not as heart centered—it is also possible to understand the importance of grooming across areas of medicine in which lifestyle changes and assistance from paraprofessionals, and not interventions, are central to quality. Specialized cardiologists use their referred patients to maintain a training program, run trials, and maintain relationships with their colleagues in a city. Without seeing how important patients are to maintaining the fellowship program, and to sustaining ties to local clinicians, it would be hard to understand why EP attendings would fight so hard to keep them. And in seeing how standard-setters manage to make it so they can accept referred patients—thus helping their own reputation and the needs of their clinician colleagues (we'll see them more frequently in chapters ahead)—we can see the important role served by patients when used as tethers.

Interlude

Multiple Stakeholders in Nonhospital Venues

Chapters 2–4 showed us the ways that physicians control tasks, and the consequences that they perceive, should they lose that control. The first half of this book has mostly focused on standard-setters who are, through teaching and research, working to strengthen their location in the occupational project. In those chapters, talk of clinicians largely arose in relation to referral relationships. In the second half of the book we exit the hospital to follow the standard-setters to what we might call EP's public sphere, where everyday doctors attend conferences headlined by top doctors in electrophysiology, where knowledge and skills are acquired and circulated, and where standard-setters make a case for the work they do on the shop floor.

Focusing on EP's public sphere can explain several questions that are more specific to the problem of consuming and spreading knowledge, competing for status, and consolidating authority.

1) The first set of questions has to do with the processes by which current and past fellows in a training program stay connected to new ideas from their former attendings, while also informing those teachers of their new observations and ideas based on everyday practices. How do fellows continue to follow their teachers' work, to know, for instance, that they will be able to send them puzzling patients? How do those standard-setters maintain their relationships with those they once closely instructed at the bedside? And how do those standard-setters demonstrate the validity and legitimacy of the approaches organizing indeterminacy they use in their niche?

2) The second set of questions has to do with the awareness of clinicians of the innovations and standards of those in the broader occupational project. In chapter 6 I show how clinicians initially learn about innova-

tions during industry-sponsored hands-on meetings, small events with only one or two speakers. These doctors need to remain aware of how they can reinforce the defensibility of their approach to organizing indeterminacy for those inside and outside medicine. Where do they learn about the multiple new technologies available? Where do they gain updated validation for existing practices? How do they hear about changes in their school of thought?

3) The third set of questions has to do with the concerns that preoccupy those leaders who must institutionalize knowledge and standards in the field. How is information shared that might shape the way that attendings are able to gain buy-in for their approaches? How do leaders establish the key subjects about which standards should be set? What steps do they take to increase the legitimacy of the process through which they form these standards?

In the second half of this book I describe three venues where physicians share information on their practices that might be helpful to colleagues as they work in different venues. Activities at the fellows' programs and hands-on meetings are centered on establishing content on what should be done in practice. But medical work also involves staying attuned to publics beyond its referral and patient base (e.g., advocacy groups, the FDA, new companies). And so, in the annual conference, a venue even farther removed from the lab than the other venues, it is possible to see how a range of doctors and industry reps interact with each other in ways that strengthen the occupational project.

five

Fellows Programs

Maintaining Status, Validating Knowledge, Strengthening Referral Networks, and Supporting Peers

If the doctors are being influenced so strongly by their training, and then by their initial experiences in their organization and community, how do they get their knowledge validated? As we move outside the hospital, oddly enough, the first venue we visit is a meeting supported by technology companies. We come back to where we started, in the vignette, to begin to better understand something: what they do to cultivate and strengthen a referral network, and how they validate and legitimate their modes of organizing indeterminacy, so that they can reinforce the occupational project.

Dr. Stimm shared with me an email invitation he received for a conference sponsored by the medical device company Medscape.

```
Dear Dr. Stimm,

On behalf of Dr. Steven Ellston, we are pleased
to share that Medscape will once again be
conducting EP 101, our program for incoming
EP Fellows who will be initiating their EP
Training in July of next year. This will be our
10th year conducting this course which has
become a highlight of the Fellows academic
year and historically draws nearly 75% of all
incoming Fellows.
    I am writing to invite your participation
on our esteemed Faculty and would very much
appreciate it if you could join us June 4th–
7th, 2012 in Boston. I have attached the
```

```
preliminary agenda for your review. I know
this can be a busy time of year, thus you need
only to participate on the day of your lecture
(Saturday).
     Please let me know of your interest and
availability, and thank you for your support of
the Medscape Fellows Program.
```

These invitations emphasize that invited speakers will have an audience of both new and respected EPs, and implicitly indicate that Dr. Stimm deserves this visibility. Dr. Stimm has been invited because Medscape is dependent on standard-setters at their fellows programs. Medscape invites standard-setters to showcase cases and methods at these conferences, seeking to ensure that its programming is led by the top doctors in the field; by doing so, Medscape is able to associate itself with the adeptness and agility of these experts. Medscape must present itself as an invaluable tool to standard-setters, but for legal and ethical reasons this underlying message must only be alluded to, not stated outright. Thus, medical device companies provide other experiences that EPs find invaluable—an arena to mediate and organize indeterminacy, network connections, and legal training—in order to prove their value to physicians. It is the hope of medical device companies that this training is valuable and that this value is associated with their brand in the minds of potential users.

As the invitation boasts, these programs attract nearly all fellows, as well as many early-career clinicians. Regardless of the national economic circumstances, expensive two- or three-day training programs happen frequently, allowing attendees to learn about new discoveries in case studies presented by top standard-setters. According to the schedules posted on their websites, Medistar and Medicore each held twelve fellows courses in sites all over the country during the 2007–8 July–June academic year. The third competitor, Medscape, offered just as many. In the nine meetings I have attended, all of these events were sponsored by medical technology companies, and their subject matter usually was independent of the company's technologies and strongly focused on the research and practices of the speakers.[1] Doctors at the meetings are drawn from all over the United States, and sometimes from areas without the same opportunities (e.g., South America). The companies incur costs because they must coordinate meetings and travel as well as pay for faculty and fellows' airfare, lavish dinners, and expensive drinks. According to a Medscape event planner, each fellows program costs approximately $250,000. Even though the costs are considerable, they are trivial compared to the profit margin they anticipate from being doctors' first choice in medical technology. The programs must be sustained because all the other companies will continue holding their events even in the face of the deepest recession.

From the fellows programs we can see that this platform lets standard-setters generate status by offering a case for the validity and legitimacy of their approach to organizing indeterminacy, allowing them to mix with interdependent clinicians, and enabling them to pass along advice and cautionary tales that strengthen the occupational project. The slides described in chapter 3 return; standard-setters use their slide-based tethers to legitimate their approach, as they make sense of observations that most doctors find difficult to explain, and seek to gain the attention of the occasional journal editor among the other standard-setters in the audience. Because standard-setters can showcase their abilities, it's a platform that also affords them the chance to gain both attention and patient referrals from existing and soon-to-be clinicians, who attend the meeting to learn about developing and managing a referral network, and take steps in building and strengthening their own. And because these venues offer space for advice and cautionary tales to be shared by standard-setters—but also professionals from other corners of the occupational project, like lawyers and company executives—these courses represent an important venue in which the occupational project is strengthened.

Fellows' socializing and socialization with industry

After being picked up from the airport in a stretch SUV, I arrive at the boutique hotel reserved by Medscape. I see the lobby is decorated with colored projections of waterfalls and prairie scenes. The radiant colors and the techno music filling the room, combined with the New York City skyline, present a sharp contrast with Superior Hospital.

In the lobby, I see these doctors on their way out the door. These fellows and new clinicians are in their late twenties and early thirties, and are walking together to the restaurant that has been reserved for the Medscape dinner. I follow and we arrive at a steakhouse, one of those places where the desserts are sliced off a cake three feet high. Standard-setters from the top centers in electrophysiology are all there. Now in their late forties and fifties, they are beginning to produce their own disciples to exchange. Standard-setters circulate among the fellows, who angle for their attention. But these standard-setters group together when we are corralled to the tables. Later they will teach, but now there is news to share and gossip to trade. Arriving at their tables, they quickly refocus to discuss future conferences and compare policies of their hospitals regarding time off for speaking engagements.

Following a full day of learning from the gurus at the fellows program, at the breakfast the next morning the fellows are telling a late arrival about the previous night's status performances at the bar. "Last night somebody bought a $2,000 bottle of Belvedere. I didn't drink it; I told them 'I'm a rum and Coke kind of guy.'"

Putting his hands about two feet off the table, he says, "They bring a bottle that's this big, they put a light in it, because the whole point is to sit down in the club and tell everybody in the club that you're special. Puff out your chest, spread your feathers. A cute woman comes by and pours you all glasses, she hangs around, there's a light near the bottle so everyone can see it. It's glittery, it's a cockfight—that's what it is."

The hotel and festivities feel very little like what I imagined from the invitation to the fellows, which centered less on partying and more on professional development. The invitation to the conference includes brief descriptions of the talks that will be presented and the speakers that have been recruited.

> You are invited to attend Medscape Medical's Symposium on Electrophysiology. In this program, top electrophysiologists will present leading-edge clinical and scientific information in a format that encourages maximum interaction. Our faculty will address extremely complex, challenging and clinically relevant subject matter, including interpretation of pulmonary vein tracings, lead extraction techniques, genetic arrhythmia syndromes and device implantation techniques for patients with congenital heart disease. Participants will engage in case study discussions, debate with leading physicians and enjoy world-class presentations on modern electrophysiology.

Also, Medscape's organizers list a set of specific professional payoffs, using language that mirrors how doctors are taught in their home hospital. The invitation reads, "Upon completion of this symposium, participants will be able to . . ." and presents learning goals that correspond to basic knowledge and areas of controversy the standard-setters will discuss: "Describe key principles of entrainment," "Name important landmarks in paced electrograms and systematically analyze them," and "Discuss the differences in ischemic versus nonischemic ventricular tachyarrhythmias and understand the treatment options for each arrhythmia type." The payoffs, which range from the practical to the theoretical, reflect the company's interest in positioning itself as offering consequential content in a venue that should be treated by the fellows with the same degree of importance as that of trainees' grand rounds lectures. Thus, medical technology companies seek to embed themselves in the minds of conference attendees by emulating established and highly heralded forms of learning and prestige.

In the same document, with the invitation and the payoffs, we find the agenda. The speakers have been influential in organizing indeterminacy in their area through their presentations and publications. The topics reflect a cocktail of clinical knowledge categories. There are often sessions too on avoiding malpractice suits, opening up a private practice after fellowship, and "doctor shopping" (when a college or professional athlete pursues a diagnosis that will return them to competition).

7:45 a.m. Welcome and Opening Remarks
   Tim Kray, Vice President of Academic Affairs, Medscape
   Steven Ellston, MD Program Director
7:50 a.m. Course Overview
   Steven Pillor, MD, Joe Forens, MD and Dan Trammel, MD
8:00 a.m. Principles of Entrainment
   Michael Mueller, MD
9:00 a.m. Fluoroscopic Anatomy for Electrophysiology
   David Stevens, MD
10:15 a.m. Ablation of AVNRT [atrioventricular nodal reentrant
   tachycardia]
   Jeff M. Wilson, MD
10:45 a.m. Unusual Device Tracings and Case Studies
   Kevin A. Endo, MD
11:15 a.m. EKG Tracing Review
   Bruce S. Stambler, MD
Noon. Lunch
1:30 p.m. Lead Extraction
   Michael C. Bender, MD
3 p.m. Biophysics of Catheter Ablation
   Rakesh L. Shah, MD
4:00 p.m. Pearls for the Graduating Fellow: From Academic Training
   to Consultant Electrophysiologist
   Alex Steinman, MD
4:45 p.m. Medical Malpractice for Electrophysiologists: Mistakes to
   Avoid
   Michael T. Goodstein, JD
5:30 p.m. How to Implant Devices When There Is Difficult Anatomy:
   Occluded and Stenotic Veins and Occluded SVC [Superior Vena
   Cava]
   Steven Mitchell, MD
7:00 p.m. Group Dinner

Even in this abridged schedule we can see Medscape, in collaboration with the program director, reinforcing important features of the field's knowledge base through its list of topics and speakers. Only a few years ago, the content of many of these talks was the stuff of live case presentations. Today it is considered best practice. By also inviting experts on subjects like malpractice law or managing money, Medscape also wants to provide fellows advice that doctors value. With its list of standard-setters pulled from the authorship of EP's clinical practice guidelines, the agenda promises to update and train doctors on the latest developments, improve the visibility of these new practitioners through helping them form new connections, and thus put these new doctors on the road to independent practice and building their own distinguished reputations. This is how medical device companies use conferences to embed the idea that their brand is synonymous with excellence in the field. And, with the names and affiliations of the doctors at the end of the list, the agenda reaffirms to trainees that these doctors set the standards. The mutual dependence of Medscape and doctors is a focus of the printed page.

At the end of the invitation, Medscape reminds the invitee that it too is accountable to the federal government, and also anticipates and responds to requests to pay expenses that might be scrutinized by regulators.

Attention Healthcare Practitioners

By participating in this Education Event, I acknowledge that Medscape may be providing reasonable value in the form of travel, meals, and/or lodging associated with this event and that this value will be disclosed in accordance with applicable Federal and State Laws. Medscape will report all meeting related expenses unless you notify the meeting coordinator that you choose not to participate in the planned functions.

The program participant is responsible for compliance with individual conflict of interest or other institutional policies as well as any applicable state regulations regarding industry-sponsored educational events and associated expenses.

AdvaMed Code and Guest Policy

AdvaMed governs relationships between healthcare providers and members of the medical products industry. Under this Code, Medscape is prohibited from paying for any expenses associated with a spouse or guests accompanying a program participant such as meals, transportation, activities, etc. If a guest accompanies you, please make advanced arrangements directly with the airline and hotel to cover their expenses. If you wish to make reservations for a spouse or guest through the Medscape travel agency, you may do so, but you will need to pay the agent's fee directly to American Express Business Travel. In addition, Medscape is not permitted to cover a participant's nonprogram related expenses.

So, even if it feels different, it looks like Medscape is establishing this event as education, not vacation. Like the physicians, it seeks to adhere to a code established by peers. Reminders that this conference should not be framed as leisure are reinforced in the program; even though many fellows' programs may offer a period labeled "afternoon on own," preceding which the program director encourages fellows to enjoy Fifth Avenue for a few hours, the doctors are expected to return for dinner. Allowing doctors to treat these conferences as pure frivolity would undermine the association with professional preeminence that they work so hard to build.

At a breakfast at the hotel the next morning, where the industry representatives intersperse themselves among the fellows, the conversation turns to other forms of shop talk. Fellows banter about whether or not their attendings are "handy" or if they are actually permitted to manipulate the catheter at the bedside. The industry representatives laugh. All appear to be having the best of times.

At the coffee break after the first set of sessions, I sit with Dr. Stimm, and ask him why he came. "The reality is, I don't know what the honorarium is for this stuff, but it's the same as it was 25 years ago." Shrugging his shoulders, Dr. Stimm continues.

> But I still do it though. It helps you build things. So I was referred a patient this week from Paris. She is a United Airlines flight attendant who had a cardiac arrest in Paris. Fortunately survived, got a subQ [subcutaneous] defibrillator. And the guy in Paris said, go back to [Dr. Stimm's city] and follow up with this guy. And he knew me. So it's not just like you care about your status in terms of your reputation, as much as you do your status in terms of building a program, spreading the gospel.

After I follow up, Dr. Stimm says he's talking about building the social infrastructure necessary to bring in patients, attract companies who might sponsor and let him design trials, and help sponsor his fellowship program. By "gospel," he is referring to the idea that EP—and maybe his approach of organizing indeterminacy—offers the best solutions for problems commonly observed in patients. Having given me a glimpse into the field's global nature—in particular, that there are referral ties across the ocean strengthening the field—he points out that the events offer a chance to demonstrate that he is also receiving puzzling cases in his home lab: "I think that it's a very important strategy to remain credible by showing your experiences. When you can show bizarre cases, it's an indication that we are clinically active and we are doing a lot."

Still I inquire further, curious that the head of an established EP program must work so hard for referrals. He also notes the value he places on getting feedback about initial findings, as well as eased access to publication. Sometimes the experts know that a case is unique based on his extensive experience with referred patients, but other times a case's novelty is affirmed by colleagues they can access in the meeting and who might be able to assist with publication.

Dr. Stimm notes that he has presented cases at meetings in which he is later approached by editors who will ask him to "consider submitting this to *JACE* [*Journal of Cardiovascular Electrophysiology*]." He says,

> You know that if you send it, it will get in. [The meetings] are a kind of proving ground. You have to come up with interesting cases. And when you present it, you get feedback from the faculty and audience members—you know, it's kind of like a comedian trying out new jokes—and if people ask enough interesting questions then you think you should write this up.

This channel to publication, facilitated in part by Medscape, assists the standard-setter EP with sustaining the reputation that prompted their invitation to the meeting, strengthening their capacity to establish and even solidify their reputation in a particular content area.[2]

The Features of Validating and Legitimizing One's Approach to Organizing Indeterminacy

By organizing medical conferences, medical device companies attempt to become synonymous with pioneering medical knowledge. To do so successfully, they rely on the innovations of other actors—namely, standard-setters. In turn, standard-setters use conferences to promote their method of organizing indeterminacy in order to legitimize their approach, thereby gaining status and, ultimately, referrals.

Because descriptions of problems and solutions in EP involve visual cues, standard-setters must visually exhibit how they organize indeterminacy. Thus, the body of the conference is conducted largely through images in the form of slides. These performances utilize images and commentary to demonstrate effective techniques, encode the benefits of their teachers' approaches, and therefore reinforce what the best practices are.[3] They seek to show that the old problems and solutions are less compelling than their own, and to provide a way for the next generation of doctors to learn to read the signals of anomalous and puzzling cases in the same way as standard-setters.

Puzzling patients are referred to Dr. Wilson, the speaker; these perplexing cases facilitate discoveries important in electrophysiology. He is from an academic institution and has dozens of publications to his name. The fact that he holds a top position at a top program helps in validating his approach, but since EPs feel they can see success and failure from EKGs, validation requires visually demonstrating success in slides.

As the talk begins, the reputation of the speaker grants him an initial allocation of deference from the audience. The introduction of the standard-setters invokes, and even amplifies, the reputation of the standard-setter. To make space for the expert, Dr. Wilson, the music fades.

> The program director, Dr. Ellston, steps up to the stage and begins: "There probably is not a single guy who is nicer, more honest, and has more hands-on experience in the EP lab in a variety of areas. I continually learn when I hear him talk, and this is an area he has been working on for the last couple of years and is a very important area in terms of EP."
>
> Dr. Wilson strides to the podium amidst thunderous music from loudspeakers on each side of the stage. As with all the other presenters, he opens with, "I've been asked to speak about AVNRT." He thanks the director for the introduction and fumbles with the laptop and laser pointer.

Introductions such as these highlight the doctor's past accomplishments and amplify his or her status among peers. The doctor, in noting "I have been summoned," signals their flexibility, expertise, and duty to the collective.[4]

During the inevitable technological glitch, Dr. Ellston salvages the situation by asking the speaker questions, a process that permits everyone to consider how knowledge and indeterminacy are produced, especially in a world full of unpredictable and messy electronics. Set against the backdrop of a conference put on by a medical device company, this technological snafu reinforces the interdependence between the conference sponsor and the profession, creating a dance around disclosure.

This presentation is on the ablation of AVNRT, and Dr. Wilson is one of the most prominent authorities on the subject. His talk begins with a disclaimer also seen at the professional association meetings, one that signals his openness to ongoing peer review.

> Dr. Wilson presents a list of four companies on his first PowerPoint slide. "I need to tell you I have research relationships with a number of companies, including the sponsor of this program. I appreciate that they have put this together and allowed me to speak. But, you know, you'll have to decide whether or not there are conflicts of interest."

These disclosures work to enhance the legitimacy of the speaker and represent the only time the speakers mention the ethics of industry ties. The disclaimer provides a sense of trustworthiness; this explicit reference to industry funding addresses the contemporary concern in medicine about undue influence.[5] Indeed, the highest-status standard-setters will on occasion flaunt their independence by talking about the problems experienced with the technology developed by the meeting's sponsor. Nevertheless, both industry and standard-setters are mutually dependent: industry needs leading physicians to use their venue to demonstrate their innovations in order for the medical device company to become synonymous with excellence, and standard-setters need the venue provided by industry to compete for and maintain their status.

To reinforce his preeminence, Dr. Wilson first primes his audience. He asks the audience to see the case in the way he does, and in helping them see how he has organized indeterminacy, he shifts the scene on the monitors to present the mediated data that EPs interpret in the lab with colleagues and fellows. He shows one of these sets of "tracings," or EKGs, and begins to describe the tracings as consistent with the accepted wisdom in the field. These are subjects most physicians have learned in their EP training and that are also noted in textbooks and other literature published by his center and those of his colleagues. In his presentation, he maps out his observations from the very start, coding abnormalities from the stacked jagged lines on the screen, and noting to the audience the "conventional" ways of understanding the problem and solution, before he suggests they are the wrong way to think about these observations. For instance, in noting a piece of anatomy, he points out, "Your natural inclination is that you're looking at one homogeneous structure. And this is what had always been assumed."

Dr. Wilson guides us through the EKGs, pointing out phenomena he thinks participants know already, or will soon see in their labs. Medscape has already printed and distributed his slides in a large Medscape-branded folder that audience members will take home. Furthermore, the learning is hands-on—when eventually asked questions by those speakers, participants will measure the spacing on the EKGs using calipers Medscape has placed on their table. Dr. Wilson's account of the medical problem and his approach to validating his observations resemble the kind of rigorous inquiry and proof his colleagues expect.[6]

> Dr. Wilson continues. "Watch what happens when you look at the next two stimuli of this burst of pacing. You start to see separation here in the roof and in the floor. The second one, the separation is greater. Look at the difference between them. The timing of these potentials." He grabs the laser pointer and flashes toward the screen. "This is early, this is late."
>
> After describing part of the tracing according to his definition of the medical problem at hand, he focuses his laser pointer on apparent abnormalities that may raise potential audience questions, and that his perspective might explain. Even then, however, there are data that reflect the opportunity for the further organization of indeterminacy. "But you could even go so far as to say,

'Wait a minute. What are these beats?' You see that this moves out.
I have no earthly clue what it is."

This narrative, one we also saw in Dr. Torstal's live case, reflects a register often adopted by standard-setters when making a case for how they are organizing indeterminacy. He reproduces the confusion the referring physician probably felt, and demonstrates the mentality felt in his lab, taking his time in puzzling through the phenomenon that he is reading into and off of the screen. This puzzlement has been recognized in the literature on scientists as an important process through which analyses of anomalous observations reveal new discoveries. Many link this attitude to the capacity to make discoveries such as that of the eminent Bordeaux physicians who changed practices worldwide in 1998 with their *New England Journal of Medicine* article in which they demonstrate a new solution to the problem of atrial fibrillation, showing that it has its source in the pulmonary veins and can be eliminated by ablating the relevant vein.[7]

For legitimacy in proposing his approach to organizing indeterminacy, Dr. Wilson situates himself in an invisible college—a network of like-minded colleagues who, here, share an approach to organizing indeterminacy—in offering up his allegiance to an ablation technique. These techniques are sometimes controversial, and speakers will often put their stake in the ground early in the presentation, saying, "At University E we use PVI," and sometimes backing up their claim with a citation. But one is positioned in a network of like-minded colleagues according to whether they use the approach of pulmonary vein isolation and thus burn a circular scar around the left pulmonary vein, rather than, for instance, using CAFEs [complex atrial fractionated electrograms] to identify and target specific signals. Situating oneself is a way to gain legitimacy, as we saw in chapter 3 with the case of Dr. Bellard's friction with his previous hospital. There is no dominant perspective; doctors can gain legitimacy through expressing membership in one of several schools of thought. The important factor is that they adopt a practice consistent with one or another of these groups, or they have developed an approach that has commonalities with accepted ones.

With his approach to coding these EKGs, Dr. Wilson walks the audience through his process of organizing indeterminacy in his publications. In particular, he highlights how his approach differs from others with whom he competes for status:

Dr. Wilson: "Debartoli showed that the two potentials are recording here and here." He points to several lines on the tracings. "And everybody thought they were hurting my feelings, saying they're not AV-nodal potentials. I needed to know what the heck those things were! But retrograde, it's late there. And so you see it as a very tiny far-field potential. See, it's very clear. So if you look at this, this is what you see over and over again."

Dr. Wilson acknowledges more controversy in his claims. "This is an argument I've had before. Look, Mark Jefferies is one of my favorite people. People think we fight all the time, but privately, it's not that way at all. We feel very differently about AV-node reentry—and I'm waiting to see what John's going to say—but Mark always says to me, 'So you never know in av-node reentry, whether activation is earlier in the CS [coronary sinus] than it is in the His [His bundle branch {heart muscle cells}].'

Dr. Wilson then grounds his approach to organizing indeterminacy in research, after anticipating the questions of his audience. "People say, 'Well, you never see that.' Well, actually, it's not true. We looked at 650 consecutive patients with short HA AV-node reentry, 83 percent were slow-fast, 17 percent were slow-slow."

Dr. Wilson situates his perspective relative to that of his colleagues and the other tough cases he sees. He shows that there are others who follow—or at least engage with—his approach, and that he will revise his perspective when new data arrive. In doing so he, like other standard-setters, may contextualize his findings and anticipate critiques.[8]

Nearing the talk's end, Dr. Wilson describes the case's contribution to knowledge. His claim is that he can take credit for organizing indeterminacy with cases like this; he implicitly argues that this answer will allow the doctors to answer some key questions in electrophysiology and to account theoretically for the success of some of the field's key practices.

"If you look at this, you can understand why AV-node reentry ablation is so darn successful! Think about this. You've got a huuuuge area that you can ablate. We didn't understand this in the beginning. Our first paper on this actually showed one of the sites was below the CSOS [coronary sinus ostium]!"

Dr. Wilson lowers his voice, puts his hands on the podium, and speaks slowly. "It doesn't connect to the right atrium. . . . So if you walk away from today with only one thing—and this is going to raise some eyebrows, and people aren't going to agree, and that's OK—but the rightward inferior extension doesn't connect to the right atrium. It connects to the left atrium, through the CS myocardium, to the floor of the CS."

Dr. Wilson then points out another open space in which others can organize indeterminacy. "And there's a form of fast-slow arrhythmia that uses a fast pathway that I only remember seeing twice. It activates the atrium just above the fast pathway region.

> And I don't understand that. And I've been afraid to try to ablate that. But it's distinct in its behavioral characteristics. Thank God it's really really rare. Who knows how many there really are, and how much variability there is."

Finally, then, twenty minutes after Dr. Wilson was told there were five minutes left, the question-and-answer period arrives. Dr. Wilson then receives a brief opportunity for self-promotion by showing expertise in another area. It constitutes an important moment, for speakers often fear they will become seen as narrowly specialized because of the categorization system and the tendency of companies to invite speakers repeatedly to discuss only one area of expertise.

> Dr. Stevens, a standard-setter who has conducted research on tissue-catheter contact, asks: "Jeff, why is the range of 25-75 so different here? Is that because of the tip orientation? I think as you put more force, everything gets deeper. It's one of the reasons why I have issues with the Stereotaxis system. Because the magnet is only so big, it's only so strong."
>
> Dr. Wilson uses this as an opportunity to claim the Stereotaxis technology, a competitor to Medscape, as a tool in an area of research in which he is aiming to organize indeterminacy. He discusses their work in the animal lab. "We did a set of experiments with a Stereotaxis catheter that had a contact force sensor in it made by Endosense. . . . And we were really surprised, in a dog heart, that sometimes with the magnetic maneuvering we got actually reasonable forces of 40-50 grams, and sometimes less than 2 grams."

The questioning gives Dr. Wilson a chance to begin making a case for why colleagues might allow him to organize indeterminacy in the area of contact force, his research area and a current area of much interest in EP. His ability to continue providing EPs problems and solutions depends on not being seen as a shill. Here, Dr. Wilson orients his comments to his peers and future EPs who may use this technology.

By answering his colleague's question, Dr. Wilson has a chance to show his ability to teach—an important factor in one's subsequent invitation. Both the individual talks and the entire program are evaluated by the program director and medical device company. Immediately after each presentation, the audience is asked to rate the lecture's content, presentation, and relevance to practice. Company representatives will fly across the country to share scores personally with the standard-setter. According to the program director, regardless of the friendship between the program director and speaker, if the ratings are consistently low, the company will not invite the speaker to future programs.

Soon the presentation ends and the program director returns to the podium to reinforce the company's role in providing the fellow access to the standard-setter: "Jeff is going to be here through Sunday, so you'll have plenty of time to get your crack at him and I know he's more than happy to sit down and spend some time with the electrograms."

Medscape wants their conferences to be a venue where relationships are cultivated between the new doctors and existing leaders in the field, so in the invitation the program director usually reminds the speakers through email that they should attend for at least one whole day of presentations. Once again, this act serves to synonymize Medscape with pioneering medical knowledge.

Following the presentation, interested in whether Dr. Wilson's efforts to define problems and solutions have registered, I ask a fellow about the talk. Fellows expect the program director to have invited respected peers, so they enter the venue with little resistance to validating a procedure. I find that with Dr. Wilson's presentation, as in other talks, the standard-setter's message has resonated, with his presentation coming to provide a template for the fellows to validate their own observations; fellows will emulate the speakers' practices and question their own execution if they do not observe the same results as the experts.[9] An example of fellows' attitudes toward speakers can be seen in Joe, who has come to learn the latest advances before heading into private practice.

> Everybody knows David Stevens and Mike Mueller; these are the gods of entrainment. So if you're going to learn entrainment, you go and learn from one of those two. So you can come here and hear David Stevens and you're like, "check." And that stuff that Shah was talking about—that's his thing. Like Wilson's AVNRT. If you can get that [in these meetings], you can check that off of your list of things you need to get before you can say, "I'm trained." You can make the literature searches, read the articles. But those are certain people that you know you need to learn certain things from.

The importance of being able to have access to communicated knowledge is seen when the fellow distinguishes between the people who really know (the true experts or "gods"), and the people who don't (fellows such as Joe). He reinforces the standard-setters' totemic quality and accepts their observations as valid.

Industry-sponsored meetings and similar venues appear to foster new clinicians' reliance on standard-setting experts, suggesting to novices that the occupational project will be strengthened because they observe and adopt their problems and solutions. Underpinning these events is the implicit suggestion that clinicians will be able to conduct the work as it changes, if they use these experts as tethers both in this venue and when they return home and have questions. Because Joe also mentioned that fellows can gain knowledge by reading articles in the field, I ask him what percentage of articles by these "gurus" he will read. Joe quickly responds, "Very very few."

> 'Cause I hope that they've condensed it down to the pertinent things, and have told it to me. Now, if what they are saying is not making sense, or there is something more when I go and apply these concepts in the lab and it's not all jibing, then I gotta go back to their article, and figure out where I'm getting lost. But if here they say "A, B, C," and then I go to the lab and I see a patient and I do my thing and go, "oh it's A, B, C," there's no reason for me to go back and read it, *because what they tell me is working.* But if I go to the patient and it's like "A, B, D," I think, OK, I missed something, I gotta either go call them, email them, or go find an article and read it, and bridge the gap, figure out what I missed.

From this fellow's account of a case of indeterminacy successfully organized, we can see there is a relationship between training, status, and standards. These high-status doctors' ideas are consequential; they change what the next generation is socialized to see, and also shape their ideas of the field's norms about what is right and wrong. These doctors are resources who use their talks as tethers that make practice efficient and effective. Further, they are doing work that is changing things periodically. And so, others can figure out how to practice differently by calling them, if necessary.

In the audience, the company's director of education sits alongside clinicians, noting the slides' key strengths and weaknesses on a legal pad. Running down the margin, he carefully notes the feature of interest along with the slide number (e.g., "31—no citation"). He goes through these presentations slide by slide. Later I'll see him in the waiting room of Superior Hospital, waiting to share with Dr. Stimm his feedback on ways to enhance clinicians' learning.

As noted in chapter 3, those with esteem in a niche will seek to organize indeterminacy by subjecting a case to a series of tests. When preeminent EPs like Dr. Wilson are at the bedside and find new data in an investigation, then they are expected to use these data as proof for an argument being made in the expert's talk. The new information generates a lot of maneuvering when it comes to status; on the one hand it's good, because it can lead to discoveries and opportunities to raise status. On the other hand, such new information is challenging because it requires applying, and sometimes generating, new tests.

Situated on the cutting edge of a shifting field, standard-setters structure the hearing of participants through their argument and their status. By understanding how speakers have organized indeterminacy, when back in the lab fellows can confidently assert "the arrhythmia has been eliminated." Furthermore, simple exposure to these individuals leaves fellows feeling trained: fellows feel trained after seeing Dr. Wilson work through a case, someone "everyone knows" as a mandarin of the field. Speakers' presentations prime fellows to validate their own observations; fellows will emulate the speakers' practices and question their own execution if they do not observe the same results as the standard-setter.[10]

On occasion another standard-setter might have a different way of doing the talk. The doctor may use these events as an opportunity to exhibit how difficult his cases are. For instance, Dr. Mason, whose presentation immediately followed that of Dr. Wilson, began his talk with a picture of the fastest-beating heart that had ever been described in a human, that of a twelve-year-old girl who had been referred to his clinic. Or the presenter may simply post EKGs on the PowerPoint and quiz the audience on the conditions they reveal.

Regardless of the exact information presented at these conferences, they are an invaluable venue where credibility and expertise are established, as well as a place where experts differentiate from others in their niche their approaches to organizing indeterminacy. These standard-setters, and not others who are also publishing and attracting patients, have been invited to speak as faculty in these meetings, because they were the ones receiving the cases their subspecialist colleagues were unable to treat. These performances, then, are part of the stratification order that sustains reputation-maintaining referrals.

The Network of Interdependence among Standard-Setters and Clinicians

Above I have highlighted one of the profession's brightest stars, and the way he makes a case for his approach to organizing indeterminacy in his niche. What keeps their reputations polished? The answer to that question lies in the relationships between him, clinicians, and his standard-setting peers— and sometimes companies—comprising the social structure of the field. The meeting lets us see this network-based interdependence between doctors with standard-setter and clinician career types, and how their interdependence is strengthened. And, as we will see, the network helps standard-setters organize indeterminacy by ensuring that complicated cases make their way to the proper physician. The ties of the referral network enable practical connections in the field and compel standard-setters to seek status in their niches. There are two key kinds of referral-reinforced ties we've seen: EPs' ties to general cardiologists and their ties to other EPs.

When in training, EP fellows have a steady stream of patients in light of the prestige of their hospital. But when EPs enter into their own practice, they discover that there are no hearts to burn without an active referral network, and that this network may have some say over whether or not, and how, those hearts are burned. Fellows are unprepared for the process of attracting patients and working within the network. Their academic hospital drew patients through internal referrals or because of its relative level of specialization in the city and consequent ability to tackle the tough cases successfully. Here, fellows simply relied on the hospital to bring patients to them, letting them learn and observe as their standard-setting attendings organized indeterminacy. Yet, once they leave their training hospital, they must cultivate a referral network of their own. By connecting with young fellows early in their career, established EPs and, as shown in the next chapter, medical device representatives work to ensure that difficult cases are referred to competent doctors.

Industry, then, is part of this network, holding it together, but also at times straining colleagues' relationships. In the same way that industry serves to help train EPs and facilitate networks by putting on these meetings, the representatives also play an important role in the processes of connecting candidates with available jobs. Representatives help doctors change jobs and assist EPs in getting on their feet in their early years of practice. Yet their influence on cardiologists can translate into challenges for the clinician EPs to whom they send patients, whose referrals might come with strings attached.[11]

If doctors are dependent on referrers for patients, then they can be controlled by them. Patients are referred from internal medicine doctors, to general cardiologists, to EPs. How do EPs manage these relationships so that they have control over their tasks? As I will show, some can't control these tasks because they don't have the tethers that will allow them to attract patients, some control the tasks by using the tethers represented by referral partners, and some control tasks by having tethers of a sufficient number of relationships with companies.

Consider the profiles of new clinicians that Medscape has invited to the meeting, each clinician different in career stage and number of experiences: Andrew, who sits outside the patient-referral network; Michael, who sits inside it; and several clinicians with more experience. To examine network ties, we will first look at Andrew, a clinician who has been unable to attract referrals from general cardiologists. To investigate how the network is organized, we're then going to look at Michael, a clinician who has the referral flow and must decide which patients to treat and which to pass along to standard-setters. Finally, we look at the stories of several more-experienced clinicians to see some of the skills involved in managing the perceived overreach that accompanies referrals.

Andrew, a new clinician, has come to the Medscape meeting hoping to find information and generate contacts that will lead to a new job.

> I circulate among the representatives and the doctors during one of the meeting's many between-session breaks. I meet Andrew, who is two years out of his fellowship and sports a receding hairline and a hangdog posture. He lives in Florida but is looking to move north. "I hear North Carolina is nice." As he tells me, his problem is getting the trust of the referring doctors. He is a single man in his mid-thirties, can't socialize with the general cardiologists in the community, mostly men in their fifties. Without a wife or kids, he can't schmooze at church or soccer games. So cardiologists don't refer patients to him. "They are too afraid of lawsuits." The general cardiologists ultimately then just give the patients anti-arrhythmic drugs.

Andrew is an example of a doctor who has no ties with general cardiologists. Andrew depends on positive words from the medical device company to general cardiologists to help him generate referrals. He is the rare nonfellow participating in the meeting. He wants to meet colleagues and standard-setters, but is especially interested in meeting with the company representatives, because they have flown in from around the country and generally have more accurate information on vacancies than doctors. Andrew has been unable to build trust and status with general cardiologists who would send him referrals. Without having attracted these referrals, he can't demonstrate good patient outcomes. Without good outcomes to show, he can't build his standing in the community.

Clinicians like Andrew who are outside of academic settings recognize the tightened constraints of a referral network. They are confronted with the informal system of accessing patients, one long demonstrated to be organized by class, religion, and ethnic group.[12] They know well that there is no one-to-one relationship between condition and treatment; general cardiologists can simply give patients medication rather than send them forward into the hands of an unknown quantity who might open them up to a lawsuit if a procedure fails. In the meeting, clinicians like Andrew can inquire about regions in need of EPs that are less competitive than his current one.

Job-seeking doctors such as Andrew are interested in resources prepared by the medical device company. For example, at the meeting, the company distributes a booklet entitled "practice profiles." It has eighty pages of job listings in private and academic practices around the country. For electrophysiology fellows, especially those following the clinician's path, industry is hugely influential in getting a job. The local and regional representatives know the gossip about openings as well as satisfaction and dissatisfaction on the ground. In an effort to foster long-term ties, the company doesn't want to place someone in a site where they will fail. Representatives are extremely important information brokers; their networks often make them far better placed to assist in a job hunt than the fellows' past or current teachers. Thus, depending on the new doctors' experiences starting off, they may come to rely on industry to improve their position in this network. So, in addition to being a venue synonymous with medical excellence, medical device companies use meetings to provide unrivaled career resources. For individuals like Andrew, these resources are vital, and providing them allows medical device companies to be seen as a lifeline for physicians. Yet again, facilitating the careers of physicians facilitates the positive image of the company.

Once a clinician is established in a practice and gets referrals, their practice is affected by their successes and failures with these patients. Michael is firmly situated in this position. He is tall and square-jawed, with a black suit and impeccable posture. And he thinks hard about maintaining referral relations with standard-setters.

Michael, a clinician, founded a private practice on Long Island, NY, and, in the two years since his fellowship, has achieved the enviable position of being able to choose among patients to treat, and of referring complex cases to standard-setters with more expertise and interest. Michael is a clinician with strong ties to both the company (which has invited him to speak), and standard-setters to whom he can refer risky cases. Furthermore, he has a very good sense of when and where to refer patients in a way that protects his reputation. His capacities to work within the network results in more status; program directors will often invite doctors like Michael to share their own experiences.

A crowd of fellows has circled a young doctor who opened his own practice after fellowship. Drawing on a napkin he makes three columns to diagram the issues he thinks EPs will need to be aware of when they start practicing independently. The three columns are procedure type, amount of reimbursement, and length of time required.[13]

Table 5.1. Decision Criteria about Referrals.

Procedure	Reimbursement	Time
Afib ablation	$2,500	4 hours
AVNRT ablation	$2,500	2 hours
Bi-V ICD	$2,200	1 hour
ICD & DFT	$1,800	45 minutes

The table compares more- and less-complex procedures by revenue, to physician and time necessary to complete the procedure. Michael's table emphasizes that the routine device implantations are more lucrative than the more complex procedures. These cases are also more likely to bring him status; he is less likely to make a mistake and damage his standing with general cardiologist referrers like chapter 2's Dr. Walker, who will refer to EPs and interventional cardiologists patients needing procedures. However, beyond emphasizing the financial rewards, he emphasizes that the reputational risks involved in ablations motivates him to refer cases to academic medical centers. Since academic physicians gain more status for conducting ablations than for implanting devices, and since ablations offer more opportunity to innovate, these standard-setters value being referred the more risky and time-intensive ablations.

Thus, accessing a patient flow for clinicians involves the correct mix of patients, and the ability to strategically refer patients to appreciative top practitioners. Michael, joined by Dr. Steinman, reinforces this point to the new fellows.

"When you are a resident you are in a socialist society, and you basically get fed cases. If you are working with Dr. Mueller, and you're there as his fellow or resident, then you really don't care if the patient comes in or not. You may not care much about the service you provided. When you're out there on your own, you're not fed cases. And I think the obvious thing for EPs is that the last thing you want to be labeled is a stroke machine or a complication machine. So if you're not sure you can do it safely, don't do it."

Dr. Steinman, a more experienced clinician, echoes this point. "Once you begin independent practice, there is a more service-oriented approach, where as a resident or fellow you're dreading the next hit–the next consult. Now, the more people that come to you, the better. You know, they talk about the triple A's: being available, being affable, and being able–and in that order of importance. I think the other thing, from a practical standpoint, is not being worried about asking for help. You're under a microscope the first year, where you're being watched [by colleagues in your practice] to make sure your comp [complications] rate is comparable to the average, if not below. So you have to be sorta judicious about picking, in terms of cases. You don't want to do, as your first case, a pulmonary vein isolation. You want to have at least a couple of devices under your belt so that people know you have some set of hands that are reasonable, and then move on from that point."

When these clinicians urge these new doctors to pass on cases about which they are uncertain, he means they should send such patients to the standard-setters such as Dr. Stimm's group at Superior Hospital. These network relationships are important for sorting patients into the hands of those most motivated and able to manage them. The venue of the conference allows these networks to understand their positionality and relationality to each other. Additionally, it encourages attendees not only to be realistic about their positionality but to thrive within their designated space.[14]

Another prerequisite for reaching a sufficient number of general cardiologists' referrals is being willing and able to use multiple brands of technology. Success for a new EP like Michael depends on whether or not the EP can manage pressures from referrers to use a certain brand, a fact that becomes clear in my conversations with two other clinicians, Irv and Tim.

> Talking to Irv, a former Superior Hospital trainee of Dr. Stimm, several years after he had finished at Superior and begun work in a large private practice, he tells me about pressures faced from referrers. "There is a [general cardiologist here] who won't let you put in anything but Medscape. If you don't, it's over."
>
> I ask Tim, an EP from Florida who also trained with Dr. Stimm, if his referring doctors act similarly. "Everybody does. South Florida's a sleazy area."
>
> He gives a resigned shrug when I ask him how he responds.
>
> "You pick your battles. Say you're a referring physician. You're getting God knows what from the Medscape rep—maybe he's giving you money on the side, maybe he's providing you with real good service, maybe he takes you to dinner. Maybe she blows you on Thursdays. I have no idea. You call me up and you say, 'Mr. Jones needs a pacemaker, use a Medscape device.' Unless I feel like it's inappropriate for the patient, I don't care. I mean, for me, it's all a joke. Because I rotate—you call me up and ask for a Medscape device, the next person doesn't get a Medscape device. You try and keep things straight. But that's the way they play the game."

Because new clinicians must depend on general cardiologists for patients, their practices may also be highly structured by it; they might be expected to use their referrers' technology preference, or even feel pressures to do procedures they do not believe are appropriate. Additionally, they may lose some control over their capacity to practice in a way that represents what they believe is most appropriate for their patients. These highly specialized doctors, while seeming to be at the top of the medical hierarchy in light of their expertise, remain highly dependent on those who bring them work, and accept the influence of referrers (and industry) to practice.

Standard-setting EPs have far less trouble with being controlled by referrers. In chapter 4 I showed that even if they might have trouble securing beds, standard-setters in hospitals that support their position atop the status order have little trouble with referrals, and they don't have the problem of being told what procedure to do. They also feel buffered from pressure to use particular practices or technologies. After feeling forced to leave Superior Hospital, Dr. Stimm reinforced this matter. "We don't have an issue with docs calling and telling us to use their device. Because they have a problem and want our discretion." Standard-setters use the fellows conference to get attention and referrals, especially of those patients who will help them compete for status.

We also see here the dynamism of being embedded in a referral network; referrers may control the EP, but the EP also has counter-controls to even out the longer-term appearance of bias. EPs I spoke with uniformly reported seeing only modest differences between devices; as Fred Malcolm put it: "a defibrillator is almost like a commodity now—there's wheat, soybeans, and defibrillators." Consequently, so long as reps are competent, the doctors are relatively comfortable with the existence of these controls. (Working with private practice doctors, reps participate in device programming and patient education far more than they do in the academic setting, where fellows do much of this work.) Consequently, coming to the fellows' programs sponsored by different companies is a valuable learning experience for those who will need to work with referring general cardiologists with different commitments, ones that may organize EP behavior as much as, if not more than, the onetime socialization occurring in the hospital where they trained.

Cautionary Tales and Advice on Managing Patients and Choosing Procedures

We've seen how fellows courses involve the interlinked goals of the maintenance of individual status and of validating and legitimating individual EPs' efforts to organize indeterminacy, all set against the backdrop of a venue designed to synonymize the sponsoring industry with medical excellence in light of their strengthening of the occupational project. We've seen how referral networks act as a source of control. At these meetings, too, a considerable amount of time is spent on strengthening the occupational project. There, older and wiser doctors socialize younger doctors to practice EP in line with their beliefs and navigate the EP referral structure through cautionary tales. These tales, which sometimes take the form of advice, are a mix of practical tips and moral exhortations that connect standard-setter and clinician—but also, perhaps, industry members and members of another profession—through accounts of personal experience of what kinds of bad things can happen. Cautionary tales serve to strengthen the occupational project; they place doctors at the interface with the public and a network of other doctors and also confirm for them what should be regarded as extraordinary and what is commonplace. Just as our examination of the clinicians' travails offered us a sense of the challenges they must navigate in accessing and managing patients, through advice and cautionary tales it is possible to see the implicit reinforcing of the EP social structure in cautionary tales about being judicious. These tales involve attempts to strengthen EPs' collective efforts to be the occupation that organizes indeterminacy around the arrhythmia tasks.[15]

The first kind of cautionary tale involves encouraging an arm's-length relationship with industry. Senior physicians will also urge judiciousness in financial relationships with companies that might damage the occupational project and the ability of doctors to sustain their ability to organize indeterminacy.

> The standard-setter organizing the program takes the mic. "Medscape, in my personal experience over the years, more than other companies, has fostered education. But you got to be fair about it; they're not the Pew foundation. They are doing it for a reason, and their reason would be that a better-educated EP would do things right." He continues with advice about letting a company pay them too much for a speaking engagement. "Are you getting paid above your fair market value? Give yourself the *New York Times* test. Do you want your name smeared across the *New York Times*? These are not worth the extra money to you."

In some interactions with companies, then, the point is not to reach out, but to back away. Those at the top of the field are highly aware of the public attention paid to industry funding, and are especially sensitive to any implication of impropriety.

The senior physicians encourage arm's-length relations, then, but at times, an executive from the sponsoring company will address the meeting's participants to specify the company's vision of an optimal relationship. This speaker reminds EPs of the value of the relationship for making technology that advances the field, and urges physicians to advocate on industry's behalf—though not that of the specific company—with other doctors and the administration.

> After the program director leaves the stage, a Medscape vice president comes to the podium. "I want to reinforce that the major innovations in EP came out of collaboration between industry and doctors." The executive goes on to talk about new pressures on

consulting relationships. "Deans want us to send money to them to divvy up, whether it goes to gynecology or whatever. So I think they're living in a fairy tale land. There's not a lot we can do as a company because it's seen as a conflict of interest, but it hurts the specialty. Unless you go back to your program chairs, [meetings like these] can all go away."[16]

Stories like this are framed to bolster the new EPs' understandings of the ongoing partnerships between industry and physicians, which influence the process of running clinical trials and inventing technology that benefit standard-setters, but also the availability of training opportunities. Messages such as these reinforce an implicit message of the conference: although discrete entities, industry and medical professionals of all strata depend on each other for success both independently and collectively.

A final type of cautionary tale warns of the consequences to the occupational project from disparaging peers in malpractice cases. Peers may, sometimes inadvertently, hurt their peers by not allowing them to control cases in the way they see fit. Standard-setters use these stories to reinforce that since failure is unavoidable, new EPs must learn how to prepare for lawsuits that follow these failures. Thus, the program director brings in professionals such as lawyers (and, at times, financial advisers). At this meeting, the doctors have an opportunity to benefit from the lawyer's expertise before they ever have to meet a malpractice lawyer under more uncomfortable circumstances. These talks give another perspective on the perils and challenges of being in the position of organizing indeterminacy, doing procedures others may not attempt.

> Dr. Ellston, the program director, returns to the stage. "I wanted to tell you all, a couple of weeks ago I got back from vacation after Labor Day, and went into my office to check the mail before work on Tuesday. I opened up an official-looking envelope and it said, "This is a second request for a subpoena, please check off the following, if you have the following records." I looked through it and thought, "God, I know that patient, he's a patient of mine." Always sends a shiver down your spine when you see one of those envelopes requesting medical records. I opened the envelope and boy, was I relieved when I saw, "Oh, it was a [Medistar] lead." Patient had about twenty-five inappropriate shocks. And I took a sigh of relief when I realized it was one of those class action lawsuits." After describing his relief that the lawsuit was directed to the company, not him, he gestures to fellow standard-setters and continues. "So I think Steve, Michael, and I spent about an hour

talking about the legal issues that affect us as invasive cardiologists that do procedures on patients. And the good, bad, and ugly–there's a lot of bad and ugly and not too much good, and I think that the only good is that we have Michael Goodstein today to talk to us about some of the legal challenges we're going to see–if you practice long enough, hopefully you will–and how to manage them, how to deal with them, how to react to them, and, if there's any way to avoid them, how to do that. So, Mike Goodstein is a senior partner in a law firm in Indianapolis that handles a large amount of medical practice, and I'll look forward to his comments."

Dr. Ellston reinforces the multifaceted relationship between industry and doctors, a relationship that both distributes and spreads risk. Pressures on companies by competitors and pressures on the state by patient advocates mean that companies will need to modify technologies in response to flaws identified after reaching a market. As inevitable as the occasional patient death, technologies will fail, and colleagues will share these stories of the resulting vulnerability. Dr. Ephron's story of the failure of the Medistar lead shows the value to doctors of being able to distribute risk; in this case, the liability falls on the device maker and he does not have to testify against a colleague. Yet doctors are far from buffered from risk—if a technology does fail, doctors will have to deal with lawsuits until fault is established.

The lawyer's cautionary tales are intended to prepare new doctors for these failures of both technology and technique and to help them think about how to ready themselves for accidents.

Goodstein, the lawyer, steps up to the stage. "For a brief moment–I apologize–but let's mention the *m* word." He pauses for two full seconds. "It's malpractice. The best defense is a good defense. And we assume all the way down that you are at the top of your field, you know what you're doing. . . . A lot of people think a bad outcome means it's malpractice, but that's not necessarily the case. The bottom line is"–and here he slows down and raises his voice–"do you really want a jury deciding that question?"

The lawyer continues, sharing cases where the patient might have fared better if referred to a standard-setter, and in which those standard-setters' attempts to organize indeterminacy–during which they defied manufacturers recommendations–went poorly. "What cases are actually getting to court? I'm going to run through five or six cases . . . this one's an angioplasty with a new device. The physician broke the guide wire upon removal.

The broken wire caused rapid restenosis. This is one that's currently in suit. No outcome yet." He continues, with an example of a lawsuit from the family of a deceased patient, whose standard-setting doctor was seeking to offer a new solution. "Here's one on improperly sized devices. The plaintiff contends that the defendant cardiologist utilized an oversized balloon, and exceeded the maximum balloon inflation during angioplasty stenting procedure. The late plaintiff's coronary artery ruptured. The defense argued that the manufacturer's recommendations were outdated, and an oversized balloon was appropriate. And the jury thought a lot and gave a verdict of 1.6 million dollars."

Goodstein then presents a case with the subtext that doctors should be careful about not weakening the occupational project by throwing colleagues under the bus. "A patient was treated with a permanent pacemaker for a rheumatic heart disease with second-degree AV block. A second physician stated to the patient that he didn't know why this treatment was chosen. Now, the jury returned a verdict for the defense, but the case may have been avoided had a colleague not said those unkind words. In other words, do not do your colleague in, even inadvertently. It happens all the time, you go in, go for a second opinion, the doctor says, 'I don't know why Dr. so and so did what he did. I don't know why he used that sized catheter, that sized balloon. I don't know.' And it leaves that feeling in the patient's mind [that] 'something wrong must have happened; this is not good.'

"So think 'there but for the grace of God go I,' when you're talking to a patient about what a colleague did. Be cautious. Choose your words carefully, because you can make a lawsuit for that other physician."

In some respects, we saw this ecumenical stance modeled earlier in the chapter by Dr. Wilson when he discussed during his lecture about how another standard-setter, Mark Jefferies, might differently organize indeterminacy. All doctors know that accidents happen due to chance and new technologies, and that developing new knowledge involves organizing indeterminacy. Given the constant threat of an accident, and the potential impact, Goodstein reinforces the importance of maintaining the reputation of colleagues. This involves monitoring every word uttered when a patient seeks a second opinion. The subtext is clear; if you don't support their approaches in organizing indeterminacy, you're hurting the profession. These talks are intended to convey that when accidents do happen, the doctors will take judicious care not to tarnish electrophysiology's standing by inappropriately impugning a colleague.

Conclusion

When doctors attend fellows programs, for two days they leave behind the schedules and patterns organized by hospital hierarchies and immerse themselves in a haze of booze, food, and fun. Whether one is a decorated standard-setter or struggling fellow is made temporarily irrelevant. They socialize with their textbooks' authors and chuckle over a mentor's retelling of early missteps. As a result, the doctors feel more charismatic, autonomous, and fully involved in everything around them, including their occupational project.

For the standard-setters, clinicians, and fellows, the fellows programs are formatted for presentation of claims both to knowledge and to strong and ethical support of the field as a whole and its best interests, showcased in presentations of the complex procedures the experts may have pioneered and the cutting-edge research they have conducted. We saw that these venues are important visible forums for communication. By creating and organizing them, industry contributes to standard-setters' capacities to sustain what they have worked to define as best practices, all while cultivating a synonymous relationship with medical excellence—an implicit message they hope the physicians carry back home with them. The chapter also demonstrates how status is co-constructed by company and speakers: the company wants to highlight the eminence of the speakers, because their presence is a tacit endorsement of the company.

The meeting comprises standard-setters' highly visible performances amid a large group of peers and new initiates, permitting the exposure and ongoing evaluation necessary for establishing and shifting status. It allows speakers to present details on their activities in other venues, and to build their status through defining the problems and solutions to be followed by the next generation of doctors. Like the world of academic science, the standard-setters have venues such as journals, conferences, and direct communication channels of email and lab visits, channels through which they can choose to share hunches and research. This chance to give in-person performances is important to keeping the status system fluid because they can generate impressions and feedback in a way impossible elsewhere, except perhaps at the kinds of spectacles like the live cases illustrated in this book's introduction.

Speakers create a socially organized way of seeing and understanding clinical information that is answerable to the interests not only of their professional group but also more specifically of the high status members of this group. Because these meetings are so well attended, they provide standard-setters with the chance to observe and differentiate their own approaches to organizing indeterminacy from those of their peers, seeking to making a case for how their approaches are more compelling than those competing in their niche. Fellows here are further socialized into the field through learning to see their work in ways resembling standard-setters' problems and solutions. Their status with peers and fellows is tied to this process of validating onstage their efforts at organizing indeterminacy. Thus, status determinations are reestablished through presentations among peers and the next generation of doctors, who are a prized source of referrals.

In showing us some features of the network structure of stratification in EP, these meetings let us see the social structures through which standard-setters can diffuse their approaches to organizing indeterminacy. In doing so, it shows us how standard-setters and clinicians are connected. The doctors at the top of the field seek to validate their personal practices as best practice, and sometimes link them to clinical trials, so that they are able to attract referrals from younger physicians. And the cases of Andrew, Michael, and other clinicians show us that career paths of these clinicians may differ according to an individual's opportunities, networks, and traits—features that may influence the longer-term success of these doctors.

Further, the venue is an important one for sharing advice and cautionary tales intended to instruct the next generation in how they should protect their own and others' reputations through judiciously choosing patients and making decisions to refer. Standard-setters are helping ensure the quality of medical work, while also seeking to avert lawsuits that have the potential to hurt all.

In the processes through which EPs organize indeterminacy in the fellows conference, the event also reveals much about the role of industry in the occupational project. Sponsoring companies participate in the status competition, and benefit from it as well. The sponsoring companies need speakers, all of whom have used their products at some point, to convey the efficacy of their practices with individual patients and in randomized clinical trials. The company wants the standard-setter to have a high level of status because such a star spokesperson raises the profile of its products. Industry sees these standard-setters as a conduit of a reputation for medical excellence and seeks to ensure that participants closely associate the pioneering medical advances of standard-setters with the brand's name. Because both the company and standard-setter want the latter's status to be enhanced as much as possible, their interests are aligned, making it unsurprising that the companies take so much care to evaluate and provide feedback to the experts, a practice that implicitly implicates them in the socialization of fellows. Standard-setters have the patients; people at the top places get a high volume of tough referrals. Because it gets credit for strengthening these referral relationships, Medscape benefits from bringing the different parties together. Therefore, they can do the research that industry needs to support the promotion, and refinement, of new technologies. There's little question, too, that it is interested in minimizing the number of patient lawsuits; the companies have the deepest pockets of stakeholders in EP, and are frequent targets of class action lawsuits.

Finally, the chapter lets us see where tethers come from, and how relationships are formed that afford the referring of patients between general cardiologists, clinicians, and standard-setters. Specifically, the company's venue helps solve problems in connecting clinicians and standard-setters. Even though the home lab is important for doctors to be able to develop a reputation for careful practices and to enable others to observe and learn, it is costly for doctors to serve as tethers by traveling to others' labs to learn, transmit, and adjudicate the knowledge they produce. At the fellows conferences, standard-setters demonstrate the merits of their approach by offering accounts of previous successes with patients, using referred patients as tethers to their home lab, ones that help them strength their approaches to organizing indeterminacy. As suggested in Dr. Bellard's objection to more senior doctors' efforts to control his practice (chapter 3), the way doctors interpret an EKG is shaped by one's work in their home lab. It also represents a kind of language-based tether; the way one reads an EKG reflects how one wants others to understand the data they are receiving, and that reflects a problem you think the profession is capable of solving. Observation across venues is enabled by both the director's use of a speaker and the speaker's use of slides (taken home in a Medscape-branded folder), as tethers. These tethers encourage relationships in which, during the weeks and months that follow the meeting, people share news of each other's practices.

six

Physicians and Medical Technology Companies at Hands-on Meetings

Strengthening the Occupational Project

This chapter takes us to an important venue where physicians confront new technologies and their needs for them: industry-sponsored hands-on meetings. Each of the three dominant EP device companies holds approximately seven hands-on training meetings around the country each year, for a collective total of about twenty-one events.

What is it that brings some of the standard-setters here to talk in these conferences? And why do clinicians attend, when the new technology is a risk for their skills and professional project? It's because, even as these technologies are created with considerable input from standard-setters, for many, adopting them is a risk that may change the nature of their occupational project. And even if a new technology will be used by only some of the doctors, with others referring patients to those leaders, they all want to evaluate the new thing and be in control as their work changes.

As with the fellows programs we looked at in chapter 5, new clinicians come to these gatherings in order to stay apprised of what's going on in the field and who can do it. But in this particular kind of industry meeting, these and more experienced clinicians get their hands on the technologies and cultivate referral relationships with standard-setters who have organized indeterminacy using these technologies. Some will learn the new techniques and others will find a knowledgeable colleague to whom they can refer patients. It's in part a shopping trip, in part a sortie into new territory, and in part a chance to extend a network.

In choreographing the hands-on training programs, companies immerse the doctors in two or three days of interactions with existing colleagues and provide introductions to new ones, offer opportunities to try recently approved technologies, and sponsor lectures from EPs who frequently use or conduct research with the technology. There, outside the hermetically sealed apprenticeship venue of one's home laboratory, standard-setters are charged with training practicing doctors to appreciate—if not use—new technologies. In contrast to the fellows programs, the standard-setters are not necessarily the most eminent on a profession-wide level. Instead they are considered experts with the technology. They will be either investigators on the early trials or "super users," doctors who use the technology in at least two procedures per month. Clinicians might want support in the case of complications, and they might need the financial investment that others in the workplace may not be prepared to make immediately. For this reason, companies promoting new techniques implement a teaching strategy in which the standard-setters serve as surrogate mentors of sorts, reasserting while reaffirming the value of the best practices they have pioneered and teaching clinicians how to follow their approaches. In these meetings, the clinicians will learn not only medical practices and associated technologies that interest the company and the standard-setters, but also whether the technology will be financially reasonable.

Clinicians use meetings to stay updated and build networks. They come to meetings knowing that even if they don't adopt a specific technology, they must at least be cognizant of technological changes in order to "keep up" with developments in the occupational project. Thus, they come intending to discover the newest gadgets rather than to challenge opinion leaders. For these doctors, coming to the event is necessary because the big companies don't approach them with their latest innovation, and their hospitals may not be frequent stops on standard-setters' lecture circuits. The event is also helpful for network building: at the end of the meeting, the speakers will almost invariably invite the other doctors to visit their lab for firsthand observations or to call if they are stuck in a case.

The companies use the meetings to get technologies into the hands of the doctors (through the standard-setters), but they are also seeking ongoing feedback on technology. According to representatives, they listen closely to why people won't adopt, because they want to learn about the sources of resistance. Medical device firms' concerns are to pass along not just the new knowledge, but also doctors' interpretation and application of it, so they want the potential users to assess and critique the technology. These companies want to understand if the doctors consider knowledge of this technology necessary or consider it just a fad.

The events begin with the program director working to justify the day's activities, slowly progressing to the details of the procedure, and finishing with a presentation about how features of the technologies used in the hands-on sessions distinguish the company from its competition. The speeches move from the textbook knowledge of medical school to the insider expertise of the applied stages of training. There is a formal curriculum that conveys the importance of the event for the field and the technical practices that will be addressed, but it is interconnected with some other material that is justifying the varied nature of the course.

When doctors are deciding if they should adopt new technologies—and thereby accept companies' solutions, at least in part—how do doctors factor in their reputations and their social relationships with others in their field, including their referral networks? How do standard-setters seek to control the way(s) those in the post-fellowship stage of their training understand the heart and how it should be managed? Because companies are providing these technologies and sponsoring the talks from standard-setters who are there to teach their approaches to practice, the key puzzle is how companies gain acceptance from those whose professional role appears antithetical to the profit motive.

In this chapter I investigate how a medical technology firm convinces physicians that it is in their professional interest to change their behavior— either by adopting a new technology or by coming to accept its benefit for their patients. To understand how companies are granted permission to work alongside standard-setters to shape the work of their potential clients—the clinicians—I describe traits of training that are paramount to strengthening ties between companies, standard-setters, and clinicians. I then look at participants' different impressions of training sessions organized by two different companies in order to examine how and when industry strengthens or weakens the occupational project. Through this, we can identify key features underpinning when and how physicians evaluate claims of industry.

The Hands-on Industry Meeting

We pass through an unmarked gate at the sponsor's mirrored building in a Minneapolis suburb, to the facility where hands-on workshops occur. The bus is full of clinicians, traveling from community hospitals and private practices. They may spend their days working in three or four hospitals, covering the northern third of a rural part of a state. They are too busy to follow the latest research of standard-setters, don't work in venues where they will hear grand rounds or collaborate in clinical trials, and have yet to get their hands on the latest technologies.

I'm walking step by step toward my own hands-on experience with new technology. I have joined in the 7 a.m. trip to the training center from the new downtown boutique hotel. After the program director has described the plan for the day, I slide on the pale blue scrubs and the booties over my shoes. I walk through the locker room door, which is covered by a poster: "Every 4 seconds, someone, somewhere in the world is helped by a Medistar product." Below the images of a pig, dog, and rabbit, the poster continues: "Research animals help make this possible. Please respect their contribution." On the other side of the door is a poster outlining the various zoonotic diseases, and instructions for reporting concerns to the Institutional Animal Care and Use Committee. Entering the room we'll work in, I note that it is set up as an EP lab, almost identical to Superior Hospital's.

And, from its size and heaving chest, I know this patient is a pig. We've walked into a sterile operating room and are handed lapel clips that will record the amount of radiation we are exposed to. We assemble on the right side of the patient, who is covered with the blue paper that usually drapes an anesthetized person during procedures. The administrator begins the procedure with a display of deference toward us. "Let's take five minutes each, so you can choose if you want to do an ablation, put up a couple quads [four-electrode catheters], or if you want to do the CS [coronary sinus vessel]; whatever you want to tackle, you can tell me what you want and I can queue things up for whatever you want to work on." The administrator hands the catheters to the invited faculty and steps outside our line of sight. We then wait, taking turns to feel and see how the wires interact with the body. The procedure we're learning is commonplace to most standard-setters, but few clinicians—especially those over fifty—were trained to perform afib ablation. And those who were trained may not have learned the approach the observing standard-setter developed.

I watch a clinician attempting the new approach, and Kim, one of the physician-educators working for the company, talks about how if she sees a clinician not performing well in the lab meeting in Minneapolis, she will tell the local reps to watch that doctor. Also, she tells me that when she's in the field, like those reps, she herself may push the emergency shutoff button on new cooling ablation technology if it's kept on too long and is likely to injure the patient. At the same time, she knows that not all device reps are comfortable giving orders to those doctors performing the procedure.

I'm approached by a Medistar representative. "You want to do this?" Emboldened by having watched dozens of procedures, I'm surprised to hear myself say, "OK, maybe I'll manipulate it a little bit." The faculty member stands beside me and walks me through the procedure. I snap on the gloves, I wrap my right hand around the handle, I squeeze the trigger. The MasterBurn catheter head bends, showing me that it will ease my access across the septum to reach the pulmonary veins. I ask how I get "there," gesturing to the image above the pig. He says, "You'll feel it, just put [the catheter] down in the hole." And I'm in.

"R on" he says, pointing toward the pedal on the floor that activates the X-ray that will enable us to see the pig's innards on fluoroscopy. "So then you want one hand up here, like this." He moves my left hand to the knob, and places my right on the handle of the catheter. "And you want to push on the left pedal to see what you're doing."

Stepping on the switch, I feed the catheter about two feet into the patient but cannot yet see anything on the screen. The Medistar representative is watching me closely.

The machines are beeping. Good, the swine's alive, still has a pulse.

I warily continue pushing the catheter forward. The standard-setter, somewhat impatiently, says, "Right now you're not even seeing—push push push push." The catheter appears on the monitor.

"Wow!"

To show me how to move into the atrium, he bends his finger into the shape of a C. I pull the trigger, and the catheter bends to touch the lining of the heart. "Yeah, that's it. So let's see if you can put it into the ventricle." He points at the screen. I go too far, poking up against the wall, and he guides it to a site where he can interpret the EKG in a way consistent with how he has organized indeterminacy, "Push it down here."

As the jagged lines of the EKG become more closely spaced and rapid, the standard-setter gently provides more hands-on guidance. "You're getting these extra beats because you're touching the free wall of the right ventricle."

Feeling my movements blocked, and with a swagger like that of the surgeons I've seen, I show I know the consequences of a misstep. "Well, I don't want to keep pushing, because then I might perf."

The doctor nods. "Yeah, you'll perf."

I have crossed the septum into the right pulmonary vein, where, if I pushed the button to turn on energy, I'd be able to perform the gold-standard procedure for ablating atrial fibrillation.

The pig is still alive.

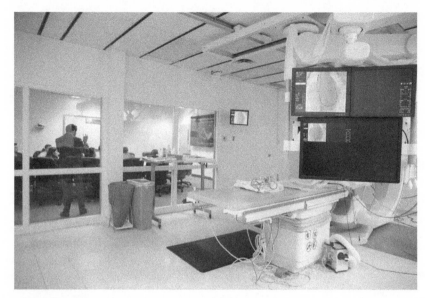

Figure 6.1. At an industry venue, a standard-setter shares his slides of the procedure that the clinicians will soon practice with a pig, as part of a hands-on training in a new ablation technology. Photograph by David Schalliol.

Figure 6.2. At the hands-on meeting, clinicians take their turns navigating the ablation catheter into the heart of the pig. Photograph by David Schalliol.

The Medistar rep reminds me that we will not be ablating the pig, for ethical reasons. I remove my gloves and step past the observing clinicians, who appear unmoved by my performance. With my turn over, I watch with secret pride as the next one fails to identify the vein.

How do clinicians learn new knowledge and a set of skills in a venue that many doctors are suspicious of? In this section I offer a general overview of industry hands-on meetings as well as describe the network formation and mentoring they afford. The model of training looks like that found in the fellowship—if somewhat more ethics centered—with competition between standard-setters and focus on strengthening the occupational project. This snapshot suggests that companies are not stakeholders external to medical work but instead are internal to the occupational project and intimately involved in maintaining quality control within the field.

Overview of the Meeting

I've arrived at the hands-on meeting, one I learned about when Dr. Stimm forwarded a confirmation email he received after agreeing to speak.

Dear Dr. Stimm MD,

We are pleased to confirm your participation in the Medistar Program on Friday, September 5, 2014 in Minneapolis, MN.

As a presenter at this Medical Education event, Medistar will provide an honorarium, and an appropriate travel allowance based on your existing Master Services Agreement (MSA) and/or Work Order Agreements with Medistar. Medistar will also cover your travel expenses (please submit all receipts).

The Program Manager, Emily Davis, will be reviewing the agenda and the content for the presentation with you.

Medistar cannot promote or otherwise encourage off-label use of its products at Medical Education events. As a faculty acting on behalf of Medistar you must follow the applicable provisions of the Medistar policy for interactions regarding the On-Label Use Requirements for Medistar Training & Education

Programs, which is attached as Exhibit A.
During your presentation the information that
you provide about Medistar products and
therapies must be limited to uses that have
been approved by the U.S. Food and Drug
Administration.

All presentations will be reviewed to
ensure they are consistent with the approved
labeling, including:

1)   Legal and Regulatory Requirements.
Presentations containing Medistar device/
therapy related content will be reviewed by
Medistar to ensure the content is consistent
with approved labeling.

2)   Disclosure—Please provide a disclosure
slide to advise the audience of all of your
relevant industry arrangements and that you
are a paid faculty member for AF Remedies.

Please do not hesitate to contact me if you
have any questions.

The focus on ethics is familiar from the fellows programs, but here the stakes are especially high; companies are responsible to ensure standard-setters are not teaching clinicians to use technologies in ways that have not been approved by the federal government. While off-label use may occur in individual clinics, the company itself must promote only the uses that have succeeded in clinical trials. The company makes sure standard-setters understand the importance of discussing federally approved uses of technology, and that the doctors know the company considers this adherence to be important. While chapter 5 introduced us to industry-sponsored fellows' programs, where fellows and clinicians are able to evaluate the validity and legitimacy of standard-setters' practices, the relationship between doctors and industry in this venue (the hands-on meeting) is different because doctors are being introduced to new technologies in a hands-on way. With the monetary interest and the regulatory implications, there are potential conflicts of interest and violations of laws about discussing off-label uses of technology.

When done well, as shown below, to clinicians the event feels like the formal didactic training they received in their fellowship programs. It is an event that is advertised as providing the solution to a clinical problem that clinicians often see, but which they typically treat with drugs: atrial fibrillation. The new solution of catheter ablation is offered in a model that closely resembles the format of their early training.

This course provides instruction with contemporary approaches to ablation for Persistent Atrial Fibrillation. The course focuses on mastering stages of three essential steps of the procedure: 3D mapping (Map), ablation (Ablate), and use of a circular mapping catheter (Validate). The course is conducted by our respected faculty of physicians and industry experts and will provide you with the practical knowledge and know-how for the procedure. Information presented will guide you from the early steps of patient selection all the way to the final stage of discharge and follow-up. This includes how to avoid transseptal complications, optimal anticoagulation settings, tips on how to shorten procedure time, increase efficiency and settings for using the MasterBurn® Catheter. The MasterBurn® Catheter is the only catheter that is FDA approved for the ablation of the symptomatic drug refractory paroxysmal atrial fibrillation when used with CATHO® Systems.

Faculty:
The course is run by a renowned faculty, physicians performing more than 250 AF ablation [*sic*] annually.

Covered topics:
Background to PAF ablation
Pre, peri and post procedure considerations
Workshop on Ringo® Catheter tracings
RF ablation biophysics and hands-on
Procedure complications—how to avoid and how to deal with
Hands-on: Mapping the LA using the MapperSound® Module,
        Mapper® 3 System, MasterBurn® Catheter and Ringo®
        Catheter

This advertisement, an example of those used to attract participants, emphasizes interactive contact with standard-setters and hands-on contact with technology to teach the theory and the practice of ablation EP. The sequence of subjects is similar to the early stages in medical training more generally, where two years of textbook instruction ultimately give way to patient encounters. The company, dissatisfied by the fact that only half of the field conducts ablation procedures, wants to demonstrate the severity of the problem of arrhythmias for which catheter ablation provides an effective solution.[1]

Once they arrive, the standard-setters weigh in on the program's knowledge in several ways. Before faculty begin to lecture at eight o'clock, the conference begins with an introduction from the program director. The forty-five-minute talks have titles such as "Biophysics of Ablation" and "Cardiac Anatomy: Fluoro and EGM Guidance," emphasizing the event's specific topic. The doctors then move into the hands-on workshops, which,

Figure 6.3. At the hands-on meeting, clinicians will use these simulators to practice inserting and navigating the ablation catheter in human anatomy. Photograph by David Schalliol.

for meetings on the subject of ablation, tend to involve performing an ablation on a heart, dissecting it, and inspecting how catheters have produced lesions.[2]

The afternoon workshops usually involve a simulator that takes participants through a transseptal procedure, or, as in the vignette, actually performing the procedure in the heart of a living pig. Here standard-setters teach clinicians to recognize important qualities in the ablation procedure, often hoping to enlist them into accepting how they've sought to organize indeterminacy profession-wide, and teaching them to feel the anatomy as they do.[3] The final session will be an overview of the newest technology produced by the company.

Competing for Status and Constructing Networks

Looking closer at the interactions in this venue, it's possible to see that it's a place where doctors put different ways of organizing indeterminacy into conflict with each other, competing to get their approach into play. Such competition can be seen in the attention they pay to contested language.

Beyond their function in conferring technical skills, many of these events are platforms for developing and strengthening collegial relationships among and between standard-setters and clinicians. Daily life doesn't afford many opportunities to interact with people on the cutting edge of the field, and the rank-and-file doctor has a very narrow view of the ideas and problems in the profession's core. While these learning experiences also include an expensive dinner, which allows the doctor to interact with colleagues and fellows in a more relaxed environment, the platform is highly attractive for other reasons.

For standard-setters, the conference is an important venue in which they can shape clinicians' ideas of competing approaches to organizing indeterminacy. As with the fellows program, the goal of each standard-setter is to legitimize their approach. There they compete with standard setters not present to establish problems and solutions for the next generation. It's a venue in which they frequently discuss existing standards and their contested nature. For instance, field-wide controversies are signaled when the faculty discusses how they interpret EKGs in their personal laboratory. It is common to point out that some people will ablate atrial fibrillation solely by isolating the ostium, the most recent approach being pulmonary vein isolation, while others will use wide-area circumferential ablation or left atrial catheter ablation. Others will use a combination.

For clinicians, the conference diminishes the probability they will become frozen in amber, as it gives them a glimpse of the ongoing debates among standard-setters. And so, within the formal curriculum, an informal curriculum is presented by standard-setters hoping to teach clinicians to understand controversies in the field and possibly adopt the experts' perspectives. They also walk away seeing the event from the standpoint of standard-setters as they see it *that* day—in a way represented by *those* physicians.[4]

Learning directly from the standard-setters also helps clinicians stay in touch with the capabilities and preferences of experts. So, even if clinicians don't want to ablate atrial fibrillation, they will know when an ablation might be needed as well as a person who can provide one. These events help prevent the social aging of the community.

One place that evidence of competition can be seen is in discussion of what might be called "contested anatomy," which may be defined as features or landmarks on an organ that some in the profession feel hold medical significance. If a practitioner convinces others to recognize the significance and location of one of these landmarks, he or she is then able to describe a procedure or account of disease processes that implicate this anatomical feature.

Much like naming a trail or cliff face, naming a piece of anatomy allows others to organize around it, thereby propagating a dialogue centered on— and mediated by—the label originator. In many ways, standard-setters are acting as physiological taxonomists. When a doctor names these features and landmarks, it reflects the use of a tether, and creates notoriety and recognition for the person who has used it in their approach to organizing indeterminacy. Names are necessary for reasons internal to a field—expertise must be passed down in textbooks, discoveries must be duplicated in scientific studies. Given that there is conflict in any field over matters such as the best ways to treat conditions, or over priorities in science, one might expect that the people who name parts of the body will clash. The naming process entails the doctors claiming they are people who know the body *and* want their terminology used in patient-doctor interactions.

Such labeling may occur in the context of an individual's attempt to shift medical practice toward their approach to organizing indeterminacy, an attempt that may not be deemed legitimate to others in a field. Naming a piece of anatomy, for instance, is not a value-free utterance and reflects different viewpoints of experts. The antrum is a particularly tendentious example of such a tether. To refine the approach of pulmonary vein isolation for ablating atrial fibrillation, a group of electrophysiologists argued for the crucial importance of ablating this anatomical area.[5] Naming this part of the heart was necessary for teaching others to perform a procedure Dr. Northern developed for ablating atrial fibrillation.

> I'm surprised when Dr. Naron describes an approach to ablation in terms of belief. "You'll want to ablate [burn] the antrum—if you believe in it!" Later, Dr. Stimm interprets this comment in an interview. "That term [antrum] was used probably first with Andy Northern, who always uses [the technique of] PV [pulmonary vein] isolation. It's a good way to describe what you're doing, I have no trouble, I use that term all the time. But if you don't like him, you might say, 'that term's dead to me . . .'"

When another doctor uses the term in a description, he indexes his association with a perspective—one, in this case, about which the cause-and-effect relationship is questioned. If the legitimacy of that sect is contested, then the user's status can be contaminated by association. And so, colleagues use language in their presentations to signal their acceptance or rejection of the practice that Northern uses in his everyday lab.

Additionally, a doubter might reject terminology in the interest of competition. Dr. Stimm describes the case of a well-respected EP who coined a term for a process that others wanted the credit for discovering.

> Frank Miller was the first person to describe, I think, concealed entrainment. Well, that's not really the right term, it's really entrainment with concealed fusion. So people that are excited that Frank described that—such as people who trained with Frank—will use the term "concealed entrainment." People who think *they* should be getting credit for that con-

cept use a different term: entrainment with concealed fusion. Steven Jacobs, who's probably in a different camp, uses a different term. The terminology that people use sometimes is reflective of what camp they come from.

And so the standard-setters use language that reflects their approach to organizing indeterminacy—and others who have adopted it—language they would like to be quoted to patients. Although it depends on alliances, experts will debate over whose terminology is most appropriate.

Beyond these lectures, the standard-setters present their personal techniques in the hands-on portions of the meeting. They are there to give their experiences and show the clinicians how to do their techniques and what they will result in. Because procedures are so important, it is unsurprising that the majority of every hands-on meeting involves touching catheters and dissecting anatomy, feeling in those catheters how various corners of the heart respond to their touch, and seeing on the fluoroscopy how the catheter looks in the heart.

Just as the standard-setter asserts that EPs should define the terms for EP knowledge, they also want to define what techniques and abilities are appropriate and constitute good hands; knowledge claims include recognition of appropriate techniques and abilities. Developing good hands in fellowship happens under the close supervision of an attending physician, where that teacher demonstrates a technique representing some component of their approach to organizing indeterminacy.

> Dr. Stimm stands before the dummy and the Medistar employees are out of our sightline. His incisions on the model are projected on the screen. Amid these gamified interactions the doctors help each other, and share their personal techniques for tying suture knots.

Through this hands-on teaching, the clinicians are able to get a sense of how the standard-setter conducts a practice for which he or she is known, as well as how his peers perform other related tasks that have been successful with their patients.

Experts like Dr. Stimm participate in the events because it helps them teach clinicians how to use a new technology to treat a condition they're esteemed for, which reinforces their status. These events also provide them with the opportunity to influence how other doctors interpret patients' conditions, label and speak about contested anatomy, and possibly attract new referrals. As Dr. Stimm puts it, "If you're up there teaching, it kind of puts you on the map a little bit as an authority in the technology, too, because [it shows] you know what you're talking about." By using the meeting to enhance their level of esteem in their niche, standard-setters can start establishing themselves with the clinicians and also send a message to the company of their importance. Standard-setters get to develop the language the company will have to take for granted as it develops and describes its technology in both marketing and discussions with doctors.

How Companies Seek to Protect Themselves and the Occupational Project

While standard-setters seek to mentor clinicians in ways that strengthen the occupational project, they are not alone in using the venue for quality control. Company reps, too, are concerned about the risk that inexperienced physicians may pose for their ability to compete. Thus, part of the purpose of the hands-on meetings is to allow technology reps to vet and try to gain some control over the potential users of their technology.

Physicians and representatives from medical technology firms observe each other because each is potentially a liability or a boon to the other. Additionally, and as shown in chapter 5, the doctor's referring physicians may expect them to have the ability to perform certain procedures or install specific devices. Also, EPs are wary that, should the device fail, their reputations will suffer with patients and referrers. When a device fails, it damages the patient-doctor relationship and may also strain collegial relationships with referring general cardiologists, who may become reluctant to refer patients. These failures also leave doctors vulnerable to accusations of misconduct: electrophysiologists are concerned about their reputations being vandalized by a company found to have given them "consulting fees"—payments that are legal but, given attention by the press, deemed unwarranted.[6]

At the same time, the stakes are also high for the company. By making new technology, the companies are competing with each other for market share, status, and money. While companies can improve their status and financial statements by recruiting doctors who can use or recommend products, they are also liable for failures. The profit margin for each implanted defibrillator is approximately 23–28 percent, and productive doctors in private practice will implant four or five devices per day.[7] In the area of leads, companies seek to make them thinner and thinner. When there is a failure—and that failure is identified—they lose market share, revenue, and may have to pay money in lawsuits. Additionally, such failures damage their reputation among doctors, insurance companies, and patients (in fact, they may later need to merge with another company to regain their status). Profits for mapping and ablation catheters are considerably lower but, unlike similar laboratory implements, such as a stethoscope or an electrocautery device (an electronic scalpel), each is nonreusable and involves a more substantial investment in a mapping system (to convert cardiac currents into visual representations) or a compatible ablation system (to deliver radiofrequency currents for creating cardiac lesions). Thus, when a physician adopts a company's system, his or her hospital also makes a capital investment of approximately $250,000 and a commitment to purchase compatible catheters. This motivates companies to get their products into the hands of as many EPs as possible. Yet the sellers, too, must exercise restraint and choose only successful doctors; the companies recognize the reputational and financial costs if a physician uses their technologies incorrectly. They are highly concerned about creating a "007," a "license to kill." The physicians thus serve as liabilities as well as lucrative consumers.

Because performing some techniques require using a particular technology, standard-setters are also motivated to ensure that clinicians learn how to use the technology; through this process, the doctors gain status and the company gains customers. However, damage can occur to the occupational project when physicians are poorly trained. A question remains, then: what prevents poorly skilled physicians from practicing in ways that damage the occupational project?

Companies, who depend on the strength of EPs as a community, recognize the problem. There is a cost associated with putting technologies into the hands of the inept: they may fail in practice, reflecting poorly on medicine and the company. For this reason, and similar to the kind of screening physicians experience (by other physicians) before they become residents, fellows, and attendings, the company seeks to identify and deter doctors from practicing procedures with which they are at risk of error. This concern for their company's reputation is lucidly described by a key company's director of hands-on programs.

> Educational director (Medicore): "I must say that I did have a couple of failed doctors in the program—we spent a whole day with them and we spent any amount of time with them that they needed. We realized that they should not do procedures. They should—they better not do it. And we always have people like that."
>
> DM: "Okay. Because you think that they might make a mistake?"
>
> Educational director: "Different reasons. So one of them we failed at [teaching] is really old and set in his ways and he just doesn't look. Another one is actually young and very arrogant and thinks that he could do it but it was a disaster during the course. He was just not listening. He was doing whatever was in his mind. He wasn't really trying to implement what he was taught.
>
> "[After he went home and wanted to do the procedure] This guy asked us for a proctor and asked to do the procedure with

our help. The faculty at that point said, 'No, we don't want to go there.' They didn't want to do it because they don't want to take the responsibility. So we are kind of a jam because what do you do? How do you say no to a doctor that asks for your help? We're still in the process of trying to figure out how to do it. And some of those doctors are going to do it anyway. We never have [newly trained physicians] do new procedures without our help but still I can't ask one of my fellow faculty to go there if they don't believe that they should."

DM: "And it's interesting that some of the responsibility is landing on you."

Educational director: "Well, I can tell you that doctor is going to do procedures. And he's going to do it because I cannot tell him not to do it. It's not my job and I just hope that his patients are going to be OK.

"There's nothing else I can do. If we see we have a person like that in the course, we make sure the faculty [reinforces] that being through the course doesn't mean that [they feel] you are ready to do this procedure. That you need to go step by step. That you need to make sure that you're feeling comfortable, without saying explicitly, but [saying] in general that you should be very cautious about doing the procedure. It's something in order to make sure that we are not giving [a] license to kill."

Although they sometimes put technology in questionable hands and hope for the best, companies do not want technology in the hands of those likely to fail; thus, they require a strategic relationship with standard-setters. The company's long-term reputation is bound to those doctors who use its technology. They look to the faculty at the meetings to report to the company doctors who might end up as a liability. They use the standard-setter for the dirty work of regulating those doctors who the company thinks will harm its reputation, asking them to dissuade the clinician from using the new technology. One program director explicitly tells me how the company expects this dirty work from standard-setters: "I would ask an expert to be a proctor for a few sessions [in the clinician's home lab]. So it's coming from him." In this sense the company helps the expert maintain their status and, more important, help maintain the authority of medicine—the profession suffers when failures occur.

Alternative Meeting Models and Their Success with Clinicians

As described above, hands-on meetings serve multiple purposes for a variety of actors. Ideally, participants leave having gained new knowledge they can take back and apply in their clinics, standard-setters create and reinforce tethers, and more clinicians choose to use devices made by the hosting firm. Below I describe the hands-on meetings of two medical technology firms: Medistar and Medicore. For one company, the hands-on meeting was a resounding success. This success can be attributed to the company having a complete understanding of the medical hierarchy and their role as a tool within it. For the other, an attempt to establish a new role for itself within the system toppled the medical hierarchy and resulted in an aversion to their products by physicians.

In a race among medical technology firms to create thinner leads for implantable defibrillators, Medistar's widely adopted lead led to a series of failures in 2007. As Dr. Kellogg put it, "A wide range of doctors expressed ill will [because they] didn't admit problems in their technology." Electrophysiologists felt that these failures, in which defibrillators deployed at inappropriate times or failed to deploy during an arrhythmia, were not reported rapidly enough by the company to physicians and the FDA. Medistar had lost credibility with doctors, and the public. Since pulling the product off the market, the company has largely focused on attracting the highest-status standard-setters to lead programs and giving them full control over the design of training events. They have lost credibility with older doctors, so they seek a more positive relationship with the next generation of practitioners. As a consequence, they have left the structure up to the standard-setter leading the conference. The standard-setter, too, is interested in developing ties with the next generation of practitioners.

In contrast, Medicore has seen some success in recent years and seeks to maintain their status. Having put their technologies into the hands of many physicians, they are confident in their capacity to make and diffuse products that physicians will value. In the wake of this success, they have taken a stronger hand in structuring the meeting.[8]

Each company structured its meetings differently based on these particular goals and past experiences. Medistar promoted the position of standard-setters, who used the event to establish tethers. Here the medical device was a tool used to strengthen the authority of their practices. Medicore, in contrast, placed itself in a position of educational authority, thereby sidelining standard-setters. The effect of this displacement of traditional modes of education and power was that clinicians felt much more negative toward the company; some clinicians even vowed not to use their technology. Comparing these meetings shows that trainees felt more positive about the company's supporting a mentoring relationship that strengthens the occupational project.

Based on post-meeting interviews, Medistar was regarded in a positive light by physicians because the company was perceived to "[care] about education." In contrast, the impressions of Medicore were negative because the company was seen to be "pushing product." The implications of these meetings were tangible: clinicians said they would decline to use Medicore technology, which also has consequences for the referral network. What informed the EPs' perceptions of the companies and drove them away from Medicore?

Below we can see the impact—and associated behavior—of these companies' market positions and the associated meeting structures they use.

Medistar

Clinicians at the Medistar meetings are taught beside the faculty in a way that mirrors their initial training experience as fellows: hands-on and with space to ask questions. The teaching fits how standard-setters see themselves. These doctors don't see themselves as slavishly recording details of a procedure, and they think of themselves as working in an inductive manner; they take fresh observations, and then study whether they can be more generally observed. Then, they disseminate their findings to other clinicians less interested or, capable of, the science. As Fred Malcolm, one of the highest-status EPs in the profession, put it:

> Mark Jackson taught me that you question everyone else's work. He used to tell me, "Fred, we're not scientists. We're phenomenologists. We're in the business of observing and relating the observations and telling people the phenomenon we observed. And how to make things better because of it. . . .
>
> "If you're in an academic environment you think, 'Do I need to learn everything? Or do I need to get a comfort level, and then get used to it?' Making the judgment about something new takes a little bit of extra effort. And you have to be reeled in, and put in an environment where you feel, 'Hey, it's not that bad and it's not that hard, [and] I can see from a practical standpoint where it might have an advantage, and that's why I might want to use it. So I'll go back and use it.'"

This model of discovery resembles that enacted by the naturalist scientists who did not seek to fit everything they saw into existing theory.[9] For this inductive work, their labs must offer an environment that facilitates the development and use of their good hands with the technology.

Medistar put trainees in an apprentice-like environment where they could learn about the signals that should be considered significant when conducting the procedure once they return to their labs. Medistar gives standard-setters the freedom to teach the clinicians their mode of practice. During their instruction, there was no trace of the company representatives. Everything necessary for a smooth procedure had been put in place long before the doctors entered the laboratory. The standard-setters, who are in

Figure 6.4. A medical technology representative places a hand on a clinician's hand to orient his fingers properly on the sheath used to insert a catheter into the heart. Photograph by David Schalliol.

control of the lab, expect deference. Thus, the industry representatives need to give the doctors space to facilitate their focus on the lab's central tasks and demonstrate the expertise that gives them status.

> The faculty member leans over his first short-term protégé. Like much of the guidance the company has enabled him to offer, this instruction seems intended to strengthen his relationship with his trainee. "So the key is, whenever you have your hands on the catheter, you usually have two fingers on the sheath and you transmit your torque." The doctor moves his hands atop those of the clinician. "So your natural instinct when you see that on fluoro is to do ninety more. And if you do not see it moving you do ninety more. So then you have 270- and 360-degree views."
>
> The significance of this snapshot is in its familiarity. Clinicians, even those who completed fellowship long ago, are placed in a similar apprentice-like role configuration. The representative is largely invisible, arranging the catheters, checking the pig's blood pressure; in the background, invisible to the others in the lab. He is informed but deferential, himself also taking on a familiar role—the one he plays in laboratory visits. In the same way that he gives

the faculty the chance, earlier, to depart from textbook knowledge in the lecture, he lets them convey their own "pearls" at the bedside. The clinician, standard-setter, and industry representative all act in ways that resemble their practices in the training venue.[10]

With Medistar, the doctors are given ample time to learn how to read the screens, building up their ability to perform for their temporary teacher. The faculty member is able to emphasize the perils of perforation without overstating the difficulty of the procedure. (He avoids spooking the doctors into passivity in the procedure or making them think they should simply revert to providing their patients with drugs.) As in the academic setting, he is able to take however long he feels is necessary to walk through the steps. In facilitating this teaching, the company uses him as a tether to a well-respected lab.

The trainees ask questions whose answers can only be learned at work. Inevitably the faculty answer most questions, then, with "it depends," or by teaching their personal strategies to the doctors. Thus, questions such as "Can you pretty much do the same manipulations whether you're transseptal or retrograde?" lead to answers such as "This is one of the most difficult things, when you're in the left atrium, because you go around the corner there, which tends to catch the catheter. One of the tricks you can use is to lock the catheter when you go into the atrium." In its highly personal quality, the expertise conveyed here mirrors the skepticism conveyed in the hospital in the morning meetings.

This teaching model can be seen in the weekend's most interesting exchange, at the end of a lecture and provoked by a set of questions from one of the faculty members on the subject of validating a new catheter technology. The episode involves the same type of evidence-based and skepticism-driven colloquy we've seen in previous chapters, but it has transformed to accommodate the presence of the technology representative and the role of the technology. Here the representative has claimed its new catheter to be as effective as the one this faculty member currently uses. Yet the kind of evidence that has been deployed to this point is clearly not adequate, and the standard-setter seeks something more. Specifically, Medistar's previous technology failure had left Dr. Shah, a speaker at the meeting, wary of whether he and his colleagues had a sufficiently strong legal defense if the technology were to fail again. Medistar plays an important role in the doctors' ability to maintain their capacity to defend themselves in legal proceedings and thus strengthen the occupational project with patients and referring physicians in a region. Dr. Shah uses the technology but is not satisfied with the data available to support it. Having research findings at hand helps physicians feel more confident upgrading to new technologies.

Solid data are critical in court cases should complications arise. As shown in the previous chapter, this concern about legal action is widely shared.

> The representative is describing a new catheter that is cooled internally to prevent the accumulation of "char" on heart tissue. Medistar considers this catheter, the "Cooler," an upgrade from one that prevented char through constantly spraying cold water through its tip.
>
> Rep 1: "It is incumbent upon Medistar to use the scientific studies to prove to you that this has the same efficacy as well as having minimal problems in terms of its complications compared with the open-irrigated catheter."
>
> Dr. Shah, the faculty member, jumps in. "So, why don't you compare?"
>
> Rep 1: "The reason, Doctor, to be perfectly candid with you, is that *the company* thought rather than to go directly into a clinical study and do the head-to-head, let's give the physicians the choice. And *they* took the path of least resistance, to be perfectly honest."
>
> Dr. Shah responds: "So you're going to do a head-to-head with your open irrigated versus Cooler, right?"
>
> Rep 2 intervenes: "Possibly. And it should be done, *we* should have a head-to-head, in my opinion. *We* should do an 8 millimeter, *we* should do internal irrigated, *we* should do the competitors of the MasterBurn catheter."
>
> Dr. Shah: "I use the Cooler 2 for afibs and think it works better than MasterBurn, but if I ever get into trouble I'll be sued for sure, because some idiot's going to come and say I should be using an open-irrigated catheter because there's no data for Cooler. But you guys don't want to do that study."
>
> Rep 1: "There's no question, doctor. It's a mea culpa on *our* part. *We* should have done the head-to-head between the open irrigated and the Cooler. *We* should have. *We* didn't do it."

Beyond its emphasis on responsibility, this response from the Medistar representative is satisfying to the doctors also because of the deferential sentiments it exposes. The use of status markers such as "Dr. Shah" reflects the language a representative would deploy in a lab visit. "Doctor" is the Elizabethan "thou" in public displays between company representatives and the physicians from whom they desire legitimacy. By taking the trainee role in the pimping administered by the standard-setter, the representative provides clear signals of deference. This compliance is important because it tempers the information asymmetry—and its potential consequences for inconsistencies in status—between the representatives and the doctors.

According to conversations with clinicians after the meeting, the representatives' deference—exhibited through vocabulary and awareness of the desire for head-to-head testing—strengthened their company's veracity, because it appears that their interests aligned with the standard-setters'. Beyond showing that the company knows the evidentiary gold standard, the representative's use of language shows them actively resisting overstating their claims and plainly admitting they can fail. The company is doing that because the standard-setter has pursued the issue. To these doctors, the company shares the sense of responsibility they feel for the patients they treat.[11]

As a result of the autonomy given to the standard-setter, and the company's reenactment of the expert-trainee and expert-representative lab relationships, the doctors were very positive about experimenting with Medistar's technologies and techniques, a sentiment reflected in their framing the meeting as an educational experience. Consider the following evaluation by a fellow, who said he came to the meeting even though his teachers would not.

> DM: "Does this meeting make you feel better, the same, or worse about Medistar as a company?"
>
> Fellow: "Overall, their marketing strategy is, in part, to improve their goodwill. Because they fucked that up a few years ago. They are not going to change the minds of attendings that were out at that time. What they can do is increase the goodwill with us. This is good because they are probably one of the least biased companies out there. 'Cause you know that even though they are trying to be unbiased and not talking about their products, there are still some subliminal—you're still improving goodwill. But, I think it's fine to improve goodwill if you're doing stuff to support education. Nothing wrong with that."
>
> DM: "So you don't have any reluctance to use their products in the same way that someone four or five years ago would have?"
>
> Laughing, the fellow continues: "Well, it's not like it's our choice though. It's our attendings'. But that's the thing—my attendings don't use them at all. That shows an immense amount of goodwill, that they're still supporting me despite the fact that we don't use any of their devices."

As shown here, the doctor feels that the company is "supporting education" because it is willing to teach them without concern, from his perspective, for financial gain. The tethers Medistar used were acceptable. The word *ed-*

ucation came up repeatedly that weekend; it was clear that the clinicians were more than willing to defer to Medistar, who had facilitated a strong relationship with standard-setters. Another symptom of the positive feelings Medistar elicited was that the doctors were willing to begin giving it feedback, which could inform the development of new technologies, an often time-consuming activity involving periodic trips to company headquarters. Several young doctors said they would consider sitting on an advisory board. Finally, clinicians also allowed Medistar to organize an advice-giving email list in which they subsequently exchanged stories about tough cases in their labs. As expressed in post-meeting interviews, good feelings about the company were nearly universal.[12]

For the participating clinicians, the Medistar meeting was a success. Medistar arranged educational opportunities for clinicians that cleanly mapped onto their expectations for teaching and industry relationships. Students freely manipulated the catheter and how it was represented on the monitor, all under the watchful eye of a standard-setter, who provided them useful tips. During the lecture portion of the meeting Medistar was prepared with responses to experts' provocations; they took ownership of shortcomings and acted deferentially. In an attempt to overcome past failures, Medistar organized the event as one that promoted the didactic relationship between standard-setters and clinicians and positioned itself as a helpful tool to this relationship. As a result, the doctors felt that the meeting was organized to reinforce the relationship between clinicians and the experts, strengthening the occupational project.

Medicore

While the lecture components of both Medistar's and Medicore's meetings were similar, the hands-on portions differed. Unlike the faculty-led teaching that Medistar provided, Medicore's educational director shepherded clinicians through various activity stations that were, at best, pantomimes of clinical work. One station had an ablation catheter that was submerged in water in order to simulate its performance when submerged in blood. Another station had a pig's heart pinned to a board—the anatomy was labeled as if in a high school biology class. At a third stop was a simulator in which participants could move a catheter into a plastic blue box shaped like a coffin, watching on a screen as the catheter navigated through its pseudo-anatomy—the experience was more like an arcade than surgery.

During these activities, faculty members were largely out of slight. Thus, the apprenticeship relationships—the one that clinicians touted so heavily at Medistar's meetings—were absent, the company and standard-setters exerting no control over indeterminacy. Instead, Medicore's meeting felt more like a high school science fair than an opportunity for professional development.

Clinicians came to Medicore's meeting with the expectation of interacting with standard-setters who would guide them through approved uses of the technology. They anticipated seeing how standard-setters had organized indeterminacy with these tools; they sought to learn their technique and conclusions rather than personally scrutinize Medicore's devices. Thus the Medicore meeting placed clinicians in a position that is outside their wheelhouse and contradictory to the medical hierarchy in which they function. In many ways, Medicore's efforts were off-putting. When clinicians asked questions during the lecture before the activity sessions, the leader of the meeting often responded: "Write it down and test it tomorrow!" In response to a later question she repeats the message: "This is a very nice experiment you can do tomorrow."

The administrator's repeated invocations made her intentions clear: the clinicians were to experiment. Her answers positioned clinicians as researchers who were to engage in a process of inference and hypothesis-testing. But, for clinicians, this position was antithetical to their role. In their practices, they are not supposed to experiment with new technology to test hypothesis. That is the work of specialized standard-setters who have access to laboratories and have devoted their careers to this kind of inquiry. Instead, clinicians had come to the meeting curious about the new technology and hoping to learn directly from the experts, the individuals who have organized indeterminacy and mastered a skill. From the perspective of the clinician, if there was a scientist in attendance, it was the invited standard-setter. Consequently, they wanted to hear about the technology's merits as a tool in achieving a successful operation from a seasoned practitioner, someone able to show them what to do in their everyday work scenarios.

Rather than see the event as educational, then, based on their perceptions shared with me after the meeting, the clinicians came to see it in the same way the company did—as promotion and as singularly serving Medicore's feedback needs. According to doctors, the tasks then seemed like they were intended to reinforce the relationship between the clinicians and the company, rather than clinicians and standard-setters. The clinicians were expected to learn new skills without the expert's guidance. These expectations erode the work of the field, because it does not resemble the practice of medicine. In their meeting, Medicore asked all attendees to be responsible for a leadership position in terms of the organization of indeterminacy, a request the clinicians felt was incongruent with their social location.

Because there could only be up to four doctors at each of five stations, and because a company rep continuously needed to maintain the more technology-intensive stations, there were some less compelling tasks to occupy the doctors between stations. The company had the doctors watch a movie in which a German scientist dissects a heart. One of the EPs made the doctors' reaction to the movie clear: "Am I the only one who can't pay attention to this?" One of the administrators came into the room where we watched the movie. "Did you already watch this?" Another EP responded, "We could never watch this more than once." This didactic approach to learning, conducted in the absence of a standard-setter, bore no resemblance to the kind of instruction to which participants were accustomed. Not only did the doctors find this mode of isolated and passive knowledge transmission deeply unattractive, they were not reticent to share this dissatisfaction with their peers.

At the Medistar meeting, faculty members were foregrounded and the administrators were invisible. In contrast, at the Medicore meeting, company representatives were continuously involved in tasks related to preparing the lab: assembling, dismantling, and maintaining the stations; resetting the simulator; replacing dissected hearts with fresh ones; repairing the frequent malfunctions from the ablation catheter. In designing a situation where the doctors were to learn from personally experimenting with the technology, the company repeatedly came between the standard-setter and trainee.

In sessions, Medicore's actions did not allow standard-setters to develop control using tethers. Both the faculty and company employees gave lukewarm responses when the technology created by a Medicore competitor was mentioned.

> During a presentation a clinician asks, "What do you think about the balloon?"
>
> The standard-setters mutter, "I'm skeptical of the data." They respond in a similarly guarded fashion when asked about a product from another company, Medivac.
>
> Later, in the swine lab, a frustrated clinician unhappy with the technology's performance asks about a product made by a competitor. "I need a sheath [from a competitor]."
>
> The head of the program, Hanna, responds with "Shhh, can't say that."

In interviews, the clinicians said they believed that these discussions—in stark contrast with Medistar's demonstration of success in practice and their openness to the idea of a head-to-head trial with their competition—involved a high level of company control, rather than faculty control, of the meetings. Clinicians wanted to see Medicore engage an accurate, measured conversation about their products. Instead, the response from Hanna precluded the neutrality and adjudication the field expects of practitioners, especially its standard-setters. The deferential persona expected of industry was absent, and the standard-setters were not put in a position where they could protect clinicians from undue influence.

Beyond interrupting the traditional mentorship model between standard-setters and clinicians in its training session, Medicore also simulated a different kind of laboratory relationship between the EP and the representative. The relationship between the representative and doctor is never one of equality, yet, in the meeting, Medicore situated itself as a source of expert knowledge by saying, for instance, "We'll help you learn . . ." For clinicians, medical device companies are facilitators, not teachers. In her approach, the director attempted to convey a personal relationship, distancing the company from any impression of seeking undue influence on clinicians. For physicians, keeping industry on the sidelines of medicine is a necessary goal. Generally, attending meetings allows clinicians to learn from high-status sources, who have at least the appearance of neutrality. But, by injecting itself into the meeting as an educator, Medicore bluntly toppled accepted convention.

Ultimately, Medicore's efforts created lasting damage. Doctors gave extremely negative evaluations of Medicore. For example, clinician Dr. Balstin declared that he was not able to see the distinct advantage of its technology over drugs; Medicore and its standard-setters were not sufficiently compelling in their efforts at organizing the indeterminacy around the idea of performing ablation for atrial fibrillation.

> "Sometimes the more you know about a procedure, the less emphatic you're going to be about what a decision is." Lowering his voice, he continues. "It's not like somebody's got appendicitis, it's ruptured, and the way to fix it is to get the appendix out. [In that case] it's clear, that's what you should do.
>
> "I mean, we're talking about a procedure with complications. The risks are greater than trying an antihypertensive [drug] that doesn't work. So [in those cases] you stop and change. Big deal. So when you're considering a procedure with up-front risk that is going to change your patient's quality of life, then you need to be sure the risk is worth it. This isn't the only way to treat the problem. And the cure isn't known. So it demands a much harder decision than appendicitis, where the known cure is to get it out of there. Broken bone, you fix it. Or nose, you don't. I think ablation for afib opens up a whole can of worms."

As this example shows, Medicore influenced the practice of medicine, but not in the way it had hoped. Dr. Balstin would not accept the practices described by the company and standard-setter, a surprising outcome in light of his self-selection into the training. At the end of the meeting, Dr. Balstin remained unconvinced of the benefits of using catheter ablation over drugs or implantable defibrillators for regulating atrial fibrillation. Other doctors, too, were consistent in their skepticism of the company. For Medicore, it is damning that their technology is seen as excessively risky rather than promising, especially in light of the field's generally favorable disposition toward risk.

While Medistar was able to harness the influence standard-setters hold in the field—and display deference to them—Medicore, in contrast, attempted to topple the traditional medical training structure and assert itself as an arbitrator of indeterminacy. By doing so, Medicore uncomfortably positioned participating clinicians outside their normal location in medicine's stratification structure.

Medicore's program looked little like the training venue clinicians are accustomed to, which hampers learning. Additionally, the company didn't put standard-setters into positions where they could use tethers. To be successful in their role, standard-setters must be able to teach new practices to clinicians. Ultimately, had Medicore recognized the mutually beneficial relationship between standard-setters and clinicians, it might have been able to position itself as a valuable link between the two. Instead, it was seen as superimposing itself onto the role of educator, decimating its chances of being widely embraced by clinicians. Ultimately, Medicore's approach also has the potential to have a negative impact on the field more generally. By not harnessing the power of standard-setters to gauge the capacity of participant clinicians, Medicore runs the risk of putting its technology in the hands of a "007." By sidelining standard-setters at the hands-on meetings, Medicore stripped itself of a valuable intermediary.

Conclusion

For EPs, the adoption of technology is constitutive, thereby requiring them to adjudicate solutions. This chapter has described a venue for this task. The venue is purposefully constructed to facilitate mutual observations between industry and physicians. The impressions clinicians have of the sponsoring firms shape the approximately $200 billion medical devices industry.

The hands-on meeting, where clinicians come to remain literate with cutting-edge technologies, involves a reinstantiation of how doctors are taught from the beginning. How doctors see medicine is how they have always done it—even in the conference venue, they are doing what they always do. They work in an interdependent network relationship, where standard-setters organize indeterminacy, and clinicians have access to them.

Like many other physicians, electrophysiologists have long looked to industry for lessons on new technologies—after all, medical professionals

Figure 6.5. Clinicians at the hands-on meeting watch a slide presentation by a standard-setter, at which they take notes, sometimes pose questions, and compare their own solutions to what is suggested here. Photograph by David Schalliol.

rarely create the treatments they recommend. Rather, doctors mediate between private companies and their customers: companies offer new technologies, and customers request new treatments. Whereas celebrities and professional athletes choose whether to endorse a product, party, or person, physicians endorse new (and old) products simply as a consequence of their state-mandated gatekeeping role.

Beyond the doctor's experiences, a set of relationships between industry, standard-setting doctors, clinicians, and the state determine if a physician adopts a technology. The hands-on meeting represents a key place where new technology and its associated practices are introduced. Before doctors are even allowed to adopt some technologies, the FDA requires they complete a training program that is sponsored and organized by industry. By law, new drugs and technologies cannot be promoted without physicians' assistance as prescribers and operators. Even if referring physicians and patients have heard about and requested these technologies, the clinicians need to be trained before using them. To get the endorsement of doctors and introduce them to new technologies in a way approved by the FDA, a company invites standard-setters and clinicians from all over the field to its physician training programs, offering a key interface between clinicians and standard-setters.

The different attitudes of trainees toward companies and their technologies, if we compare the two sample meetings, suggest that this stratified mentorship structure is an important influence on clinicians' attitudes about company technologies. The effectiveness of the company depended on how it supported the use of tethers. In one case, the company set up architecture supporting the field's internal processes of training and technology evaluation. In the other, the company tried to impose its own processes. The Medistar meeting clearly facilitated industry's deference toward participants as well as faculty members' apprentice-like teaching approaches. To establish hierarchy between the standard-setters, the fellows and clinicians, and the industry reps (as we saw in chapter 3 on good hands and the hierarchical structure of the lab), the company representatives took a deferential position to the faculty speakers when they presented their content. The company also encouraged the same turn-taking linguistic structure of exchanges during talks as in the lab or at the fellows programs. It produced autotelic experiences where clinicians could fluidly learn to see how the patient's anatomy was featured on the fluoroscopy's black-and-white monitor. As a consequence, they could easily handle the tools and assist each other.

In the Medicore meeting the clinicians were less positive toward the company and its technologies. It put the doctors in the role of standard-setter, a role inconsistent with how they view their tasks. Instead, the clinicians expected to be able to learn at the foot of their instructors. They attended the meeting to be put at ease with the technology by trustworthy mentors.[13] Clinicians don't want to do independent work outside of the purview of the faculty—their goal is to learn enough from these doctors to repair a common condition or diagnose and refer away a complex one. When not given this opportunity, the doctors felt negative about the new technology. These cases suggest that for doctors to take on new technologies and practices in the years following formal training, it is important for associated knowledge to be communicated in a way that reinforces the preexisting stratification system.

Ethnography and interview-based research always has its limits, and causality is always challenging to identify. The two meetings described in the latter half of the chapter reflect a small number of respondents. Yet they do describe some of the processes seen elsewhere in the occupational project. For this reason, my deductions of the "success" or "failure" of these companies are intended to be weak inferences; the perfect data would involve longer-term adoption rates by those attending the meetings. Still, the interviewees offered up informative accounts of the more or less positive experiences that shape their attitudes about the company. Such observations, while perhaps not sufficient for conclusive claims about what works or doesn't, offer an important look at the factors organizing the management of authority.

This chapter demonstrated that whether and how a company allows for the use of tethers is important to standard-setters who bring in their approach to organizing indeterminacy. The ability of standard-setters to use tethers also assists in the development of relationships that lead to the adoption of technology and the strengthening of authority. This chapter showed how tethers are used to improve the status of standard-setters and protect the reputation of companies, thereby contributing to the occupational project. Standard-setters describe and promote contested anatomy (e.g., the "antrum"), thereby diminishing the standing of status-seeking peers. By questioning the terminology others have used, they embolden their own approaches to organizing indeterminacy. Standard-setters also use technologies as tethers when they show clinicians how to carry out everyday techniques. And company reps, in contributing to the occupational project, use standard-setters as tethers to try to prevent the use of their technology by clinicians who might fail with it.

seven

The International
Annual Meeting

Global-Local Feedback, and Setting Standards for

Problems and Solutions

As we've seen, medicine's standard-setters meet in an array of venues to socialize the next generation of trainees and clinicians, to access and spread new ideas, and to try to raise their standing. Yet the views of cardiology that these venues offer are partial: there, only some players attend. The next step for understanding how authority is managed is to return again to how physicians strengthen the occupational project as a whole, which occurs as they compete for status and other resources, which will let them use tethers to control tasks.

A central place where this competition is observed, and the focus of this chapter, is the annual meeting of the professional associations for electrophysiology and cardiology. In the two venues previously described, doctors have access to only a select few others with whom they might generate and share observations. In contrast to their hospital's home lab and industry-sponsored meetings, the annual conferences of the American College of Cardiology (ACC) and of the Heart Rhythm Society (HRS) are events where big names gather. Each meeting runs for four days and is held annually. The annual conference might be closest to the electrophysiologists' "public sphere," in which they meet to share their accomplishments and discuss new practice-related changes that are used as tethers to connect venues. Cardiologists from around the world attend to hear about new technology and research findings, reunite with friends and colleagues, and hold meetings for groups that have been communicating virtually for months. Attendees who are not doctors are leaders of advocacy organizations seeking to collaborate with standard-setters, as well as industry reps trying to sell products and services. Activities include competitive games, lectures, debates, committee meetings on guidelines, and gossip—and in all of them, physicians and industry reps are strengthening the occupational project.

The annual meetings' tasks also have a range of doctors and industry reps interacting with each other to strengthen the occupational project. Here standard-setters can integrate influences from the state, companies, research, and even activist communities, in organizing indeterminacy. Participants in these venues reiterate knowledge developed in hospitals, but they're also providing doctors with knowledge to use there. In some venues (like the exhibition hall), stakeholders seek to gain material for everyday practice; in others (like the guidelines committee meetings) they are seeking to establish the contours of such practices. At these annual meetings, interpersonal evaluations are developed in industry-organized sales pitches, structured debates among opposing camps, person-to-person interactions, and in colleague-structured gossip networks. It shows us some of medicine's many stakeholders who are vying for influence. These stakeholders include individuals and groups inside of medicine (e.g., cardiac surgery), those who want to be recognized by medicine (e.g., social movements), and those outside medicine (e.g., the state).

On the face of it, such meetings are surprising. There are a range of stakeholders, much of the information can be shared through other means, and they are very expensive to attend and enact. And it has been said that these annual meetings are not good for much. As we'll see, there is a lot of advertising and socializing going on, which certainly makes this perspective plausible. However, in spite of these seemingly extraneous activities—or, as I'll suggest, in part because of them—these meetings offer an informative window into the overall social organization of medicine. And beyond the event's value for the sociologist, the physician also walks away from these conferences with experiences that feed back into their work and that offer both individual and collective benefits.

This chapter, then, while set in a specific place and time, gives us a 10,000-foot view of EP. First, on the floor of the exhibition hall, it's possible to see that companies are involved in supporting how indeterminacy is organized, and that they do so by reiterating with clinicians the latest understanding of problems and solutions involving their drugs and devices. By displaying key values of the occupational project—good hands, quotable statistics, quickness, and communal success—these companies are able to engage clinicians in familiar modes and arm them with information to bring back to their hospitals in order to argue for investments in technology. Second, in the debates, we can see multiple ways this indeterminacy is organized, and how standard-setters argue for one or another way by reflecting the research agenda that brought them status in the occupational project. Third, status competition is a preoccupation in these social events, where the

Figure 7.1. The exhibition hall of the venue of the annual meeting, seen from outside. Photograph by Carlos Javier Ortiz.

Figure 7.2. A complex display on the floor of the annual meeting's exhibition hall. Photograph by Carlos Javier Ortiz.

standard-setters, clinicians, and fellows share stories about companies and other doctors. The standard-setters tell stories in ways that enhance status—especially relative to those in other, similar venues—through telling horror stories about other companies (from whose failures they have protected colleagues), and through disparaging other standard-setters (whose research they think is suspect). Finally, doctors' overarching concern about status is revealed in the measures taken in setting the guidelines; because all have their own approaches to organizing indeterminacy, a central goal is to create a document that appears to be neutral.

In these venues, multiple interactions are going on that reinforce the occupational project, but the organization of those interactions is less clear. The doctors must collectively communicate with those outside the occupational project about how they have organized indeterminacy as a part of managing their authority, while also consolidating power and reinforcing best practices from the inside.

The Annual Meeting's Pastiche of Tasks

I am here at the American College of Cardiology annual international meeting. I hear the song "The Rhythm Divine." More so than in any other venue, when I walk in to the convention center, it is made immediately evident that medical work involves a range of activities that don't immediately appear to be what we think of as "work."

> The exhibition hall is buzzing with the efforts of industry. Hanging banners praise the virtues of companies that will have booths in the exhibition hall. Stands provided by the sponsor encourage me to connect by uploading the conference program into my Blackberry. Signs beside the escalator with walking animated heart images read, "Be heart healthy, use the stairs!" Shoeshines are five dollars.
>
> The shoeshines are the least expensive component of the event, at least from the perspective of those industry reps seeking to catch a doctor's eye. All of the companies at this venue want the physicians' attention. Companies with $25,000 to spend have chosen between putting up a banner in the lobby of the convention center or sponsoring the turn-down service at the conference hotel. The device company with the deepest pockets has spent $542,000 to rent a booth in the center of the exhibition hall. Another company, selling a high-end blender they hope cardiologists will promote with patients, makes its case from a $3,500 booth in a location farther afield. And, in the hall's distant corner, a lone representative stands at the $100 booth of the Association for the Advancement of Medical Instrumentation.[1]

If expensive for sponsors, I cringe in recalling how much it cost me to attend. Some of this money goes toward subsidizing the development of the program; as I learned when invited by the organizing committee to speak about the diffusion of medical innovations, invited speakers pay neither the modest $30 submission fee for those wanting their paper or poster presentation considered, nor the hefty registration fee, which ranges from $725 for ACC members to $1,999 for those who do not practice medicine.

In the convention center's exhibition hall, I hear noisy game playing, excited shouts in unexpected meetings among old friends, and the hushed tones of gossip. I also glimpse doctors discussing that evening's parties, as well as entering closed and branded doors off the exhibition floor.

There, device companies seek physicians to study their products: "Interested in being involved in a trial as an investigator?" Former college cheerleaders with dime-size diamond rings hand out free pens and personalized mouse pads. These are not the ex-nurses and ex-engineers who work with EPs in the home lab. They stand near shirtless male models with electrodes on their chests. In addition to the conference swag, free smoothies are handed out and large brass espresso machines dole out generous shots.

Stimulation is not the sole marketing tool; there are also articles. I am handed a USB drive that later turns out to have thirty clinical research studies supporting a company's new technology. Sales representatives distribute folders full of journal articles with initial findings from clinical trials their companies have sponsored. Results have been framed in a highly usable fashion, wielding unambiguous recommendations that sweep aside the variation of patients' everyday lives. They indicate how study findings have been integrated into practice guidelines. As they tell me, these articles can serve as artillery for physicians needing support for new purchases.

In booths where the more valuable—but still free—products are given away, the space has been designed to keep you around for a few minutes. In one booth, the representative snaps your picture in a lab coat, converts the image into a sign for communicating office hours and policy ("Cellular phones are not permitted to be used inside the office"), and takes a moment to frame it. Many give you a pen engraved with your name. These customized freebies are not without strings: the delay for their production costs five or ten minutes of your time, usually spent waiting alongside the company's exhibits. Choosing to sit down puts one in the representative's territory, and a moment of rest usually leads to an introduction by someone looking to talk technology.

These more affluent companies work hard to capture attention in terms that doctors can understand by appealing to their competitive natures. When they meet you, they introduce you to the quizzes they would like you to take and the information monitors they would like you to see. Their booth has plush carpeting, contrasting with the more austere booth for the "high powered, heart healthy" smoothie machine.

Seeking to avoid being recruited into participating in a game show—and thus averting my eyes like so many students after a professor's question—I wander from booth to booth, between the plush, padded carpets of the rich companies to the hard floors beneath the tables of the advocacy groups. I meet Mary Teller, an activist and the founder of a patient advocacy organization, in a booth donated by the Heart Rhythm Society. She stands beside a laptop computer, which is displaying a web page link to videos of standard-setters who have volunteered to explain their approach to organizing indeterminacy, describing the problems and solutions involved ("Afib Master Class with Evan Price"). She is talking to one of the many clinicians who have expressed curiosity. Dr. Banth says he had recognized her name and that he has directed his patients to her website. After the doctor leaves, and before our conversation is once again interrupted by interested physicians, she proudly points out, "One of the comments that I hear from patients all the time is, 'Doctors say stay off the Internet, only listen to me.'" As another physician introduces himself, she continues: "Would you like some cards to take to give to your patients to send them there to the site? It tells on the back what kinds of resources they'll find on the site. And here are the instructions for getting a free listing in our 'AFib services locator.'" Mary directs me to a monitor displaying her website, on which she points out a video of an interview she conducted with Dr. Evan Price, a standard-setter interested in describing the benefits of his approach to ablation. She gives me a tour of her website, taking particular care to point to the policies for maintaining a "brick wall" between the site's corporate donors and those who provide the news coverage on developments in EP.

As I leave the exhibition hall, I find a television, this one featuring standard-setters, including Dr. Stimm, who had been interviewed by CTV (Cardiology TV). A mustached interviewer asks Dr. Stimm about opportunities for EP practitioners in the conference. He engages in an extended discussion of the conference's features, pointing out the special live broadcasts of colleagues' labs, the cases that will be discussed, and the meeting's centerpiece: the "late breaking trials" sessions where the findings of clinical trials are released.

The applause and excited talking from a nearby conference hall suggest that the results of those late-breaking trials will soon be announced. These sessions, along with the live cases and the expert debates, are the conference's most popular events. As I move from the exhibition hall to the conference hall, I move from a venue organized around selling, and into one organized around emulation. Once there, not long after seeing Dr. Stimm on CTV, I see him at a podium in front of thousands. With the exception of the "conflict of interest" slide, which has a built-in ten-second timer and unreadable 12-point font, these talks share little in common with others at the conference. The moment the presentation begins, the information presented here is going to be published simultaneously on the site of a top journal; three of the sessions are co-sponsored by the *Journal of the American College of Cardiology* (*JACC*), the *Journal of the American Medical Association* (*JAMA*), and the *New England Journal of Medicine* (*NEJM*). But these clinical trial results are being offered to clinicians directly at the conference. And so, doctors hold up their digital cameras to catch shots of the slides projected on the forty-foot-tall screen.

This performance is as much rock concert as it is scholarly presentation. The lights fade in, focusing everyone's attention on the screens hanging above. The loudspeaker blasting "All I need is the rhythm . . ." quiets as the presenting doctors take the stage. The statistical tables and bar charts all have a musical accompaniment. At the talk's close, the applause is heavy.

At the conference, the clinical trial results are offered to a professional public, but they do not scoop the journals—the first speaker points out that the trial was published in the *New England Journal of Medicine* just two minutes ago. The legions of clinicians in the audience would be reluctant to try the new technologies and practices until they come out through these presentations, and the association's embargo arrangement also protects the standard-setters' standing by ensuring that findings are reported through appropriate and long lasting channels. The reporting of the details of the trials is itself dramatic. Statistical significance is reported slowly, with their levels arriving individually on the screen. Point. Zero. Zero. One.

Figure 7.3. At a slide presentation at the annual meeting, an attendee preserves an image of the slides. Conference attendees often capture images of slides so that, for instance, they can contact the presenter later or share with colleagues in their home hospital. Photograph by Carlos Javier Ortiz.

Cell phones rise with each slide. Even though the presentation's figures and tables are immediately published online, the doctors and drug representatives tell me they will use their cell phone images–rather than the cleaner ones available online–in their own presentations; clearly they want to highlight their presence at this venue. Some say they will use them to relay conference highlights. Others indicate they will use them to make a case to their hospital for investing in a technology.

My cell phone buzzes with activity. Medistar is tweeting the positive news: "the long awaited CYCLONE trial: Cycle ablation is non-inferior!" "lively discussion on whether cycles can move VT-ablation from 2nd line to 1st line therapy" "Just announced: Cycle and PVI had similar consequences. Learn more @ our booth." I open a browser and see that Medistar's stock has just risen 1.7 percent.

After the presentation, it is time to discuss implications for practices and the field's knowledge base. The PIs of the study answer questions about their thoughts regarding changing everyday medical care. What I'm seeing is very much like the description of his own experience that Dr. Bellard had offered in an interview:

They have five huge screens [and] like 10,000 people, and then there was a panel of people from all around the world that just grill you—it's almost like your dissertation defense. And then they have a five-minute rebuttal and somebody from Europe gave his perspective—whether he agreed or disagreed. It was a big deal, it was a really big deal. The *New England Journal* [*of Medicine*] loved the paper so much that they embargoed it, and wanted it to be released the day of the presentation—a simultaneous release. And I finished the final revision a week before, and one of the editors said that they had never turned a paper around in the *New England Journal* as fast as they had for this one.

> The knowledge in the trial results is not left in an abstracted form. The talks involve a discussant who turns these trial results into normative claims that can inform clinical practices. Discussants—who are either general cardiologists or EPs who embody the roles of scientist, clinician, and editorial writer—contextualize the finding with respect to some of the other trials, as well as the usual conditions observed in the clinic. They are sense-makers; they help the doctors in the audience connect and make inferences from the trial about their own patients. In this session, the discussant intervenes, saying, "With this, we should revisit the guidelines, considering also the findings from the COURAGE trial, the ADVANCE trial and others." The speaker responds by mentioning other trials and restates the need to revisit the guidelines. In the clinical results sessions, it is impossible not to notice the constant reassertion of the importance of the evidence and predictions about shifts in practice that are the consequence of such groundbreaking trials.
>
> I've been told that the big names in EP spend little time in the hallways and exhibition floor, knowing that many people want something from them. While their names are in the program, I see very few of them indeed in sessions outside of the keynotes, live cases, and debates. My fellow attendees are mostly doctors with badges from private practices and lower-tier academic medical centers.

In these venues the occupational project seems to be in constant flux, with its future linked to the acceptance of its problems and solutions in its most remote clinics—reminding us how medicine is organized in a dynamic fashion.

The Annual Meeting and the Occupational Project

With all the flash, one might wonder: What is this for? Why would there be a game show at a professional conference? Why would physicians make the trip and take the time to attend a crowded conference session rather than simply open the *New England Journal of Medicine*?

Indeed, a leading medical researcher recently published a piece in *JAMA* entitled "Are Medical Conferences Useful? And for Whom?" In it, he argues that there is little evidence that these meetings effectively train, educate, set evidence-based policy, and disseminate and advance research.[2] "In the electronic age in which information can be shared around the world instantly, the contribution of large medical conferences to the dissemination and advancement of science is unclear." When the meeting is seen as a site for blasting new findings to an undifferentiated mass, this perspective makes sense. However, the merit of these meetings is more evident when viewed as an event organized to feed back into—and reinvigorate support for—physicians' practices. By focusing on just one or two venues, we are unable to explain how the physicians maintain an approach to organizing indeterminacy and establish rules for trainees. This chapter reinforces that not all of peers' regulation and affirmation of practices happens in the laboratory and hospital. Much of it exists in exchanges among colleagues onstage and while socializing. But in contrast to fellows programs and industry-sponsored meetings, the annual meeting's venues demonstrate how standard-setters' approaches to organizing indeterminacy directly interact with one another.

Cardiologists' annual meetings reveal key processes for the management of authority in medicine. Company representatives are engaging the ambitious young and bored older doctors, advocates are seeking to attract attention to their causes, and the principal investigators of major scientific studies are releasing findings, which in turn will be interpreted by their similarly notable colleagues. These characters, and many others helping medicine reconstitute itself, work with the hope that physicians will return to their home labs with a changed or reinforced understanding of medicine's possibilities.

Simulating Clinician Competition and Reiterating Problems and Solutions in Corporate Game Shows

At first glance, trivia games at the conference might seem misplaced, but these contests have important payoffs for the occupational project. In fact, contests work to familiarize the venue for clinicians; the competitive spirit of the game is similar to the rivalries produced in medical school and that may exist at their own hospitals or practices. Because industry is not able to

Figure 7.4. At the annual meeting, a different game show built into the program, on the model of *Jeopardy!*. The fellows are motivated to compete, even if it puts them on the spot, and they choose to engage in this competition. Photograph by author.

Figure 7.5. The *Jeopardy!* game show at the annual meeting. The teams are composed of fellows from different regions, who train in labs with different ideas of optimal problems and solutions. Photograph by author.

use a "hard sell" of technology with EPs at the conference, the game show allows them to inject stats about their products and technology into a learning and socializing opportunity. They do so by communicating to clinicians the problems and solutions developed by doctors who have organized indeterminacy around their drugs and devices. Meanwhile, the doctors are engaging with industry and others on the exhibition floor differently, to mirror practices taking place at the doctors' many other venues. Competition persists—in this venue it's between clinicians. Indeed, the competition can be seen in a kind of microcosm form at the floor's most attractive exhibits. These booths involve hands-on engagement, the kind of action-oriented processes these doctors appreciate. In this section I examine how industry's interactions with doctors are entrained in a way that syncs with the EPs' tasks and their modes of interpersonal engagement generally.

The relationship between doctors and industry is highly interdependent, and even after the multiple days of interaction held, for instance, in the hands-on industry meetings, companies may not win doctors' trust. In a different venue, where companies have only seconds to compete for doctors' attention, who wins and how?

To answer this question, we can investigate which booths attract the most doctors. In the same way that EPs value a deliberate and assertive style with patients and colleagues, their highly interactive nature attracts them to certain industry representatives' booths, and not to others. The most popular booths are highly interactive in a way that parallels chapter 6's well-received hands-on meetings: by providing active, engaging, and relevant lessons.

At the conference I am attending, the most popular site has a game show format and is led by a man with a suit, hair gel, and hands-free microphone. Each of the ten contestant podiums before him is briskly filled, and no seats remain empty across the five rounds of play I observe.

> The game show host launches into his introduction. "Now, folks, up here on the screen is the leader board. You need to have a score higher than 941. Once you get here, the endorsement deals will be rolling in. Nike, Gatorade, Adidas. It will be amazing. These guys in the last round had a bunch of record-breaking scores, it was amazing." Sweeping into a panel in front of a podium, he continues. "In a second I'm going to explain how to up your scores, and will tell you a hint on how I'm going to do that in a moment. . . . If you are familiar with Angiostar, raise your hand." The speaker pauses a beat. "If you're not familiar with Angiostar, raise your hand." Looking very earnest, he continues: "If you've never raised your hand before, raise your hand."

The language of hands predominates, a subtle reminder that good hands are the calling card of any notable clinician. The opening question of the game show reiterates details in the research base supporting the use of Angiostar.

"In the HEALTHY-AMI selection process, patients with cardiogenic shock or left main disease were not excluded. True or false?" The host paces for a few seconds, stopping to glance at a computer screen on his podium. "You have ten seconds to get your answers in. You want to be first, you want to be right, you want to be fast. One second to go. Eight of you said true, two of you said false. Eight of you are correct."

After the players input their answers, he goes straight into the player statistics. Success rates are crucial in the work of EP's, and this is no exception: "Other than Player 4, everyone's still in the game." He points at a doctor in the front row, Player 6, who is elbowing a rival. "Let me remind you that the key to being a high scorer, like this doc, is being a split second faster than everyone else."

The game show host introduces tests contestants on a study that will offer the solution. "HEALTHY-AMI was a prospective double-blind, open-label trial of 3,000 patients undergoing a percutaneous coronary intervention. True or false.

"Oh yeah, the whole board lit up on that one. One hundred percent of you said true, 100 percent are correct. Let's give us all a round of applause. It's always great when everyone gets it right. Player 6, you're on your way to a record-breaking score, you got to keep it up."

The game show music builds up the energy of the contestants. Their engagement with the game allows the speaker to pass along information about the product without running into the trouble of "teaching physicians" that Medicore experienced (as shown in chapter 6). The host is adept at using the language of physicians to drive the competition. His commentary focuses on praising hands, the stats of the players, the quickness of their action, and communal success; in many ways, this game is propped up on the principles of the occupational project.

The second set of questions describes a research study that yielded what this evidence-based trial could fix for patients. Its mode of problem formation is one that is argued to characterize contemporary medicine, where people who feel healthy can be defined otherwise through new tests and treatments that define medical problems without incorporating personal experiences.[3] They begin by establishing factual material on which others can agree.

> "Disrupted atherosclerotic plaque are found beneath approximately what percentage of thrombi responsible for acute coronary syndromes. Is that 19 percent, is that 43 percent, is that 75 percent, or is that 82 percent?" More positive reinforcement follows the answer. "There you go, nice work, some of you are even changing your answers, smart move."

The problem is not self-evident; there is no initial reason to think that electrophysiologists would care about the percentage of thrombi representing disrupted plaque. But this kind of presentation binds the existence of a sole anatomical trait to a health outcome that EP doctors think is negative.

The questions and answers continue, with the doctors quizzed on problems that can be solved with the company's medication-based solution. The quizzes always finish with the implications of failing to use their technology for treatment. Further, the act of highlighting that some contestants changed their answers is an important one and reminds clinicians that medicine is not static. Instead, medicine is iterative. As standard-setters continue to pioneer novel approaches and techniques, clinicians work to adopt and adapt.

> After five minutes of play, the last question arrives. According to one researcher's calculations, how many neurons might be lost for every minute's delay in treatment for an ischemic stroke? Is that half a million, 1.2 million, 1.9 million, 3.2 million?
>
> This final question reflects what nondoctors would consider to be the critical costs of inaction, and the competitors exchange determined glances before buzzing in. "Here we go. Start the timer on this one. You want to be first, you want to be right. This will give you those additional points you need to get onto the leader board. Two seconds left, one second. One person said 500,000, no one said 1.2 million, four of you said 1.9 million, five of you said 3.2 million—and four of you were correct."

Risk has been diagnosed and treated in terms of technologies. The company rep uses findings from the labs of faculty investigators with whom they have developed research partnerships. In the same way that the teaching described in the hands-on meetings is never punitive, there is no pimping of these doctors; reps from technology companies are not attendings. Yet the delivery remains consistent with the Socratic model of education long experienced by the doctors up to this point in their education. Ultimately, this sequence pieces together condition and treatment in a competitive register.

Furthermore, this presentation fits the cognitive template of a field that, in calling out their knowledge and techniques, draws out key features underpinning their tasks and, thus, the terms underpinning their competition.

Electrophysiology, and cardiology more generally, developed alongside changes in diagnostics and treatments. In addition to creating new tasks, jurisdictions, and even professions, technology brings a mindset that emphasizes the process of measurement. Yet the most attractive interactions involve lit-up screens and buttons; they have a visual, technological, and competitive component. Interactions are visceral, too—the doctors have to reach for those buttons. Thus, capturing and keeping the attention of the doctors in the exhibition hall involves activities that require fast hands, as well as being fast with numbers, rates, and other statistics.[4]

By choosing a mode of interacting with clinicians that mirrors their medical training and works to serve the occupational project, industry in this example has successfully achieved their goal of highlighting the advantages of their technology while avoiding the teaching pitfalls Medicore encountered at their meeting. After participating in or watching the game show, clinicians are armed with a repertoire of trivia to make a compelling case to their hospital or clinic's administrators about purchasing technology. As the last question of the quiz show demonstrates, if they are to stay competitive and viable, time is of the essence.

Standard-setters Debating Best Practices
Developed in Their Home Labs

I enter an immense ballroom with rows of chairs, where the most established electrophysiologists are again in view. In debates, some of the meeting's most popular events, two standard-setters will spar about a topic that the moderator has assigned them, but about which they are considered experts. These interactions are sometimes formalized into face-offs between two treatment modalities for a given condition, or they may take a less structured format, intended to showcase different perspectives. The problem, in this episode and others, is the same (ventricular tachycardia), the management approach different (medication or ablation). Overall, the debate is not oriented to one answer; at its end, there is no vote or other way of declaring a winner. Such a resolution is consistent with what we've seen in the home lab: multiple accepted approaches to organizing indeterminacy exist.

Centered around a carefully chosen case, each standard-setter lays out the purest illustration of their approach to organizing indeterminacy. The process of the debates is highly stylized; speakers move from their idea or position to the proof of principle, from there to a set of studies and to the way it is done in patient care (often with their own patients). The structure of interaction moves from general principles into specific practices, in which speakers seek to discuss accounts in the scholarly literature but also hope along the way to show that they appreciate the particularities of everyday clinical practice, often even signaling that they feel their recommendations of "what we should do" may fall closer to their colleague's position than initially indicated. Each debater has twelve minutes to make their case and a three-minute rebuttal period. After the debate, audience members have an opportunity to ask questions.

Debates are valuable for fellows, clinicians, and standard-setters, as all are thinking about how indeterminacy is organized. Fellows are starting to differentiate between experts they have valorized relatively equally in industry meetings. For the clinicians, knowing the latest practices and their evidence base offers a way to think about and talk to patients about treatment options. These rank-and-file physicians in the audience, who have trained with standard-setters who vary in their approaches to organizing indeterminacy, can use these debates for updates on what others in their school of thought are currently doing in terms of both clinical decision-making and technology use. And for standard-setters, creating methodological statements lets them justify practices on the shop floor. As they describe their approach to organizing indeterminacy, there is never a resolution, because they can define multiple outcomes as being high-quality.

The subject of the debate is the "best practice" for managing ventricular tachycardia (VT) and, in particular, whether ablation should be the initial choice for treatment. Gunther Breen, whose position is in support of using medication, led a task force entitled "Pro-arrhythmia and Nonantiarrhythmic Drugs: Regulatory and Clinical Consequences." Although he does not exclusively favor using drugs for arrhythmias, he uses them frequently. Breen's most-cited work is about evaluating the outcomes across different types of procedures. His opponent, David Willets, wrote a textbook in the same year that describes best practices in catheter ablation of atrial fibrillation. Willets's research primarily involves performing ablations. Though both of them conduct both types of work, their most-cited pieces are in the area they will discuss (eight out of ten of Willets's most-cited works are in ablation of atrial fibrillation, while nine out of ten of Breen's most cited works are outside the area of ablation). Each is well respected and highly invested in the position taken in the debate. They hold different commitments in their research lives that anchor the approach to organizing indeterminacy for which they advocate.

The speakers are introduced with the same verve as in the fellows programs, and all of their accolades and research accomplishments are mentioned. Dr. Willets is arguing in support of ablation. Alternative treatments to ablation include medication and device therapy. Dr. Breen has been asked to defend medication-oriented practices, so he heightens the concerns about—but not the benefits of—devices by starting out saying that devices are problematic.

The debate opens with Dr. Breen. "Thank you for coming. This is an extremely important question, the issue of whether VT ablation should be done as a first-line treatment for VT." He begins by anticipating the criticism of one of the alternatives to ablation, the use of devices, which at times shock patients inappropriately. "So, patients who have a single shock are at increased risk of heart failure. All of these things you can ask yourself, 'Is this cause and effect?, Is this simply a heart that's transitioning into a less functional mode, such as ventricular dysfunction?' Certainly for the patient who has a single shock, that is the most reasonable thing, but once one starts getting multiple shocks, it raises a concern that the shock itself may be hazardous . . . one inappropriate shock doubled your mortality. So there's something about shock therapy that is perhaps directly concerning."

Dr. Breen seeks to establish the problem of device-based treatments, which differ from the treatment he is to support (medication). As his presentation continues, he uses studies to heighten skepticism about device therapy, another treatment that the audience might be considering, while raising the audience's concerns about the benefits of ablation, for which Dr. Willets will soon advocate.

After Dr. Willets introduces his talk in the same way, he similarly works through the evidence, deploying and interpreting published findings from his own center, drawing on studies that have occurred in the last three years. (Studies from more than ten years ago are "older.") With the acronyms of their studies running along the bottom of the screen like a stock ticker, the speakers also cite and display diagrams from other papers, pointing out that the same phenomena can be seen at high-status centers.

> After his introduction, Dr. Willets continues, discussing his research. "OK, we saw a highly sick population, advanced disease, nonetheless, pretty good outcomes for patients—marked reductions in VT. And that's typical of many centers, not just ours. The mortality that we saw was about 10 percent for one year, it ranges up to 18 percent for the MasterBurn multicenter trial."

Dr. Willets describes the results of his center's trial, one that he believed reflected a convincing test of his approach, ablation, since it involved patients with extreme conditions. The proportion of patients who died after his trial was lower than the one for his opponent's approach. As he has done this research himself, he is well aware of the work in the area that informed the development of his questions and the areas in which he has contributed. Like his opponent, Dr. Willets presents statistics that the rank-and-file practitioners can give to patients and others for which they might need to defend their decisions. Thus, both speakers hope their talk will rally disciples.

The presentations include a normative component: recommendations of what cardiologists "should do" with a particular diagnosis, based on their own and colleagues' research. In beginning his rebuttal, Dr. Breen recasts Willets's data in an effort to support his own position.

> "Well, ladies and gentlemen, dear David, I think you made the case for antiarrhythmic drugs, if I understand this correctly. Initially when I was invited I was a little bit sorry that I could not talk about catheter ablation, because I would have loved very much to talk about catheter ablation. But actually now, having listened to your talk, I think there are more arguments for drug therapy as a first-line therapy. We are not talking about secondary steps after initial drug therapy. Your data, which you presented from your group, were based on patients that were 86 percent on amiodarone. So everyone was on first-line therapy. So I think we are really lacking valuable data."

He continues, drawing on his opponent's studies to undercut his opponent's argument for his preferred solution. To do so, he chooses endpoints (such as inappropriate shocks) that help strengthen his case that there are bad consequences that stem from Dr. Willets's recommendations.[5]

> "So, David, you made the claim that you would like to have your patients get their ablation earlier than is done today. I sometimes think it takes too long to make a decision to send somebody to the appropriate group to do catheter ablation. But I would like to point out a few things, because you said antiarrhythmic drugs are bad—that is, they are pro-arrhythmia. How should I interpret this here?" Pointing to his slide Dr. Breen notes, "If you look at the EuroVT study, the fail rate at the beginning was 20 percent and if you look a year later, less than 50 percent are really free. So I don't think the success rate is so, so good."

For Dr. Breen, a positive recommendation for treatment arrives, one that is consistent with what he has at stake. Dr. Breen recognizes the multiple ways in which the data Dr. Willets presents can be interpreted, ways that allow him to make his own case. Only at the end of the interaction comes the admission that the recommendation is not straightforward. In reaching a conclusion on a treatment, scientific findings are nonetheless deployed to support a more personally advantageous decision. "I'm going to continue to do x," is a statement that reflects the commitments he has as a researcher, and the kind of practices for which he gets referrals and will be disproportionately rewarded for conducting.

Physicians receive patients one at a time, and when they organize indeterminacy, they need to manage these patients using personalized assessments, not population-based data. The audience expects assistance
with this task from the speakers. Dr. Willets closes:

"Obviously as in any debate, the same data can bring up different conclusions. The future's hard to predict, and I think we can
certainly say there's some uncertainty with the data we have, and
that perhaps we can't make a conclusive argument. Unfortunately
I need to make a decision for my patient today, and the results of
the CEASE-VT trial will be available in about five years. But let's
reassert the basic arguments—I would say that the optimistic predictions about what has happened on drug therapy are not carried through once you get one shock. We certainly need better
data than these suggestive findings. We have bits of information
but we need a definitive trial. As Dr. Breen has already mentioned,
CEASE-VT will start soon, which will answer more definitively all
the things we've raised here in terms of uncertainties for these
treatments [of arrhythmia]. But in the meantime, until I have all the
findings from those studies, I'm going to advise my patients to get
their ablations earlier rather than later."

Dr. Willets has recognized some of the merits of Dr. Breen's position, but
he does not change his own choices. He need not do so to remain credible.
He concedes that drug therapy can be helpful, but only to a point—it may
not be the optimal treatment once a patient has already experienced a shock
from a defibrillator. But he remains unmoved.

The debates finish with questions from the audience, composed largely
of clinicians. Frequently, the moderator will jokingly acknowledge that
questions are partisan, from doctors representing one approach to organizing indeterminacy: "The Penn group has exceeded their quota for questions today." Playful comments such as this help demonstrate the networks
the standard-setters have created. It is understood, however, that those doctors taking a position in the debate may not personally feel that strongly
about the actual position, and are just trying to "win" the debate (even if, as
I was surprised to learn when initially encountering these events, that there
was no formal winner crowned). No winner is necessary, however, for observing clinicians to be able to use these debates for support when they return to their labs. In many respects, acknowledging a debate within the field
and forming an opinion assists clinicians in building respect and resources
within their home institution.

Sparring by using the results of clinical trials shows the importance
of these trials in justifying standard-setters' approaches to organizing

indeterminacy. The use of this evidence is, in some ways, predictable; because of his reputation in the field for certain practices, Dr. Willets has been asked to take his position in the debate by the conference's program director. Colleagues are constantly reinforcing peers' reputations for organizing indeterminacy in a particular way.

The value of these events is that they draw out the range of ways standard-setters have organized indeterminacy on an issue and end with proposing a solution based on laboratory experience, where usual work tools have given the physician a comparative advantage with the position they have taken. For the audience, nothing is ultimately settled. Rather, this is a collegial debate: competitive and focused but not hostile. The physician's choice to use a technique—one that they often have practiced since training and might differ from one that their colleagues have learned and believe in—is validated in this presentation.

The debaters' decisions, at the end, remain consistent with initial positions. And at the end, when it gets to the patient, it's a matter of conducting more trials; everyone supports the conclusion that more research is necessary to support their efforts to organize indeterminacy. In part, this equivocality can be expected, since population-based journal evidence is predictably unhelpful with the individual. Consequently, personal experiences related to professional research can become decisive factors.

Yet, why should the personal experience with a specific patient end the interaction, regardless of the cachet of the randomized trial? In a conversation after his own debate, Dr. Price reinforces the importance of the preponderance of one center's evidence.[6]

> So I like to debate. Having said all that, the one thing I've learned in life, never argue with anyone's personal experience. It's a lost cause. I can't tell you how many times—and years ago, I get to the microphone. I would give a lecture. I would do maybe sixty-plus, eighty lectures a year. Who knows? And you get there. Someone says, "You know, Evan, I know you said that. But in my experience . . ." I've got to pad answers to that, because what am I going to do? If I say, "I don't believe you," then I'm calling them a liar.
>
> You just can't do that and be a nice guy. So what I usually say to people when they start that crap is, "Well, that's interesting. It sounds to me like whatever you're doing is working for you, but I stand by my comments. These are what we feel are the preferred ways to do it. I think if you found out a way to do it that works for you then I'm perfectly comfortable with that. Next question, please," because you can't argue with someone's experience.

Clinicians expect standard-setters to recognize, and build theory from, their personal experiences. These clinicians see success with their solutions;

even if the three-catheter and five-catheter solutions provide different data, each has indications of success. Respecting and accounting for those clinicians' experiences while organizing indeterminacy is necessary not only for the profession's standards but also for the individual, to be seen as a "nice guy." Personal evidence comes in at the end of the doctors' exchanges, because Dr. Price can't make inferences for individuals based on populations. Nice guys get adherents and referrals from all over the country. In a public setting, then, one cannot challenge the experience of a colleague.

Dr. Price's response, while reinforcing the idea that consensus is a fiction, also reinforces that he's not going to accept all personal experiences equally. In his depiction of people who "start that crap," we see Dr. Price has a personal opinion and he does what he does. People who question it by bringing up their own cases are questioning his position. He can't publicly challenge them at a conference, but it bothers him nonetheless.

And so, if children recognize a local social organization through conflict itself, experts like doctors recognize it through enacting conflict. The speakers defend practices and research that represent their long-held commitments, built up from years of research and leadership in the area, and for which they are widely known. They do not want such work to be forgotten or fall out of favor. The opposition expressed in the debate contains some rhetorical flourishes, but it's ultimately rooted in professional research tasks.[7]

For clinicians, the debates tie together the problems and solutions that standard-setters have sought to develop. Standard-setters support approaches that are consistent with their own practices in a home lab and provide warrants for rank-and-file physicians' everyday patient management. Material from these events can be used by doctors to connect the bench and bedside in their interactions with patients, administrators, and, in the worst case, lawyers, like Dr. Goodstein. At these meetings, members of opposing sects place perspectives into relief. Venues where difference is expected involve similar language as that seen at the fellows programs and hands-on meetings, where doctors frequently say, "In Oklahoma we do . . ." Yet here, too, the attacks on one's status are relatively oblique and impersonal, directed more at the practice than the person. This stands in sharp contrast to the status-deprecating and -enhancing gossip that also occurs at the conference. Gossip has much more potential to diminish the standing of individuals.

Strengthening Relationships in Invisible Colleges and Reinforcing Status in Social Events

Establishing one's mode of organizing indeterminacy is not simply a matter of asserting in a crowded amphitheater what the best practices are. Rather, it's about ensuring that across the profession as a whole there is some distribution of what has been adjudicated in venues, such as the debates, but also what can only be discussed in confidence among colleagues. Trusted standard-setters offer clinicians news about technology that they are unlikely to hear in industry-sponsored events. Additionally, everyone will exchange the gossip accessible from their particular social location. Interpersonal interaction is an important mode of communicating news that diminishes the status of those who might potentially give EP a bad name. Like other forms of informal news, these interactions have a normative subtext: "this is what you should do."[8] In showing the standard-setters puffing up their own reputations while disparaging those with alternative approaches to organizing indeterminacy, they show status competition at work.

The meeting's more private social gatherings enable standard-setters to maintain relationships that will enhance their status through attracting referrals and spreading word about their accomplishments, enable them to grow their program by attracting promising new recruits, and let them share information about others who risk diminishing the profession's standing. Private gatherings maintain clinicians' personal reputations and that of their labs more generally, strengthening personal and institutional credibility in the field. Departments host cocktail parties near the conference site that are attended by alumni; colleagues from other universities; and past, current, and prospective fellows. They will also use these social gatherings to replenish the ranks, recruiting new fellows and attendings by reinforcing that their approach to organizing indeterminacy is a compelling one. These leaders seek to build the status of their own and their labs by showing that they and their colleagues have reputable "filters" for evaluating the technologies they are offered by industry, and that they are unique and special in their capacities to foresee the benefits and risks of practices and technologies. And sometimes they disparage others. Clinicians may bring their former teachers questions about what kinds of new practices are warranted, sometimes with concerns about their merits given other circulating rumors. Further, in this venue, all of the doctors gossip about what's happening in other laboratories—including those that are using different techniques—while meeting new fellows and socializing with current or old ones.

Such gossip might involve showing that someone has such a personal stake in a practice that it is plausible their interest in personal gain is stronger than their interest in the profession's development; that they are hasty in making decisions; or that their fellows put the field at risk because they have been denied learning opportunities. Much of the matter discussed in these back channels, then, is gossip of the "let's remember what he did" variety—for instance, when people at a school regulating industry funding talk about how someone at a prestigious school received heavy funding from a company under dubious conditions. And so, a typical topic of discussion is the believability of others who are not present in the venue, and the reliability of the solutions they offer for difficult problems in the profession.

Parties at the annual conference are venues where standard-setters socialize and gossip with former students and shared (invisible) college members. An EP in private practice in New York, Dr. Kahan, points out that the recently deceased director of his EP fellowship, Dr. Rothfeld, was also deeply involved in basic science research, and frequently organized dinners at the Heart Rhythm meetings. At these dinners, researchers and clinicians currently working in his lab, and the lab alumni now in research and clinical positions, each discussed their work. "[At these dinners] he concentrated on getting a deep connection between these fellows and his scientists in his lab, [making sure] we all know each other. It created a 'bench to bedside' feeling. [After the meetings] the researchers are all going to NIH and all over the country, and the applied scientists are all coming back to their practices."

At these parties, which are composed of mostly those sharing a particular take on organizing indeterminacy, informal conversations among standard-setters and clinicians develop and strengthen their skepticism and support for new technologies being peddled. As noted in chapter 6, doctors recognize that technology failures occur. but they resent it when companies do not inform them promptly enough. This resentment is especially acute among clinicians who, in competing with other local EPs, may be especially eager to generate local status through having used new technologies. Standard-setters help buffer their former students from the negative reputational consequences of these failures, through one-up sessions in which they demonstrate their foresight with respect to matters such as problems and solutions.[9] Dr. Marcus, a clinician who trained at Superior Hospital with Drs. Buntin and Stimm, discusses one such solution.

In front of several fellows, Dr. Marcus is describing how Dr. Buntin foresaw a widely publicized failure of a new technology with negative reputational consequences for doctors using it. He points to Dr. Buntin and says, "This guy was clairvoyant. We've been burned a few times by new technology, and we're a little bit wary. The thing is, I stopped putting in [Medistar's leads] about four years ago. I have no doubt that having suffered the Medistar fate recently, we will all do it again."

Dr. Buntin smiles, offering, "History repeats itself."

Dr. Marcus: "Absolutely. Because [companies] come up with a reason to sell the story to us that we should be putting them in. We don't have the time to wait and see what everyone else does for a while. Everyone wants to be the first one hundred to put them

in. [After working with Buntin], you know how many of those leads
I've put in? Three."

When Dr. Buntin replies, "History repeats itself," he identifies himself with
an elder's wisdom in the field. He also demonstrates his ability in foreseeing problems; he has judgment and insight and is going to tell others about
it, in light of the damage done to EP by the lawsuits and distrust following
the technology failure.

He takes another step to respond to Dr. Marcus's validation of his judgment, with a story that positions him as distant from the device companies
and shows he is not "on the take."

> Dr. Buntin: "I'm on the advisory board for Medistar. And every lead
> advisory board they say we gotta go smaller, we're getting killed,
> our reps are getting pissed off about this. And I would say, you're
> crazy to go smaller right now. You gotta look into it a little more.
> This is not going to be a long-term thing. They didn't listen to me.
> And the best part about it is that this guy Chris Franken, who is an
> EP out in Seattle, comes out to me and says, 'How were you so
> goddamn clairvoyant on that thing? We were all just begging
> them to go smaller and smaller: give us smaller leads. We all
> thought you were a crazy academic.'"

Dr. Buntin's efforts extend to a venue that is outside a place where most of
these doctors will meet. By being on an advisory board, Dr. Buntin has an
opportunity to forestall problems as an adviser. In sharing his observations,
he reaches outside the field's upper echelon, and can begin gaining the benefit of the doubt; doctors in community hospitals will be especially grateful
for Dr. Buntin's foresight and communicated insight, as they have less access to comparative information on technologies.

These displays resemble the "horror stories" that residents in medical
school use to impress one another while warning them about the attendings
with whom they will soon work. Horror stories exist as moral parables of
things that have gone wrong in treating patients, reminding all that heal-
ing is difficult and should be done with care. Here, Dr. Mitchell is telling a
horror story about a company. With their stories of negative experiences
with industry, doctors demonstrate lessons learned in practice while preventing technologies from diffusing. Expertise is always enacted, and
these interactions are important for making Dr. Buntin an international
authority.[10]

Knowledge about the work conducted in the home lab reaches physicians
at conferences in other ways. They will discuss the doctors whose asserted
success rates are "too good," pointing out the impossibility of reproducing

these results. Through this, they develop and confirm informal standards about what constitutes an acceptable success rate. For something to be acceptable in this context, it must also show validity.

> One fellow, interested in pursuing an academic career and considering joining Superior from "University C," contrasts the practices of his well-known teacher to a doctor whose practices have received scrutiny in recent years. "I never quote Pantos's data to patients. I quote our success rate. It's basically eighty-seventy-sixty: 80 [percent success rate] for paroxysmal AF [atrial fibrillation], 70 for symptomatic, 60 for chronic. And that's very basic stuff. It's always slightly different. Pantos, everyone knows he makes up his data. Five thousand cases and no strokes? The complication rate should be .5 percent even if you manage things correctly. The way Bill [at University C] does it is like a textbook from John Milten."

Here we see a fellow invalidating an absent expert by claiming that, relative to his teacher, this expert's research findings are "too good," due to the impossibility of reproducing results he seeks to have represented as standard practice. This assertion is particularly compelling, because doctors who present such high success rates do a disservice to the occupational project, as others will not be able to reproduce these results with their patients.

At the same time that they are here to learn, then, they are also here to gossip about other doctors and their practices. Gossip, a powerful form of social control, is a way for members of the community to construct others' standing in a field by populating communication networks with information that has the potential to elevate or diminish status.[11] The doctors discuss what they have seen in their own labs when they carry out a well-known doctor's trademark approach and, sometimes, how those personal experiences contradict claims from the more famous physician. The doctors are embedded in a network of people who share the approach, taking in the information and considering different paths of intervention.

The importance of gossip in this venue was reinforced later, when Dr. Pantos was mentioned in my interview with a standard-setter in his office.

> He had a series of patients who he did use Stereotaxis [on], and it seemed to one of his antagonists in Germany that the series was too large because she had gotten the technology at the same time he did, and the company had told her how many catheters were out there. So she dug into it, and there is no way that he could have done seventy-three. He said seventy-

three, and when she confronted him he said, "Oh, that was just a typo. It really should have said thirty-seven." . . . He publishes results that are too good to be true.

As we've seen, publicizing results that are "too good to be true" is bad because it makes everyone without those results appear to be poor performers. Sharing their intel regarding those deviants becomes a virtual obligation of standard-setters.

The meeting gives the attendings a chance to show everything is running smoothly in the home lab, signal the program's health to doctors in and entering the field, and point out those who might be putting the occupational project at risk. Where it might be said that a manifest function of gossip in this venue is to strengthen credibility with the rank-and-file (many of whom are former fellows), a latent function is in the recruitment of fellows and faculty. The storytelling that occurs in these social venues is an important process, which underpins decisions to adopt, adapt, and reject technologies, as well as to identify and confirm that certain practices would be best conducted by senior physicians. These senior doctors, while protecting their reputation, also gain feedback regarding durable lessons they've conveyed.[12] The head of the lab strengthens credibility by building up the home organization. In doing so, he reinforces the standards organizing the invisible college in which all are embedded, in a setting—like the fellows programs and scientific conferences more generally—where hierarchical rules used to regulate conduct in the lab are temporarily suspended.[13] Finally, this venue offers sufficient privacy in which one can suggest that a colleague is posing a threat to medical authority. If it is possible to suggest at the fellows' program that someone's findings are "too good to be true," here it is possible to say, "I don't trust him."

Immunizations against Politics in the Guidelines Meeting: Processes That Neutralize the Disproportionate Influence of Physicians' Status-Seeking Efforts

> The guidelines are hardcore, worked-out things, and while they're not always the evidence we'd like, they're the best we can do. And they're a good starting point. So, they aren't the Sefer Torah, coming out during Kol Nidre. They're not quite that level, but they are the Talmud. They are a reasonable interpretation of the laws. And I think that's how people should view them.
>
> —DR. EVAN PRICE

By comparing professional guidelines to the Talmud—a central basis of Jewish law that was recorded from oral laws debated among scholars—Dr. Price points toward the living and contested nature of these documents. If the spirit of the law is important to the doctors, for sociologists the politics are crucial. There are three of the types of guidelines the society endorses: expert consensus statements, clinical competency statements, and practice guidelines. A key problem in establishing guideline topics and content is developing processes that serve to reconcile the points of view of different technical specialists, who hold divergent interests, in order to make compromise possible. Decisions are difficult because of the diversity of organizing principles that might potentially be enacted for determining whose practices inform the document—after all, the committee includes both the senior and mid-career members as well as community and research leaders. Furthermore, bias must be deterred in light of the fact that many standard-setters have their own approach to organizing indeterminacy, and they compete with each other to get them institutionalized in the documents. And because standards have to change, these documents must also flex and bend. The question asked in this section, then, is how standard-setters establish the set of rules for going from published knowledge to discussion among standard-setters to panel discussion to guidelines.[14]

What kinds of objects help to affirm the solidity of medical knowledge? Guidelines and protocol documents are potentially powerful ways for medicine's many actors to communicate the current state of the problems as well as the solutions they have arrived at. Physicians have long sought to standardize the training and practice of medicine, an effort that stems back to the Flexner Report of a century ago. Protocols for standards are institutionalized in textbooks, insurance company reimbursement criteria, and, most recently, guidelines statements. These latter statements are usually assembled by committees comprising either medical practitioners or a mix of medical and political stakeholders.[15] The US National Institutes of Health, the UK National Institute for Clinical Excellence, the UN World Health Organization, the American Medical Association—all of these organizations develop guidelines. They reflect dominant ways of organizing indeterminacy on a subject, ways intended to capture the will of many stakeholders. Because they are used across institutions—as protection in court, support for hospital investments, and justification for insurers' reimbursement decisions—they serve as a kind of "outward face" for the profession. As we saw earlier, physicians may be reluctant to depart from guidelines because they may be vulnerable to a lawsuit or concerned about whether their care will be reimbursed. Beyond being consequential in physicians' everyday interactions, guidelines are collectively consequential; for instance, whether a guidelines committee classifies a tumor as cancer or not can determine whether hundreds of thousands of patients will undergo surgery.[16]

But the presence of a range of physicians with competing ways of organizing indeterminacy suggests that such objects are not easily constructed.

What is the social organization underpinning the construction of these guidelines? What are the rules intended to keep them credible? This section shows that they are organized to strip influence from individuals and their politics in order to maintain credibility for the doctors individually and collectively.[17]

There are as many types of guidelines as there are ways these documents are used in practice. All of them are likely to maximize multiple groups' interests, but also to be a bit more weighted in one direction. For instance, professional associations' guidelines will likely be focused more on matters such as training, safety, laboratory design, and defending the jurisdiction from other professions. In contrast, guidelines created by state agencies will be focused more on whether the financial costs of medical practices or technologies justify their benefits. And, as we have seen, both doctors and industry use these guidelines to further their shared and individual goals; the tie between articles reporting scientific findings and everyday practice is quite contingent, with reasons hinging on factors that range from trainees' interest in avoiding embarrassment to experienced doctors' interest in furthering their status.[18]

Guidelines are used in areas inside and distinctly outside medical domains. They are cited in introductions of journal articles, described in the computer systems physicians consult to check on best practices, and deployed to defend decisions at the bedside and in the boardroom. They are used to assist practitioners in decision making when clinical trials are unrepresentative of a patient base and are, therefore, thought of as being of limited help in decision-making.[19] We see them when our doctor or Internet-hosted health record reports whether our blood tests place us in a "normal" range. Additionally, guidelines touch an immense audience that reaches far beyond the shop floor. Plaintiffs quote guidelines in the courtroom, even if at times they have been considered hearsay. State officials use guidelines in reimbursement decisions. And they reach the marketplace, too: the packaging materials of new cell phones contain pamphlets quote National Cancer Institute guidelines on whether cell phones cause cancer.[20] And the Heart Rhythm Society committee for these guidelines intends them to be used that way—to guide inside and outside stakeholders: "The purpose of HRS documents is to provide guidance to our membership as well as other entities (FDA, industry, healthcare providers, and others) on issues that are timely and for which guidance is currently lacking or needs to be updated."[21]

But the divergent invisible colleges in medicine mean that the process for creating guideline documents is both important and challenging to develop. Before anyone can use those guidelines, the standards for their creation need to be settled.

To diminish the appearance of politics in discussions on the processes of formulating guidelines, the chair of the group must implement approaches that ensure they will not be unduly influenced by individuals' status-generating efforts. Instead, they must rely on processes that will make the guidelines valuable and compelling to those inside and outside medicine. Physicians know that within EP there are divergent schools of thought. Nonphysicians may be concerned about financial conflicts of interest. To be compelling, then, these audiences need to trust that guidelines are developed in an unbiased way.

The structure for making guidelines must account for the unmistakable fact that this is a group of high-powered people who value status and who have to manage divergent approaches and personalities. Standard-setters assemble one morning each year to reinforce and reconsider both the process of creating guidelines and the agenda for what guidelines should be updated or generated.[22] The committee's primary problem in the institutionalization process involves managing divergent approaches among many strong personalities. In an anecdote about the final stage of writing a guideline, at which point the committee had received input from physicians in the professional association, Dr. Price offers a clue for why they need processes:

> So the chair wrote a very fair piece that he worked on, and he sent it out to a few of us, and it said, "These [conditions] are met." We all agreed that isolating the pulmonary veins was key. Then he had a bit on each section. If you look at the document you'll see we didn't say one was better than the other. We were on a conference call, and as soon as the conversation is off the ground for ten minutes, Pantos blows up. "None of you know what you're doing. You need to be following my method. I've done 20,000. If you want to know how to do it right, come see me and I'll teach you how to do it." And then people just started yelling at each other. Stevens accusing him of falsifying his data, and on and on it went. I thought, "Wow." Harry, the chair, called me after and said, "Evan." I said, "Harry, I prepared you. I have prepared you. Don't worry about it. Keep on track. Give everybody their fair due. You don't have to change a bunch. You knew this was going to happen. Just basically have a statement that there's no one, proven technique."
>
> Stevens was really pissed because he had been sitting for two days in Pantos's labs and watching, and Pantos never checked for some things. Then he gets on the call and says, "I was checking." Stevens said, "I was there two days. I've watched you do four or five cases. You never once checked for this. Why are you lying to us?" This big fight broke out. I'm telling you. That's the background that you never see. So there's all this

kind of stuff. The fact is that is why there is no 1a approach to atrial fibrillation.

Dr. Price's comment points out how individual perspectives and strong personalities can make consensus elusive and fractures frequent in the committee's negotiations. The chair must neutralize the effect of individuals' objections on the discussion while simultaneously finding a way to integrate respective perspectives into the document. The committee must also assign a rating to the work that captures the strength of both its evidence and its level of recommendation; an 1a rating is only given to recommendations based on evidence from meta-analysis of randomized controlled trials. Using lower levels affords the committee the ability to hedge.

Dr. Price intends his anecdote to reflect the scenarios the guideline meeting's leadership and its members seek to avoid. The leadership in the meeting seeks to diminish the impression that the guideline is seen as reflecting the interests of just one person. In this scenario, the committee comprises many high-status people in the area of ablation who had published on the topic. Findings must be made to appear compelling to those who read the published findings, but also to those who visit a lab. So, it is also problematic that Pantos's claims were not validated by another high-ranking doctor. Because knowledge is what brings committee members esteem in their niches, personal knowledge is always involved in the process of developing the guidelines—and so practitioners will commonly place blame on the physician rather than the technique when their signature practice fails. Thus, ego, as much as expertise, is embedded in the expert documents.

When dealing with these fractures, as well as the problem of disproportionate influence by a single member, committees tend to implement more rationalized decision-making process than those formally expected of them by their professional association. The American College of Cardiology's guidelines mandate using formal and confidential votes for the approval of guidelines, drawing their principles from Robert's Rules of Order as well as a strict peer review process.[23] In terms of the further measures they implement, the first is to use technologies like survey instruments. As one committee member put it, "We're all used to meetings in which the dominant people win the day. And most of us in this room are included in this group of dominant people. And the survey tool really lets everyone have their say, and cuts off some of the arguments." The survey tool mentioned here is highly endorsed on the set of documents handed out to the meeting's membership. Included as part of each of these documents: "the use of a survey tool to detail consensus among the writing group is expected."

The second measure is the use of disclaimers in the beginning of these documents, passages that describe an ecumenical formal process for making a decision. One sign of splintered perspectives is in the preamble to one of the most recent guidelines. This passage demonstrates how the group seeks to resolve the problem of multiple camps:

> This statement is not intended to recommend or promote catheter abla-tion of VT. Rather, the ultimate judgment regarding care of a particular patient must be made by the healthcare provider and the patient with consideration of the individual patient characteristics that impact on risks and benefits of the therapy. In writing a "consensus" document, it is recognized that consensus does not mean that there was complete agreement among all Task Force members. We identified those aspects of VT ablation for which a true "consensus" could be identified. Surveys of the entire Task Force were used to identify these areas of consensus.[24]

This statement is similar to the opening paragraphs of many guidelines doc-uments, yet reflects a change from guidelines statements developed soon after a procedure has been developed, statements simply containing a dis-cussion of the condition. It reflects that the field has progressed to a point where deep fissures exist over the belief systems recommended for any pro-cedure, and it hints at the networks of support among those satisfied with their approach. Few multicenter studies of ablation exist—but even with those, the authors disagree about endpoints and procedure. The presence of these deep disagreements is well understood; hence the author's use of quotation marks.[25]

The third measure in response to the problem of individual influence, and one mentioned in the initial passage, is that members selected for the committee are those who are standard-setters in the discipline's core, who have visited one another's labs and can report on those experiences. As Dr. Malcolm puts it:

> Most important is reputation based on work that is empirically verifiable. People talk, reps talk, if a guy does 500 ablations and you trust him, then I think that person is accorded more credibility in the guidelines discus-sions. [These doctors gain respect] even if they don't publish much; there are people who you know publish a lot but aren't very experienced—it comes under the rule that if you aren't doing much clinically, you've got lots of time to write. And there's some truth to that. And I'm sure you've found rules about how people accord status and weight activities accu-rately. The fact that a lot of people have gone to Bordeaux heightens the credibility of everything [Bordeaux doctors] say.

Because procedure volume and veracity of experiences are important, peers examine clinical practices and experiences of those making assertions. Virtually all EPs accept the work of the Bordeaux group, which made the field-transforming discovery in 1999 identifying that atrial fibrillation could be identified (and thus treated through ablation), from the left pulmonary vein. The circuits of communication between industry and the field mean that those bedside experiences matter when it is time to create standards.

Beyond the issues tied to the disproportionate influence of a single person, and despite the measures developed in previous meetings of the committee, a fourth measure taken by the group is to negotiate the rules of precedence. In clinical trials there exist norms for first and last authors, but principles for authorship in guidelines committees are less institutionalized. And, despite their eminence in the profession, authors remain preoccupied with priority. Given the influence of these documents, there are likely to be disagreements over credit that have implications for the structure of leadership. Such a concern came up a half dozen times in the two years I observed the committee. In one meeting, the chair both brings a question to the group, and indicates the inevitability of eventual hurt feelings.

> "Do you think it would be better to have a chair and co-chair, or equal co-chairs? I think it would be better to have a chair and vice-chair. Somebody's going to end up being first on the document. And people, obviously in our group, end up getting their feelings hurt by the way we say we're going to order the authors. My co-chair is not happy being a second person instead of being the senior person."

As we have seen, the people at the top of this constantly shifting field think they should be cited for their contributions. They seek to maintain their leadership status in a profession that has recognized contributions of others. These elites made early advancements, developing systems for ablating atrial fibrillation. To some, there has since been a major shift in the field, with the Bordeaux group's invention of pulmonary vein isolation. But others, like Pantos, have methods for building on Bordeaux's ablation approach that they felt were not being recognized by the field.[26]

The proceedings of the meetings are, in some ways, reiterative of what we've seen in other venues. The challenges faced by the committee relate back to the technologies and practices that people are using in the home lab. What the physicians see and do in the home lab is going to confirm their school of thought; their practice is going to help them figure out new methods; everyone in the field is going to have their own position. So the process of choosing and making standards is going to have to quietly account for that, and find a way to prevent the personal aspect from skewing the proceedings of making standards that will work for all. One consequence of the processes used to create these documents is that, because they seek to strip out bias toward a particular invisible college, they offer some capacity to facilitate individuals' divergent efforts to organize indeterminacy on the shop floor and in their research.[27]

Getting complete consensus on a set of "right" answers, the point of guideline documents, is an impossibility. But the committee must ultimately report an outcome back to its constituency. For this reason, compromises are necessary. Beyond their value in moving a document to completion, the compromises that result may ultimately enable doctors to feel validated in following their own traditions at the bedside.

Conclusion

In venues constituting the "public sphere" of medicine, the appearance, evaluation, and spread of new practices occurs. Recurrent patterns of reciprocal influence among specialty leaders shape the local practice of EP internationally. Medical practice is shaped at venues organizing bedside-, hospital-, and national-scale tasks. When an EP is at work in the lab, at times they have in mind the entire world of industry stakeholders and professional peers, none of which can be seen but is, nonetheless, present. In the EP lab, then, even if they must at times make on-the-fly decisions based on rapid feedback loops, decisions are made as much on the basis of subtle observation of patient anatomy and symptomatology, as on informed interpretation of nationally standard devices.

At the conference, there are two processes occurring that are complementary in terms of space. A lot of interactions are out in the open. These are in contrast to other conversations, which are closed. The closed conversations happen among those who seek to strengthen the influence of a single invisible college, and those who seek to ensure that multiple perspective are heard. The annual conference, then, involves a range of venues important to medicine.

At work in these venues are many of the competitive processes we've previously seen among those seeking to organize indeterminacy. For instance, the opportunity to highlight one's own practice, and the ongoing work of adjudicating expert knowledge. In this chapter we add some attention to another feature: social gatherings. On the exhibition floor, through game shows and other spectacles, industry tries to establish what positive results might be expected with their technologies, and other industry stakeholders seek to influence doctors to consider their interests. Physicians in debates offer methods that can serve to recast others' interpretations and validate their seemingly idiosyncratic practices occurring at the shop floor—their own practices and those of the like-minded. This recasting and validating helps them personally with status, but also serves to provide observers at the debates with material that might help them justify their own practices. The social gatherings enable standard-setters to maintain relationships that will enhance their status and strengthen the hold of their practices through attracting referrals and spreading word about their accomplishments. Finally, the meetings on developing guidelines focus primarily on cultivating processes intended to strip away the possibility of undue influence from standard-setters who hope that their own, and not others', efforts to organize indeterminacy get codified. Those leading the guidelines meetings regulate themselves through an awareness of the expectations of medicine more generally.

The chapter also demonstrates that medical practices are far from atomized, undifferentiated, or unorganized. There are exclusivities and traditions, but those need to be reinvigorated in light of the new agendas discussed at meetings. In these places, they learn from leaders and peers what of their current practices are acceptable, and also what might profitably be tried. Amidst this strengthening process, doctors share news of deviant behavior that may reinforce their personal status and marginalize those potentially undermining the profession.

The annual meeting benefits both standard-setter and clinician. First, the meeting's venues offer spaces for standard-setters to integrate influences from the state, companies, research, and even activist communities, in a way that helps physicians' knowledge dominate while contending with other stakeholders who seek to govern practices in their home clinics. This is where standard-setters try to compellingly state their expert knowledge, reiterate that they have it, and generate the status so that practices in other venues will be supported. We observe in these events a space for standard-setters to promote their lab's standards and shape circulating gossip about their trustworthiness and judgment. Further, by giving fellows information about their skills and foresight, they can attract fellows they will be able to train in their lab and send as practicing physicians to their peers' labs. They can also benefit from their efforts to shape the decisions of other actors to whom clinicians' access is limited, such as technology companies. Standard-setters at this conference are aiming to have their approaches adopted as the standard across many shop floors, and the conference offers a venue where they proffer changes to those standards as political winds shift.

Like standard-setters, clinicians gain some benefits from the meetings, as they are reminded that there are those at the top who have the right, somehow, to set standards for all the rest of them. At the same time, these meetings also offer them the material to reinvigorate support for a range of practices that are ultimately less uniform than might otherwise be expected. Consequently, these places are for building and reinforcing a wide understanding of the way indeterminacy has been organized.

Their debates, some of the annual meeting's most popular events, show us the relationship between the practices of individual EPs and their collective group. These standard-setters know, but may not admit in this venue, that the ideas that inform their most innovative research frequently originate in personal experiences. Physicians in these debates offer methods that can serve to validate their seemingly idiosyncratic practices occurring at the shop floor, practices of their own and the like-minded with whom they compete for status. In delivering their side of the debate, those with international standing replicate one aspect of discourse on the shop floor: that of being "strong and wrong" about the applicability of medical practices and research findings that are understood as being relevant for larger populations rather than for specific cases. And they show that there may be differences in the way that, say, Dr. Stimm and Dr. Bellard operate in the lab, but they can still work together. Furthermore, they have support for how they do cases and teach fellows in their home hospital; there they can point toward the practices of their medicine-leading colleagues. Doing it "my way" becomes warranted, then, with the debates connecting expert practitioners with everyday professionals. Ultimately, the passages show that each standard-setter has their own approach to organizing indeterminacy, and, by describing their own research and others', they demonstrate a process through which one's home lab can inform a profession's best practices.

In helping refine the basic concept of organizing indeterminacy, this chapter also reinforces the importance of the status competition for adjudicating knowledge claims, by refining the relationship between interdependence among career types, individuals' practice-related interests, and public interactions in the venues. The annual meeting is one where we can see processes described in other chapters, suggesting both their pervasiveness beyond the particular venues observed in this book, and their capacity to enable not fragmentation but coalescence.

Finally, we see a range of tethers being put to use. In their head-to-head debates, the standard-setters use examples of patients from their labs to strengthen their case for their approach to organizing indeterminacy. And those tethers are compelling; as Dr. Price noted, no one questions peers' use of such tethers as evidence. We also saw that by being on an advisory board and going to annual meetings, Dr. Buntin is allowing himself to be used as a tether to Medistar. High success rates are presented, and doctors who present the tethers of unreasonably high success rates hurt the occupational project, as others will not be able to reproduce these results.

eight

Conclusion

Managing Medicine's Authority into the Future

The patients who benefit from medical work expect it to be well organized. And those patients have come to expect from doctors that they can provide good outcomes. It might then be surprising that only one chapter involves stakeholders' in-depth interactions with patients. Other scholars, whose subject is directly or indirectly concerned with medical authority, have given more attention to patients. I spend little time on patients because my field-work observations—in not only inpatient wards but also in outpatient clinics and guidelines meetings—did not reinforce the importance of patients to the management of medical authority. In addition to the wards, described in chapter 2, I spent many months observing the outpatient clinics of residents, fellows, and attendings. There I observed no evidence that those interactions shape the ongoing management of authority, except to the extent that training and freshly minted physicians needed to develop task-specific interactional skills. The concerns of those on the gurney, and those accompanying them, were firmly rooted in the immediate personal needs of their own or their family members, concerns which were soon organized by their hospital providers. There were, to be sure, a few patient-activists at the annual meeting, as well as a patient advocate at the guidelines meeting. And patients had some importance in the field, if indirect; the referral chain was important to physician success, patient insurance types were discussed by clinicians in the industry-sponsored meetings, and their potential lawsuits were discussed. Yet the data showed them to be a distant reference point in the overall management of authority.[1]

What I saw was that, in addition to patients, doctors too expect that the tasks of their work will be organized—and an underlying point of this book is that they develop processes for doing this. Some situations in work involve obvious problems; for instance, seeing water on the floor indicates a pipe is leaking. But other situations require expertise, even to identify which of a set of conventional problems the expert faces, and which of a set of solutions should be applied. As medical sociologists have well documented, these complex situations can involve great uncertainty for those charged with managing them.

It is the work of the individual doctor to make the decision about what the problem is and how it should be resolved. But this book reflects that that kind of work is not shouldered by the individual alone. Part of physicians' work, together with others in their occupational project, is to use the established processes for making sense of why a patient would live or die, whether that has to do with luck or age. The doctors perform their tasks in different venues formatted for different purposes. In and between the venues, through tethers, they create and share evidence for validating their approach to organizing indeterminacy, to make a well-supported case for it, and to help others in the future do their work of identifying problems and solutions more effectively. From medicine, we expect explanations for patient experiences, and medical professionals weave narratives for both individual patients and a community of colleagues by producing and working with knowledge to produce reasonably durable understandings of problems and their solutions, to create, fill, and re-open an open space.

Because this space is so open, and is marked strongly by indeterminacy, it makes sense that members of the occupational project will try to organize the indeterminacy by developing processes for managing these relationships. Physicians and medicine's other stakeholders have created those relationships that support medicine's constant renewal, which results in a certain interdependence through which authority is managed. As demonstrated in the outsize role played by allied nonphysician stakeholders, such as hospital and industry actors, in managing the occupational project, it is clear that physicians do not dominate all other stakeholders. And even among the physicians, the variety of tasks on which excellence can be demonstrated, the existence of gossip networks, and a lack of strong sanctions all reflect and continually reinforce that there is no single, strong, future-shaping leader. For standard-setting physicians, this dependence on nonphysicians can create a problem because other stakeholders in the occupational project have a strong say in medicine's direction. Yet, at the same time, this dependence also enables them to, for instance, access a way of overseeing the difficult-to-observe clinicians, and to draw on the resources of these stakeholders to create and access technological solutions that strengthen their authority. Their authority is managed by establishing, revisiting, and reestablishing the nature of their work and how it should be done, in what I have called an occupational project: the constellation of forward-thinking stakeholders involved in the range of tasks associated with establishing problems and solutions.

Taken together, this book claims that doctors manage authority in part by having developed a process that allows them to address indeterminacy, which is a source of potential challenge that could fracture their profession in light of the expectations placed on doctors. Specifically, what we have seen beyond these episodes within and across venues is that authority is managed by those engaged in a collegial competition for status and other resources across venues, in which doctors and others in their occupational project label problems and solutions by using tethers to control patients and colleagues. After all, we've seen ways of interacting across venues that have harnessed some of the features of competition for these resources. These processes of managing indeterminacy represent work that makes this competition not corrosive but relatively constructive. Practicing these approaches to organizing indeterminacy lets them use the knowledge, skills, and techniques acquired in multiple venues, gain resources for performing these specialized practices, and deter disastrous outcomes for which they will be largely held responsible. To excel in this competition, they use tethers such as carefully created slides, the legitimizing ratification of their capabilities by conference peers, and patients referred by clinicians that afford the use of their approaches. These tethers help them organize work conditions in venues where threats to their approach to organizing indeterminacy come from those whom they must depend on in carrying out the task (e.g., administrators, technology companies, etc.). If they have this control, which comes from using tethers in carrying out tasks, they can continue to practice and influence others in practicing their approach to organizing indeterminacy.[2]

It may not seem sensible that this competition would strengthen the occupational project, but it is possible to see it that way when we recall that standard-setters' engagement around problems and solutions involves presenting successful cases across venues, discussing clinical trials, teaching techniques, and developing guidelines—activities that they work to keep highly connected, broadly visible, and widely observed. They take extra time to meet and discuss their work, ensure that others see these events, and accede to a situation that is not organized by rules that feature either competition or the spotlighting of an individual. Together they are doing work such as teaching modes of interaction, ensuring they can receive patients with whom they can do research, spreading good news about their program, sharing slides with those inside and outside their invisible college, promoting technological innovations, and ensuring that guidelines involve participatory processes. This work happens within and between the venues, as a part of attending to, and investing in, the future of the group. This book's demonstration of how these professionals seek to organize indeterminacy, then, is a first step in reconciling their individual self-interest with their mode of practice, which reflects that doctors collectively orient to the profession, and develop the kind of reliable and actionable accounts we expect.[3]

The Significance of a Focus on Occupational Project, Efforts to Organize Indeterminacy, and the Use of Tethers to Exercise Degrees of Control

If physicians were only doing tasks at the bedside or in the clinical consultation room, then it would be difficult to say that what they are doing contributes to managing their authority as an occupation. But once we see that they are doing multiple tasks that contribute to an occupational project that is future-tending, we can account for the management of authority. The occupational project is oriented toward the future—that is, to the ability of doctors to keep doing their work in the face of change, disagreement, and a degree of competition that has characterized medicine since the days of eclecticism, homeopathy, and Christian Science.

We can account for experts' management of authority by noting that the occupational project is set up to allow interpretation and vetting of a range of stakeholders and social changes for which their expertise is relevant; the interactional affordances of venues give recurrent opportunities to incorporate contributions of multiple stakeholders, and consider changes in technology, patient needs, and even the legal landscape. This lets them reduce indeterminacy, and allow the competition that keeps them responsive to the challenge of new knowledge and keeps them talking to each other about what's happening.

This conclusion is supported by the chapters taken together, which illuminate processes operating across venues and electrophysiologists, and offer three key findings about how physicians and other stakeholders are managing authority, reinvigorating and strengthening the occupational project. A central finding is that the leadership structure among physicians is multiheaded, characterized by a governing plurality, in which it is possible for different approaches to exist. A second finding is that multiple nonphysician stakeholders in an occupational project play important roles in a process of organizing indeterminacy, and that there were roughly three types of this organizing. A third finding is that EPs are engaged in work in addition to their tasks at the bedside, in multiple venues that are connected with tethers, in which they are working on organizing indeterminacy at the same time as they are engaged in a collegial competition for status and other resources. This multiheaded leadership is related to the fact that one of the things they are doing is organizing this indeterminacy that so strongly marks the work they do. Here I am using the term *control* as prosocial, exercised in the furtherance of the occupational project, where doctors are not giving orders, limiting choices, or directing behavior, but rather managing how others should understand problems and solutions. Control involves not only the shaping of anatomy, a disease process, or an approach or technique, but also shaping expectations and understandings of categories of people.

First, we can see that their occupational project's leadership structure is multiheaded, because we saw that standard-setters are engaged in a competition for status, among other resources, at the same time as they are organizing to allow for vetting and responsivity to change. It remains the case that individuals, whether doctors or device reps, care about personal success. They have novel experiences that will necessarily affect their perspectives on what is possible and what should be done. They name anatomy. They also have novel commitments; they belong to invisible colleges to which they themselves were introduced in training, and they want their invisible colleges recognized in the problems and solutions they construct. They angle for support by cultivating a set of believers in their work and share the informal news of gossip in an effort to undercut the standing of those with the potential to steal thunder. As knowledge is passed down to them, they remain connected and are passing down this knowledge to students and colleagues who help strengthen their personal legacy. And they seek to have indeterminacy organized their way, using as tethers slides with descriptions of their approaches, training fellows and clinicians to work in their way. In addition, they seek to ensure that they maintain a stream of patients and collaborators from local, national, and international communities. And they use industry reps and can even accommodate that the industry reps use them. Industry reps, too, are careful about those with whom they develop alliances. They benefit from industry reps who evaluate and provide feedback to standard-setters who speak at their events, and they seek to keep their technologies out of the hands of clinicians they perceive as likely to make mistakes.

The EPs I studied and company reps, then, operate in a multiheaded model of managing authority. The observation that individual stakeholders are pursuing their individual interests might lead us to think the group would be torn apart without a single head. The competition we have seen is not corrosive but relatively constructive, which suggests that it is a non-zero-sum competition. And admittedly, this competition is indeed like others that center on outcomes of individuals, in which certain individuals gain opportunities at the expense of others in the group. But it is important to emphasize that outcomes here are different; stakeholders are making and adjudicating expertise that contributes to an occupational project. And the outcomes involve being in a place where one can shape the ways indeterminacy is organized in that occupational project. As a process it also works differently than a typical competition, because space is continuously reopened for different people with different opinions to propose and support their problems and solutions, involving many individuals striving to be right and pressing their case (and those of others behind them), while letting others be "virtual witnesses." Debaters at industry-sponsored and annual meetings demonstrate the process in microcosm; when standard-setters demonstrate the benefits of a modality, they are careful to ensure they are seen not as dogmatic but as just working from the data, trying to validate associated practices. The debaters are expected to be empiricists and use data from their actual practice, the kind of evidence espoused by philosophers Robert Boyle and Francis Bacon; the doctors performing presentations must have treated enough patients to be able to supplement their discussion of their procedure with sensory details. There is no final vote determining a victor. We can see that this competition is not inimical but rather intrinsic in an occupational project organized in a way that can produce high-quality outcomes.[4]

A second finding is that physicians and other stakeholders are organized in an occupational project that works into the future—one in which they organize indeterminacy across multiple scales and reference groups. Not only are they working to shape others' understandings of a range of tasks, but they are organized in multiple venues where people are able to work in specific ways and with different stakeholders, who are interconnected. All of these stakeholders in the occupational project were involved in managing authority, and often in interdependent ways, as they participated in organizing indeterminacy. Multiple stakeholders have venues centered around different tasks, each affording the chance for offering evidence of success with a task, whether it involves caring for patients, training the next generation, or leading clinical trials. With this broader lens, answering the question of how authority is managed, at least in this particular area of medicine, requires accounting for the contribution of a range of stakeholders, and recognizing how important individual actors and the venues they have created are in organizing indeterminacy. The management of the occupational project, then, does not happen in a way that is top-down and static.

Indeed, as we saw in chapter 7, there are conditions in place that actively preserve an open space and prevent dominance of an individual, such as the extensive measures that exist to ensure diverse viewpoints in guidelines documents. The effort to maintain an open space with this competition, which is also characterized by individual efforts to organize indeterminacy and support the occupational project, suggests it might be better described as a collegial competition. To be competitive, doctors carry out tasks that strengthen their approach to organizing indeterminacy—and implicitly those of their invisible college—such as running clinical trials, training fellows, meeting clinicians at conferences, and shaping a set of guidelines documents. The individual comes from a tradition, as we saw from Bellard's reassertion of his onetime mentor's ideas, and willingness to move across universities. But, as we also saw, tradition cannot rule completely because of the importance of clinical trials. And they trust their hands, and know that they can carry out those practices successfully. From the lawyer's presentation to fellows in chapter 5, we could see that the doctors' interest in carrying out practices according to the occupational project's dominant problems and solutions was so they could get results that are considered positive according to guidelines, and not get sued. And we saw that they sought to attract patients that would help them "spread the gospel," thereby improving their standing.[5]

Across the chapters, many examples of the processes of organizing indeterminacy were described, taking place in venues like periodic conferences, and involving the use of tethers for the flow of relevant information. These processes shared an emphasis on constructing new understandings of observations, but they can be differentiated into approximately three types, each comprising its own reference groups, scales, and processes. The first type is scaled for a reference group that comprises large groups of experts—including medical subfields and professions themselves. These groups were distinguished by, among other qualities, their differences in training programs, technologies, and journals. For instance, we saw differences between general cardiologists and electrophysiologists, who differ respectively in terms of their tendency to treat an arrhythmia by either providing pills to the patient or burning their heart tissue. We also saw EPs organizing indeterminacy using ablation and catheters, while cardiac surgeons used a procedure involving open-heart surgery. A second type was characterized by differences across smaller groups within electrophysiology's occupational project, such as the invisible colleges. For instance, we saw differences in how indeterminacy was organized by electrophysiologists who trained in different programs, or those opting to conduct their research on medication or ablation. Among those EPs who conducted ablation, they had strongly differing beliefs about the optimal number of catheters that should be used. A third type could be seen in differences across individuals, each of whom had to work across venues to validate their approaches, and compared themselves to doctors who consistently saw different patients. One example included the fact that the "antrum" was recognized as real only by those physicians who accepted the claims of the physician who coined the term. Another was that physicians are reticent to argue with a practice of a clinician that is rooted in their personal experiences. Similarly, standard-setters seek to provide strong evidence for those experiences, seeking to validate with research studies the advice they provided to rapt fellows and clinicians, as clearly seen in the industry-sponsored training programs.[6]

It is also important to note that these are flexible categories, and that there could be switches across the categories described here. They should not be seen as static, as we could see in certain situations, such as this book's opening vignette, where stakeholders left space for others to push at their understandings and shared slides. There we could see that groups that could otherwise be understood as competing over a professional jurisdiction involving arrhythmias (cardiac surgeons and cardiologists) were engaged in close collaboration. And so, as these examples show, this book suggests that the entities involved in organizing indeterminacy should not be considered to be overly "durable."[7]

A third finding is that venues and tethers, used in the context of collegial competition, were important to strengthening the occupational project. What I saw was that multiple venues are tethered, in a number of ways, and the consequence is that people remain alert and sharp about the possibility that their work may need to change, and their expertise as well, to deal with new understandings necessary to do the work in the future. The finding raises a range of questions. Why, then, is it that the occupational project has not been taken over to allow the corrosive influence of nonphysician third parties to damage the project? And why isn't it a Hobbesian "war of all-against-all," one whose resolution necessitates a Leviathan? How is it that the authority of the profession itself is managed? One of the keys is that the processes allow some diffusion of possible tensions that might otherwise prevent the management of authority. And venues are the key to understanding that doctors' self-interested work to organize indeterminacy is managing authority. Venues allow stakeholders to divide labor, demonstrating excellence with a range of tasks. In competing across venues, each affording the demonstration of prowess with a different task, they can develop the strongest support possible for their approach to organizing indeterminacy, and test others' approaches. Venues helped foster collegial competition because the work in an occupational project comprises many tasks beyond arrhythmia ablation and pacemaker implantation, tasks for which those venues are formatted. Specifically, venues allowed individuals to demonstrate individual skills, and do different tasks with the potential to support the occupational project.

Venues function in another way in the management of authority: they are staging places for interactions that develop visible relationships between seemingly different stakeholders, such as industry actors and physicians. Looking at the tasks involved in creating problems and solutions that fill the open space, we see kinds of work that call for a broadening of how we should understand shop floor tasks. In addition to the work with patients that we think of as the prototypical work of doctoring, these other tasks may involve recruiting students, training and building alliances with peers, navigating organizational politics, and managing arm's-length relationships with companies. Venues ensure that the relationships involved in performing these tasks are made public in ways that demonstrate that doctors are in control of their own profession. Moreover, because doctors seek credit for their approaches, venues were important because competition needs to be visible: doctors observing others' labs, being present in industry-sponsored meetings, and attending events in the annual conference.

Having a mode of organizing indeterminacy is trivial when one lacks the means to control tasks in a venue and across venues. Without these means, and the control they afford standard-setters would be unable to demonstrate the benefits of their approach. Doctors have such a mode for asserting control over tasks: tethers. Tethers used to connect venues are important for managing authority because they allow for professionals' control over features of work, such as scarce resources and the presence of multiple stakeholders, that happens inside venues. For standard-setting physicians, managing authority demanded keeping control over accessing resources and controlling attention in venues that will let them get their work done. For this control, doctors often used tethers such as carefully created slides, or language that indexed and reinforced affiliation with certain approaches and not others. Tethers helped doctors control work conditions in venues where threats to their approach to organizing indeterminacy come from those whom they must depend on in carrying out the task (e.g., administrators, technology companies, etc.). In every one of the six key venues where EPs do their work, they do their best to manage the immediate face-to-face situation by using tethers to preclude or control challenges to their preferred approaches to organizing indeterminacy. They do so by steering the immediate proceedings in a way that conforms to their interests, tastes, competences—their preferred problems and solutions. Beyond those situations, as the case in chapter 4 showed, when they lost control over beds and patient referrals, they felt they had no choice but to leave the hospital, moving to another organization in the occupational project. Losing control of these resources limited their ability to carry out clinical trials and practices consistent with their modes of organizing indeterminacy, and moving across town let them continue to strengthen their occupational project. In their hands-on meeting, clinicians were less accepting of the technology of the company that, while using the newest techniques and technology, did not let standard-setters run the meeting. This case of the bed management program and the episodes at the hands-on meetings show that physicians aren't the only stakeholders involved in managing authority; the company representatives—and the hospital, in its pursuit of prestige and reimbursement funds—influence the ability of physicians to develop and impose their approaches to organizing indeterminacy.[8]

In addition to affording control in local venues, tethers are valuable to let stakeholders stitch venues together, letting them control what others do across venues. Attendings use language to shape subordinates' practices, in the wards and lab, but also in ways that can reach into other venues, such as the industry-sponsored and social events. Standard-setters like Dr. Buntin managed others' sense of key problems and solutions in the occupational project by referring to the prescience he exercised in other venues and also by reinforcing the merits of his own approach through disparaging those of a competitor. Other standard-setters cited articles written by faculty who trained them, they asked for others' slides and distributed their own, they attracted patients on whom they could perform their procedures their way, and they sent their trainees to other labs to spread their approach. They visit and ask peers about work in the labs of those with whom they are considering a collaboration. In their referral relationships, standard-setters felt they needed ties to clinicians, those occupying a different tier of the occupational project, in the same way that scholars of the medical profession describe referral ties in a city that sustains the flow of patients from non-specialist to specialist. But, looking outside of the city, we see that using tethers can offer a less local and more durable payoff; that of strengthening the efforts of EPs in their occupational project. Doctors value having patients, and without getting patient tethers as referrals, they felt unable to continue "spreading the gospel," to use Dr. Stimm's term, and took the step of moving to a lower-ranked program and hospital.[9]

The control afforded by tethers both inside and across venues resolves a key unanswered question in the sociology literature on the creation of individual professionals: Should we, like Merton and colleagues, understand professionals as socialized similarly from training days, or should we, like Becker and colleagues, understand their professional development as emerging from conflict with other stakeholders such as nurses, and even peers? The answer is that both early socialization and ongoing local competition matter, but to understand how, we must study professionals' many tasks and the venues where stakeholders use tethers to shape the future.[10]

I argue that this connection between venues afforded by tethering is important for understanding products of collective behavior, such as coalescence and the management of authority. Overall, what we are seeing is a complex, semi-coordinated—but also free and loose system—in which people are exercising enough control with enough flexibility to allow others to succeed, so that they can begin to coalesce. The result is that, since most of their activity is directed at being successful, they are now managing authority.

Attention to the tethers affords us not only insight into how individuals are controlling each other, but also into the relationship between managing indeterminacy and the occupational project, and the competition that still persists. There is little contestation among stakeholders across jurisdictions who organize and perform different tasks. In other words, these physicians are working to establish relationships that help them avoid conflict inside venues, even as they are competing across them. Individuals paying attention to organizing indeterminacy cared more about their personal reputations than about the protection of their jurisdiction; relationships with industry help individual careers, and no one wants lawsuits. Of course, our ability to infer the importance of individual efforts comes in part from the blinders accompanying the method used; ethnography is the study of individuals. And ethnographers can study a decade at most, not the centuries studied by Abbott, in what he referred to as his "turf war" model. However, this ethnography took us to venues where sparring over turf could have happened, like the conference, and showed little evidence of such warfare. And it showed us unlikely collaborations such as those between those EPs and cardiac surgeons, relationships that we might expect to be characterized as adversarial. Close scrutiny of venues, then, exposed at work not jurisdictions comprising an inside and outside of a professional system but an occupational project at work in maintaining an open space. It also helps us make sense of unexpected relationships, such as those between pattern-identifying programmers working with radiologists, and new fields like "neuroendocrinology."[11]

Overall, venues and their tethers provide a window into the nature of the occupational project itself, and its role in the management of authority. In this book, they showed that a central quality of the occupational project is maintaining control of the acceptance of problems and solutions, and the collective recognition of an occupational project, and in it, a process of social control. With respect to individual physicians, tethers focus us on those who refer cases to them, those who absorb their new knowledge, and those who hold their own opinions different from the key stakeholders but continue to practice successfully.

The Tethered Venues Approach

In the early days of this project, I observed in venues studied most by sociologists interested in medicine: the hospital's residency teams and operating rooms. Yet this book's approach emerged from an unexpected opportunity, one that ended up placing me in a position to rethink how I should conduct this ethnography. I received invitations, and then cultivated opportunities, to go into the other venues. Moving into these spaces was ultimately key to understanding how authority was collectively managed. I realized that the administrative venues in the hospital, and the industry and professional association venues outside it, had value because they allowed me to observe the stark differences and interdependencies among stakeholders who considered themselves to share an occupational project. The discussion of tethered venues introduced in this book offers a further payoff beyond its ability to expose key relationships underpinning how authority is managed: it suggests a methodological direction for ethnographic scholarship that begins to address a core problem in sociology. Specifically, attention to tethered venues uncovers some of the individual-collective relations that are hard to observe in one venue—such as processes of coalescence—by focusing our attention on how interactions at a distance shape collective behavior. It afforded a range of benefits, including ways to understand: the management of medical knowledge, the stratification in medical work, and the way medical work is organized not only within, but also across venues.

And so, the opportunities I was offered and then cultivated in the field can provide new insight into some of the questions raised by the Chicago School about studying how geographically and temporally distant events and places influence and are constituted by "local" practices. Specifically, my efforts to understand the relationship between individual and collective was well served with ethnographic data across venues. Such data allowed us to interpret how medicine's stakeholders collectively ensure that medicine does, and continues doing, what it takes to afford medicine a position of social prestige. These ongoing processes were revealed in my observations of the recurrent events of teaching on the wards, presenting in professional development meetings, and engaging in gossip in conference parties. It was possible to relate physicians' behavior to their different career stages and social locations, as they work to validate and revalidate their definitions of how medical work should be executed and interpreted. It was also possible to interpret the behavior of companies that benefit from an authoritative decision about a technology, even if it happens at a patient bedside, one distant from their headquarters. In addition to showing how this work of validation is organized, this book revealed individual doctors' efforts to raise their own standing through competing over resources such as patients, clinical trials, and positions on prestigious guidelines panels. And it demonstrated how certain individuals reinforce their social authority in a way that affords everyone's ability to manage authority in medicine into the future.

These findings suggest that studying tethered venues can push forward "shop floor" studies to account for more complex, global linkages beyond the single field site. This book has taken a further step beyond efforts of those in the Chicago School, to observe and identify connections between the multiple places where work is done. A key contribution of this work is to illuminate how people create and use relationships between those places, which I call tethers. By using an approach centered on tethered venues, this book demonstrated the active role of interdependent and stratified professionals in managing the structure and the content of their work. If solely focused on Superior Hospital, this study would most closely resemble the model of institutional ethnography that Everett Hughes and his students pioneered. This model facilitates general claims yet remains vulnerable to critiques of the decontextualized world it appears to represent. The tethered venue approach expands on the Hughesian tradition by showing how people use tethers to strengthen venues' interdependence across their geographic and social locations in the city and collective. This approach, then, engages Robert Park's development of an ecological perspective that connects disparate corners of a city, as characterized by the "First Chicago School," but it also addresses critiques of the Hughes-centered "Second Chicago School." Beyond studying the city, as did Park, studying tethered venues exposes more distant linkages in an occupational project that order hospital work.

It constitutes a response, then, to the claim that the Chicago tradition cannot offer a theory of globalization.[12]

In the sociological understanding of professions, the nature of professional coalescence and the processes involved remain largely unexamined. In the case of doctors, examining tethers allowed some understanding of how doctors carry out and shift pioneering practices—practices about which they might, at times, feel personally uncertain—while strengthening the occupational project through remaining in close contact with others they see at periodic and recurring events. This kind of strengthening of connections is evident in work on political groups, where a shared perspective emerges from interdependent party members showing up in the same place multiple times, to talk about the same thing. It is also evident in religious projects, where a shared understanding of a religious community emerges from the interdependencies involved in a venue's rituals.[13]

When past investigations observed one clinic, they did not see collegial control in the profession; they saw, as also shown above, that physicians rarely sanction coworkers. In this investigation, we did see some social control through local divisions of labor, exerted when physicians accept their peers' efforts to maintain esteem in a niche. But scrutinizing medicine in terms of tethered venues provides more occupational-project-wide evidence that physicians observe each other, have opportunities for durable exercise of some control even as they compete, and in a limited way, perform self-regulation through gossip, encouragement, and observation of and discussion about potential collaborators in other labs. As discussed in chapters 5 and 7, in venues where reputations are shaped will be found criticism of peers, informal asides, and whisper campaigns. Admittedly, direct sanctions are minimal outside the residency and lab setting, where expectations are clear and levers are conspicuous; there, attendings are expected to teach and residents and fellows are expected to comply under the threat of formal punishment. And the effects of sanctions among colleagues are difficult to observe in the short run, with ethnography. In this criticism—if sometimes subtle—physicians are willing to share accounts of peers who perform in ways they think might pose problems for the occupational project. But these activities have the potential for durable effects, occurring as they do in the context of a competition across venues, in a way that strengthens the occupational project. Once we move outside a single venue and recognize there is only so much space on panels, money from companies, and space on committees, we realize they must compete for this space at the same time as they are going to compete for status. Consequently, we are able to see some self-regulation at work.

A contribution of this book, then, methodologically speaking, is to make the concept of place more robust by providing an approach for understanding the effect of different places on a group, and by finding a way to understand disparate influences through examining how the spaces are spatially tethered and used to organize the occupational project as it moves into the future. It allows us to see interactions we couldn't otherwise see, for example, interactions in which people are controlled by the doctor if they are to be effective in carrying out their professional practices, and ones in which other stakeholders manage potential and actual threats to their control of work-conditions in these venues. By looking at the way tethers are used across venues, we can see the fissures and connections in a group that appears to share a homogeneous perspective, while also offering how perspectives stay stable. Compare this approach to the typical "negotiated order" approach of looking at the organization of professional work by evaluating negotiations among groups who share a professional task but understand it differently—say, in the case of nurses and physicians who all work in the NICU, each with a different view of optimal problems and solutions. The negotiated order approach papers over differences we have seen among those who consider themselves as sharing an occupational project. Examining tethered venues solves that problem, because it exposes connections between venues by looking at tethers such as language (contested anatomy, "antrum"), in venues where many individuals can be influenced (international conferences). It focuses on both a variety of tasks and their management in venues. It lets us see that as physicians performed those tasks afforded by the venue, they were able to build support for their modes of indeterminacy through working across venues and using tethers. Paying attention to venues and tethers lets us see how individuals could solve problems and be influential in ways that are obscured when we simply observe a single venue or compare multiple ones.[14]

Another benefit for sociology of moving across venues is that a tethered venues approach adds to our understanding of the process of managing uncertainty, the theoretically useful concept of organizing indeterminacy. The payoff of differentiating these concepts is clear if we compare the sociologist's focus on indeterminacy to a sound, single-venue study. In her ethnography of standard-setters struggling with innovating while leading the profession, Renee Fox observed physicians' managing of uncertainty in their efforts to conduct research and treat patients, raising the important issue of how individuals are related to their collective circumstances of medicine more broadly. Fox's study was an ethnography of individual actors with local interpretations; and it strongly affected subsequent understandings of the concept of uncertainty, which similarly described it in terms of the application of expertise to very particular situational circumstances. In this study we saw some individual expressions of uncertainty—for instance, in the live-case vignette, the fellows conference, and at the conference with the debaters who know their data are imperfect. But what couldn't be seen by Fox was the way the physicians she studied interpreted their work and recast it in different ways, depending on the context. As discussed above, the future is shaped on the shop floor, with patients and colleagues, but also in reference to more distant groupings. The concept of clinical uncertainty has been useful for understanding how training and practicing doctors apply expertise in very particular individual actions with knowledge. But using the tethered venues approach let us see physicians' collective action with knowledge, as we need to in order to situate the management of uncertainty in a broader context. As we saw, when surrounded by other standard-setters, each felt uncertainty on the wards but made advances with others inside and outside of their invisible colleges, in venues affording a broader scope of influence. Without the tethered venues approach, we wouldn't be able to see how uncertainty was particular to certain tasks, was transient, and could perhaps even be explained by its rhetorical value. Specifically, we would not be able to see how those transient individual sentiments served more collective processes of organizing indeterminacy. The tethered venues approach to ethnography lets us account for a broader set of voices in the doctors' community and allows us to see how an individual feeling of uncertainty is compatible with the act of organizing indeterminacy for an entire occupational project. If we focus on one venue, then, it is possible to get an incomplete impression; rather than simply coping with uncertainty by working with colleagues in a single place, these physician-researchers are managing indeterminacy by actively retaining open spaces, proposing and establishing problems and solutions across venues.[15]

The tethered venues approach also allows us to understand larger scales of stratification than can be easily seen in one venue—in particular, the kind of interdependencies among career types spanning venues. For instance, it would be hard to see a stratification system by studying medical schools or hospitals because they disallow observation of the way that doctors stratify with respect to each other. In EP, there are two career types of doctors, standard-setters and clinicians, who make different amounts of money and have different opportunities. It would be hard to see this distinction in medical school or residency. This is because selection factors are likely at work; it's quite possible that different types of incipient doctors select into different medical school and residency training programs and continue in those tracks. Stratification processes could also operate after residency, when we see where they are placed in fellowship, when they make a decision about with whom they will ally, or when they find their passion ultimately lies in research or clinical practice. It is also the case that making claims about hierarchy is not straightforward, as each position is more or less desirable to different people; standard-setters will often experience more autonomy, but make less money. And so, in light of the fact that those with different career types hold different goals, this stratification is not necessarily unjust.

A final benefit of the tethered venues approach is that it can show that processes working across venues might differ from those operating within venues. That there are differences in processes is important, because it alerts us to a perception that what stakeholders are doing is managing authority. For instance, processes of managing authority across venues had more to do with competition for status. Among the many examples presented, we could especially see status as a preoccupation in standard-setters' storytelling about patients being cared for in an especially compelling way. At the same time, the competition within venues often involved competition for quality, although there were exceptions. To maximize the chance of positive outcomes, they must set up the lab the right way. They know that, for their hands at least, there are better and worse ways of performing procedures that represent the solutions described in a mode of organizing indeterminacy. And within those venues, doctors did pay attention to whether a proposed approach to organizing indeterminacy has been validated by a strong level of evidence. That is, in some important ways the doctors' competition resembles what can be described not only as a status competition but also a marketplace of ideas.

Some Final Payoffs and Next Steps

This book follows a tradition of paying attention to the relatively durable features of professional work most iconic of the "official" profession, from the shop floor to the annual meeting. But it is an effort to expand the Chicago tradition—especially in terms of places to observe—and it has given us a broad view across medicine's *terroir* to explore a range of features that structure medicine, features that sociologists don't typically understand as internal to the occupational project's self-regulation. Some of these features are, for instance, contacts with disparate professions. The book has shown us the importance of looking in multiple ways—looking at individuals and their venues of interaction, and looking across those venues, even those venues that seem insufficiently "professional."

When we look at venues like an annual conference not only as a place to expand one's knowledge base but also as a place that is differently used by individuals to serve their own ends in the interest of organizing indeterminacy amidst a competition, we are given a different way of understanding expert work itself. A valuable expansion of this work, then, would be to take account of venues where physicians and nurses mix, or venues in which they interact with pharmaceutical companies. It might also mean observing other venues that lend themselves to potentially consequential social interaction, like the golf course. Or, reflecting that I noted trainees' and attendings' often instrumental use of the Internet to access deployable research findings, and the fact that these doctors also promote themselves on

Twitter and in virtual curbsides, future work might incorporate observation of virtual venues. Just as scholars of wine and artisanal crops have come to examine the features of a crop that emerge from all the environmental factors that affect its epigenetic qualities, including its environment contexts and farming practices, we have seen the benefit of including in our purview those habitats in which a range of factors contribute to a collegial order.[16]

Although a focus on tethered venues emphasizes not comparison but connection, in this work I have nonetheless intermittently compared EPs with those in occupational projects whose problems and solutions are different, showing processes that are similar in form if not in content. These comparisons suggest parameters for understanding other occupational projects in light of the theory of authority management sketched here, the benefits of centering on tasks, and ways they facilitate the uses of tethers. To choose only a few, in chapter 2, I show that general cardiologists also must groom patients, but their solution involves a different kind of grooming; rather than groom the patient into submission for a surgical task involving short-term feedback loops, they encourage the patient to take initiative to care for themselves in light of the longer-term feedback loop involved in their care. In chapter 4, I show that internal medicine doctors, because they are at the referral chain's beginning in contrast to its end (with EPs), have tasks whose solutions—which involve collaboration with social workers and case managers—diminish the impact of the hospital's administrative programs. And in chapter 6, I show comparisons between companies whose task structures for training differed. There, when reps changed the tasks that connected standard-setters and clinicians, the company shifted clinicians' attitudes toward their technologies.

The kind of expanded unit of analysis reflected by the occupational project may also be useful for observing other professions because it lets us see arm's-length relationships that would otherwise go unexamined. The care with which these relationships are managed is signaled in the ethical codes of professional associations, whose extensive attention paid to the matter of arm's-length relationships indexes their ongoing concern about these other stakeholders. Accountants consistently face expectations from companies to alter their audit practices. Police departments have extensive processes of managing donations so as not to appear as if they are taking bribes. The AAUP's code of ethics involves extensive discussion of the liabilities of professors' service on corporate boards. Accounting for the individuals trained outside of the profession's formal institutions is also consistent with recent work in the sociology of knowledge, which recognizes the input that parents have had on the knowledge base of physicians. Moreover, analyzing arm's-length relationships lets us see that in working with companies, professions can take on more complicated tasks with a greater chance of success.

Another payoff of examining the occupational project is that it offered a way of interpreting case studies of work not neatly contained within the concept of "profession." It let us bring together the many scholars of expert work whose attention has shifted from attention to "professions" as a unit of analysis, to examine episodes much like those we observe in the vignettes, which center on the actual foci of peoples' attention in their venues of work. Recent research on work has focused less on a profession's core and general tasks, to attend to professionals' work outside what is usually covered by the term *jurisdiction*. In reading this work and observing these venues, it has been impossible to ignore that work has a much larger scope than we might casually pay attention to, and that occupations involve collaboration around shared tasks, assessment of others' capacities, and a range of interests that are focused within and across different venues. Today, we see some of the highest-status corporate lawyers work in accounting firms, venues which, for the lawyers themselves, are becoming more determinative of work tasks than is their professional association. The economic sociology literature, too, has demonstrated the importance of expanding the scope of how we should understand professional work, showing the intermingling of financial, organizational, and medical processes in work on dying, variations in hospital ownership, and markets for eggs and sperm.[17]

At the same time, examining the occupational project also offered a payoff more central to classical theoretical traditions, ones engaged by scholars of professions and medicine. Specifically, this approach of focusing on the occupational project, a more dialectic or dynamic way of talking about collective processes and authority in work, let us reconcile professionals' individual goals and interests with collective interests, by attention to processes necessary for shaping the collective's understanding of medical work. To understand how these individual interests are tied to collective concerns is not only to revisit concerns of those in the classical liberal tradition, interests of those from Hobbes to Locke to Rousseau, but could also be the key to 1) unlocking the problem of coalescence, 2) building a theory about how expert work is organized in a well-managed way, 3) accounting for multiple career paths alongside at least some semblance of a shared knowledge base. It remains to be seen how this work would be undertaken, but one promising direction for further studying these individual-collective relations might be to track the effect of a core group of individuals on the nature of the project itself, examining which individuals' efforts to organize indeterminacy end up being influential collectively, and teasing out the conditions in which particular individuals are more or less successful.[18]

Another contribution of the approach, one relevant for studies outside of medicine, is that doing ethnography in multiple tethered venues can offer implications for how we understand the process by which knowledge diffuses. Close attention to venues will allow us to identify which venues are disproportionately important for presenting ideas, and how the extent and cadence of diffusion will be tied to venues' temporal or geographic proximity to each other (and thus to the potential frequency of contact). Tethered venues let us make sense of place-based social structures that support mixing among those with multiple group memberships, which can lead to the rapid and effective spreading of a message. This theory involves periodic events in which higher- and lower-status professionals mix, and thus addresses some of the issues related to diffusion bottlenecks produced by high-status actors, who will be reachable at predictable venues at predictable times. Circulation is happening in venues that are constantly referencing something that took place before in that venue and others that are periodically visited, resulting in emanating chains of circulation. By examining tethered venues, we can study these structures of emanation and circulation, allowing us, for instance, to substantiate claims about the associations that make up scientific facts.

This study can say little about individual careers, because its approach to ethnography centers around venues and their connections, rather than individuals and their biographies. At the same time, scrutinizing tethered venues suggests the potential for new directions in the study of careers. For instance, this study is suggestive of how standard-setters' work to organize indeterminacy yields benefits across a career, in what may be a kind of a cycle of behaviors that ultimately yield positive impacts. Among EPs, the cycle is marked less by sequences of jobs than by events that afford individuals a platform for distinguishing themselves. Specifically, the study suggests that standard-setters, perhaps in connection with a device company and others in invisible college, develop and strengthen their approach to organizing indeterminacy in a niche. They groom patients on wards and treat them in a lab, also training fellows in their approach. They go to industry-sponsored venues to explain and teach approach to fellows and clinicians and gain adherents and referrers, and to annual meetings to argue that their approach is better than others', shape guidelines, and disparage the competition. In carrying out tasks in all of these venues, they use tethers that let them support work in other venues (e.g., getting slides, sending out fellows, using [or dismissing] specific terminology) and raise their standing. This research suggests that examining physicians' different capacities to work across these venues successfully would be fruitful for those interested in the social organization of individual mobility.

Theoretically speaking, it is not possible any longer to reduce the way that authority is managed, especially as it relates to so-called "external" stakeholders, to simply a story of either professional supremacy or corporate capture. On one hand, Abbott, in early work, would say that a professional group would co-opt those with different expertise into their group. Latour, in his case study of Pasteur, described a similar cooptation. Yet physicians' relationship with industry involved much more dependence; they depended on fellows programs and industry meetings to build networks and learn skills, as well as to provide a visible venue for demonstrating the merits of their approaches to organizing indeterminacy. Those same device reps helped standard-setters keep new technology from the hands of the inept. On the other hand, Conrad and Light point attention at corporate capture, a situation where prevailing problems and solutions are established by private corporate interests, which differ from those of physicians. But physicians were frequently taking control of their clinics and even venues that were organized by companies, while companies put meeting agendas and invitees in the hands of physician program directors, and device reps sought to distance themselves from physicians whose use of their technologies put their own and their company's reputations at risk. Ultimately, this work confirms that industry reps and medical professionals mix in interdependent ways. Indeed, while sometimes industry is kept at arm's length, other times it facilitates self-governance in the occupational project. What we have seen, then, is a multiheaded mode of governance, characterized by mutually beneficial relationships. Authority is not managed by professionals or industry alone, and that fact, rather than being understood as separated by boundaries, should be understood as a hallmark of sharing an occupational project.[19]

Even as I address this literature on medicine and the professions, I acknowledge that I have approached the subject of managing medical authority less as a scholar of the professions, and more as an ethnographer and theorist. As a sociologist steeped in a tradition of ethnography focused on groups of people doing things in single spaces, I was motivated in part by an interest in working out a different kind of ethnography, one that involved tying together these places. I saw that the same people visited venues, ones that differed completely in terms of the activities they permitted, and asked: What were the relationships between these people and spaces? This different approach to fieldwork—one that remains continuous with but overcomes limitations in "Chicago School" ethnography—not only helped me better understand connections between people and connections between places but also showed the way these connections are actively managed as a part of an overall process of a social project—here, the maintenance of medical authority.

Still, beyond the potential value of this ethnographic approach for studying other social projects, it may be useful for those whose work falls outside the tasks and concerns of sociologists, in particular those who are interested in policy matters. It could be productive for others who are concerned with how work gets done in the health care professions, with a range of interests from public policy to medical ethics. In particular, this ethnography of tethered venues may be useful for thinking about small-area variations in health care, as it suggests a way to understand some of the studies showing that physicians practice in many substantially and ethically different ways, ways that, even when holding constant patient acuity, vary across geographic areas, organizational forms, and salary versus fee-for-service systems pay-ment arrangements. Nationally representative studies have shown that those with similar medical training practice differently. These studies re-flect, in part, that doctors are focused on their everyday venues, and have their personal ways of organizing indeterminacy. This study has similar findings; EPs come to different conclusions because of the kinds of cases they see in their labs, cases that may vary according to whether they are standard-setters or clinicians. Practices also may vary in light of the connec-tions physicians make and strengthen at venues like the fellows programs and industry meetings, where device companies put on a show and seek to convert clinicians to a particular emerging technology or technique. We have also seen how doctors are differently taught in venues outside the lab, looking at how those physicians may use what they have learned in other venues when confronting pressures faced in home labs. We also saw some variations are particular to EPs, such as whether they use the three- or the five- catheter approach to ablation, and these variations and differences have to do with tasks and relationships made in periodically visited venues, and constituencies of particular EPs who come to a consensus about prob-lems and solutions in EP. Yet it will not be the case that attending these events will necessarily account for use. A broad focus on venues, then, may show how small-area variations in health care can persist. And so, this study helps us account for the heterogeneity of practices in a way that is dif-ficult when using administrative or survey data, because not all doctors are pulling the occupational project in the same direction, or with the same ability.[20]

In this book I write about how doctors, as one set of stakeholders among others, seek so carefully to identify and shape the nature of problems their expertise can address, and the kinds of solutions they can support as a pro-fessional group. I've come to appreciate the work of doctors in other ways. Doctors should be given great credit for managing their occupational proj-ect so that it is not overrun by the push for powerful individuals to take over, a choice that has preserved the possibility of an emphasis on quality. They can also be given credit for creating relationships with those outside the field that can benefit their occupational project. While wearing a lead vest and apron, and standing beside them, and while observing them share their ma-terial with colleagues, I came to see how their efforts to give peers this free-dom to manage one's own work is potentially socially productive. I came to admire their ability to maintain their relationships at the same time that they are fiercely critical about their contributions to knowledge. Their drive to seek excellence is not only important for how they manage the occupa-tional project to emphasize quality, but may also have positive implications for policy considerations about the place of medicine in society.

appendix

Methods

The very difficulties of carrying out field observation—the resistance
of his subjects, the danger that his very success as a participant may
later prevent him from full reporting, even the experience of getting
thrown out of town—are facts to be analyzed sociologically.
—EVERETT C. HUGHES[1]

We can think about ethnographers as working in an occupational project
that involves constructing problems with their methods, while also actively
developing solutions. This appendix is where some of the details of that process are offered. Any statement of method serves as both a confessional
about the nuts and bolts of the ethnographer's personal experience (so as to
demonstrate rigor [and trust]) and as a set of lessons learned (so as to offer
potentially helpful insights for fieldworkers). Below I describe some problems fieldworkers face, and the solutions I arrived at, while sharing lessons
from my experiences. My aim is to convey the rigor of my methods and, ideally, generate trust in my account.

To understand the shaping of any ethnography, it's necessary to understand the shaping of the relationships described. It is said that some minimal degree of trust is necessary. But, as Duneier notes, we never know just
what trust we have received from those we observe. At the same time, it is
possible to get some signals of overt distrust. I was not always trusted, and
there was much hidden, and much I could not see, let alone understand.
These challenges related to trust, as well as other issues, created particular
lessons and led to particular strategies that I will spend the remainder of this
section addressing. My approach to managing these and other challenges
exposed what are likely to be only some of the social features of medical and
other venues that shape the ethnographic work that can happen there.[2]

In this appendix I will seek to clarify my involvement with the people and
venues I observed, and then describe the methodological problems I faced
and the insights I came to about ethnography, including the casting of the
ethnographer as a problem, using tethers to help with access, deidentification, and subject self-consciousness.[3]

The Fieldwork: Sequence, Time Spent, and Relationships Built

According to my records, the data presented in this book were collected over the course of more than twelve years. For me, doing ethnography was less about the amount of time I spent with subjects than about the relationships built. In this section I describe my methods not only as a chronology but also as a survey, and by including not only the particular relationships I formed, but also what I had to be careful not to do, and what I was welcome to do.

Chronology

I will start with the chronological. In my third year of graduate school, as I was finishing my required coursework, I was given initial access to observe a residency team in Superior Hospital, after I was introduced to an attending there. Fresh from reading Weber on bureaucracies alongside scholarship on professional social control, when introduced to the attending I thought would be helpful, I described my interest in studying how medical knowledge makes its way into practice, in light of the vertical controls of the hospital bureaucracy and the horizontal controls of the medical profession. I also indicated to this person my interest in the adoption and rejection of medical technology. As I met other attendings, I gained the opportunity to conduct my initial exploratory fieldwork with the other teams to which these attendings provided access—the internal medicine residents discussed in chapter 2—and that fieldwork extended into a second year. I gained approval from my university's Institutional Review Board (IRB), in the College of Social Sciences. I was introduced to other attendings by a colleague of the first attending I had observed, who described me—and implicitly, my style of research—with a quick introduction: "this is Jane Goodall." For eight months, over two years, I would "take call," or follow residents' thirty-five-hour shifts. This brought credibility; residents would brag to each other about my commitment. It also showed me why the residents were in no mood to discuss my observations the morning after. I also went to drug company–sponsored dinners and journal clubs, where trainees discussed the latest research findings. In my second year of observing residency teams I made my way into teams led by cardiologists, because they were led by two kinds of attendings, which afforded me a look at influence of each type of attending's different tasks. Because of Dr. Walker's bedside manner, a resident suggested I observe his team, which was co-led by Dr. Kellogg. At the end of the month, Dr. Kellogg suggested I observe Dr. Stimm's team.

In year three I gained access to more venues, partly in response to some resistance from those in the position of "chief resident," and partly in response to an offer from Dr. Stimm. The resistance coincided with a problem involving an overdose on the wards. Someone unknown to me contacted Superior Hospital's HIPAA board about privacy concerns. I was interviewed by the police. The hospital sought, unsuccessfully, to take control of my IRB protocol. Nonetheless, the hospital was able to require that I perform an extensive introduction to patients being treated by those residency teams I was observing. (I describe this episode in greater detail below.) With this increase in expectations about informed consent, I felt my ability to observe was impaired significantly. The director of the residency program asked me to take some time off from observing. I felt that I was being kicked out.

I then began to think about what new venues might be available that would allow me to continue studying authority. I remembered that at the end of our month on the wards, several months earlier, Dr. Stimm had offered me the opportunity to study his lab. In light of my interest in the adoption of medical technology he had said, "You should study us; we're rejecting technologies all the time." I took Dr. Stimm up on his invitation in a more full-time capacity after I was interviewed by the police in year three—I had previously been visiting only on occasion—and I found the electrophysiology laboratory to be a small society within the hospital, and EP to be a field with a multiplicity of influences on its practice. Once I was kicked out of the residency program and began observing in EP (chapter 3), I also observed the "bed throughput and fill" meetings of administrators (chapter 4). I continued observing in these venues through years five and six (when the three Superior EPs left for Cityview). After I mentioned that other attendings had used it, Dr. Stimm incorporated the Dr. Goodall description when introducing me to lab members and colleagues in Superior and at industry events and the annual meeting.

In year five, my fieldwork focused primarily on venues outside of Superior Hospital. To gather background information on electrophysiology I visited labs of influential standard-setters, for observations and interviews, in Philadelphia, Milan, Indianapolis, Ann Arbor, and Bordeaux. I began traveling to observe fellows programs (chapter 4), hands-on meetings (chapter 6), and annual meetings (chapter 7), and continued doing so, on and off, until year twelve. During year eight, I began asking those I studied to read chapters of my dissertation, and I sat beside them to ask their opinions on my interpretations. And during years eleven and twelve, I observed two in-person meetings, and silently participated in biweekly conference calls, of a joint American College of Cardiology and Heart Rhythm Society committee creating a guidelines document for ventricular arrhythmias. Dr. Stimm made me a member of an email listserv where people consulted each other in "virtual curbsides," and I also followed Twitter accounts with advice requests and humble brags. I continued to conduct interviews for clarifying and confirming details until the manuscript was submitted for publication.

Survey

Now that I have presented the chronological arc of my activities in multiple venues over the twelve years, I will now survey my fieldwork activities in the years 2005–18. My fieldwork was centered on six venues: the inpatient wards; the home laboratory in which EPs perform procedures and teach their trademark approaches; the administrative meetings to manage beds; the industry-sponsored meetings where fellows and clinicians learn about advances in EP; the industry-sponsored meetings where clinicians are able to learn new technologies; and the international conferences where they describe these approaches as best practice, evaluate each other's performances, and exchange gossip. In these venues, I made recordings, conducted interviews, and performed observations; my days took different forms depending on the venue I was studying. I also conducted 121 interviews with members of the occupational project from around the world. I used a standard set of questions tied to my interest in the management of authority, though I at times asked questions of particular relevance to my interviewee. When the venues I entered were set up for visitors, as was the case with some of the high-profile labs I visited, I faced the challenge of ensuring that I asked questions the doctors and administrators did not have ready answers to, and thus needed to think about.[4]

I used interviews to get otherwise inaccessible information, and transcribed most of them myself. Of the 121 interviews I conducted, 109 were in person. I asked the subjects I could reach to provide their comments on the text after I wrote up key passages. When describing medical procedures I consulted physician friends I had made during the process of fieldwork, asking them to share expertise in exchange for coffee, dinner, or, in one instance, a free tennis lesson.

The sequence in which I did the fieldwork largely followed that of the manuscript, with the within-Superior observations preceding those in outside venues, though I often interspersed observations in multiple venues inside and outside of the hospital depending on the timing of relevant events. My observations inside Superior Hospital took place primarily from 2005 to 2009. I was fully immersed in eight teams total on the wards, across six four-day call cycles a month, for a total observation time of about 3,840 hours on the wards. I conducted one-on-one interviews with the members of the team that I focus on here and also conducted follow-up interviews approximately one year after my initial observation. I followed all teams' four-day "call cycles," which comprised two days of twelve-hour shifts followed by a thirty- to forty-hour stretch of being "on call." During the night of call, team members admitted patients to the service, followed up on existing patients, responded to "codes" (the emergencies, usually fatal, occurring throughout the hospital), and attempted to steal a few hours of sleep.

The team then received twelve to sixteen hours off before returning to Superior and restarting the cycle. I observed in the Superior electrophysiology lab two to five days a week for two years, for a total of more than 2,880 hours. Across my four years at the hospital I also frequently attended meetings of the bed management program, including, but not limited to, the days I observed residency teams (whose more junior members were required to attend those meetings).

My observations outside of Superior Hospital took place primarily between 2008 and 2018. During that period, I observed a total of ten industry-sponsored meetings in Boston, Chicago (five meetings), Cleveland, Minneapolis, Flint, and New York. Four of those meetings were fellows meetings, and six were hands-on meetings; most lasted two days. I also attended nine of the three- or four-day meetings of the American College of Cardiology and the Heart Rhythm Society, in Boston, San Francisco, Chicago, and Denver.

Of course, the heartbreaking reality of fieldwork is that only a tiny fraction gets into final published form. There was material from some venues I observed that did not make its way into the book, because the book is organized by venues and pertinent to the problem of managing authority. I observed these venues, which ultimately provided extensive background information and context, during the process of winnowing down places to observe from those to which I had been given access.[5]

I attended events periodically, both independently and with Superior doctors. Coming to the events periodically meant I could observe changes in EP's occupational project, by comparing snapshots of the ideas and technologies dominant at each time. As with a filmstrip, by splicing these snapshots together I could see the field in constant motion. After a while, I could see patterns, but in a way I had not expected. I set out to study how people moved across venues, and what they did in them. But what I ended up seeing was patterns of change—as a record of how their practices were responding to change.

When I started going to these events, I had already invested three years in understanding EP "from home." By the time I arrived in a limousine to the fellows' conference, I had been briefed on what was at stake for the elite EPs participating in debates, and I knew what the attendings had published and their positions on controversial matters in EP. When I got to the industry training programs I knew the history of the companies. When I was invited to speak at the annual meeting and an esteemed cardiologist asked for my slides, I felt that I was not a total outsider to the field of EP. Once there, I went to the most popular events in the hall, and the most well-attended events on the program.

I ensured I attended events that lasted no longer than the short periods for which I visited. Short events, such as fellows meetings, hands-on meetings, and international conferences, are designed to operate over two to four days. In a certain way, I was not "helicoptering in," as everyone helicopters in. This temporal quality creates dynamics of interaction (reunion parties, compressed sales pitches, etc.) that must be observed through the eyes of participants. Therefore, the equivalent of being fully embedded was sampling the universe of events, which allowed me to ensure that the patterns I observed were truly general phenomena in the event or site. It would have been impossible to study groups whose patterns of interaction vary daily over such short periods. Within residency teams, for instance, on call days, interns are busy, the residents are less busy, and medical students may not even be in the hospital. Observing for only a few days would offer a completely unrepresentative view of their work. I had to spend time with members of the residency teams outside rounds and the often stylized case presentations. In addition to offering access to "unscripted" interactions, doing so also showed me how they collected information and translated patient traits into symptoms. My being there from the beginning of the month also made them take for granted I would be part of the team.[6]

Further, for each kind of site I covered the universe of possible configurations in the field; I observed how Medistar, Medicore, Cardiacore, and other companies held their fellows programs and hands-on meetings. They asked and I disclosed who I was and why I wanted to attend. According to industry officials, the FDA now sends undercover observers to industry meetings to ensure no one discusses off-label usage of technologies. I was concerned that officials and speakers would change their behavior based on concerns over whether this non-EP was, in fact, a mole. Therefore, I made sure to attend—and to inform other meeting participants that I attended—events sponsored by a range of companies. In doing so, I demonstrated their peers' belief in my integrity while sampling from the universe of settings distant from, but influential on, my home site.

Relationships

In spending so much time in EP's various venues observing, and in discussing my observations with physicians curious about the project, I began to form longer-term relationships, and build some trust. Among many other modes of participation in these venues, I wore scrubs and the white coat, taking notes on notebooks and scraps of paper. I "took call" with trainees including sleeping in Superior Hospital where residents squeezed in a few hours between admitting and treating patients. I wore a twenty-five-pound apron made of lead as I stood for hours watching electrophysiologists implant a defibrillator into a patient's chest. I watched them extract infected pacemaker wires from a patient's arteries, or burn lesions into their heart. I sat through meetings where attendings negotiated with administrators in their pursuit of the resources necessary to attract patients they could treat, study, and discuss in the other venues they frequent. I joined doctors to socialize with current and past colleagues, dine with industry representatives, and wrangle over the content of the guidelines.

After a few months of my full immersion there, I came to be accepted as more or less a part of the laboratory. After a year in the EP lab, I was invited to the end-of-year celebration to honor departing fellows. After two years, I was included in the EP lab's Christmas party celebrations at Dr. Stimm's house. And with my eyes opened to EP culture's informal order, I began to perceive many aspects that had previously been rendered invisible by my theoretical blinders. Like most fieldworkers, I made choices to build relationships of trust, and to afford the clearest picture I could get of what they were doing.

I also learned that, even though Dr. Stimm's assistance was valuable for initial access, getting into some venues relied on having relationships that were sufficiently weak. Dr. Stimm opened some doors for me outside Superior Hospital, such as fellows programs and hands-on meetings, and other doors I opened myself. These introductions afforded me a chance to build relationships that would let me open doors for myself both during my dissertation research and long after the dissertation was complete. However, like the doctors I studied, I sought to have arm's-length relationships with companies. Company reps usually allowed me, and sometimes invited me, to attend many meetings outside the hospital, provided I was willing to foot the bill myself (which usually meant finding a couch of a local friend). To them, the benefit of having Dr. Stimm's goodwill far outweighed the cost of an observer.

Overall, I was impressed with the EPs' openness and willingness to provide access to venues. It has been argued that it is challenging to "study up" because of the resources that socially powerful subjects have available to prevent "prying eyes." I was able to gain access to professional meetings of physicians that enabled me to move unnoticed among both physicians and the vendors and hawkers of medical wares, for four reasons. First, having spent significant time bedside, I had learned the patois of this group. Second, similar to those atop the pecking order of the hospital, I wore a white coat. Third, I was the same age as many fellows, so was assumed to be a colleague or student. Fourth, I had the sponsorship of the powerful. Fifth, I could be used as a tether; Dr. Stimm, then the program director of the annual Heart Rhythm Society conference, invited me to speak at the annual meeting in Denver, where I spoke on the diffusion of medical innovations.[7]

Although it is impossible to confirm unambiguously, the extensive access to electrophysiology activities I was afforded and the opportunity I had to participate in those activities suggest that some trust was gained. My immersion would likely not have been possible otherwise; for instance, I would not have been invited to graduation ceremonies and dinner parties as I was. And, to be sure, I did not have a medical degree or experience the EP's training as an insider, but I suspect that my standpoint in this regard was as much a benefit as a hindrance. In any case, this deep embeddedness gave me sufficient time and exposure to be able to see key episodes in the field, and to ruminate over and later pose questions to their key participants.

Casting the Ethnographer as a Problem (or Their Management as a Solution)

I mentioned above that in year three I thought that my project had ended due to resistance from certain physicians I had been observing. Chief residents sit in the middle of a hierarchy, sandwiched between the residents and attendings, and are given responsibility over key dimensions of the residency program: organizing faculty speakers and other activities, giving residents time off, and assembling and scheduling teams who conduct the "rounds" I described in chapter 2. Charged with protecting both those leading and those participating in the training program, they occupy a vulnerable social location. My presence, as far as I can tell, was seen as exacerbating their vulnerability. So they constructed me as a problem, and got me kicked out. But I did regain access. This episode suggested to me the importance of knowing the particular foci of people you are studying, and taking the opportunities extended to you, being aware that you in turn might become the subject of their own occupational project as they figure out how you might help them with their goals.[8]

I also learned that there's not just one social entry point that might enable me to answer questions. Specifically, I learned that having relationships underpinned by mutual intellectual curiosity, and not considered potentially threatening to the occupational project—like my relationship with Dr. Stimm—was important to gaining access to venues where I might answer my questions. I learned that it may be necessary to look hard at one's relationships, to avoid threatening their project, and to cultivate relationships with individuals who are in a location in their occupational project in which they are less vulnerable. In order to provide an account of how it is that I eventually ended up having access, and the kind of access I had, I'm going to talk about how I was constructed as a problem, and how I was also later constructed as a solution.

My realization that I had been constructed as a problem began when I arrived at a hospital auditorium planning to observe a year-end parody of attendings and colleagues by the outgoing interns. The parody was going to poke fun at superiors and peers as well as the stresses of the job. I had been invited by an attending who was a senior member of the residency program administration; they thought it would provide a great perspective on the culture of the program. But one of the chief residents asked the director of the program to ask me to leave before the event started. He did, and I left. Clearly, I had not yet earned admittance to this playful mockery; the doctors did not want me to see their caricatures before seeing the professional identity they wanted to present.

One month after I was asked to leave the parody, steps were taken to subject me to some scrutiny to see what sort of problem I was. After I had begun to occasionally observe the electrophysiology lab, I was invited to meet with the three chief residents, who said they hoped to learn more about my project. Prior to meeting with them, I had—with IRB approval and the verbal permission of the attendings and team members I observed—spent two years following teams. The chiefs began with an audit of my fieldwork, saying they had spoken with some of the residents. One chief said, "When the residents said you slept in the on-call room with them, they said they sometimes felt they were expected to talk to you during times they would have preferred sleeping." Another said, "We spoke to a resident who was conducting a procedure, and he felt uncomfortable when you were in the room when there were complications." Next came two genres of questions pinpointing concerns both particular and general.

First, the chiefs cast me as interfering in the everyday tasks residents are asked to accomplish. Before meeting with me, the chiefs asked residents a set of questions that framed the ethnographer as a problem in light of the expectations of attendings; the chief residents are charged with taking care of residents, and must scrutinize whether anyone might impose on those residents. Chief residents feel charged with ensuring that students transform into professionals in the way medical culture has always enabled. This pedagogical role was first voiced in concerns they expressed to me regarding resident workload. As one chief put it, "They have a very busy job, and we are concerned that you will occupy too much of their time. It would add a considerable amount of time to their work if they had to page you before rounding every morning." They were also concerned about the residents' ability to form collegial informal relationships with other cohort members. The same chief asked, "Will they feel comfortable being uninhibited with you around?" I argued for my ability not to interfere with the residents' work. I reported that I had gotten consent through the residents independently of the attending. I also said that I urged the residents not to feel uncomfortable rejecting my request for access. I answered these questions as I had with the IRB. The chiefs said that some residents mentioned that, in my early days of fieldwork, I asked them questions in the bleary-eyed postcall mornings. (I learned the inadvisability of this practice after taking call.) I was being "pimped," subjected to questions with different content but the exact same rapid-fire form as these residents had experienced during their years of training on the wards.

Second, they identified ways in which, for them, the way I was carrying out my research was problematic for the way they carried out their work. One way the ethnographer can be framed as a problem is if others who think of themselves as researchers—as well as professionals subject to HIPAA— can frame the ethnographer as carrying out their research in a problematic way. For instance, the chiefs cast me as a potential threat to their efforts to protect their own reputation and that of the hospital. And residents, like others on the cusp of leaving a training program and launching a career, seek to advance their own goals in part by strengthening their occupational project. Along these lines, the residents expressed general ethical concerns about obligations of researchers to their subjects. Since they scheduled—but did not participate in—the teams I observed, they knew little of my work. And so, their questions resembled the usual battery delivered by IRBs. The chiefs asked, "How will you make your data anonymous?" "How will you remove from your observations those who have not provided consent?" They even expressed discomfort with the consequences of my becoming an insider: they worried that I could not observe the ethical code of the physician while wearing their emblematic white coat. "I don't feel comfortable with you 'being invisible' on a team. Doctors are supposed to participate in patient care under any circumstance." Finally, the chiefs asked questions that evinced an assumption that I occupied a privileged position in the hierarchical teams I was observing: "Since you are getting access to the team through the attending, how do you keep the rest of the team from feeling pressured to participate?"

In preparation for this meeting, the chiefs had come up with a solution for the problem they had constructed: to include my mentor in a meeting either over the phone or during a visit to Superior Hospital's residency program, perhaps to help in their efforts to remove me. Even as I later realized that he might have served as a helpful tether for me, I felt that since the chiefs and I were approximately at the same age and stage in a graduate program, it was more ethical not to pressure them through using a high-ranking attending. So I suggested it would be better to discuss matters as colleagues. I did consult privately with my mentor about potential approaches to future sampling, and responded to the chiefs' points via email, suggesting multiple approaches I thought would address their concerns. One of my responses was to develop a complex strategy that involved gaining informed consent from team members using a checklist of events I could observe and making sure that 100 percent of the team consented, and even then not participating 25 percent of the time to ensure that no one was blamed for opting out. I felt that these and my other answers were detailed while not being overly intrusive to the ongoing working of the program. Yet the email did not alleviate the chiefs' concerns, for reasons that were not immediately clear to me. In a meeting soon after, the director of the residency program suggested

I take some time away, and I headed home that day to ponder how to salvage my dissertation.

Ultimately, someone—I never learned who—contacted the hospital's HIPAA board. I also learned that the IRB of the university's College of Medical Sciences had contacted the IRB of the College of Social Sciences, and had argued that gaining consent from the physicians (my approved authorization) was inadequate. On November 16, 2007, the IRB announced that future observations on all residency teams were to involve the assent of their patients. The residency program had circled the wagons, having successfully cast me as a problem.

The chief residents' decision is understandable if we think about their roles as gatekeepers. According to the residency program director, chiefs see themselves as advocates for the house staff community, and would want to keep potential distractions out of the program. As that director told me in an interview, "If you aren't on their good side, you won't make inroads," and added that they see themselves as "protecting the residents."

Specifically, the chiefs' success in securing the hospital's backstage influences their future recommendations and opportunities with powerful administrators. My particular challenge with the chiefs made me sensitive to the importance of accounting for the fact that my insertion into a community might harm someone else's position in it. Chiefs are responsible for protecting the hospital from having the often messy details of patient care publicly exposed. Residents provide the bulk of care in an academic hospital, and chiefs are the most consistent source of their oversight. As an attending put it to me, chiefs are in a position that is "metastable"—meaning that it is short-lived and capable of tolerating only small disturbances. Anyone who has seen a medical television show knows the uncertainty under which trainees and even experienced physicians operate. (The popularity of these shows relies on the belief that medicine has an intellectual coherence that is not experienced in practice.) For real hospitals, when publicized, these dramas can be costly in reputational and financial terms.

I realized that a researcher could be recast as a problem even amid their efforts to produce knowledge within an institution with the mission of doing precisely that. Yet, when a patient at Superior Hospital experienced a morphine overdose, the same chiefs may have seen me as a solution to the hospital's problems. The idea I had then, though it is impossible to confirm, was that because they occupy such an unstable situation, stuck between the residents and the faculty, they felt they were doing something for their reputations in the program by passing my name along to the police. In any event, soon after the chiefs pimped me, I received a letter from hospital administrators: "As you know, the Medical Center is working with the Police Department to conduct an investigation of recent events that occurred with some of our oncology patients. Based on our medical record review, it does not appear you had any direct contact with the patients, however you may have been on the Unit in question during the time period under review. As such, the police and our internal investigator need to conduct a very brief interview with you."[9]

Even if my social location might have been a liability with the chiefs, it could be an asset with the EPs. At the time of my interaction with the police, I had already turned to observe the EP lab, which positioned me less as a problem and more like a solution. My continued access came from the fact that I came prepared to help. I was able to move into place the laser for extracting damaged leads, alert the doctors when visitors came to the operating room, help tie gowns in a way that maintained the wearer's sterility, and serve as a sounding board for spurned device representatives. I studied up on the news and told the doctors what was happening in the outside world. Because my subjects spent sixty to eighty hours at work each week, once my classwork was complete and I was studying the residency teams, it was sensible to follow their schedule, 24/7. Beyond my own learning, this approach had the virtue of teaching the subjects a little bit about ethnography. So, later, when patients or their families told Dr. Stimm that they wanted to discontinue treatment, he no longer announced to anyone within earshot, "Can't the sociologist do a talk about end-of-life issues with our patients?" Instead, he had learned what a sociologist did. Everyone involved had learned about each other's work.

Beyond the minor appreciation I likely received from the EPs for the everyday help I offered, it is possible that companies also saw some benefit in trying to help me with my research. Specifically, it was clear that they sought to generate goodwill with Dr. Stimm. Allowing me access was a low-cost gesture that would be appreciated by a high-status doctor they clearly wanted using and saying positive things about their technologies. One caution to an ethnographer who would adopt a multiple-venues approach, then, is that you have to find venues where you can be received and might be used as a tether. As does any failure, this episode reveals fundamental features of social life; groups create problems and solutions, and the ethnographer can be implicated in this process.

Taking Few Pictures, Leaving Few Footprints: On Deidentification and Sociology's Occupational Project

Though answering my research questions required I observe venues where hierarchy is inescapable, it is possible for me to take measures to protect subjects upon publication. There is another fiduciary duty, then, and that is mine, to my field. The measures I took involved a principle I refer to as "taking few pictures, leaving few footprints."

Were it only so easy. Fieldwork involves not only discovering new venues but also encountering unexpected gatekeepers and unexpected alliances. It involves continuously reinterpreting one's project for outsiders while also discovering improbable forms of empathy. Effective ethnography, perhaps more than other methods, involves reading the subjects' evaluation of the personal character of the speaker—Aristotle's "ethos" mode of persuasion. The observer asks from those observed a kind of leap of faith. Gaining access from the chief residents was about getting in the door, getting their provisional trust, and endeavoring not to cause harm to the subjects. Yet this effort was also important to the authority of sociology itself.

In thinking about protecting electrophysiology and sociology, my mind often turned to a message for hikers: "take few pictures and leave few footprints." The adage, as I understand it, is meant to communicate responsibility. In writing about what I observed, I felt some responsibility for the people and venues who let me in. I did not want their lives to be adversely affected. In publishing, there is much we cannot control. But we can control whether we make our subjects public. Although many people have told me that I have their permission to use their names in the book, I have chosen to protect the innocent, choosing to mask people and places. I have also taken pains to maintain this confidentiality by changing university, city, and company names—as well as descriptive details and statistics (by a standard increment)—when not important to my argument. When I utilize quotations from publicly circulated documents, including emails, I reproduce them largely verbatim, intervening only for changes to identifying information and not for grammatical or spelling corrections.

By opting to take few pictures and leave few footprints, I provide no trail that will lead others to retrace my steps. It is true that a focused Internet search may reveal the identities of central characters and venues in any carefully constructed and thoughtfully reported ethnography. Yet I felt I owed it to my subjects to make such a search difficult. My approach to presentation did not arise from participants' own concerns—most of the EPs were disappointed to hear I would deidentify them. But privately held opinions and private behavior, even if exemplary by the standards of the group, might be misunderstood by those outside of the group. And once a book leaves an author's hands, they cannot control its use. Others reading the book can impute their own agenda in such a way that individuals might be harmed. I chose to protect those who were doing their work with the best intentions, who might not be able to have a say in how their accounts were used. I felt this was especially important in light of my subject matter, and the possible deployment of my book by those with an ax to grind; there are many ideological discussions of medical knowledge. I knew that my book might be used as a tether by those in other disciplines or professions with social projects that might benefit from disparaging electrophysiology or sociology. At the same time that I sought access, did not want my project to increase the work necessary for them to maintain their authority.

I err on the side of confidentiality not only because I want to protect people, places, and disciplines, but also because identifying individuals would be inadequate for validating my argument. Individuals are inconsistent in their behavior, and forgetful of their utterances. Under the very best circumstances, having the names might allow verification of whether the people in my book were in a particular place at a particular point in time, but it will rarely allow you to confirm why they said what they did, or even what they said. My claim is that confidentiality is not opposed to rigor because, as ethnographers, we study the recurring, stable, and persistent forms of interaction that comprise social structures. We are there not to transcribe the lived reality but to study a specific question. As the sociologist Hughes once noted, most social processes that occur once are likely to be seen again. I maintain that if a work-based interaction happens once, it is likely to happen again. It is my job to situate the characters of these stories in a context that shows that they, like the rest of us, are caught up in systems that are not of their own choosing, and face certain pressures that are not easily overcome. Ultimately, specific individuals in our work should be substitutable.[10]

Wherever possible, I documented interactions using a digital recorder, but only when authorized by individuals or their organization, and after I felt a relationship of mutual trust had been developed. The presence or absence of the recorder seemed, for the most part, to have little effect on the content or the progress of the discussion. I made extensive use of this recorded material because such evidence is more direct, vivid, and self-evident in its implications than the narration of observed incidents.

It is often said to scholars of medicine that their failures are never as severe as those of physicians, whose custody over the life on the operating table is whole. Yet, the ethnographer, if they fail at their craft, threatens to destabilize the reputations of those who accepted the considerable risk involved in holding them in confidence. Moreover, the ethnographer who unmasks participants can be judged for betraying people, making the work of all ethnographers harder. Ultimately, then, I felt the benefits of providing identifying information—such as allowing others to follow up with subjects, and letting subjects see their names in print—were far lower than the potential costs for those identified, as well as the potential difficulties for future fieldworkers in their fieldwork venues of choice.

On Perspectives

You know, it's interesting—I don't know if you thought of this. Now this is an observation of mine about you. It's sort of the transformation in terms of thinking about your work. When you first came and talked to me it was sort of about this abstract, you know, information and hierarchy thing. And, you know, the core concepts are probably similar, but with the way you talked about them, the way you imagined it working, part of me was like, "Whoa, no, you gotta just go see it because it doesn't go like that, you know?" And, you know, how you think about things now, I mean the sophistication, the depth of understanding is—it's a remarkable change, whether you know it or not. Um, so, if there's a way that after you do your dissertation you could write about that—about your own transformation—I think that would actually be very interesting. I've seen something—it's dramatic. It's been really enjoyable and fun to watch you change over the years. So I do hope you write that part up.

—DR. WILLIAMS, SUPERIOR HOSPITAL PHYSICIAN IN
INTERNAL MEDICINE

Everett Hughes describes the medical trainee's professionalization process as a transformation in perspective. "One may say that the learning of the medical role consists of a separation, almost an alienation of the student from the lay medical world; a passing through the mirror so that one looks out on the world from behind it, and sees things as in mirror writing." The fieldworker undergoes a similar change. Although other fieldworkers have shown how this transition happens in the course of immersion in one particular place—whether school or street corner—my experience was that it was necessary to leave the hospital in order to understand the multiple experiences during training and practice that explain how knowledge is mobilized for practice, in the process of managing authority.[11]

Ultimately, the ethnographer is always a nonexpert coming in, with assumptions that must be examined immediately, and then repeatedly through the observations. So too must the ethnographer examine the effects of doing ethnography. It is not only that the ethnographer's experience will be broadened. In some ways, so might the experience of those observed. An important lesson, one likely known by experienced fieldworkers but worth reiterating, is that one must make an effort to understand the world as the subjects understand it. Some central dimensions of ethnographic work generate empathy, such as physical closeness, sharing of tasks, and sharing experiences. And that is something that ethnographers can offer—empathy for those we study, even if we cannot fully understand the world as subjects understand it.

In the notes above, a dominant theme and implicit argument is that we ethnographers have a duty that is very much like a fiduciary one, in which someone who values something entrusts it to the care of another. Even more, for an ethnographer, socially speaking it is a relationship of respect. It is up to the person who owns what is transferred to determine its value. It is up to the fiduciary to respect that determination, and not to harm whatever is entrusted. Fiduciary responsibilities are ones of protection, as is well understood by lawyers, bankers, teachers, and doctors. Those I observed place strong value on free exchange, new knowledge, and the ability to speak up, and, most important, on patient welfare. Sociology benefits when fieldworkers accept similar fiduciary responsibilities for those they study. In the end, I have tried to maintain my fiduciary duty to those I spent time with, who trusted me, and let me report on the facts as I saw them. I cannot say how much they saw me as protecting them, and how much protection my account will ultimately offer. But I have drawn from my observations only what I think they could bear. I am aware that by presenting quotations, I've selected examples, but I have tried to use representative ones while at the same time recognizing that one of the key features of the occupational project is that there are many different career types and modes of practice accommodated. I have been careful about generalizing based on particular comments, and use them only as illustrations. And I can only hope that physicians, sociologists, and others reading this will find that the footprints that I have left have not marred either this presentation or the occupational project I was studying.

Changing Relationships: Matters of Self-consciousness, Standpoints, and the Temporal Problem in Ethnography

> Watch out for the sister-in-law with the notepad. You've seen it a lot, I'm sure. There's always that instance where someone in the family is writing down everything you say. As I said, it's usually the sister-in-law, somebody who is quietly there in the corner asking lots of questions and you wonder why they're there to begin with. But, after it's all over, and things don't go well, and you're trying to recollect what you said and did not say, you have that person who has written a book on you. So choose your words carefully.
> —MICHAEL GOODSTEIN, MALPRACTICE ATTORNEY

This comment, from the attorney speaking in the fellows program, reminds us that doctors who perform procedures are aware of the ever-present possibility of lawsuits, and need to be seen as experts; documentation of anything that suggests otherwise brings liability. Thus, doctors will be especially concerned about how they are being interpreted. This comment also raises the question of how participants perceive the ethnographer. I too had a strong sense of the doctors' concerns. I found that their concerns about self-presentation differed according to the stage of research, as did mine.

And the question of whether I was an insider or an outsider depended on the situation in which I found myself. Consider how, at different stages of a project, fieldworkers have different access to their subjects' opinions on getting put into print, opinions that might influence these gatekeepers' behavior. Once through the initial gates at the beginning of the research, ethnographers find their subjects guarded with defenses that are oriented to protecting their self rather than their site, and that differ according to the situation. In discussing changes in the medical student's standpoint, Becker (1956) compares what is often termed the "idealist" and "cynical" perspectives toward their work, and warns against treating the latter as the "real" perspective. Similarly, it is likely common for fieldworkers to favor "insider" disclosures that occur later in their relationships with subjects over those that happen earlier. Given this, and the fact that one can expect that subjects unsure of the fieldworker's motives will attempt to display their best public face, at the beginning of our relationships in the field we are at risk of portraying people according to their valorized persona, while at the end, we may be inclined to portray the "real" perspective based on our ability to have seen insider interactions. An obvious symptom of this phenomenon of context-specific treatment is the ubiquitous plea of subjects: "Be sure to get that in the book."[12] Accounting for these situational changes is always a problem for ethnographers—especially so for those whose subjects have high social prestige—because it must be said that getting past guardedness doesn't mean that what you get is what you would call "reality."

Insiders have an agenda for why they provide access. If the ethnographer is aware of this, it is possible to sort out the agenda might shape the subject's performance, and to discern what may be revealed while watching the agenda unfold. Doctors, at least those I studied, are conscious of how they will be portrayed, and early in my observations I found they would seek to portray an attractive professional self, whether presented as thoughtful, ethical, gentle, noble, heroic, or scientific. Others, such as the technician, who occupies a different status hierarchy, may not share that concern. I could make this claim with confidence, based on my ability to observe conversations like this one:

> Dr. Stimm: "Did you check the final numbers?"
> Dipu, the first-year EP fellow, warily responds: "I thought if I did you might yell at me."
> "Have I yelled at you since you've been here?"
> "No."
> Dr. Stimm turns and looks at a cardiology fellow working in the lab that month. "Helen, have I yelled since *you've* been here?"
> "No, you haven't yelled."
> One of the techs suggests the fellows are appeasing Dr. Stimm. "Bunch of liars."
> Dr. Stimm: "I haven't yelled. I haven't yelled. It's a great atmosphere here in the EP lab at Superior Hospital. Come on, spread

the word. How (is he) to portray us?" He turns back to the monitors displaying the ablation catheter. "Don't whine. We're taking
care of sick people, man."

As this vignette suggests, Dr. Stimm is conscious of public presentation, and
seeks to put on a certain kind of performance to strengthen the occupational
project. Over time, I came to agree with his characterization of lab dynamics based on what I saw—he corrected people he was officially charged with
teaching; he pointedly asked for tools necessary for procedures when those
were not immediately given; and he ignored people when they asked something of him while he was conducting a procedure; but sanctions were delivered without yelling.

It also became clear they were certain of how they did not want to be perceived by someone outside of the social space of electrophysiology. In some
of my first interviews, the doctors would say something along the lines of
"don't make us out like the orthopedists," who the EPs see as being "on the
take." In a profession and period where government attention is directed
toward conflicts of interest, they were concerned about whether I would
portray them as solely profit-seeking, kickback-taking, self-interested actors. Orthopedists have seen intense scrutiny for being paid by firms selling failed replacement hips. Although the profit margin for EPs is lower and
the field has had fewer publicized technology failures, some of its practices
can potentially be sensationalized. For instance, when discussing companies' payments to doctors for conducting clinical trials, one of my respondents put it this way: "Cardiacore will pay 5k for each pacemaker implanted
as a part of its studies. Put in 20 of those a year and you're making big money."

Further, what the doctors wanted me to write in the book seemed to depend on their social location. Once you are in the room, subjects often try
to shape how you represent them. In the first stage of the EPs' interactions
with me, their concern about self-presentation had much to do with their position in relation to others they were training. Later, when I had developed
some trust, and they had moved from Superior to Cityview, their interest
in my attention to their self-presentation shifted to their larger story. They
wanted their story of mobility told, the subtext of Dr. Stimm's comment
after his group moved to Cityview: "We want you to come with us and write
about me." Others wanted me to tell of their challenges accompanying mobility, like the fellow who wanted me to show how harrowing his transition
to independent practice felt: "Get in [the book] how scared we are."

I also learned that my authorization to observe changed as my spatial location, and our temporal location, changed. When I observed the EP lab, I
was not in the operating theater; I sat in an observation room with a speaker
that broadcast discussions that took place inside. Because of this, my subjects did not always feel the weight of my presence in the room. If we think

about it, this makes sense; if you are studying a football team, there is a big difference between studying them on TV, from stands in the bleachers, in the front row at the fifty-yard line, from the bench, or on the field.

Still, at times I was also very definitely excluded; there were ways that I was not authorized to participate in their presentation of self. The EPs were very vulnerable with regard to my first impressions, and it took them a lot of time to express less self-consciousness. The vulnerability might be why the chief residents resisted my attendance at their satirical event before they knew me well; I was not authorized to pick up on the irony. To create a place of irony, the audience must share a perspective—outsiders will not "get it," making the targets of satire (in this case, the attendings and program) potentially vulnerable. Similarly, while the doctors would quickly discuss members of the field who they respected, it took several years before they would name those who engaged in questionable practices. Notoriety for an unethical standard-setter is bad press for an occupational project.

Ultimately, all ethnography is of a particular social time and place. Occupations, venues, and the events in each will come and go. When an ethnography is conducted over a long period, and across places, the world changes for the ethnographer as well. As I wrote this book, I had a different sense of what problems I was seeing, and what the solutions were. Subjects changed their minds about me and about their work colleagues. There were places where I could see those changes happening, but it was challenging because I was there not very long. People came in and out, and I could only be there so often. My approach to these inherent problems of time and place was to study recurrent situations. Centering my analysis on the way tasks were carried out over time thus afforded a benefit beyond that of letting me identify distant influences on a group: it enabled me to view their changing standpoint toward me.

Notes

Chapter 1

1. Hughes 1963.

2. On historical shifts in the standing of physicians, see Rosenberg 1962, Stevens 1998, Whooley 2013.

3. Before getting too far, some definitional preliminaries seem necessary with the use of authority here, although I define it further below (n18). In studying authority both inside and outside of medicine, some have chosen to distinguish social and cultural authority. As discussed further below, social authority has been described in terms of rank orders, while the cultural has been described in terms of symbol systems. See Goldhamer and Shils (1939), Goode (1978). In professions, see Laumann and Heinz 1978 versus Abbott 1981 respectively. I have chosen not to distinguish these types, largely because they empirically overlap in ways that make unclear the value of a conceptual distinction. This book is focused on the collective authority of medicine's stakeholders rather than individual authority of doctors and others, even if these are in many ways inseparable. On the latter literature which describes "authoritativeness," see Menchik 2020a.

4. To eliminate these heart rate disorders (arrhythmias), EPs ablate (burn or cool) the heart and leave dense scars. A macroscopic channel is an area where ventricular tachycardia (a fast heartbeat) travels through the scar, and isolated diastolic potentials are the electrical signals, ones that are thought to reflect surviving tissue that conducts tachycardia circuits, in that channel of scar.

5. On physicians at the top of their professions, and stratification in medicine generally, see Fox (1959, 1974), Freidson 1985, McDonald 2012, Menchik 2017, Jenkins 2020. Eakins painted himself taking notes from the seats in this classic work (Farago 2020), making its use in social science scholarship still more appropriate.

6. On the "it's complicated" conclusion, see Collins and Pinch 2008.

7. An extensive literature on medical uncertainty describes a range of different ways medical professionals make decisions about these individual, particular cases. Although too vast to review here, it includes: Parsons 1951, Light 1979, Light 1985, Timmermans and Angell 2001, Menchik 2014, Timmermans and Stivers 2017. The exemplar of the way the individual patient case is understood as being managed by the uncertain individual practitioner is Fox 1959. An exemplar of the way the individual patient case is understood to be managed by an uncertain small group or team is Bosk 1980. Sociologists have described uncertainty in similar ways around weather forecasting and economic policy-making decisions (Daipha 2018, Beckert and Bronk 2018).

8. See Freidson and Rhea 1962, Bosk 1979 [2003], pp. 122–27, and Hunter 1991. The live case is in many ways the opposite of the relatively local "degradation ceremony" described in Bosk's account of mortality and morbidity conferences. Differences in ways of identifying problems, and making decisions on solutions, were powerfully pointed out in Bloor 1976.

9. See Becker 1963, Blumer 1971, Abbott 1988.

10. In sociology, scholarship on the construction of disease and treatment, and the authority represented in their construction, began with the work of Parsons and Freidson, and came to be understood as medicalization. A key intervention of Freidson's (1970) synthetic work, in describing what came to be called medicalization, was to propose that illness can be understood as a parallel form of deviance to that described by Becker, even if he provided few clues as to how the process was continuously organized. And Abbott implicitly noted the centrality of this process, adopting medical parlance in describing a range of professions, and using the language of diagnoses and treatments (see Hughes 1959, Becker 1963, Freidson 1970, Abbott 1988). Those focusing specifically on medicalization or biomedicalization are Zola 1972, Conrad (who also at times uses the terms of problems and solutions [e.g., Conrad and Schneider 1992; Conrad 2005]) and Clarke et al. 2003. See also Brown 1995, Jutel 2009, Horwitz 2011. Many scholars, in recent years especially, have paid attention to the role that advocacy groups have played, more or less successfully, in seeking to shape these problems and solutions. For case studies of successful efforts including Epstein (1996), Eyal (2013), Navon (2019). For cases in which the influence is short-lived, see Decoteau and Daniel (2020), who found that in their case study, "genomic explanations for autism retained power, but only through their reconfiguration. Dominant field members ceded on the importance of the environment, but they managed to subsume its causal power into the body, therefore negating the threat of vaccine injury" (472). There also exists a long tradition of scholarship in the history of medicine on the social construction of disease (e.g., Rosenberg 1962, Aronowitz 1999, Wailoo 2000, Greene 2007).

11. On their qualifications about the particularity of their accounts to a particular period, see Freidson (on medicine's "golden age" 1970 [1988], p. 383), and Starr on the limits of his account for offering inferences about the future (1982, pp. 381–449).

12. The work most evidently positioning these stakeholders outside of the occupation—and not inside an occupational project, as is done here—is Light's (2000) work on "countervailing powers."

13. The language of jurisdiction comes from Abbott 1988.

14. Among the many other works on expertise in medicine that give due appreciation to the connectedness of internally and externally facing expert content, see Epstein 1996, Carr 2010b, Kempner 2014, Buchbinder 2015, Eyal and Pok 2015, Eyal 2019, Decoteau and Daniel 2020. Gusfield 1981 offers a careful demonstration of the qualities that the insides and outsides of political movements share.

15. My choice of the term *occupation* follows that of Freidson (1970), who emphasized that his primary interest in studying medicine was to study "an occupation whose objective was to serve as the discoverer, carrier, and practitioner of certain kinds of knowledge, but which is not a body of knowledge as such . . . it is an occupation first, and only on occasion a profession" (5).

16. Given the diversity of stakeholders, it would seem like the way to understand the scene would be through the literature on communities of practice (Lave and Wenger 2001). Yet, in occupational projects some tasks might involve joining together actors such that they identify as part of a community, while for other tasks they might not identify that way. Physicians, hospital administrators, and company reps may at times share a domain of interest, learn from each other as a community, and interact repeatedly around a set of stories. But the physician only

sees the administrator as part of their community when the administrator seems to be concerned about helping that doctor or their profession. In this dimension of work, an occupational project's constitutive parts are closer to the kinds of "professional segments" described by Bucher and Strauss (1961) yet include a far wider range of stakeholders. Ruit and Bosk's (2020) revealing case study of patient safety officers demonstrates the great degree to which certain professional segments must respond not only to each other, different professions, and clients, but also to policy shifts.

17. A video of the procedures, and commentary on their performance, was soon published on YouTube. The URL is omitted for reasons of deidentification.

18. At least since Parsons's hand-wringing over translating Weber's (1947, p. 152) Herrschaft, there has been constant discussion around defining authority (see also Goldhamer and Shils 1939, Goode 1978). The definition I use retains Weber's (1978) interest in control—"the probability that a command with a given specific content will be obeyed by a given group of people"—and the focus of scholars of professions on the shaping of content (Hughes 1959, Freidson 1970, and followers, e.g., Starr 1982 and Conrad and Schneider 1992). One of the book's readers took issue with this departure from how Starr defines the nature of medical authority, "the probability set particular definitions of reality and judgments of meaning and value will prevail as valid and true" (1982, p. 13). As helpful as a concept such as "particular definitions of reality" is in capturing the cultural control that medicine may hold, a particular affordance of the definition used here is that it reflects the diversity of stakeholders scholars have demonstrated are centrally involved in shaping medical work, and the fact that the standpoints of those comprising medicine differ too much to reflect a single way of understanding medical "reality" (see Anspach 1993). Further, it retains the emphasis on the profession's "sovereignty over reality," without narrowly centering that control around economic exploitation (Navarro 1976), resorting to polemical accounts of medicine's iatrogenic effects (Illich 1976), or rejecting the idea that authority is human-created (e.g., Foucault 1978, 1985). Finally, the definition used here has the virtue of better capturing the ways in which problems and solutions are organized and imposed beyond medicine, and also reflects what we see in social science scholarship on management and governance outside of medicine. See approaches to authority extended by Goldhamer and Shils (1939), Goode (1978), and especially Banfield's treatise (1961) on the social organization of political authority in processes of urban governance.

19. These search results were obtained on March 2, 2020.

20. On the conceptualization of culture's location that is used here, see Silverstein 2004, 2013.

21. The quote is from Pessin 2017, p. 98. On convention, see Becker 1982, chap. 2. Another step toward the multistakeholder conceptualization can be seen in the idea of "linked ecologies." The linked ecologies concept depends on the idea of a professional ecology operating in relation to only one other ecology, or to an "environment" outside the profession (Abbott 2002, 2005). A tethered venues approach is different because it incorporates a range of members into an occupational project whose members are place-based, and are actively managing and using connections. Such a conceptual understanding foregrounds the value of ethnography for capturing the whole occupational project, though it's possible to imagine possibilities for using other methods.

22. Merton and colleagues (1957) propose that medical students and residents are "socialized" into a profession, taking on certain traits, habits, and values. See Abbott 1988 on the ambiguities in scholarship on professional coalescence.

23. On venues, see Zussman 2004, Delbridge and Sallaz 2015. The most specificity given to the subject is provided in Menchik 2019. On the work these places do to build and strengthen relationships, see Breiger 1979, Feld 1984, Small and Adler 2019. In the scholarship on venues, there is less work on medicine, but on the importance of the lab in psychotherapy, see Craciun 2016.

24. When I refer to authoritativeness, in contrast to authority, I refer to this as an instance of control in the immediate interaction. Elements of the relationship between scholarship on culture and authority, in literatures centered on both medicine and work, are suggested in Menchik (2019, 2020a). For scholarship on the *where* of culture, see especially Silverstein (2004, 2013).

25. On this contestation among those experts around the DSM, see Schnittker 2017 and Whooley 2019.

26. On physicians' hands-off relationships with each other, see Freidson and Rhea (1965).

27. See Freidson 1970, Abbott 1988. See also Larson 1977, Krause 1999.

28. The list of book-length hospital ethnographies, even if we count monographs alone, is very long. Exemplary single-hospital ethnographies include: Fox 1959, Becker et al. 1961, Bosk 1979, Zussman 1992, Anspach 1993, Chambliss 1996, Heimer and Staffen 1998. Exemplary comparative treatments include: Mumford 1970, Kellogg 2011, Jenkins 2020.

29. A long tradition of conversation analysis scholarship examines these patient-physician interactions. See Heritage and Maynard 2006.

30. By using venues, it is also possible to conduct ethnography in a way that prevents the "under the lamppost" problem that, as Bosk notes in his study's second edition, served as a limitation of his study (1979 [2003], pp. xvii–xx). Studying medical authority requires being in a venue where the authority of those under study may in fact be placed at risk. This need for variation in part motivated my decision to study venues that the physicians in the top hospital I focused on didn't attend, and to observe not only standard-setters but also clinicians, physicians who were lower in medicine's pecking order (see Martin 2017).

31. I follow the language norms of those I studied in using "EP" (and "EPs"), to interchangeably represent both individual ("electrophysiologist") and collective ("electrophysiology") units of analysis.

32. Because the international population of EPs comprises more than the membership of the Heart Rhythm Society, the field's main professional organization, it is difficult to access an accurate count of the population of EPs. In 2020 there were 7,120 members of the Heart Rhythm Society. That number represents 4,788 physicians (and 80 percent of the EP-certified physicians are members), 1,781 non-physicians, 459 scientists, and 92 emeritus members (Jay Vegso, personal communication, May 11, 2020).

33. On career types, see Hall 1949. A close comparison of these types and their interdependence, primarily via referral relationships, is in Menchik 2017. Decoteau and Daniel (2020) pay particular attention to the role of those leading medicine. Sociometric studies of science demonstrate the presence of a similar core-periphery structure (Hagstrom 1965; Crane 1972, pp. 49–58) although the

existence of referral relationships in medicine means these ties necessarily involve more interdependence.

34. These critiques are developed more extensively in Menchik 2020a.

35. I take up the question of doctors' differential motivation as being driven by money, status, or other resources, in the concluding chapter.

36. An incomplete list of other scholars who used medical work to build theory would include Parsons, Merton, Hughes, Coleman, Gusfield, Goffman, Freidson, and Bosk.

Chapter 2

1. Parsons (1951) noted the importance of patients' belief in physicians' success, even if he gave a more theoretical than empirical account. Craciun (2016) noted the importance played by charisma in this process (see also Menchik 2020a).

2. See Berg 1992 on similar processes physicians use in outpatient clinics.

3. At Superior Hospital, the cardiologists' patient population comprised approximately half admitted with chest pain, one-quarter had heart failure, and the rest suffered from arrhythmias or needed a heart transplant.

4. Brada (2013) calls this "productive fear."

5. Sociologist Katherine Kellogg (2011, pp. 70, 78) describes the pervasiveness of the "strong and wrong" philosophy among surgeons. The fact that her tasks share much with surgeons makes it unsurprising that Dr. Kellogg's teaching resembles that of Dr. Arthur in Bosk 1979 [2003].

6. "Pimping" is a process interns dread due to the interrogation's persistence (see also Anspach 1988, p. 361; Kellogg 2011, pp. 78, 117; Prentice 2012, p. 154). Its traumatic and anxiety-producing nature makes pimping a common target of satire in medicine (Bennett 1985, Detsky 2009). The analogue in the United Kingdom is "bollocking" (Pringle 1998, p. 192). Its efficacy for learning surgical tasks is periodically reinforced in the medical literature (Antonoff and D'Kunha 2011).

7. See Rier 2000.

8. His style is improvisational, in a way not unlike many doctors involved in patients' end-of-life decision making (Stonington 2020).

9. Pedagogically speaking, then, if Dr. Kellogg is an example of what Weber (1968, pp. 439–51) called the *ethical* prophet who has received authority from God and expects obedience as an ethical duty, Dr. Walker is an example of the *exemplary* prophet, one who demonstrates the way to religious salvation.

10. See Shilloh 1965.

11. Unsurprisingly, deliberators are thought to project the "nice guy" persona that residents describe as common in fields with tasks that have similarly long feedback loops, such as psychology (Stelling and Bucher 1977, p. 104).

12. See Connell 1987.

Chapter 3

1. Because they describe their group as a "lab," I will use this term to refer to the people as well as the operating room where they perform procedures (e.g., ablation, device implants, lead extraction).

2. The EPs also see patients once per week in outpatient clinics, following up with patients they have treated. These venues are less critical to understand for capturing how authority is managed, as, in contrast to the patients of general cardiologists like Dr. Walker, these patients may only see EPs for a few visits following a procedure.

3. These "good hands" judgments usually refer to the kind of tacit abilities described in Polanyi 1958. Bourdieu (1977, p. 72) describes the general process through which an environment influences principles, habits, and ways of being. In surgical and medical training more generally, the importance of learning and maintaining good hands is discussed nicely in Prentice 2007. Hands are so valorized in this area of medicine that the association of former surgery residents at Johns Hopkins calls itself the Old Hands Club (Timmermans 2003, p. 218).

4. When I noted the frequency with which EPs used the compliment "good hands," several interviewees noted that "good brain" or "good mind" should also be tied to the phrase, because of the importance to EPs of the task of carefully interpreting EKGs. However, when observing them at work, I never heard these latter compliments given in the same breath.

5. Pope (2002, pp. 377–78) also shows the importance placed on competent assistants for facilitating good hands. See also Smith et al. 2003.

6. In their interrogation of the value of Goffman's metaphorical vocabulary in settings of mutual coordination, Hindmarsh and Pilnick (2002, p. 148) illustrate well how anesthetists "work with patients as opposed to treating them as objects to be worked on."

7. See also Bosk 1979 [2003] on quasi-normative errors.

8. Attendings who educate fellows, like physicists who educate graduate students (Collins 2000, p. 836), want new generations to ensure carry forward their practices or research traditions. Death of medical practices happens much more slowly because, relative to experimental physics, for example, practitioners are less easily monitored and less dependent on well-endowed institutions that can fund expensive experiments. Medical departments will often hire their own fellows, or those of other like-minded standard-setters, so procedures can all be done the same way, in research studies for instance. This process of teaching students to see in ways particular to a professional group is well described in Goodwin 1994.

9. See Bosk 1979 [2003] on socialization.

10. See Bal 2009 on malpractice.

11. This role-based division of labor is effective because the person given responsibility for a niche tends to be more suspicious of new data. They are expected to be suspicious of something that is framed as "new," with suspicions allayed only once they put new discoveries through a set of tests. This is because they usually have previous knowledge based on experience and observation about, for example with new devices and leads, the characteristics of a specific kind of material—rubber, plastic, metal—that has proved useful for his usual task. "Although inventions originate in response to a social demand, in all conservative societies it has been considered dangerous as infringing upon the existing order, be it magical, religious, social, or economic . . . even the technical leader is not supposed to take unnecessary risks" (Znaniecki 1968, p. 56).

12. Heath (1998) also describes such slide-circulating networks. Blau (1955) describes this key mechanism animating the status competition; high-status indi-

viduals give favors, which creates obligation. In the scenario described here, standard-setters share status by circulating slides, which, in turn, help them and clinicians. As the latter group benefits relatively more because they have fewer followers—whereas top doctors can always find more supporters—we can expect them to feel relatively more obligation.

13. This positive relationship between the strength of role segregation inside the lab and ties to doctors outside the hospital is similar to the findings of Bott (1957, chap. 3) on the interconnections between the role relations of husband and wife and the density of their professional networks.

14. Doctors informally polled about top programs named anywhere from five to eight of them. Respective university names have been changed to A, B, etc.

15. This dynamic is consistent with Perrow (1965), who argues that with complicated technologies it will be physicians—rather than administrators or trustees—who dominate decision-making in a health care organization. Nonacademic hospitals will likely afford physicians less decision-making power. As seen in the following chapter, however, decisions on other matters, such as beds, are led by administration.

Chapter 4

1. Academic physicians are especially interested in tough cases. But this taste is developed even in medical schools where physicians are unlikely to follow an academic route; all trainees relish the opportunity to gain clinical experience with cases unfamiliar to them (Becker et al. 1961: 329–30, Mumford 1970).

2. Efficiency is a predominant concern for trainees, who often feel pressure to comply with contemporary work-hour restrictions (see Szymczak and Bosk 2012). A lighter patient load, which efficiency affords, also offers residents more sleep. Because of this overarching concern, trainees focus on the meeting's attending physician, who is involved in the bed management program; with the nineteen students who attended the forty-four meetings I observed in internal medicine, only four interacted with a nonattending (usually the social worker).

3. In the emails and hospital documents I have preserved grammatical, capitalization, and typographical errors. Most emails were shared by authors. I interpret emails in a way that reflects authors' intentions, as discussed with me in interviews.

4. By and large, patients with high-quality insurance tend to be better resourced in general, and are thus better able to seek out hospitals with stronger reputations. And the hospital's reputation is indirectly affected by its reimbursement rates, because higher reimbursement means the hospital has a higher budget for personnel and technology, which help boost its success rates.

5. If we removed the Honor Roll formula (or if hospitals were unconcerned with it), it would be the case that the incentives of the hospital and the specialties would be similarly aligned as those of doormen and tenants. The doorman wants all of his tenants to be high-status—leading the doorman to treat and present them accordingly—because it raises his own status (see Bearman 2005). The Honor Roll makes it so that such mutual dependence exists only with certain professionals' tasks.

6. It also, through a process of reactivity, perpetuates organizational structures intended to maintain dominance in an area (Espeland and Sauder 2007).

7. See Commonwealth Fund Task Force on Academic Health Centers 2003.

8. Presentation on hospital finances, Vice President for Planning, Superior Hospital, summer 2007. All of the other numbers on Superior Hospital's bed allocation and budget were obtained through personal communication with financial officers and data managers at the institution.

9. On organizational slack, see March and Simon 1958. It is worth pointing out that the meaning of "profitable activities" or "making money" differs when used in describing a firm. Superior is a nonprofit organization and redistributes its revenues within the organization.

10. Most of these patients leave Superior insured; the hospital makes about two thousand public aid applications each year on behalf of uninsured patients, and gets about 60 percent approved.

11. Examples are taken from episodes described in the meeting. Bosk et al. (2011) describe the burden placed on community hospitals to convince academic hospitals that patients who are transfer candidates aren't dumps.

12. Although many trainees mentioned this critique of the program, I was unable to track down the reason that ob/gyn students felt they were getting these limited opportunities. Potentially, beds that would have been used for deliveries were allocated to patients with other conditions, or the ob/gyn department wasn't allowed to admit any patients.

13. This strategy has long been in place. Although Superior Hospital has expanded physically, its number of beds has risen by only approximately one hundred beds between 1976 and 2010. The hospital's reticence to open new beds is justified in light of its goals; the availability of bed supply leads to additional utilization (Freedman 2016).

14. Such projects are more commonly described in terms of state- and city- than organization-building efforts. See Scott 1998 and Venkatesh 2001.

15. Five years later Superior Hospital renewed this grant for an equivalent sum.

16. Such meetings are necessary in any health care organization; administrators need to constrain physicians enamored with the idea that "everyone is entitled to the best possible care."

17. Extracts from primary documents are unedited as much as possible to keep the voice of the original.

18. Sharing information about work-arounds is an important and well-documented dimension of student culture in medical school (see Shem 1978, Conrad and Schneider 1992, Szymczak and Bosk 2012, and Menchik 2014.)

19. These strategies are similar to Davis's (1960) description of doctors' strategic statements of uncertainty, and to Hughes's (1928) points about the rights of professionals to declare emergencies.

20. In part because of the fallout, Dr. Wilson left Superior soon after this episode.

21. This cascade effect resembles what happens when departments are recruited from universities or law firms. It is not the case, however, that the whole

group was necessary for carrying out tasks; EP does not require the model, necessary in some surgical procedures, of distributed cognition among team members (Hutchins 1995).

22. Others felt that a move would help Dr. Stimm and the field more generally. Dr. Stimm had consulted his old fellowship adviser, Dr. Frank Moore, one of the most renowned practitioners in EP, who has trained hundreds of EPs. His teacher recommended he leave.

23. See Erikson 1976, Klinenberg 2002.

24. In producing work that was of high quality but relatively less able than other specialties to attract prestige to Superior, the cardiologists held the equivalent of the "forty-first chair" in science (Merton 1968, pp. 56–57; Zuckerman 1977, pp. 42–50). I thank Ned Smith for pointing this out.

Chapter 5

1. The independence of this subject matter follows from the fact that it is in the interest of the companies that host these meetings to appear to have a strong arm's-length relationship with the presenting physicians. However, in the fellows programs and in the hands-on programs discussed in chapter 6, a company rep did perform a short presentation on the affordances of the company's newest technologies.

2. Based on my observations, and my interviews with standard-setters, faculty tend to be monomorphic, acting as opinion leaders for only one topic. On the importance of scientific conferences for cultivating ties to journal editors, see Mody 2011. On serving as an opinion leader, standard-setters' monomorphism resembles Katz and Lazarsfeld's (1955) finding that housewives turn to one another for information on topics like baking or detergent. And, like the "two-step" model used to describe how ideas flow through media channels to opinion leaders who subsequently convert that information to influence, the company gains authority by associating with high-status physicians. See Lazarsfeld, Berelson, and Gaudet 1944, Lazersfeld and Menzel 1963.

3. The tales told at the conference differ in content but share a structure, in a fashion paralleling Propp's (1968) seminal model of the morphology of the folktale.

4. On summoning, see Tavory 2016.

5. See also Suchman 1995, p. 575.

6. Even if the description follows Dr. Wilson's particular efforts at organizing indeterminacy—replete with qualifications and hedges—it nonetheless remains pitched as objective (Daston and Galison 2007).

7. These doctors spent long days mapping signals from the atrium. As the French physician responsible for this discovery reported in an interview after I observed their lab, they would wait twelve hours for only one electrical signal, or "activation," to be sensed by the lead placed in this vein.

8. On moral legitimacy, see Parsons 1960, and Aldrich and Fiol 1994. And, as Bourdieu (1988) argues, even negative engagement is an implicit acceptance of the legitimacy of Dr. Wilson's perspective in the field.

9. Goodwin 1994, p. 609.

10. The fact that this medical knowledge has to "work" differentiates the process of taking on practices in medicine than from that of coming to engage predecessors' ideas (Camic 1992).

11. Outside of these events, industry can provide a more direct source of assistance to new EPs seeking to develop a referral base. Because referring doctors may also decline to refer patients because of their ignorance of EPs' capabilities, device companies may also organize dinner programs for general cardiologists to inform them about innovations (and help EPs carve out an informed referral base). The importance of this practice is reinforced to me by Dr. Santo, an EP from Delaware, who has practiced for four years. Medscape organizes dinner events that allow him to present both the general capabilities and new developments in EP for general cardiologists in his hospital.

12. Lieberson (1958) and Hall (1948, 1949) demonstrated how opportunities for practice are influenced by referring networks, which themselves are influenced by nonprofessional traits such as ethnicity and geography, and access to sponsorship by a senior physician.

13. AFIB = atrial fibrillation; AVNRT = Atrioventricular Nodal Reentry Tachycardia; Bi-V ICD = biventricular implantable cardiac defibrillator; DFT = Defibrillation threshold testing.

14. The three-A mantra described in the quote is also shared among surgeons, suggesting that EPs similarly subordinate technical to moral forms of self-regulation (Bosk 1979 [2003], p. 176).

15. Christakis describes cautionary tales in detail (1999, pp. 99–103).

16. An index that EP is male dominated is that gynecology is almost always mentioned in examples of how institutional funds are spent frivolously. Earlier, the program director discussed the meeting's funding source: "AAMC [American Association of Medical Colleges] have laid out recommendations for reducing the role of industry in symposia. The AAMC has suggested that the money from industry go to some central planning agency in a medical school. That's not even just going to cardiology, it could end up being used for some gynecological program or something, I'm not kidding you."

Chapter 6

1. I confirmed that, at the time of this conference, according to data provided by the Heart Rhythm society, 49.9 percent of the field performed ablation.

2. When companies can afford a sheep's or pig's heart they will often seek some symbolic advantage over their unnamed competition by pointing out its advantage over chicken breast. (Chicken breast is typically used for the ablation and dissection if a heart isn't available.)

3. Standard-setters' goal in training is for clinicians to develop sensitivity to these signals. As William James (1890 [1950], pp. 417–18) put it, "A faint tap *per se* is not an interesting sound; it may well escape being discriminated from the general rumor of the world. But when it is a signal, as that of a lover on the window-pane, it will hardly go unperceived."

4. Standard-setters' interactions before the clinicians are not unlike those which occur among sociologists promoting Introduction to Sociology textbooks, in which

they discuss their teaching practices (and sometimes distribute handouts) in front of a crowd assembled to learn about the books. In their industry-sponsored events, they distinguish their textbook from "the old one," which introduced the theoretical perspectives of the previous generation.

5. "Studies of PV anatomy from pathologic specimens and three-dimensional CT have shown that the PV is funnel shaped, with a tube that fans out into a proximal 'cup' that blends into the posterior atrial wall, which we refer to as the *antrum*" (Verma et al. 2004, p. 1337. Italics in original).

6. Many doctors are justifiably concerned about their public reputations after contentious episodes over undisclosed support by pharmaceutical firms to the faculty of Harvard Medical School (Wilson 2009) and, more recently, confirmation that device manufacturer Biotronik made side payments to doctors to encourage hospital adoption of the company's heart devices (Meier 2011).

7. On profit margins, see Meier 2009.

8. Because the details of a meeting let us see the process through which a company makes a case for a procedure and the use of their technology, I report on two meetings. However, as reported in the appendix, I attended many others organized by each company around the same time, which had a broadly similar structure.

9. See Shapin 1996.

10. A "pearl" is experienced-based personal knowledge (Polanyi 1958), usually shared by senior physicians in training settings.

11. The specifics of the company's language suggest why clinicians considered it to strengthen the occupational project. The words in italics above represent what linguists Brown and Gilman (1960) refer to as "pronouns of power and solidarity." In their pattern of delivery these pronouns parallel the movement from collective responsibility to personal responsibility expected in the professional socialization process in EP. As shown in chapter 2, such a presentation of accountability is a core value for intensivist, hands-on areas where tasks involve fast feedback loops and leadership over a team. Note the movement from the use of "Medistar" or "they" to the "we" also used by the program director at the beginning of the meeting, when introducing "the community's" problem of atrial fibrillation. In training, these doctors are expected to report all complications to their attending, and when they become attendings themselves they must, as Bosk (1979 [2003]) puts it, "wear the hair shirt," ritualistically describing unexpected failures before colleagues.

12. Beyond the fact that they don't remember the field's past failures, younger practitioners are also still developing the senses involved in procedures. Targeting this group is a strategy also pursued in other industries where "feel" is important. For instance, tennis racquet companies seek to get their new technology into the hands of the younger players. Interviewer for *Tennis Magazine*: "Will there be any players on tour using SpinEffect racquets in 2013?" Head of Tennis for Wilson Sporting Goods: "I do believe we'll have players using the S eventually. The pros are looking for any advantage that they can get. But it's going to take time; it's likely not going to be in the Australian Open this January. The adoption of racquet innovations most always starts off with younger players. They try it and get used to it, and then as those players come up, the technology makes it on tour" (DiFeliciantonio 2012).

13. These figures, especially those who speak at the previous chapter's fellows meetings, are what Weber (1946, p. 189) meant when he discussed how individual castes develop distinct cults and gods.

Chapter 7

1. See Nguyen 2011.

2. See Ioannidis 2012, p. 1258.

3. See Greene's (2007) compelling analysis of the process through which new technologies inform definitions of health.

4. See Prince, Frader, and Bosk 1982.

5. Dr. Breen here uses a common strategy. Dr. Price, a frequent debater, draws a vivid picture: "I usually come very prepared, and more prepared with their own data than my own. I've always told people when you do a debate to know your opponent's side better than your own because then they have no choice. Then you will frankly take their data and upend it on top of their head. And you don't care about yours because you know they're going to go after you. As long as you can take their data and put it in the toilet, they have lost their footing."

6. The inability to reach a conclusion also suggests why the interactions tend toward humor as they come to a close, beginning to move toward the pathos end of Aristotle's continuum. See also Reay 2009.

7. On recognizing social organization through conflict, see Goodwin 1982, and Maynard 1985. On the content of the exchange, which captures an ongoing debate, see Calkins et al. 2012.

8. See Shibutani 1955.

9. Practice in one-upmanship begins early in medical training (Bosk 1979 [2003], p. 109)

10. On horror stories, see Arluke 1977, Bosk 1979 [2003], and Hafferty 1988. On the enactment of authority, see Silverstein 2006, Matoesian 2008, and Carr 2010a, and Menchik 2020a.

11. On gossip, see Hagstrom 1965, pp. 32–33, Burt 2010, Vaidyanathan et al. 2016.

12. Offering a venue for both self-promotion and feedback, the event functions similarly to the Royal Society (Sprat 1667, p. 98).

13. On the momentary suspension of social rules at conferences and elsewhere, see Lomnitz (1983) on scientific meetings, and Turner (1977) on *communitas* generally.

14. Gellner (1992) treats much the same puzzle of legitimating belief. See also Weber 1978, p. 402.

15. As Knaapen (2013) notes, the state may guide what kinds of questions need to be answered.

16. On guidelines see Timmermans and Berg 2003, Knaapen 2013, Weisz et al. 2007. Neuman, Bosk, and Fleisher (2014, pp. 4–5), in noting the array of questions guiding the development of beta blocker guidelines—questions not only of rigor but also of larger political and professional importance that observers have assigned to findings—suggest that it's unsurprising that such documents might not ultimately be helpful for guiding practices.

17. Parallels exist with what James Ferguson (1994) calls "the anti-politics machine" of UN agencies, bilateral aid organizations, and nongovernmental actors engaged in so-called Third World development efforts, a governance strategy that aims to work around the politics of individual countries.

18. The products of these meetings are relevant not simply to the technical elements of practice. They range from the first piece, in 1994, "Report of the NASPE Policy Conference on Antibradycardia Pacemaker Follow-Up: Effectiveness, Needs, Resources" to those dealing with the field's reproduction, as with 2001's position paper: "Clinical Cardiac Electrophysiology Fellowship Teaching Objectives for the New Millennium" to "NASPE Policy Statement on Catheter Ablation: Personnel, Policy, Procedures, and Therapeutic Recommendations." (Until 2004, the HRS was named NASPE [North American Society of Pacing and Electrophysiology].)

19. See Kusumoto et al. 2014.

20. Verizon Wireless Annual Review (2013), "Consumer Information about Radio Frequency Emissions & Responsible Driving."

21. From HRS policies for development and endorsement of HRS scientific and clinical documents. See: https://www.hrsonline.org/documents/hrs-clinical -document-methodology-manual-jan-2019/download.

22. I observed the construction of a single guidelines document organized by the ACC, a committee composed of general cardiologists, interventional cardiologists, EPs, a geriatrician with expertise in terminal care and shared decision-making, and one lay representative (a lawyer). During the years I observed in person and over the phone, the nineteen of them, and I, also met every two weeks via conference call. They sought to complete the two dimensions of the guidelines: a Class of Recommendation (COR), which indicates the strength of the recommendation, encompassing the estimated magnitude and certainty of benefit in proportion to risk; and a Level of Evidence (LOE) measure that rates the quality of scientific evidence supporting the intervention on the basis of the type, quantity, and consistency of data from clinical trials and other sources.

23. See the ACCF/AHA Task Force on Practice Guidelines 2010. Galison (1997) also notes that members of large physics collaborations also use votes to confirm big decisions.

24. See Aliot et al. 2009, Wilkoff et al. 2009.

25. Of course, not everyone appreciates the focus on process. As Dr. Kelter put it to his colleagues after thirty minutes of wrangling in a meeting: "A lot of folks, me in particular, sometimes feel the process takes over. And the principles we're working towards get lost. It's like being with your grandmother going through security in the airport, and the officer wants to do a rectal on her. This is process gone amok."

26. The frustration of outliers is because some of the technologies used to execute "best practices" have techniques already locked in. Technologies come out of new approaches made by mandarins in the field. So they have built into them particular habits (see Mumford 1964).

27. The members of the committee are aware of concerns of clinicians about the politicization of guidelines, many of which parallel the assessments of social scientists (e.g., Timmermans and Berg 2003, McDonald and Harrison 2004, and Wilson, Pope, Roberts, and Crouch 2014).

Chapter 8

1. Beyond observations of their will and ability to change physicians' problems and solutions, these observations reinforced the conclusions emerging from the paltry evidence in the literature, which shows that in one-on-one interactions, the overall incidence of physicians' authoritativeness with patients being compromised is very low, at least as measured by patients' ability to shape physicians' decisions in a clinical setting. Most of the way that authority is exercised looks a lot like what we saw in chapter 2, with the physicians organizing the structure and content of the interactions. On physicians' successful work in creating consent, in the inpatient setting, see Ansbach 1993, and Heimer and Gazley 2012. Physicians, and their observers, know well that they "get consent," and do not ask for it; when doctors obtain informed consent in medicine, *consent* is a verb. Any observer will regularly hear "Have you consented the patient?" or "We need to consent him before we bring him to the floor." This interaction does not constitute one person asking another for consent, but rather more closely resembles this question: "Have you subjected the patient such that you were able to get consent?" For doctors, the meaning of this term is shaped by the medical climate where patients have worked their way through the courts to eventually earn the right to be asked about their "do not resuscitate" and "do not intubate" preferences (see Rothman 1991). Work outside the inpatient context on the extent of physicians' rare acquiescence shows that while influence does happen, it is relatively rare, and varies according to qualities of a workplace (Menchik and Jin 2014). (On varieties of interactional dynamics with the parents of sick children, see Timmermans and Stivers 2017, Gengler 2014.)

In scholarship beyond that on authoritativeness in a particular venue, scholarship on control over problems and solutions has shown well how some unusually motivated group unites to try to influence the knowledge base of an occupational project, as in the case of parents of children with autism, and AIDS activism (Epstein 1996, Eyal 2013). Although I was sensitive to the possibility of seeing these motivated participants throughout my fieldwork, I was surprised that I rarely saw them, even as I did attend a venue where I expected some index of collective action might be observed. In the guidelines meetings one position was taken by a nonphysician, but he rarely spoke, and did not make any edits to the writing of the guidelines documents. This occlusion may of course be tied to my primary method; the empirical foundation for much scholarship on medical movements is not ethnographic but rather archive or interview-based. These methods can unearth spaces difficult for an ethnographer to observe, and can also arguably be said to afford a temporal scope that is more expansive than ethnography, even when the work is conducted across the many years spanned by my research.

2. The challenge of disentangling motivations is felt by all ethnographers. The data showed that doctors had a variety of motivations. As we saw here and elsewhere, these motivations will be felt differently by individuals according to their social location; doctors at different tiers want different things. Helpfully for the motivational issue, observing six venues has afforded the opportunity to spotlight circumstances where status competition is more or less salient. We saw that clinicians, such as those discussing reimbursements (chapter 5), were relatively more focused on money. Standard-setters, whom we saw gossiping about colleagues they competed with for clinical trials, rare patients, and spots on a guidelines panel, are

relatively more focused on status (see also Menchik 2017). In any case, the distinction is more possible in conceptual than in empirical terms; one may compete in order to gain money, but at the very same time one is competing for what it is that generates money. More significantly, my concern has less to do with individual doctors' motivations, and more with broader, system-level processes that emerge from their everyday activities. Note too that in discussing status I am not articulating a new conception of status or making a claim about its allocation; to the degree that I write about individuals, like other sociologists I describe how individuals assess others' status according to their performance of tasks. It is sometimes allocated meritocratically and sometimes is not. (See Menchik and Meltzer 2010, Zuckerman 2012, Ridgeway 2019.) I thank a referee for pushing me on these matters.

3. Competition is a common theme in scholarship on scientific work (cf. Merton 1968, Hagstrom 1974, Latour and Woolgar 1986, Bourdieu 2004, p. 182, R. Collins 2000), and in first-hand accounts (Watson 1968). Scholarship in the Hughesian tradition distinguishes scientific practices from professional ones, noting the different nature of each's relationship with the public. Yet it is probably prudent to not overstate differences, especially given the role of business interests in both types of work.

4. On virtual witnesses in science, see Shapin 1996, p. 108. These observations about multiheadedness stand also in contrast to Latour's model of Pasteur's dominance, which implies that indeterminacy can be organized without much of a competition; in Latour's (1988) account, a single recognized person can organize indeterminacy and gain sufficient buy-in, so as to reshape the way a subject is understood, as in the case of Pasteur. To be sure, in what we've seen there's some evidence for the strong influence of individuals, especially in light of what we've learned about the importance of interdependence: in cultivating referral relationships with clinicians, standard-setters cultivate allies. But, beyond control exercised by industry, it is other stakeholders that shape doctors' ability to organize indeterminacy. Although individuals (such as Pasteur) can be effective in efforts to organize indeterminacy, as we saw, their abilities as individuals have limits. For instance, as described in chapter 4, organizational support—here, of the hospital—is consequential for those seeking to lead their field.

5. It also follows, due to the range of venues in an occupational project, that aggregation of these assessments into something like a "status score" cannot be done in a straightforward way; because a professional's tasks vary across venues, assessments are going to vary according to the ability of colleagues to observe tasks, or to access secondhand accounts.

6. As can be seen in other historical and sociological studies, these types of constructing epistemological and ontological understandings share some qualities beyond EP in other areas of medicine, even if the connections are not perfect. The first mode can be seen in the work on differences in professional sectors (Craciun 2018, Schnittker 2017, Whooley 2019), the second in the work of Crane (1972) on invisible colleges, and the third in the work of Bloor (1976) on practice differences across physicians, and Latour (1988) on Pasteur.

7. For a perspective that sees the composition of these groups as relatively more durable, see Abbott 1988.

8. I return here to Abbott's (2005) concept of linked ecologies, which he developed in an interest in responding to criticisms of the boundary assumptions of ecological arguments in sociology (p. 246). The multiheadedness I describe spotlights

other stakeholders with interests beyond any two single ecologies to which his model applies. The six venues demonstrate clearly that there are many more germane stakeholders internal to medicine's occupational project that organize what we call medical work—lawyers, administrators, salespeople, engineers, technicians, nurses—and that they are connected through their use of tethers. (He has conceded the possibility of these circumstances, noting the inability of this two-ecology model to capture adequately the full cast of characters in his case study of the security field [Abbott 2002]. Similarly, using Hughes's idea of "dirty work" (1962), Liu (2020) also implicitly describes these limits, observing the many more 'impure' actors than those that might comprise two closed professional groups.) The concepts of occupational projects, and of tethered venues, accounts for the way work is organized because it recognizes the existence of more than two groups, internalizes what Abbott refers to as "audiences," and reflects their codependence around tasks.

9. On referral ties in a city, see Hall 1948. On the way a scientist's standing depends on their ability to compellingly promote their lab, see Knorr Cetina 1992.

10. The dynamism in their knowledge we can see from looking at different stages of development, and the differences across clinicians and standard-setters, also raises questions about how we might explain organizational isomorphism. After all, many models of the diffusion of organizational forms rely on the assumption that professionals have a single form of knowledge (cf. DiMaggio and Powell 1991), rather than the multiple competing modes of organizing indeterminacy seen here. I thank Tim Hallett for reminding me of this point.

11. On the jurisdiction-based "turf-war" model, see Abbott 1988, 2002. On those new partnerships, see Navon 2019.

12. Hughes, a onetime student of Park, could be said to share his attention to space. For critiques, see Gouldner 1967, and Burawoy 2000, p. 14.

13. See Abbott (1988, p. 318) on the lack of understanding of professional coalescence. See Pacewicz 2016 on the reinforcement and changes in political identities, and Tavory 2016 on summoning in religious communities.

14. The "negotiated order" perspective is customarily associated with Strauss, Becker, and followers. The naming process seen with the "antrum" is not unlike that seen with those who "discover" anatomy, and whose names become recognizable to both lay and specialized audiences. Besides the antrum, or the opening vignette's macroscopic channels "that were a matter of belief," there is the epiploic foramen (of Winslow). Or instances where individuals completely rename a structure: the rectouterine pouch becomes the pouch of Douglas, or the uterine tube becomes the Fallopian tube, or the auditory tube becomes the Eustachian tube. I thank Megan Penzkofer for these examples.

15. See Fox 1959.

16. I have sought to show the benefits of studying a group through examining the venues they regularly frequent. Doing so also lets us explain why the professional association usually used by sociologists to capture the nature of professionals alone includes very different stakeholders. Even the professional association itself reflects a group doing a diversity of tasks; 25 percent of the Heart Rhythm Society members are "allied health professionals," a group comprising a range of non-nurse health professionals, but predominantly members of industry. (Those in sales or marketing are ineligible for membership.)

17. On politics, see Medvetz 2012. On science, see Epstein 1996, Callon and Rabeharisoa 2007. On artists, see Gerber 2017. On architects, see Bechky 2003. On lawyers, see Wilkins and Ferrer 2017. On accountants, see Canning and O'Dwyer 2018. On medicine, see Almeling 2011, Reich 2014, and Livne 2019. On changes in careers more generally, see Barley et al. 2017.

18. The careful guarding of autonomy by physicians described by Freidson (1970) reflects that doctors have individual interests. But an older tradition of scholarship on professional work, one developed by Talcott Parsons, reinforces that they have collective concerns.

19. The corporate-capture argument is best seen in accounts of Light (2000), and is inflected in arguments that implicate industry in the "medicalization of everyday life" (cf. Conrad 2005). See also McKinlay 1993. Arguments that have centered on rent-seeking, and claim that physicians are under the strong influence of industry, have some friction with a large literature in sociology that demonstrates that professionals have strong, collectively developed moral sentiments about individual practices (Bosk 1992, Chambliss 1996, Fox and Swazey 2008). Light has proposed that these stakeholders are related in countervailing ways, with each stakeholder operating in competition with the others. This existence of multiple stakeholders is similar to what I have seen here, in which the conceptual object is that of medicine, not professionals. However, by looking at the concrete individuals who work in and move between these stakeholders, it was possible to see a different picture: that that these stakeholders are less in competition than interdependent. Sociologists' approach to problematizing the relationship between industry and medicine is represented in what has been called "ontological gerrymandering" (Woolgar and Pawluch 1985). And see Latour 1993 on Pasteur's efforts to coopt stakeholders into his projects.

20. On using the tethered venues approach for studying subjects beyond medicine, see Menchik 2019. The population-based studies on small-area variations began with Wennberg and Gittelsohn (1973). On differences in physicians' practices, see Mumford (1970), Menchik and Meltzer (2010), and Menchik (2017, 2020b).

Appendix

1. See Hughes 1960, p. xiv.

2. See Duneier 1999.

3. Like Hughes in the quote above, I use the term "subject," though it is less than ideal. *Subject* denotes subjectification. Yet that term seems inadequate if the ethnographer can get kicked out. There is no perfect term, but when possible I use "those observed."

4. I have the late Charles Bosk to thank for advice on this front.

5. This material included two years' worth of hospital executive board meetings, 1.5 years of "morning report" meetings among residents training at Superior, 16 grand rounds lunch events, 23 mortality and morbidity conferences in both surgical and cardiology departments, 4 "town hall" meetings to gather public feedback on hospital decisions, 3 separate trips to observe interactions of the EPs I had begun observing at Superior and had moved to Cityview, and 3 visits to observe EP procedures in other hospitals in the US, Italy, and France.

6. Because these events change from year to year, this is different from what Klinenberg (2006) calls "quick hit" ethnography. My study is closer to Fine and van den Scott's (2011) description of leisure activities, where people invoke identities that are less coupled to their everyday tasks. These short-term events resemble what Goffman (1961) called gatherings or encounters, where participants are briefly engrossed in interaction processes that may only minimally resemble those in other sites (in this case, electrophysiologists' home labs).

7. The recognized significance of the white coat for authoritativeness is discussed in Vinson 2018 and in Menchik 2020a.

8. On being maneuvered out of a hospital field site, see also Casper 1997.

9. Ultimately, as fellow outsiders, the police appeared to be having their own challenges with access. The police asked me about my whereabouts and also implicitly conveyed to me their frustration with getting detailed information from the physicians. This challenge was clear as the ruddy-faced older officer said with a smile when I arrived, "You're right on time, you're the ONLY person! If we could give gold stars, you would get one." They asked if I had heard anything about the overdoses, if I ever handled medicine, if I ever had contact with the patients, and if I was ever on the ward during the months in which the overdoses occurred. I had no useful information on the problem of the overdose, and took a moment to explain my goal of noninvasiveness. I collected my backpack and jacket, and was walked to the door by the larger officer. "See how easy that was?" After I replied affirmatively, he offered a hint of the inevitable distance the closed groups of doctors and police will inevitably feel: "We don't lie like the doctors when we say that it won't hurt a bit."

10. On substitutability in light of the recurrence and stability of interaction, see also Duneier 1999. A recent case for naming names, or "unmasking," is in Jerolmack and Murphy 2017.

11. See Hughes 1955, p. 23.

12. These pleas persisted despite my claims about the readership of academic works. See also the pleas of those studied by Burawoy (1979, p. xv).

Works Cited

Abbott, Andrew. 1981. "Status and Status Strain in the Professions." *American Journal of Sociology* 86 (4): 819–35.

———. 1988. *The System of Professions*. Chicago, IL: University of Chicago Press.

———. 2002. "The Army and the Theory of Professions." In *The Future of the Army Profession*, edited by D. M. Snyder and G. L. Watkins, pp. 523–36.

———. 2005. "Linked Ecologies: States and Universities as Environments for Professions." *Sociological Theory* 23 (3): 245–74.

ACA/AHA Task Force on Practice Guidelines. 2010. *Methodology Manual and Policies from the ACCF/AHA Task Force on Practice Guidelines*. https://www.acc.org//-/media/Non-Clinical/Files-PDFs-Excel-MS-Word-etc/Guidelines/About-Guidelines-and-Clinical-Documents/Methodology/2014/Methodology-Practice-Guidelines.pdf.

Aldrich, Howard E., and C. Marlene Fiol. 1994. "Fools Rush In? The Institutional Context of Industry Creation." *Academy of Management Review* 19 (4): 645–70.

Aliot, Etienne M., William G. Stevenson, Jesus Ma Almendral-Garrote, et al. 2009. "EHRA/HRS Expert Consensus on Catheter Ablation of Ventricular Arrhythmias: Developed in a Partnership with the European Heart Rhythm Association (EHRA), a Registered Branch of the European Society of Cardiology (ESC), and the Heart Rhythm Society (HRS); In Collaboration with the American College of Cardiology (ACC) and the American Heart Association (AHA)." *Heart Rhythm* 11 (6): 771–817.

Almeling, Rene. 2011. *Sex Cells: The Medical Market for Eggs and Sperm*. Berkeley: University of California Press.

Anspach, Renee R. 1988. "Notes on the Sociology of Medical Discourse: The Language of Case Presentation," *Journal of Health and Social Behavior* 29: 357–75.

———. 1993. *Deciding Who Lives: Fateful Choices in the Intensive-Care Nursery*. Berkeley: University of California Press.

Antonoff, Mara B., and Jonathan D'Cunha. 2011. "Retrieval Practice as a Means of Primary Learning: Socrates Had the Right Idea." *Seminars in Thoracic and Cardiovascular Surgery* 23 (2): 89–90.

Arluke, Arnold. 1977. "Social Control Rituals in Medicine: The Case of Death Rounds." In *Health Care and Health Knowledge*, edited by Robert Dingwall, Christian Heath, Margaret Reid, and Margaret Stacey, pp. 108–25. New York: Prodist.

Aronowitz, Robert. 1999. *Making Sense of Illness: Science, Society and Disease*. New York: Cambridge University Press.

Bal, B. Sonny. 2009. "An Introduction to Medical Malpractice in the United States." *Clinical Orthopaedics and Related Research* 467 (2): 339–47.

Banfield, Edward. 1961. *Political Influence*. Piscataway, NJ: Transaction Publishers.

Barley, Stephen R., Beth A. Bechky, and Frances J. Milliken. 2017. "The Changing Nature of Work: Careers, Identities, and Work Lives in the 21st Century." *Academy of Management Discoveries* 3: 111–15.

Bearman, Peter. 2005. *Doormen*. Chicago, IL: University of Chicago Press.

Bechky, Beth A. 2003. "Sharing Meaning across Occupational Communities: The Transformation of Understanding on a Production Floor." *Organization Science* 14 (3): 312–30.

Becker, Howard S. 1963. *Outsiders: Studies in the Sociology of Deviance*. Charlottesville, VA: University of Virginia Free Press.

———. 1982. *Art Worlds*. Chicago, IL: University of Chicago Press.

———, Blanche Geer, Everett C. Hughes, and Anselm L. Strauss. 1961. *Boys in White*. New Brunswick, NJ: Transaction Books.

Beckert, Jens, and Richard Bronk, eds. 2018. *Uncertain Futures: Imaginaries, Narratives, and Calculation in the Economy*. New York: Oxford University Press.

Bennett, Howard J. 1985. "How to Survive a Case Presentation." *Chest* 88: 292–94.

Berg, Marc. 1992. "The Construction of Medical Disposals: Medical Sociology and Medical Problem Solving in Clinical Practice." *Sociology of Health & Illness* 14 (2): 151–80.

Blau, Peter M. 1955. *The Dynamics of Bureaucracy*. Chicago, IL: University of Chicago Press.

Bloor, Michael. 1976. "Bishop Berkeley and the Adenotonsillectomy Enigma: An Exploration of Variation in the Social Construction of Medical Disposals." *British Sociological Association* 10 (1): 43–67.

Blumer, Herbert. 1971. "Social Problems as Collective Behavior." *Social Problems* 18 (3): 298–306.

Bosk, Charles L. 1979 [2003]. *Forgive and Remember: Managing Medical Mistakes*. Chicago, IL: University of Chicago Press.

———. 1980. "Occupational Rituals in Patient Management." *New England Journal of Medicine* 303 (2): 71–76.

———. 1992. *All God's Mistakes: Genetic Counseling in a Pediatric Hospital*. Chicago, IL: University of Chicago Press.

Bosk, Emily A., Tiffany Veinot, and Theodore J. Iwashyna. 2011. "Which Patients and Where: A Qualitative Study of Patient Transfers from Community Hospitals." *Medical Care* 49 (6): 592–98.

Bott, Elizabeth. 1957. *Family and Social Network: Roles, Norms, and External Relationships in Ordinary Families*. London, UK: Routledge Publishers.

Bourdieu, Pierre. 1977. *Outline of a Theory of Practice*. Cambridge, UK: Cambridge University Press.

———. 1988. *Homo Academicus*. Stanford, CA: Stanford University Press.

———. 2004. Translated by Richard Nice. *Science of Science and Reflexivity*. Chicago, IL: University of Chicago Press.

Brada, Betsey Behr. 2013. "How to Do Things to Children with Words: Language, Ritual, and Apocalypse in Pediatric HIV Treatment in Botswana." *American Ethnologist* 40 (3): 437–51.

Brieger, Ronald. 1974. "Duality of Persons and Groups." *Social Forces* 53 (2): 181–90.

Brown, Phil. 1995. "Naming and Framing: The Social Construction of Diagnosis and Illness." *Journal of Health and Social Behavior* (Extra Issue): 34–52.

Brown, R., and A. Gilman. 1960. "The Pronouns of Power and Solidarity." In *Style in Language*, edited by T. A. Sebeok, pp. 253–76. Cambridge, MA: The MIT Press.

Buchbinder, Mara. 2015. *All in Your Head: Making Sense of Pediatric Pain*. Berkeley, CA: University of California Press.

Bucher, Rue, and Anselm Strauss. 1961. *Professions in Process*. Chicago, IL: University of Chicago Press Journals.

Burawoy, Michael. 1979. *Manufacturing Consent: Changes in the Labor Process under Monopoly Capitalism*. Chicago, IL: University of Chicago Press.

———. 2000. "Reaching for the Global." In *Global Ethnography*, edited by Michael Burawoy, Joseph A. Blum, Sheba George, et al. Berkeley, CA: University of California Press.

Burt, Ronald. 2005. *Brokerage and Closure*. Oxford, UK: Oxford University Press.

Calkins, Hugh, Karl Heinz Kuck, Riccardo Cappato, et al. 2012. "2012 HRS/EHRA/ECAS Expert Consensus Statement on Catheter and Surgical Ablation of Atrial Fibrillation: Recommendations for Patient Selection, Procedural Techniques, Patient Management and Follow-Up." *Heart Rhythm* 9 (4): 632–96.

Callon, Michel, and Vololona Rabeharisoa. 2007. "Growing Engagement of Emergent Concerned Groups in Political and Economic Life: Lessons from the French Association of Neuromuscular Disease Patients." *Science, Technology & Human Values* (33) 2: 230–61.

Camic, Charles. 1992. "Reputation and Predecessor Selection: Parsons and the Institutionalists." *American Sociological Review* 57 (4): 421–45.

Canning, Mary, and Brendan O'Dwyer. 2018. "Regulation and Governance of the Professions: Institutional Work and the Demise of 'Delegated' Self-Regulation of the Accounting Profession." In *Professions and Professional Service Firms: Private and Public Sector Enterprises in a Global Economy*, edited by M. Saks and D. Muzio, pp. 157–76. New York: Routledge.

Carr, E. Summerson. 2010a. "Enactments of Expertise." *Annual Review of Anthropology* 39 (1): 17–32.

———. 2010b. *Scripting Addiction: The Politics of Therapeutic Talk and American Sobriety*. Princeton, NJ: Princeton University Press.

Casper, Monica J. 1997. "Feminist Politics and Fetal Surgery: Adventures of a Research Cowgirl on the Reproductive Frontier." *Feminist Studies* 23 (2): 233–62.

Chambliss, Daniel F. 1996. *Beyond Caring: Hospitals, Nurses, and the Social Organization of Ethics*. Chicago, IL: University of Chicago Press.

Christakis, Nicholas A. 1999. *Death Foretold: Prophecy and Prognosis in Medical Care*. Chicago, IL: University of Chicago Press.

Clarke, Adele E., Janet K. Shim, Laura Mamo, et al. 2003. "Biomedicalization: Technoscientific Transformations of Health, Illness, and US Biomedicine." *American Sociological Review* 68 (2): 161–94.

Collins, Harry M. 2000. "Surviving Closure: Post-Rejection Adaptation and Plurality in Science." *American Sociological Review* 65 (6): 824–45.

———, and Trevor Pinch. 2008. *Dr. Golem: How to Think about Medicine*. Chicago, IL: University of Chicago Press.

Collins, Randall. 2000. *The Sociology of Philosophies*. Cambridge, MA: Harvard University Press.

Commonwealth Fund. 2003. *Envisioning the Future of Academic Health Centers: Final Report of the Commonwealth Fund Task Force on Academic Health Centers*. New York: Commonwealth Fund.

Connell, Robert W. 1987. "Hegemonic Masculinity and Emphasized Femininity." In Connell, Robert W., *Gender and Power: Society, the Person, and Sexual Politics*, pp. 183–88. Stanford, CA: Stanford University Press.

Conrad, Peter. 2005. "The Shifting Engines of Medicalization." *Journal of Health and Social Behavior* 46 (1): 3–14.

———, and Joseph W. Schneider. 1992. *Deviance and Medicalization: From Badness to Sickness*. Philadelphia, PA: Temple University Press.

Craciun, Mariana. 2016. "The Cultural Work of Office Charisma: Maintaining Professional Power in Psychotherapy." *Theory and Society* 45 (4): 361–83.

———. 2018. "Emotions and Knowledge in Expert Work: A Comparison of Two Psychotherapies." *American Journal of Sociology* 123 (4): 959–1003.

Crane, Diana. 1972. *Invisible Colleges: Diffusion of Knowledge in Scientific Communities*. Chicago, IL: University of Chicago Press.

Daipha, Phaedra. 2015. *Masters of Uncertainty: Weather Forecasters and the Quest for Ground Truth*. Chicago, IL: University of Chicago Press.

Daston, Lorraine, and Peter Galison. 2007. *Objectivity*. Cambridge, MA: The MIT Press.

Davis, Fred. 1960. "Uncertainty in Medical Prognosis: Clinical and Functional." *The American Journal of Sociology* 66 (1): 41–47.

Decoteau, Claire Laurier, and Meghan Daniel. 2020. "Scientific Hegemony and the Field of Autism." *American Sociological Review* 85 (3): 451–76.

Delbridge, Rick, and Jeffrey Sallaz. 2015. "Work: Four Worlds and Ways of Seeing." *Organization Studies* 36: 1449–62.

Detsky, Allan S. 2009. "The Art of Pimping." *JAMA: The Journal of the American Medical Association* 301 (13): 1379–81.

DiFeliciantonio, Justin. "Gear Talk: Wilson's John Lyons, Part 3." *Tennis Magazine*, September 13, 2012.

DiMaggio, Paul J., and Walter W. Powell. 1991. "The Iron Cage Revisited: Institutional Isomorphism and Collective Rationality in Organizational Fields." *American Sociological Review* 48: 147–60.

Duneier, Mitchell. 1999. *Sidewalk*. New York: Farrar, Straus, and Giroux.

Epstein, Steven. 1996. *Impure Science: AIDS, Activism, and the Politics of Knowledge*. Berkeley, CA: University of California Press

Erikson, Kai T. 1976. *Everything in Its Path*. New York: Simon and Schuster.

Espeland, Wendy Nelson, and Michael Sauder. 2007. "Rankings and Reactivity: How Public Measures Recreate Social Worlds." *The American Journal of Sociology* 113 (1):1–40.

Eyal, Gil. 2013. "For a Sociology of Expertise: The Social Origins of the Autism Epidemic." *The American Journal of Sociology* 118 (4): 863–907.

———. 2019. *The Crisis of Expertise*. New York: Wiley.

———, and Grace Pok. 2015. "What Is Security Expertise? From the Sociology of Professions to the Analysis of Networks of Expertise. In *Capturing Security Expertise*, edited by Trine Villumsen Berling and Christian Bueger, chapter 3. London: Routledge.

Farago, Jason. 2020. "Taking Lessons from a Bloody Masterpiece." *New York Times*, May 28.

Feld, Scott. 1981. "The Focused Organization of Social Ties." *American Journal of Sociology* 86 (5): 1015–35.

Ferguson, James. 1994. *The Anti-Politics Machine: Development, Depoliticization, and Bureaucratic Power in Lesotho*. Minneapolis, MN: University of Minnesota Press.

Fine, Gary Alan, and Lisa-Jo van den Scott. 2011. "Wispy Communities: Transient Gatherings and Imagined Micro-Communities." *The American Behavioral Scientist* 55 (10): 1319–35.

Foucault, Michel. 1978. *The History of Sexuality*. Volume 1. New York: Pantheon.

———. 1985. *The Use of Pleasure: The History of Sexuality,*. Volume 2. New York: Vintage.

Fox, Renée Claire. 1959. *Experiment Perilous: Physicians and Patients Facing the Unknown*. Piscataway, NJ: Transaction Publishers.

———. 1974. "Ethical and Existential Developments in Contemporaneous American Medicine: Their Implications for Culture and Society." *The Milbank Memorial Fund Quarterly* 52 (4): 445–83.

———, and Judith P. Swazey. 2008. *Observing Bioethics*. Oxford, UK: Oxford University Press.

Freedman, Seth. 2016. "Capacity and Utilization in Health Care: The Effect of Empty Beds on Neonatal Intensive Care Admission." *American Economic Journal of Economic Policy* 8 (2): 154–85.

Freidson, Eliot. 1970 [1988]. *Profession of Medicine: A Study in the Sociology of Applied Knowledge*. Chicago, IL: University of Chicago Press.

———. 1985. "The Reorganization of the Medical Profession." *Medical Care Review* 42 (1):11–35.

———, and Buford Rhea. 1963. "Processes of Control in a Company of Equals." *Social Problems* 11 (2):119–31.

Galison, Peter. 1997. *Image and Logic: A Material Culture of Microphysics*. Chicago, IL: University of Chicago Press.

———, and Lorraine Daston. 2007. *Objectivity*. Cambridge, MA: Zone Books.

Gellner, Ernest. 1992. *Postmodernism, Reason, and Religion*. London, UK: Routledge.

Gengler, Amanda. 2014. "'I Want You to Save My Kid!': Illness Management Strategies, Access, and Inequality at an Elite University Research Hospital. *Journal of Health and Social Behavior* 55 (3): 342–59.

Gerber, Alison. 2017. *The Work of Art: Value in Creative Careers*. Palo Alto, CA: Stanford University Press.

Goffman, Erving. 1961. *Encounters: Two Studies in the Sociology of Interaction.* Indianapolis, IN: Bobbs-Merrill.

Goldhamer, Herbert, and Edward A. Shils. 1939. "Types of Power and Status." *American Journal of Sociology* 45 (2): 171–82.

Goode, William. 1978. *The Celebration of Heroes.* Berkeley, CA: University of California Press.

Goodwin, Charles. 1994. "Professional Vision." *American Anthropologist* 96 (3): 606–33.

Goodwin, Marjorie Harness. 1982. "Processes of Dispute Management among Urban Black Children." *American Ethnologist* 9 (1): 76–96.

Gouldner, Alvin. 1967. "Sociologist as Partisan: Sociology and the Welfare State." *For Sociology* 1: 27–68.

Greene, Jeremy A. 2007. *Prescribing by Numbers: Drugs and the Definition of Disease.* Baltimore, MD: Johns Hopkins University Press

Gusfield, Joseph R. 1981. *The Culture of Public Problems.* Chicago, IL: University of Chicago Press.

Hafferty, Frederic W. 1988. "Cadaver Stories and the Emotional Socialization of Medical Students." *Journal of Health and Social Behavior* 29 (4): 344–56.

Hagstrom, Warren O. 1965. *The Scientific Community.* New York: Basic Books.

———. 1974. "Competition in Science." *American Sociological Review* 39 (February): 1–18.

Hall, Oswald. 1948. "The Stages of a Medical Career." *The American Journal of Sociology* 53 (5): 327–36.

———. 1949. "Types of Medical Careers." *The American Journal of Sociology* 55 (3): 243–53.

Heath, Deborah. 1998. "Locating Genetic Knowledge: Picturing Marfan Syndrome and Its Traveling Constituencies." *Science, Technology & Human Values* 23 (1): 71–97.

Heimer, Carol A., and J. Lynn Gazley. 2012. "Performing Regulation: Transcending Regulatory Ritualism in HIV Clinics." *Law & Society Review* 46 (4): 853–87.

Heimer, Carol A., and Lisa R. Staffen. 2012. "Inert Facts and the Illusion of Knowledge: Strategic Uses of Ignorance in HIV Clinics." *Economy and Society* 41 (1): 17–41.

Heritage, John, and Douglas W. Maynard. 2006. "Problems and Prospects in the Study of Physician-Patient Interaction: 30 Years of Research." *Annual Review of Sociology* 32: 351–74.

Hindmarsh, Jon, and Alison Pilnick. 2002. "The Tacit Order of Teamwork: Collaboration and Embodied Conduct in Anesthesia." *The Sociological Quarterly* 43 (2): 139–64.

Horwitz, Allan V. 2011. "Creating an Age of Depression: The Social Construction and Consequences of the Major Depression Diagnosis." *Society and Mental Health* 1 (1): 41–54.

Hughes, Everett C. 1928. "Personality Types and the Division of Labor." *The American Journal of Sociology* 33 (5): 754–68.

———. 1955. "The Making of a Physician—General Statement of Ideas and Problems." *Human Organization* 14 (4): 21–25.

———. 1959. "The Study of Occupations." In *Sociology Today*, edited by Robert Merton, Leonard Broom, and Leonard Cottrell. New York: Basic Books.

———. 1960. "Introduction: The Place of Field Work in Social Science." In *Field Work: An Introduction to the Social Sciences*, pp. x–xv. Chicago, IL. University of Chicago Press.

———. 1962. "Good People and Dirty Work." *Social Problems* 10 (1): 3–11.

———. 1963. "Professions." *Daedalus* 92 (4): 655–68.

Hunter, Kathryn M. 1993. *Doctors' Stories: The Narrative Structure of Medical Knowledge*. Princeton, NJ: Princeton University Press.

Hutchins, Edwin. 1995. *Cognition in the Wild*. Cambridge, MA: MIT Press.

Illich, Ivan. 1976. *Medical Nemesis: The Expropriation of Health*. New York: Pantheon Books.

Ioannidis, John P. A. 2012. "Are Medical Conferences Useful? And for Whom?" *JAMA: The Journal of the American Medical Association*. 307 (12): 1257–58.

James, William. [1890] 1950. *The Principles of Psychology*. Volume 1. Mineola, NY: Dover Books.

Jenkins, Tania. 2020. *Doctors' Orders: The Making of Status Hierarchies in an Elite Profession*. New York: Columbia University Press.

Jerolmack, Carol, and Murphy, Alexandra K. (2017). "The Ethical Dilemmas and Social Scientific Trade-offs of Masking in Ethnography." *Sociological Methods & Research* 48 (4), 801–27.

Jutel, Annemarie. 2009. "Sociology of Diagnosis: A Preliminary Review. *Sociology of Health & Illness* 31 (2): 278–99.

Katz, Elihu, and Paul F. Lazarsfeld. 1955. *Personal Influence, the Part Played by People in the Flow of Mass Communications*. Glencoe, IL: Free Press.

Kellogg, Katherine C. 2011. *Challenging Operations: Medical Reform and Resistance in Surgery*. Chicago, IL: University of Chicago Press.

Kempner, Joanna. 2014. *Not Tonight: Migraine and the Politics of Gender and Health*. Chicago, IL: University of Chicago Press.

Klinenberg, Eric. 2002. *Heat Wave: A Social Autopsy of Disaster in Chicago*. Chicago, IL: University of Chicago Press.

———. 2006. "Blaming the Victims: Hearsay, Labeling, and the Hazards of Quick-Hit Disaster Ethnography." *American Sociological Review* 71 (4): 689–98.

Knaapen, Loes. 2013, "Being 'Evidence-Based' in the Absence of Evidence: The Management of Non-Evidence in Guideline Development." *Social Studies of Science* 43 (5): 681–706.

Knorr-Cetina, Karin D. 1992. "The Couch, the Cathedral and the Lab: On the Relationship between Experiment and Laboratory Science." In *Science as Practice and Culture*, edited by A. Pickering, pp. 113–38. Chicago, IL: Chicago University Press.

Krause, Elliot A. 1999. *Death of the Guilds: Professions, States, and the Advance of Capitalism, 1930 to the Present*. New Haven, CT: Yale University Press.

Kuhn, Thomas S. 1962. *The Structure of Scientific Revolutions*. Chicago, IL: University of Chicago Press.

Kusumoto, Fred M., Hugh Calkins, John Boehmer, et al. 2014. "HRS/ACC/AHA Expert Consensus Statement on the Use of Implantable Cardioverter-Defibrillator Therapy in Patients Who Are Not Included or Not Well Represented in Clinical Trials." *Heart Rhythm* 11 (7): 1270–1303.

Larson, Magali. 1977. *The Rise of Professionalism: A Sociological Analysis*. Berkeley, CA: University of California Press.

Latour, Bruno. 1988. *The Pasteurization of France*. Cambridge, MA: Harvard University Press.

———, and Steve Woolgar. 1986. *Laboratory Life: The Construction of Scientific Facts*. Princeton, NJ: Princeton University Press.

Laumann, Edward O., and John P. Heinz. 1977. "Specialization and Prestige in the Legal Profession: The Structure of Deference." *Law & Social Inquiry* 2 (1): 155–216.

Lave, Jean, and Etienne Wenger. 1991. *Situated Learning: Legitimate Peripheral Participation*. New York and Cambridge, UK: Cambridge University Press.

Lazarsfeld, Paul F., Bernard Berelson, and Hazel Gaudet. 1944. *The People's Choice*. New York: Columbia University Press.

———, and Herbert Menzel. 1963. "Mass Media and Personal Influence." In *The Science of Human Communication*, edited by Wilbur Schramm, pp. 94–115. New York: Basic Books.

Lieberson, Stanley. 1958. "Ethnic Groups and the Practice of Medicine." *American Sociological Review* 23 (5): 542–49.

Light, Donald. 1979. "Uncertainty and Control in Professional Training." *Journal of Health and Social Behavior* 20 (4): 310–22.

———. 1980. *Becoming Psychiatrists*. New York: W. W. Norton.

———. 1985. "Values and Structure in the German Health Care Systems." *The Milbank Memorial Fund Quarterly: Health and Society* 63 (4): 615–47.

———. 2000. "The Medical Profession and Organizational Change: From Professional Dominance to Countervailing Power." *Handbook of Medical Sociology* 5: 201–16.

Liu, Sida. 2020. "Professional Impurities." *Research in the Sociology of Work* 34: 147–67.

Livne, Roi. 2019. *Values at the End of Life: The Logic of Palliative Care*. Cambridge, MA: Harvard University Press.

Lomnitz, Larissa. 1983. "The Scientific Meeting: An Anthropologist's Point of View." *4S Review* 1 (2): 2–7.

March, James G., and Herbert A. Simon. 1958. *Organizations*. Oxford, UK: Wiley.

Martin, John L. 2017. *Thinking through Methods: A Social Science Primer*. Chicago, IL: University of Chicago Press.

Matoesian, Greg. 2008. "Role Conflict as an Interactional Resource in the Multi-modal Emergence of Expert Identity." *Semiotica* 171: 15–49.

Maynard, Douglas W. 1985. "On the Functions of Social Conflict among Children." *American Sociological Review* 50 (2): 207–23.

McDonald, Ruth. 2012. "Restratification Revisited: The Changing Landscape of Primary Medical Care in England and California." *Current Sociology* 60 (4): 441–55.

———, and Stephen Harrison. 2004. "The Micropolitics of Clinical Guidelines: An Empirical Study." *Policy & Politics* 32 (2): 223–39.

McKinlay, John B. 1993. "The Promotion of Health through Planned Sociopolitical Change: Challenges for Research and Policy." *Social Science & Medicine* 36 (2): 109–17.

Medvetz, Thomas. 2012. *Think Tanks in America*. Chicago, IL: The University of Chicago Press.

Meier, Barry. 2009. "Costs Surge for Medical Devices, but Benefits Are Opaque." *The New York Times*, November 4.

———. 2011. "Tipping the Odds for a Maker of Heart Implants." *New York Times*, April 3.

Menchik, Daniel A. 2014. "Decisions about Knowledge in Medical Practice: The Effect of Temporal Features of a Task." *American Journal of Sociology* 120 (3): 701–49.

———. 2017. "Interdependent Career Types and Divergent Standpoints on the Use of Advanced Technology in Medicine." *Journal of Health and Social Behavior* 58 (4): 488–502.

———. 2019. "Tethered Venues: Discerning Distant Influences on a Field Site," *Sociological Methods & Research* 48: 850–76.

———. 2020a. "Authority beyond Institutions: The Expert's Multivocal Process of Gaining and Sustaining Authoritativeness." *American Journal of Cultural Sociology*, https://doi.org/10.1057/s41290-020-00100-3.

———. 2020b. "Moving from Adoption to Use: Physicians' Mixed Commitments in Deciding to Use Robotic Technologies." *Work and Occupations*,47: 314–47.

———, and D. Meltzer. 2010. "The Cultivation of Esteem and Retrieval of Scientific Knowledge in Physician Networks." *Journal of Health and Social Behavior* 51: 37–52.

———, and Lei Jin. 2014. "When Do Doctors Follow Patients' Orders? Organizational Mechanisms of Physician Influence." *Social Science Research* 48: 171–84.

Merton, Robert K. 1968. *Social Theory and Social Structure*. New York: Simon and Schuster.

———, George Reader, and Patricia L. Kendall. 1957. *The Student-Physician*. Cambridge, MA: Harvard University Press.

Mody, Cyrus C. M. 2011. *Instrumental Community: Probe Microscopy and the Path to Nanotechnology*. Cambridge, MA: MIT Press.

Mumford, Emily. 1970. *Interns: From Students to Physicians*. Cambridge, MA: Harvard University Press.

Mumford, Lewis. 1964. "Authoritarian and Democratic Technics." *Technology and Culture* 5 (1): 1–8.

Navarro, Vicente. 1976. *Medicine under Capitalism*. New York: Prodist.

Navon, Daniel. 2019. *Mobilizing Mutations: Human Genetics in the Age of Patient Advocacy*. University of Chicago Press.

Neuman, Mark D., Bosk, Charles L, and Fleisher, Lee A. 2014. "Learning from Mistakes in Clinical Practice Guidelines: The Case of Perioperative β-blockade." *BMJ Quality & Safety* 23 (11): 957–64.

Nguyen, Dan. 2011. "How the Heart Rhythm Society Sells Access," https://www
        .propublica.org/article/heart-rhythm-convention-ads (last accessed
        February 26, 2021).
Pacewicz, J., 2016. *Partisans and Partners.* Chicago, IL: The University of Chicago
        Press.
Parsons, Talcott. 1951. *The Social System.* New York: The Free Press.
———. 1960. *Structure and Process in Modern Societies.* New York: The Free Press.
Perrow, Charles. 1965. "Hospitals: Technology, Structure, and Goals." In *Hand-
        book of Organizations,* edited by James G. March, pp. 910–71. New York:
        Rand McNally.
Pessin, Alain. 2017. *The Sociology of Howard Becker: Theory with a Wide Horizon.*
        Chicago, IL: University of Chicago Press.
Polanyi, Michael. 1958. *Personal Knowledge.* London, UK: Routledge & Kegan Paul.
Pope, Catherine. 2002. "Contingency in Everyday Surgical Work." *Sociology of
        Health & Illness* 24 (4): 369–84.
Prentice, Rachel. 2007. "Drilling Surgeons: The Social Lessons of Embodied
        Surgical Learning." *Science, Technology & Human Values* 32 (5): 534–53.
———. 2012. *Bodies in Formation: Remaking Anatomy and Surgery Education.*
        Durham, NC: Duke University Press.
Prince, Ellen F., Joel E. Frader, and Charles L. Bosk. 1982. "On Hedging in
        Physician-Physician Discourse." *Linguistics and the Professions* 8 (1): 83–97.
Pringle, Rosemary. 1998. *Sex and Medicine: Gender, Power and Authority in the
        Medical Profession.* Cambridge, UK: Cambridge University Press.
Propp, Vladimir. 1968. *Morphology of the Folktale.* Austin, TX: Texas University
        Press.
Reay, Michael. 2009. "Humor." In *Blackwell Encyclopedia of Sociology,* edited by
        George Ritzer. Malden, MA: Blackwell Pub.
Reich, Adam. 2012. "Disciplined Doctors: The Electronic Medical Record and
        Physicians' Changing Relationship to Medical Knowledge." *Social
        Science & Medicine* 74 (7): 1021–28.
———. 2014. "Contradictions in the Commodification of Hospital Care."
        American Journal of Sociology 119 (6): 1537–75.
Ridgeway, Cecilia. 2019. *Status: Why Is It Everywhere? Why Does It Matter?* New
        York: The Russell Sage Foundation.
Rier, David. 2000. "The Missing Voice of the Critically Ill: A Medical Sociolo-
        gist's First-Person Account." *Sociology of Health & Illness* 22 (1): 68–93.
Rosenberg, Charles E. 1991. *Strangers at the Bedside: A History of How Law and
        Bioethics Transformed Medical Decision Making.* New York: Basic Books.
———. 2009. *The Cholera Years: The United States in 1832, 1849, and 1866.* Chicago,
        IL: University of Chicago Press.
Ruit, Catherine van de, and Charles L. Bosk. 2020. "Surgical Patient Safety Officers
        in the United States: Negotiating Contradictions Between Compliance
        and Workplace Transformation." *Work and Occupations* 48 (1): 3–39.
Schnittker, Jason. 2017. *The Diagnostic System: Why the Classification of Psychiatric
        Disorders Is Necessary, Difficult, and Never Settled.* New York: Columbia
        University Press.

Scott, James. 1998. *Seeing Like a State: How Certain Schemes to Improve the Human Condition Have Failed*. New Haven, CT: Yale University Press.

Shapin, Steven. 1996. *The Scientific Revolution*. Chicago, IL: University of Chicago Press.

Shem, Samuel. 1978. *The House of God*. Penguin Press.

Shibutani, Tamotsu. 1955. *Improvised News*. Indianapolis, IN: Bobbs-Merrill.

Shiloh, Ailon. 1965. "Equalitarian and Hierarchical Patients: An Investigation among Hadassah Hospital Patients." *Medical Care* 3 (2): 87–95.

Silverstein, Michael. 2004. "'Cultural' Concepts and the Language-Culture Nexus." *Current Anthropology* 45 (5): 621–52.

———. 2006. "Old Wine, New Ethnographic Lexicography." *Annual Review of Anthropology* 35 (1): 481–96.

———. 2013. "Discourse and the No-thing-ness of Culture." *Signs and Society* 1 (2): 327–66.

Small, Mario L., and Laura Adler. 2019. "The Role of Space in the Formation of Social Ties." *Annual Review of Sociology* 45: 111–32.

Smith, Andrew, Dawn Goodwin, Maggie Mort, and Catherine Pope. 2003. "Expertise in Practice: An Ethnographic Study Exploring Acquisition and Use of Knowledge in Anaesthesia." *British Journal of Anaesthesia* 91 (3): 319–28.

Sprat, Thomas. 1667. *History of the Royal Society*. New York: Kessinger Publishing.

Starr, Paul. 1982. *The Social Transformation of Medicine: The Rise of a Sovereign Profession and the Making of a Vast Industry*. New York: Basic Books.

Stelling, Joan, and Rue Bucher. 1972. "Autonomy and Monitoring on Hospital Wards." *The Sociological Quarterly* 13 (4): 431–46.

Stevens, Rosemary. 1998. *American Medicine and the Public Interest: Updated Edition with a New Introduction*. Berkeley, CA: University of California Press.

Stonington, Scott. 2020. *The Spirit Ambulance: Choreographing the End of Life in Thailand*. Volume 49. Berkeley, CA: University of California Press.

Suchman, Mark C. 1995. "Managing Legitimacy: Strategic and Institutional Approaches." *Academy of Management Review* 20 (3): 571–610.

Szymczak, Julia E., and Charles L. Bosk. 2012. "Training for Efficiency: Work, Time, and Systems-Based Practice in Medical Residency." *Journal of Health and Social Behavior* 53: 344–58.

Tavory, Iddo. 2016. *Summoned: Identification and Religious Life in a Jewish Neighborhood*. Chicago, IL: University of Chicago Press.

Timmermans, Stefan. 2003. "A Black Technician and Blue Babies." *Social Studies of Science* 33 (2): 197–229.

———, and Alison Angell. 2001. "Evidence-Based Medicine, Clinical Uncertainty, and Learning to Doctor." *Journal of Health and Social Behavior* 42 (4): 342–59.

———, and Mark Berg. 2003. *The Gold Standard: The Challenge of Evidence-Based Medicine*. Philadelphia, PA: Temple University Press.

———, and Tanya Stivers. 2017. "The Spillover of Genomic Testing Results in Families: Same Variant, Different Logics." *Journal of Health and Social Behavior* 58, no. 2 (2017): 166–80.

Turner, Victor. 1977. "Symbols in African Ritual." In *Symbolic Anthropology*, edited by J. Dolgin, D., S. Kemnitzer, and D. M. Schneider, pp. 183–94. New York: Columbia University Press.

Vaidyanathan, Brandon, Simranjit Khalsa, and Elaine Howard Ecklund. 2016. "Gossip as Social Control?: Informal Sanctions on Ethical Violations in Scientific Workplaces." *Social Problems* 63 (4): 554–72.

Venkatesh, Sudhir. 2001. "Chicago's Pragmatic Planners: American Sociology and the Myth of Community." *Social Science History* 25 (2): 275–317.

Verma, Atul, Nassir F. Marrouche, and Andrea Natale. 2004. "Pulmonary Vein Antrum Isolation: Intracardiac Echocardiography-Guided Technique." *Journal of Cardiovascular Electrophysiology* 15 (11): 1335–40.

Vinson, Alexandra H. 2019. "Short White Coats: Knowledge, Identity, and Status Negotiations of First-Year Medical Students." *Symbolic Interaction* 42: 395–411.

Wailoo, Keith. 2000. *Dying in the City of the Blues: Sickle Cell Anemia and the Politics of Race and Health*. Chapel Hill: University of North Carolina Press.

Watson, James. 1968. *The Double Helix*. New York: Atheneum.

Weber, Max. 1946. "Class, Status, and Party." In *From Max Weber*, translated and edited by H. H. Gerth and C. W. Mills. Oxford, UK: Oxford University Press.

———. 1978. *Economy and Society: An Outline of Interpretive Sociology*. Oakland, CA: University of California Press.

Weisz, G., A. Cambrosio, P. Keating, L. Knaapen, et al. 2007. "The Emergence of Clinical Practice Guidelines." *The Milbank Quarterly* 85 (4): 691–727.

Wennberg, John, and Alan Gittelsohn. 1973. "Small Area Variations in Health Care Delivery: A Population-Based Health Information System Can Guide Planning and Regulatory Decision-Making." *Science*, 182 (4117): 1102–08.

Whooley, Owen. 2013. *Knowledge in the Time of Cholera: The Struggle over American Medicine in the Nineteenth Century*. Chicago, IL: University of Chicago Press.

———. 2019. *On the Heels of Ignorance: Psychiatry and the Politics of Not Knowing*. Chicago, IL: University of Chicago Press.

Wilkins, David B. and Maria J. E. Ferrer. 2017. "The Integration of Law into Global Business Solutions: The Rise, Transformation, and Potential Future of the Big Four Accountancy Networks in the Global Legal Services Market." *Law & Social Inquiry* 43: 981–1026.

Wilkoff, Bruce L., Charles J. Love, Charles L. Byrd, et al. 2009. "Transvenous Lead Extraction: Heart Rhythm Society Expert Consensus on Facilities, Training, Indications, and Patient Management." *Heart Rhythm Society* 6 (7): 1085–1104.

Wilson, Duff. 2009. "Harvard Medical School in Ethics Quandary." *The New York Times*, March 2, https://www.nytimes.com/2009/03/03/business /03medschool.html (last accessed February 26, 2021).

Wilson, Nicky, Catherine Pope, Lisa Roberts, and Robert Crouch. 2014. "Governing Healthcare: Finding Meaning in a Clinical Practice Guideline for the Management of Non-Specific Low Back Pain." *Social Science & Medicine* 102: 138–45.

Woolgar, Steve, and Dorothy Pawluch. 1985. "Ontological Gerrymandering: The Anatomy of Social Problems Explanations." *Social Problems* 32 (3): 214–27.

Znaniecki, Florian. 1940. *The Social Role of the Man of Knowledge*. New York: Columbia University Press.

Zola, Irving Kenneth. 1972. "Medicine as an Institution of Social Control." *The Sociological Review* 20 (4): 487–504.

Zuckerman, Ezra W. 2012. "Construction, Concentration, and (Dis)continuities in Social Valuations." *Annual Review of Sociology* 38: 223–45.

Zuckerman, Harriet. 1977. *Scientific Elite: Nobel Laureates in the United States*. Piscataway, NJ: Transaction Publishers.

Zussman, Robert. 1992. *Intensive Care: Medical Ethics and the Medical Profession*. University of Chicago Press.

———. 2004. "People in Places." *Qualitative Sociology* 27 (4): 351–63.

Index